INDIGENOUS BUSINESS
IN CANADA
PRINCIPLES AND PRACTICES

EDITED BY
KEITH G. BROWN
MARY BETH DOUCETTE
JANICE ESTHER TULK

NIMBUS
PUBLISHING LTD
nimbus.ca

Cover design: Cathy MacLean Design, Chéticamp, NS.
Layout: Mike Hunter, West Bay and Sydney, NS.

First printed in Canada
Second printing, 2017

NB1365

Library and Archives Canada Cataloguing in Publication

Indigenous business in Canada : principles and practices / edited by Keith G. Brown, Mary Beth Doucette, Janice Esther Tulk.

Originally published: Sydney, Nova Scotia : Cape Breton University Press,©2016.
Includes bibliographical references and index.
ISBN 978-1-77108-590-8 (softcover)

1. Indian business enterprises—Canada. 2. Inuit business enterprises—Canada.
I. Brown, Keith G., editor II. Tulk, Janice Esther, 1979-, editor III. Doucette,
Mary Beth, author, editor

E98.B87I64 2017   338.7089'97071   C2017-905925-4

Nimbus Publishing acknowledges the financial support for its publishing activities from the Government of Canada, the Canada Council for the Arts, and from the Province of Nova Scotia. We are pleased to work in partnership with the Province of Nova Scotia to develop and promote our creative industries for the benefit of all Nova Scotians.

Contents

Note from the Editors

In Canada, Aboriginal is a term that refers to First Nation, Métis, and Inuit peoples. First Nation is the term now commonly used to refer to "Indians." The *Indian Act* (discussed in chapter 2) is an Act of the Government of Canada that sets out who is an Indian and, as a result, subject to the benefits and restrictions of the *Indian Act*. Those Indians who are on the official Indian Register are considered "status Indians"; however, there are many First Nations people who for any number of reasons are not on that register and are, therefore, "non-status" (and are not impacted by the *Indian Act* in the same way). The term "Métis" often refers specifically to individuals, and their heirs, of mixed First Nation and European heritage, typically of the Prairies, who developed a unique culture and language (Michif) during the North American fur trade (discussed in chapter 1); however, it may also refer to other peoples of mixed heritage, such as the Labrador Métis Nation (now NunatuKavut). The term "Inuit" refers to Aboriginal peoples who have traditionally lived in the Arctic, and, for that reason, have similar cultures. While First Nations people or Indians have been subject to the *Indian Act*, its provisions have not applied to Métis and Inuit peoples. While we tend to use the term "Aboriginal" to refer to these three groups of peoples in Canada, the term "Indigenous" may be used interchangeably. In the chapters that follow, authors use Aboriginal or Indigenous to refer to the same groups of peoples, depending on their own preference.

On April 14, 2016, while this book was being proofed for publication, the Supreme Court of Canada issued a landmark ruling that Métis and non-status Indians are "Indians" under the Constitution of Canada, 1867 and, therefore, the Government of Canada has a fiduciary relationship with them. The impacts and implications of this ruling are unknown, but could result in negotiations for land rights and enhanced social benefits for these populations.

Foreword
Keith G. Brown

When I stepped off a DC-3 in Oxford House, Northern Manitoba in August, 1977 to begin a three-year teaching and cultural experience at twenty-two years of age, I had no idea how this first professional experience and deep immersion in Cree culture would forever change me and start me on a pathway of Indigenous education. Lessons learned in Manitoba helped shape early programming at Cape Breton University as I learned to listen and to adapt to community needs.

Thirty-plus years later, in 2010, the Purdy Crawford Chair in Aboriginal Business Studies (PCC) was formed to research best practices in Indigenous business and to explore barriers faced by Indigenous post-secondary students studying business in Canada. A series of student round tables throughout Canada was held and there was an early consensus that in the opinion of the students consulted, current textbooks and case studies were sadly lacking Indigenous content. These comments lead to early discussions on whether we could respond to this identified need. Though I did not expect it, this was the beginning of a five year journey.

As will be outlined more fully in the introduction, originally, the concept was to fashion this as a textbook after existing introduction to Canadian business books but with Indigenous-focused content. The national call of interest went out and what we received is not what we had anticipated. Aboriginal and non-Aboriginal authors submitted abstracts which spoke to land, treaties, taxation, partnerships, and demographics as forming the foundation for the text. The earlier vision leading toward the more traditional approach to a business text was abandoned as we embraced a new concept as represented by the interests of Indigenous and non-Indigenous authors from across the country.

This text is unique in its inspiration and its commitment to ensuring authors had the opportunity to present what they believe to be the most important issues in Indigenous business in Canada. As you take this journey from pre-contact business practices through to modern day land negotiations, and all that it entails, be aware there are additional supporting cases in our Case Studies in Aboriginal Business series (available from www.cbu.ca/crawford). This project began almost within the same time frame as the Truth and Reconciliation Commission and responds, in part, to some of the key recommendations on education in the post-secondary sector in Canada.

Thank you to our authors and the anonymous external reviewers whose comments shaped this volume; thank you to the Indigenous business students across Canada for their input throughout the process; thank you to faculty at Cape Breton University's Shannon School of Business who have helped us test our cases; and thank you most especially to the late Purdy Crawford who believed that change in the relationship between corporate Canada and Indigenous people is possible.

Mary Beth Doucette, Executive Director, Dr. Janice Esther Tulk, Senior Research Associate, and I began this journey together and at all stages it has been a team effort. Most likely, without Dr. Tulk's commitment to keep us on track and her goal for excellence, this book would not be published.

Introduction

Janice Esther Tulk and Mary Beth Doucette

Indigenous Business in Canada: Principles and Practices addresses contemporary concerns and issues in the doing of Indigenous business in Canada, and demonstrates the direct impact that history and policy, past and present, have on business and business education in Canada. This volume shares the voices of Indigenous business leaders, officials, Elders, and other members of Indigenous communities, along with the research of Indigenous and non-Indigenous practitioners and scholars working in their respective fields.

Throughout this volume, First Nation, Métis, and Inuit content and examples are presented; however, we recognize that it is more heavily focused on First Nations challenges related to the Indian Act than the title might suggest. Contributors to this volume could not emphasize enough just how influential and impactful that piece of legislation has been. We hope that in future publications, we will be able to better represent the issues facing Métis and Inuit populations.

The format of this volume is a hybrid, somewhere between a book of collected essays and a textbook. We wanted the book to be useful in the average undergraduate classroom setting, but recognize that some content is more complex and some concepts are not necessarily accepted as standard business practices. It is our hope that through this book and our related series—Case Studies in Aboriginal Business—Indigenous students will begin to see themselves in business curricula and engage with relevant post-secondary education, and that non-Indigenous students will learn more about the challenges of doing business in Indigenous contexts and begin to think about future partnerships with Indigenous entrepreneurs, businesses, and communities.

This book is separated into four sections. The first begins with a discussion of land and the *Indian Act*, which is a central issue that has the most significant impact on Indigenous business. In subsequent chapters, foundational concepts of leadership, entrepreneurship, and partnership are presented through an Aboriginal lens.

The second section, which refers back to the *Indian Act* periodically, presents related issues of governance, taxation, and financing. These chapters engage with the implications of law and the challenges of interpreting law in Aboriginal contexts, as well as practical challenges around financing that emerge as a result of the *Indian Act*, and approaches to dealing with them.

The third section employs a case-study approach, highlighting opportunities and challenges in three sectors: tourism, fisheries, and mining. The tourism chapter introduces marketing challenges for Aboriginal tourism products and the issue of authenticity, the fisheries chapter presents strategies for addressing barriers to entry, and the mining chapter demonstrates the importance of community engagement and corporate social responsibility. These chapters bring forward important lessons learned in the practice of Indigenous business that could have broader application.

The fourth section provides background for the study and practice of Indigenous business in Canada. Specifically, it introduces and describes the different types of treaties across Canada, the Indian Residential School system, the Royal Commission on Aboriginal Peoples, and the Truth and Reconciliation Commission.

Before proceeding to the discussion of land in part one, however, we begin with a brief introduction to pre-contact economies and the new economic models that resulted from colonial encounter.

Chapter 1

Prior to colonial encounter, Aboriginal communities thrived with subsistence economies that featured redistributive or "gift economy" practices. Their social structures were kinship-based, and could be matrilineal, patrilineal, or egalitarian. When European explorers and settlers arrived in the so-called New World, they relied on the knowledge of Aboriginal peoples and adapted pre-existing Indigenous trade routes for their own purposes. The subsequent commercial fur trade increased Aboriginal reliance on trading posts for goods, and resulted in a shift from a trade to a monetary exchange system. Consequently, there was a shift from a subsistence economy to a capitalist economy, though some elements of redistributive economies are still practised in Aboriginal communities today.

Pre-contact Economies and the Fur Trade
Katie K. MacLeod

Most timelines of business in Canada begin with the fur trade, but this approach fails to account for the economic systems in place prior to contact and colonization. The pre-contact Aboriginal economies of subsistence, trade, barter, and exchange prior to European arrival that existed on what is now known as North America are the foundation of the contemporary Canadian economy. These economies differed from one Aboriginal population to another; however, generally speaking, these economies were non-monetary, not for profit, communal, and largely based on subsistence and livelihood (Gregory 1982). This chapter highlights some elements of pre-contact economies, as well as the shift that occurred from subsistence to capitalist economies as a result of the North American fur trade. While it is not possible to provide a comprehensive history of Indigenous economies in Canada in this brief chapter, those interested in the topic are encouraged to read *The Fur Trade in Canada: An Introduction to Canadian Economic History* by Harold A. Innis (1999), *Northern Aboriginal Communities: Econo-*

mies and Development by Peter D. Elias (1995), and *Economic Development Among the Aboriginal Peoples of Canada: The Hope for the Future* by Robert B. Anderson (1999).

Subsistence-based economies of hunting, fishing, and trapping operated within kinship networks. These networks controlled and governed access to territory, titles, spiritual traditions, and economic activity. Aboriginal societies could be matrilineal, patrilineal, or egalitarian; those that followed a matrilineal descent line demonstrated a significant degree of female power. Strong examples of this are the Haudenosaunee Confederacy (also known as the Iroquois Confederacy) and many of the First Nations of the northwest coast, including the Tsimshian, Nisga'a, Gitksan, Wet'suwet'en, Tlingit, Haida, and Haisla. Aboriginal matrilineal societies had clear gender roles and divisions; however, they also promoted equality in the balance of labour within the society (M. Anderson 2000).

> **Kinship** refers to relationships that are based in common ancestry or marriage.

As Aboriginal populations came into contact with one another at their borders, a medium for exchange—chiefly, trade, and barter systems—developed. These exchanges took place in what is known as a gift economy, intended to expand social relations, rather than in a commodity or capitalist economy, intended to appropriate goods and gain profit (Strathern 1972; Borrows 2005). In this perspective, pre-contact economies operated primarily on a need basis rather than one of want. This is not to say that Indigenous peoples in Canada did not possess wants prior to European arrival; however, these wants would have tended toward the particular or specific usefulness of an item, rather than the future potential exchange value. Items were not valued equally and there was no standard metric of equivalency. To fulfill wants and needs, groups were involved in trade and exchange relationships along pre-contact trade routes.

> **Subsistence economies** are characterized by the production (through hunting and harvesting) of goods such as clothing and food in sufficient quantities to address the needs of a community. Small surpluses have value for immediate and anticipated trade purposes, since the economy is non-monetary based.

For example, the Haudenosaunee had a strong redistributive economy, where wealth and goods that were not utilized by one particular longhouse would be given to another that was in need. This constant stream of redistribution demonstrates a communal economy of exchange whereby the amount of excess goods one has to share increases their wealth. This type of redistributive or gift economy was prevalent among many pre-contact Indigenous populations. When a family or community was not able to sustain itself, exchange and trade networks were activated with other clans or communities to gain access to other goods (Richter 1992).

> **Bartering** is a system of trade without the use of money.

A significant practice within gift economies is the potlatch. The potlatch is a redistributive tradition among the Aboriginal peoples of the northwest coast practised in a ceremonial setting. Gift economies and ceremonies similar to potlatch can also be found in other Aboriginal societies, as well

> A **redistributive economy** is one in which the wealth or surplus goods from one family, clan, or community are shared with others.

A **longhouse** was a traditional dwelling in which several families lived.

A **potlatch** is a traditional gathering of Aboriginal peoples of the northwest coast that features feasting and gift giving. It is a system of gift economy.

as in Polynesian and Malaysian societies (Mauss 1967). The institution of the potlatch varies by name and practice from one Indigenous language to another, yet the basic foundations and patterns of practice remain the same (Drucker 1967). At the heart of the potlatch is the gift, but it is not exclusive to physical gifting and may extend to intangible cultural practices, such as hereditary naming (Roth 2002: 145).

Wampum belts were also part of the gift economy and were prevalent among the Eastern Woodland Aboriginal peoples, including Anishinaabe (also known as Ojibwa), Ottawa, Algonquin, Abenaki, Maliseet, and Mi'kmaq. The belts have strong political, economic, and social purposes among the First Nations who use them. In some nations, such as with the Anishinaabe, early agreements pertaining to land were negotiated between Europeans and First Nations with wampum (Borrows 1997). For the Haudenosaunee, the wampum belts had a strong communicative value, as a medium for sharing messages (Murray 2000: 139).

It is important to acknowledge that our understanding of pre-contact economies has, for the most part, been constructed through post-contact, non-Aboriginal sources. This information has largely come from the early stories, accounts, and experiences of explorers and missionaries, and of anthropologists and historians, though Aboriginal oral histories exist. Despite this difficulty with the written record of history, it is common to read phrases such as "pre-sovereignty," "pre-contact," or "prior to European control" in Supreme Court of Canada decisions as a reference point in establishing what can be considered a "traditional" Aboriginal practice. The court's tendency to focus on the pre-contact era, along with legislative and constitutional issues, has an effect on Aboriginal peoples' ability to participate in contemporary economy (as will be discussed in subsequent chapters).

Encounter and Colonization

In the 15th century, explorers began to arrive on the Atlantic, Arctic, and Pacific shores of what is now Canada. While many think of the presence of John Cabot in the east in 1497 as a point of first contact in the Atlantic, the Mi'kmaq encountered Basque whalers prior to him. In 1560, the Inuit sighted Martin Frobisher in the North and, in 1778, the Nuu-chah-nulth encountered James Cook in the Pacific (see appendix A for a timeline of exploration, settlement, and development). These explorers ventured from Europe to discover new lands, the so-called New World, which was perceived as being *terra nullius*, empty land for the taking. Arriving in the New World, explorers "discovered" a land with an abundance of animals and fish that could be shipped back to Europe for an international market. Contrary to the explorer's expectations of an "empty land," Aboriginal peoples had lived, hunted, fished, and trapped here for millennia, and it had been flourishing with its own economies, cultures, and political systems, some would say since time immemorial.

After initial European exploration, French settlement began in what is now known as the Maritime Provinces with the establishment of Port Royal in 1604. This settlement was located on the shore of the Bay of Fundy in Acadia (present-day mainland Nova Scotia). Other trading posts developed in the east, with the establishment of New France (present-day Québec) in 1608, LaHave on the southern shore of Nova Scotia in 1632, Port Toulouse (present-day St. Peter's, Nova Scotia) in 1650, and Louisbourg, Nova Scotia in 1713. Early settlers in these areas worked with the Mi'kmaw and Algonquin peoples to adapt existing trade routes and learn how to live off the land. As settlement progressed into present-day Québec and Ontario, European encounter, settlement, and encroachment continued into Haudenosaunee, Cree, and more western Algonquin territories.

> *Terra nullius* is a Latin expression describing land that no one owns. In such cases, such as in international law, the first to occupy it assumed sovereignty. Today, we might more correctly say "presumed" sovereignty.

Subsistence economies were not immediately halted by the arrival of the Europeans. Relationships between First Nations and the French were often more successful given that the French followed the necessary diplomatic formalities of gift giving and coexistence that the First Nations expected of them in order to maintain a degree of peace (Borrows 1997: 158). British occupation, however, was less cooperative. There was increased struggle in terms of political, cultural, and economic power (Murray 2000: 15). In many early treaty agreements—which might be thought of as rules of trade—such as the Treaty of Niagara between the British and the Anishinaabe, it was stated that, in order to maintain coexistence, the British had obligations to the Anishinaabe, such as gift giving (Borrows 1997); however, the British often did not undertake these formalities. As a result, conflict sometimes ensued (Borrows 1997: 158). Although trade and economic relationships changed throughout the different waves of European settlement, the domination of the British brought the most significant changes to the lives of Indigenous populations (Murray 2000; Borrows 1997).

In 1713, under the Treaty of Utrecht, whatever rights of occupancy the French had established (on areas of Hudson Bay, Newfoundland, New Brunswick, and the colony of Acadia) were ceded to the British. As Acadia only included what is now mainland Nova Scotia, the Treaty of Utrecht left Île Royale (present day Cape Breton Island and Prince Edward Island) in French control. They established their capital at Louisbourg, on Cape Breton Island. Through the imposition of this treaty, the British encouraged many to migrate to Île Royale. Beginning in the early 1700s, Mi'kmaw populations

> A **treaty** is an agreement or contract that is written between two or more nations.

were also subject to treaties of peace and friendship made with the British (see chapter 13 for discussion of the different types of treaties in Canada).

Many encounters and early agreements between First Nations and Europeans were, however, interpreted unevenly by the parties involved. First Nations often understood a relationship of equality, while the European parties understood a relationship of dominance. For example, in 1760, Minavavana, Anishinaabe Chief at Michilimakinac, noted that in the Treaty of Niagara government-to-government relationships of coexistence were established. He asserted that the Anishinaabe were not conquered by the Europeans, and that their allegiance was to stay with the Great Spirit. This demonstrates that Anishinaabe understood that the two nations or governments were parallel (like the lines of a two-row wampum) in their reliance on one another for trade and peace (Borrows 1997: 158).

In 1763, the British conquered and established control of New France under the Treaty of Paris, issued by King George III, which was followed by the Royal Proclamation of 1763. With the proclamation came the establishment of rules governing British colonial relations with the Aboriginal population (discussed in chapter 6). The proclamation set aside large portions of land reserved for the "Indians," which was not to be encroached upon by settlers. It was understood that the Aboriginal population possessed rights to the land, and that the land could only be occupied by settlers if it was purchased by or ceded to the Crown. The consequences of this are discussed in chapter 2.

Development in Canada continued with the establishment of the Province of Upper Canada in 1791 and its capital, York (present-day Toronto), in 1793. York served as a fort during the War of 1812, which pitted the United States against Great Britain (and, consequently, British Canada); with an influx of United Empire Loyalists, Upper Canada was predominately British (Armstrong 1985). Upper Canada encompassed the traditional lands of the Huron (also known as Wyandot), Haudenosaunee, and Anishinaabe peoples. With British domination, exploration moved westward and settlement flourished, continuing in the west, in many cases, centuries later than it did in the east. Nevertheless, it was marked by economic motivations of trade and capitalism (Scott 2012: 46). Traditional techniques and practices became adopted strictly dependent upon the demands of trade. This included pottery, woodworking, and stone carving to produce ceramic pipes, ceremonial masks, and gunflints (Richter 1992: 86-87).

Some nations, such as the Haudenosaunee, maintained some degree of their gift economies, with economic reciprocity and redistribution. However, as European settlement and the establishment of reserve land continued, there was a shift in economic motivation for Aboriginal peoples from exchange and gift economies to a capitalistic system as introduced by Europeans (Murray 2000: 21). In some cases, this capitalist model

Ceded land is land which has been surrendered or transferred to another party.

disturbed kinship systems. European social structures influenced those of Aboriginal communities, placing patriarchal voice into some Aboriginal systems—to which matrilineal societies were especially vulnerable. Conflict arose between Aboriginal and European populations with the imposition of British dominance due to a lack of respect and acknowledgement of long-established kinship patterns of chiefs, rank, and status in Aboriginal societies (Murray 2000). In some cases, Europeans would refuse to conduct trade relations with females, thereby limiting female power in trade and early cross-cultural economies.

The wampum belt took on new meaning in the context of Aboriginal-settler relations. In the presentation of the two-row wampum belt to settlers, there was an establishment of treaty relations with a foundation of peace, friendship, and respect between the Indigenous population and the British Crown (Borrows 1997: 164). In the case of the Treaty of Niagara, which resulted from the Royal Proclamation of 1763, this agreement between the Crown and the Haudenosaunee established both the interaction and separation of European and Haudenosaunee societies (Borrows 1997). In addition, the wampum belt contained within it a presentation of the proclamation and recognition of oral statements; it symbolized both political and economic relations (Borrows 1997: 161; Murray 2000).

In other contexts, the wampum also took the form of currency. The function of the wampum shifted from a gift economy and reciprocal exchange to a capitalistic commodity exchange along pre-existing trade routes (Ceci 1990). In New England, many Europeans quickly recognized the importance of the wampum belt and its value as a medium for trade and exchange (Murray 2000: 121). They began to attach monetary values to the wampum soon after. Europeans first recognized it as a commodity and then as a form of currency, which eventually led to Europeans producing wampum belts in order to meet economic demand (Murray 2000: 121).

> **Capitalism** is an economic system in which surplus may be produced, creating a profit which is kept by private individuals or businesses.

> **Currency** is a medium used to facilitate exchange, generally a system of money.

The Fur Trade

The trade routes that had been established in the east spread westward as European settlers adapted existing trade routes between established settlements in Nova Scotia, Québec, and Ontario. Residents of these settlements were predominantly men working in the fur trade, and the settlements were established in close proximity to First Nation communities. It was no coincidence that trade routes and trade posts had close proximity to Aboriginal communities. Aboriginal peoples were key players in the trade, as they knew the routes, land, and animals better than did the European traders, hunters, and trappers (Richter 1992; Brown 1980; Innis 1999).

The Hudson's Bay Company (HBC) was established in 1670 by a royal charter that allowed the British Crown to trade on the territory of Rupert's

Land, a third of what is now Canada. In 1779, the North West Company (NWC) was developed by traders in Montréal in order to compete with HBC. The presence and development of colonial fur-trade posts did not immediately hinder Aboriginal subsistence in these territories, nor did they affect all Aboriginal populations in the same way (Richter 1992: 3). As the capitalist economy grew, there was a rise in non-Aboriginal hunting and fishing, which resulted in Indigenous populations having a greater dependence on the HBC (McKlem 1997: 102). Aboriginal men worked as fur-trade labourers for cash wages at posts assisting European traders.

As trade and demand for animal pelts increased, Aboriginal peoples began to alter the manner in which they hunted, from a subsistence model to one for trade with Europeans. This is an early example of Aboriginal peoples responding to market demand. This shift, however, led to an increased value placed on cash and an increased reliance on trading posts by Aboriginal communities (Richter 1992: 262). As a result of the intercultural interaction in the fur trade, new Aboriginal identities emerged. Relationships were fostered between Aboriginal women and European men, who were often lower-wage French workers from the HBC or NWC (Brown 1980; Rich 1967; Town 1998). From these unions, children of Aboriginal and European descent were born. Referred to in the past as "half-breeds," "mixed-bloods," and *bois-brûlé*, they are today identified as Métis.

> The **Hudson's Bay Company** was founded in 1670. Though it began as a network of trading posts that controlled the fur trade in Canada, it evolved into a major retailer and still has storefronts in Canada today.
>
> The **North West Company** was founded in 1779 and competed with the Hudson's Bay Company in the fur trade until the two companies merged in 1821. In 1987, the Hudson's Bay Company divested itself of northern trading posts. The purchaser brought back the North West Company name, establishing stores in northern Canada and Alaska.

The men who fathered these children often had wives in Europe; however, the majority of the men who fathered these children were in relations with Aboriginal women by 1812 (Brown 1980). Métis identities became stronger and more prevalent with the progression of the fur trade in Canada. Métis children were raised by their Indigenous mothers and grandmothers. This placed women at the centre of Métis communities and as major players in the fur-trade development as they built further relationships with the traders (Van Kirk 1980; Devine 2004).

In 1821, the NWC was taken over by the HBC, enabling its expansion into the North. HBC began to establish trading posts in various locations there for the trade of oil, blubber, fox skin, and whalebone. As part of the business strategy underpinning trade, posts were established in close proximity to areas of Inuit habitation, as hunting and trapping routes would be within range of these areas (Damas 2002: 17). The HBC opened a trading post on Baffin Island in 1911 because of the economic potential it represented (Damas 2002: 19). HBC's development in the North continued into the 1920s, with new trading posts established at Cape Dorset, Pangnirtung, Pond Inlet, and Amadjuak (Damas 2002: 19).

The presence of the trade posts in the North, as had occurred in southern Canada, impacted the nomadic and subsistence lifestyle of the Inuit. As a result of early whaling practices, the Inuit in the eastern Canadian Arctic had already encountered Europeans and experienced relocation to a lesser extent. However, a greater dependency on settler goods and the relocation of Inuit to new trapping areas by traders in the 1920s and 1930s resulted in the establishment of permanent settlements, which represented a significant change to traditional lifeways and has had a lasting impact.

Conclusion

Aboriginal communities that existed prior to colonization were diverse and complex. They had economic systems and governance structures that guided the way individuals and groups interacted with one another. Their experiences have shaped who they have become and the way they engage today. Over centuries, societal structures have changed and adapted as each community connected with and was influenced by other nations. Each community's past experience with traditional ceremony, governance structures, treaties, political alliances, and exchange systems continue to influence their attitudes and approaches toward businesses and partnership opportunities today.

Key Points:

- Pre-contact economies were subsistence-based and redistributive.

- Europeans used Indigenous trade routes and networks to accomplish their trade goals.

- Treaties were entered into, but not necessarily understood in the same way by the parties.

- Government policy decisions directly and indirectly impact economies.

- Women played an important role in the fur trade.

- The fur trade, along with other factors, significantly changed Aboriginal culture.

- There was a move from Aboriginal subsistence economies to a capitalist economy; however, some aspects of pre-contact redistributive economies are still practiced in Aboriginal communities today.

- Supreme Court of Canada decisions often refer to the pre-contact era to establish what can be considered a "traditional" practice. This has an effect on Aboriginal peoples' ability to participate in the contemporary economy because it fails to recognize the diverse experiences and timelines of distinct communities, and the ability for practices to adapt and change.

Questions for Review:

1. What was the basis of pre-contact business? How was it done region to region?

2. How do subsistence economies differ from capitalist economies?

3. What is a gift economy? Are there any analogous structures in today's mainstream society?

4. What impact did capitalism have on Aboriginal kinship systems and societies?

5. Why might Aboriginal and European parties have different understandings of the treaties they were entering into with one another? How might these understandings and assumptions have influenced next steps and relationships more generally?

6. What strategies did European trading posts use to enable their success?

7. What was the immediate and long-term effect of the HBC on pre-contact trade and trade networks?

Suggested Assignments:

1. Develop a map of pre-contact trade routes in Canada with principle products identified.

2. Research treaties in other areas of Canada and how they enabled or impacted trade.

3. What is the current relationship between the North West Company and Aboriginal peoples?

References

Armstrong, F. H. 1985. *Handbook of Upper Canadian Chronology.* Toronto: Dundurn Press.

Anderson, R. B. 1999. *Economic development among the Aboriginal peoples of Canada: The hope for the future.* North York, ON: Captus Press.

Anderson, M. 2000. *Potlatch at Gitsegukla: William Beynon's field notebooks.* Vancouver: University of British Columbia Press.

Borrows, J. 1997. *Wampum at Niagara: the royal proclamation, Canadian legal history, and self-government.* In *Aboriginal and treaty rights in Canada: Essays on law, equity, and respect for difference*, ed. M. Asch., 155-172. Vancouver: University of British Columbia Press.

———. 2005. "Indigenous Legal Traditions in Canada." *Washington University Journal of Law & Policy* 19:167.

Brown, J. S. H. 1980. *Strangers in blood: fur trade company families in Indian country.* Vancouver: University of British Columbia Press.

Ceci, L. 1990. "Wampum as a Peripheral Resource." In *The Pequots in Southern New England*, ed. L. Hauptman and J. D. Wherry. Norman, OK: University of Oklahoma Press.

Damas, D. 2002. *Arctic migrants/Arctic villagers: The transformation of Inuit settlement in the central Arctic.* Montreal: McGill-Queen's University Press.

Devine, H. 2004. *People who own themselves: aboriginal ethnogenesis in a Canadian family, 1660-1900.* Calgary: University of Calgary Press.

Drucker, P. 1967. "The Potlatch." In *Tribal and peasant economies: Readings in economic anthropology*, ed. G. Dalton and the American Museum of Natural History. Garden City, NY: Natural History Press.

Elias, P. D. 1995. *Northern aboriginal communities: Economies and development.* North York, ON: Captus Press.

Gregory, C. 1982. *Gifts and Commodities.* London: Academic Press.

Innis, H. A. 1999. *The fur trade in Canada: An introduction to Canadian economic history.* Toronto: University of Toronto Press.

Mauss, M. 1967. *The Gift: Forms and functions of exchange in archaic societies.* New York: W. W. Norton & Company.

McKlem, P. 1997. "Impact of Treaty 9 on natural resource development in northern Ontario." In *Aboriginal and treaty rights in Canada: Essays on law, equity, and respect for difference*, ed. M. Asch.Vancouver: University of British Columbia Press.

Murray, D. 2000. *Indian Giving: Economies of power in Indian-White Exchanges.* Boston: University of Massachusetts Press.

Rich, E. E. 1967. *The fur trade and the Northwest to 1857.* Toronto: McClelland and Stewart.

Richter, D. K. 1992. *The ordeal of the longhouse: The peoples of the Iroquois League in the era of European colonization.* Williamsburg, NC: University of North Carolina Press.

Roth, C. 2002. "Without Treaty, Without Conquest: Indigenous Sovereignty in Post-Delgamuukw British Columbia." *Wicazo Sa Review* 17 (2): 143-65.

Scott, T. L. 2012. *Postcolonial sovereignty? The Nisga'a final agreement.* Saskatoon, SK: Purich Publications.

Strathern, M. 1972. *Women in Between: Female Roles in a Male World.* London: Seminar Press.

Town, F. 1998. *The North West Company: Frontier Merchants.* Toronto: Umbrella Press.

Van Kirk, S. 1980. *Many Tender Ties: Women in Fur-trade Society in Western Canada, 1670-1870.* Winnipeg, MB: Watson & Dwyer.

PART ONE

Chapter 2

Issues concerning the use, designation, and "control" of land, and Indigenous peoples' spiritual connections to the land, are fundamental to doing business in Indigenous communities.

Prior to the Confederation of Canada in 1867, the British Crown signed treaties with First Nations on a nation-to-nation basis. These treaties oftentimes focused on the rights of settlers and of Aboriginal peoples, and accordingly, did not necessarily result in land cessions. For example, under the terms of the Treaty of Peace and Friendship with the Mi'kmaq, the Mi'kmaq did not cede any territory to the British. After Confederation, the Canadian government signed treaties with First Nations. These post-Confederation documents required Aboriginal peoples to cede land to Canadian settlers and to become co-managers with Canada of the lands they retained.

The Goverment of Canada did not pursue treaty-making with the Inuit or the Métis. Following decades of negotiation, Canada finally began to sign co-management agreements with Northern Indigenous peoples in 1990. With respect to the Métis, in 2013 the Supreme Court of Canada ruled that in passing the Manitoba Act of 1870, Canada's government of the day did not act in good faith with the Métis people. This ruling has opened negotiations in what could become one of the largest Aboriginal land-claim agreements in the country's history.

So, what does this mean for business? Status First Nations and their lands are subject to the *Indian Act*, and to its inherent impediments to private-equity financing, among other constraints. The co-management plans for the Yukon, Northwest Territories, and Nunavut appear to cede control over mineral development in vast areas of the North to Indigenous peoples. The noted Supreme Court of Canada decision on the Manitoba Métis opens up negotiations on the management of large swaths of Manitoba. Business developers working in Indigenous communities must take account of the distinct legal requirements and cultural practices that affect land use, which not only vary from region to region and community to community, but can be quite different from the requirements on non-Aboriginal lands.

Land and Indigenous Business Development in Canada
Rachel Rose Starks and Miriam Jorgensen

> There are many requirements in the *Indian Act* that make development difficult and discourage private investment and business activity.

—Ministry of Indigenous and Northern Affairs Canada (AANDC 2013a)

> The removal of the Crown in the First Nation-third party relationship, by itself, may be a positive step in allowing First Nations to deal directly with *their* land. The challenge is that First Nations also need to be able to provide the necessary certainty to licences or interests granted in First Nation land.

—Thomas Isaac (2004: 1053)

Before European contact, the Aboriginal peoples of Canada maintained, delineated, traded, and used land for individual, family, and community purposes. They were experienced land managers. For example, in a 2013 study of Mi'kmaw community land use, an Elder explained that, in the past, families controlled pieces of land, and neighbours respected that control by asking permission to cross, hunt, gather, or stay in that area (Starks et al. 2013). Indigenous peoples have rich knowledge of their territorial boundaries and have managed, protected, and defended them. In Western Canada, for instance, the Haida Nation has asserted its right to control Haida land by carefully mapping its territory using traditional knowledge (Kunst'aa guu–Kunst'aayah Reconciliation Protocol 2009).[1]

There is a strong connection between land and well-being among Indigenous peoples. Business development—the focus of this chapter—is a modern example of this connection. When Aboriginal nations manage their land with an eye toward community-appropriate business development, they enhance the opportunities that individuals and families have to make their lives, and community life, better.

Certainly, this connection is not unique to Aboriginal communities. It is evident in non-Aboriginal communities, urban and rural areas, and developed and developing countries. Even so, land management in Indigenous Canada has distinctive characteristics that warrant special attention along the path toward business development and community well-being. A leading example is the perspective that many Aboriginal peoples have on land ownership: they do not assume that land must be privately owned to be valuable as a development asset. Instead, they are committed to pursuing economic development *and* maintaining communal ownership of their territory.

How Land Matters to Business Development

It may be easiest to understand how land relates to business development by taking the perspective of a business person who wants to develop a business on private land in an off-reserve location favourable to commercial activity.

Before buying, leasing, or building on a property, the business developer will take account of the site's physical infrastructure and any laws that affect its use. Does it have road, water, electricity, sewer, and broadband access? Is the site zoned for commercial activity? What environmental regulations apply?

If the business developer wishes to purchase a parcel of land for the business, he conducts a property title search to make sure that no one else has claims on the land and to determine the property's specific boundaries. After the purchase, or if he already owns the land, the developer may use it as collateral in a business loan.

If the business owner ends up in a dispute concerning land ownership or use, he can rely on the laws that govern land ownership and use them to resolve the concern. If necessary, the issue can be heard in court, where a judge knowledgeable about property law applies the rules in a known, fair, and consistent way.

> **Collateral** is security for a loan; it is what a lender will keep if the borrower does not pay back the loan.

In the non-Aboriginal setting, business developers take these fundamental land-management arrangements for granted. Sites come equipped with water, sewer, electric, gas, and broadband infrastructure, or offer feasible connection options, especially in urban areas. Zoning and other land-use regulations, often established by municipal governments, are accessible and fixed (changes that do occur require public notice and consultation). Markets exist to buy and lease land, and to borrow against it. Centrally accessible and accurate registries, maintained by provincial or territorial governments, keep track of land ownership, property lines, and rights of access (e.g., easements and rights of way). Courts and judges are equipped to deal with the specifics of property law.

It is a completely different story on Aboriginal lands. Land-management arrangements are far too complex, cumbersome, and confusing to take for granted. There are important differences in land ownership, physical infrastructure, contracting practices, land-use approvals, registry options, collateralization, and regulatory authority. To demonstrate, this chapter primarily focuses on First Nation reserve, where numerous federal regulations and responsibilities crosscut Aboriginal communities' land- and business-development choices.

> A **reserve** is a parcel of land owned by the Crown but set aside for the use and benefit of First Nation peoples.

Land Ownership

On reserves, land title is held by the federal government ("the Crown") and is managed by the minister of Indigenous and Northern Affairs Canada (INAC). In theory, federal ownership preserves the integrity of a First Nation's land base and protects it from further encroachment. Also, in theory, INAC administrative oversight assists First Nations in managing resources in the best interests of their citizens. In practice, federal land ownership and INAC oversight distort accountability, limit First Nations' land sovereignty, and, most relevant for this discussion, introduce additional hurdles for business development.

Physical Infrastructure

While tasked with management of Aboriginal lands, INAC historically has been unable to fund investments in physical infrastructure that could support more robust, reserve-based business development. Aboriginal governments also have lacked funding to build infrastructure. Anyone working to develop and expand businesses on reserve must, therefore, consider whether a site has the transport, sewer, water, electric, and broadband infrastructure necessary for business operations, and if not, what can be done to change the situation.

Contracts

The federal government's ownership stake in reserve land means that many leases and other contracts concerning on-reserve land use are not agreements between two parties, as is typical off-reserve, but agreements among at least three parties: the land user, the First Nation government, and the minister of INAC.

Commercial Land Designation, Registration, and Lease Approval

Entrepreneurs seeking to develop a reserve-based business must first gain access to a land parcel designated for commercial use. Canadian law specifies the reserve land-designation process, requires INAC approval of land leases, and oversees the primary registry systems for Aboriginal lands (the Indian Land Registry System, First Nations Land Registry System,

Indigenous and Northern Affairs Canada, formerly Aboriginal Affairs and Northern Development Canada, is the department in the Government of Canada that is responsible for policies pertaining to Aboriginal peoples in Canada.
It has had several different names in the past, including Indian and Northern Affairs Canada, and the Department of Indian Affairs and Northern Development.

"Citizens" may be used in some communities to refer to First Nations peoples, particularly if the First Nation has developed its own citizenship code that outlines who is a citizen or member of the community. Sometimes, even without a citizenship code, citizen is used in place of "band members." Depending on the context, the two terms may or may not be used interchangeably. The same is true for "citizenship" and "membership."

Sovereignty refers to the right of a people to govern itself without outside interference.

and Self-Governing First Nations Land Registry System). If an Aboriginal government maintains its own land registry, a business owner must alternatively (or additionally) register the site lease with that government.

The processes of reserve land designation, lease approval, and site registry can take months to years. One study of First Nation business development suggests that, on average, these steps take less than a year for an off-reserve property as compared to twenty-nine months for an on-reserve site—approximately two-and-a-half times as long (Richard, Calla, and Le Dressay 2008). When a business opportunity requires faster decision-making, the lessee may opt to abandon the deal in favour of an off-reserve location (Libin 2008; Starks et al. 2013). Yet in some instances, even shifting to an off-reserve parcel can be problematic: "the requirement for federal approval also can delay development on land that is in the process of being added to reserve or that is subject to an unresolved land claim" (AANDC 2013a).

Land Collateralization

By far, the most binding consequence of reserve land's status as Crown land is that federal ownership makes it difficult to leverage the land to raise financial capital. In other words, neither a First Nation government nor its citizens can use their assigned parcels of reserve land as collateral for loans. Individuals, businesses, and First Nation governments can be granted rights to occupy and use reserve land, but, in general, they do not own the land outright. They cannot buy and sell reserve land (it is "inalienable"), and banks cannot seize it if a borrower fails to pay. Lacking the option of land-secured capital, entrepreneurs working in Aboriginal communities must find other ways to finance their businesses, which has been a challenge across all First Nation territories in Canada (Warkentin 2014). Although the issue of access to capital may be addressed through long-term leasing (by collateralizing the right to use the land for the duration of the lease; see Akee and Jorgensen 2014) or by mortgaging structures on the land, banks may not be willing to engage in such lending arrangements. Alternative financing options are discussed in chapter 8.

Regulatory Confusion

Crown ownership and the insertion of INAC administrative authority can generate additional layers of land-use regulation (rules concerning safety, waste removal, environmental protection, building standards, etc.) and, in turn, create confusion about the lawfulness of business operations. For example, which federal land-use regulations must a business operating on-reserve follow? Which provincial regulations? Which Aboriginal government regulations? What entity will enforce the rules and settle any disputes among the parties?

Under the *Indian Act*, designated land refers to a piece of reserve land that has been identified for a commercial or other purpose. It can be leased to a business partner, who may temporarily conduct business on the land, but the land remains part of the reserve.

Determining the answers to these questions is not straightforward. Provincial laws of "general application" can be applied on reserve, but if a provincial law affects the federal government's ability to manage lands reserved for Indians, provincial law will not apply (Baxter and Trebilcock 2009). Sometimes court decisions have been required to draw the line between provincial and federal jurisdiction (Mackenzie 2013). For example, "the courts regard provincial laws dealing with management or use of reserve lands, such as zoning, buildings, water and sewage disposal and regulations under the provincial Health Act, as affecting an integral part of primary federal jurisdiction over lands reserved for Indians and therefore inapplicable to First Nation reserves" (Mackenzie 2013: 21).

The *First Nations Commercial and Industrial Development Act* (FNCIDA) of 2006 addresses some of this regulatory complexity by allowing individual First Nations to opt into the regulatory system (provincial or federal) most relevant to their commercial or industrial development opportunities (AANDC 2012a). Yet even when a First Nation opts into FNCIDA, business owners also need to be aware of local Aboriginal laws: a First Nation may enact additional relevant laws itself, either as bylaws to federal law or as "community law" outside the federal process.[2]

Of course, regulatory clarification and, as needed, the requirement to gain regulatory approvals from other governments are additional sources of delay in on-reserve business development. Tsuu T'ina nation, whose reserve lands are south of Calgary, reports that their business-development plans have been subject to the review of at least six federal departments, stretching their timelines out over years (Libin 2008). More information on governance, policy, and regulations can be found in chapter 6.

Comparing Processes

Returning to the example of a hypothetical business person looking for a place to set up a business, if they are interested in securing a business site on a First Nation's reserve, they must first contact the First Nation's leasing office, if one exists, or the band's legal counsel (or other appropriate body). Reserve land may not be bought outright, so the business person must lease the parcel identified. Office staff will look up the parcel in one of INAC's three land registries, and if it is available for use, the business person will apply to use the land. INAC must approve the applicant's stated business use (AANDC 2013b). If the land is not already designated as available for commercial development, its designation must be changed. In accordance with Crown policy, the First Nation community will need to approve the new designation through a referendum in which an appropriate number of eligible voters must participate (*Indian Act* 1985 [1876]: sec. 37[2]). Once these steps are fulfilled, a contract is executed among three partners—the business person, the title holder of the land (a First Nation citizen or the First Nation government), and INAC.

To raise funds for start-up costs, some banks will accept the value of a long-term lease or of on-site structures as collateral for a loan (AANDC 2013a; Libin 2008). If such financing is unavailable, the business developer must use personal funds, borrow from friends or family, or even use credit-card debt.

Even with land and financing, the business person still needs reliable physical infrastructure. If access to public networks is limited or if there is no public provision of certain kinds of infrastructure and site services, the business person may have to develop site-specific infrastructure and services (Auditor General of Canada 2011). Finally, the business person must verify and comply with the various rules and regulations—issued by the First Nation, municipal, provincial, and federal governments—that apply to their business operation.

The *Indian Act*

What is the root of all these differences on Aboriginal territory? Why is the minister of Indigenous and Northern Affairs Canada involved in land and business transactions? The answers are found mainly in the Canadian *Indian Act*.

The Canadian parliament enacted the *Indian Act* in 1876 to define the relationship between the federal government and Canada's First Nations. Though amended over a dozen times, the *Act* is in many ways substantially unchanged from its original form and remains the central legislation affecting Aboriginal peoples in the 21st century (Hurley 2009; Hanson 2009). It stipulates that the minister of INAC is responsible for most areas of First Nations governance and, in so doing, creates a framework in which First Nations effectively have little room for true self-determination. Inuit and Métis peoples are not part of the act, but are affected similarly by other federal legislation and court rulings.

With regard to land, the *Indian Act* describes the nature of Indigenous territory and how it is to be managed. Reserve land is defined as territory owned by the Crown, but set aside for the use of First Nation peoples. While this land is a tiny fraction of the territory that First Nations used from time immemorial, it is all that the Canadian government acknowledges as remaining under their control. Yet even that control is limited in nature. First Nations governments can zone reserve land (e.g., identify which areas are available for residential, commercial, industrial, and traditional purposes). They can assign plots to individuals for housing or business development.

They can establish leases for the same. But the *Act* also requires the minister of INAC to oversee the management of reserve land for the good of each First Nation (Hurley 2009), a duty that includes the responsibility to regulate all matters concerning land tenure (*Indian Act* 1985 [1876]: s. 18). Thus, regardless of First Nation government actions, the minister is the ultimate authority on reserve land occupancy, possession, transfer arrangements, and all land assignments, leases, and contracts.

Three other important concepts affecting reserve land use that have roots in the *Indian Act* are "communal land," reserve land "designation," and "certificates of possession" (CPs).

Communal land is held by a community as a whole rather than by an individual or business. By providing for Crown ownership on behalf of all citizens of a given First Nation, the *Indian Act* (1985 [1876], s. 18) supports a communal land-holding system on reserves.

As noted above, if any reserve land is to be leased for development, the *Act* states that it must be designated for this purpose. Specifically, "except where this *Act* otherwise provides, lands in a reserve shall not be leased nor an interest in them granted until they have been designated under subsection 38(2) by the band for whose use and benefit in common the reserve was set apart," (*Indian Act* 1985 [1876]: s. 37[2]). Even after a majority vote of First Nation members required for designation, the *Act* requires that this assignment also has the minister's approval.

A First Nation may decide to allot land to individual citizens or families by granting CPs. A CP is a right to occupy and use a delineated section of reserve territory, but it is not outright ownership—the land is still owned by the Crown (Ballentyne and Dobbin 2000). Nonetheless, CP holders have a broad range of land-use rights. For example, a CP holder may build a house or houses on the land, develop a small business, engage in subsistence activities (hunting, fishing, farming), or pursue other traditional uses. Under *Indian Act* regulations, CP holders may lease their land to whomever they want, although the First Nation government and the Crown must approve the lease (*Indian Act* 1985 [1876]: s. 38).

Arguably, not every aspect of the *Indian Act* is harmful to First Nations. Broadly speaking, the act is useful in that it codifies the Canadian government's relationship with and fiduciary responsibility to Indians (Coates 2008). With regard to land, the act has helped protect remnant Aboriginal territory from being absorbed into the jurisdiction of municipalities and provinces. For the most part, however, the *Act* is colonial policy—and worse, outdated colonial policy, still replete with late-19th-century norms— that hampers First Nation self-determination (Provart 2003; Wilkins 2000; Coates 2008; Imai 2007). As this chapter demonstrates, restrictions on land management have been extremely harmful to on-reserve business develop-

A **certificate of possession** confers a right to occupy and use a parcel of reserve land, but it does not constitute ownership of that land.

ment, making it especially important for business-oriented First Nations to get out from underneath it.

Alternative Land-Management Frameworks

Given the complexity of the Aboriginal land-management systems designed by Canada, it is no wonder that First Nation peoples have developed alternative land-tenure models. Business developers on First Nations land should be aware of this expanding set of options and innovations—and know well the specific land-management arrangements that apply in the communities where they work.

Options under the *Indian Act*

"53/60" Delegated Authority and Regional Land-Administration Program

First Nations that continue to rely on the *Indian Act*'s regulatory framework may manage reserve land under so-called 53/60 delegated authority (so named for *Indian Act* sections 53-60) and through the Regional Land Administration Program (RLAP). These arrangements allow a degree of First Nation autonomy in land management. Under 53/60, a First Nation manages reserve land as the minister's agent; through RLAP, the First Nation becomes a land-management contractor for the minister (Noda 2004).

Reserve Land and Environmental Management Program

The Reserve Land and Environmental Management Program (RLEMP) updates and expands the more limited authorities of 53/60 and the RLAP. For example, the RLEMP makes it possible for First Nations to undertake environmental assessments, community land-use plans, and community environmental sustainability planning (AANDC 2014b).

Informal Arrangements

"Buckshee leases"[3] are informal leasing arrangements used by some First Nations and their citizens to work around the oversight and bureaucracy of INAC, increasing their own control over land transactions (Campo and Vear 2011). Buckshee leases are not an official leasing mechanism under the *Indian Act* and cannot be upheld in court. With that in mind, the benefits must be weighed against their potential costs. Large-scale and long-term lease arrangements in particular might benefit from stronger enforcement mechanisms.

> **Buckshee lease** refers to a leasing agreement between two parties that outlines the parameters of their relationship. However, because they are not subject to the approval of the minister of INAC, such leases are technically unenforceable. It represents the high degree of trust that exists between the two parties and is similar to solidifying an agreement with a handshake.

Options Outside the *Indian Act*

The *First Nations Land Management Act*

In 1996, thirteen First Nations successfully negotiated the Framework Agreement on First Nations Land Management (FAFNLM) with the Canadian government.[4] Canada ratified the agreement with passage of the *First Nations Land Management Act* (*FNLMA*) in 1999. Together, the FAFNLM and the *FNLMA* establish a pathway for First Nations to take control of reserve land management by opting out of most of the *Indian Act*'s land provisions and restrictions.

Under the FAFNLM, First Nations can manage their own land through a First Nations land code. A First Nation government develops, writes, ratifies, and enacts a code in consultation with the community. The process gives First Nations substantial latitude to structure land management and land use according to community preferences: each participating Aboriginal community has the authority to write laws on zoning, dispute resolution, environmental standards, land use, land allotments, business standards, and historical and cultural preservation, among other topics (see INAC 1996: part II). When a First Nation completes the process provided by the FAFNLM and *FNLMA*, the minister of INAC is no longer involved in their land management.

Land Claims

A land-claim settlement agreement typically is the result of decades of negotiation among an Indigenous people, a province, and the Canadian government. In regions covered by the so-called numbered treaties of the late 19th and early 20th centuries, comprehensive land-claim settlements have been necessary to address land rights specified in the treaties. Nation- or community-specific land-claim settlements address disputes or claims that involve one or a few named First Nations or other Aboriginal communities.[5] In British Columbia, land-claims settlements are occurring side-by-side with the modern treaty process: because only a handful of historic treaties exist regarding lands in British Columbia, Canada's courts have required the federal and provincial governments to address their historic land takings (BC Treaty Commission 2004).

Numbered treaties were made between Canada and multiple Aboriginal nations within a common geographical area. There are eleven such treaties spanning the Prairies, northern Ontario, and the Peace River and Mackenzie River valleys. More information on the different types of treaties in Canada can be found in chapter 13.

While each agreement is different, these settlements often provide Aboriginal communities with broader land-management authority than is available under the *Indian Act*—and have become an important means by which First Nations gain greater control over land management.

Self-government Agreements

Another way a First Nation can take control of its land is to enter into self-government agreements with federal, provincial, and local governments. Like land-claim settlement agreements, self-government agreements are unique to each First Nation. While most self-government agreements address natural resources, treaty requirements, or the development of First Nation constitutions, the specifics vary because "each region, community, and cultural group has different needs, opportunities, and capabilities to address through reforms of governance systems.... The shape and nature of Aboriginal self-government reflects local circumstances, pressures from non-members, and the imperatives of senior governments" (Coates and Morrison 2008: 114-15). Their content also may be affected by the preferences and capacities of partner governments: "finalizing agreements can be difficult, and controversial and promising developments at the local and regional level have often been reversed when final negotiations or implementation was attempted" (ibid.). Yet when the dust settles, most self-government agreements provide Aboriginal governments with substantial land-management authority—which in turn affects local business development.

> **Self-governance** is the control of a group's affairs by its own members. Some Aboriginal groups in Canada have successfully negotiated self-government agreements with the Government of Canada; however, an Aboriginal community may exercise self-governance even if it hasn't signed a self-government agreement.

Assessing Impact

So, do these land-management frameworks aimed at overcoming colonial policy actually work? Are they better for Indigenous nations and for business owners?

The FAFNLM and *FNLMA* have motivated a particularly active conversation on exactly these questions. Some view the FAFNLM and *FNLMA* as a great victory for First Nations' self-government. They release First Nations from the land-administration portions of the *Indian Act*, freeing them to manage land transactions (including business-related arrangements) without ministerial approval. Others have argued that the FAFNLM creates more uncertainty, especially for outside parties doing business with First Nations. With the minister of INAC no longer involved, long-established processes change.

Yet a changed relationship between First Nations and leaseholders, business owners, or government agencies is an obvious consequence—and in fact, the primary point—of establishing a new land-management framework. Certainly, new laws addressing licensing, leasing, taxation, zoning, building requirements, and so on, will have practical implications for contracting parties (Isaac 2004). Rather than viewing this change with trepidation, however, business developers might instead view it as the start of a *new* long-term arrangement: If a First Nation adopts its own land-management practices under the *FNLMA*, business developers no longer have to worry that future decolonization of federal policy (e.g., new legislation changing the scope of *Indian Act* land management) would lead to a substantial change in the rules.

One study of Aboriginal land-management frameworks—which included Aboriginal communities operating land-management regimes based on the FAFNLM and *FNLMA*, land-claim settlements, and self-government agreements—found that, in general, land transactions (leases, CPs, permits, etc.) could be executed more easily and more quickly under a First Nation-led land-management system than under the *Indian Act* (Starks et al. 2013). Land managers also reported that having a land-management system alone did not increase business activity on reserve. They noted that it was crucial to clearly communicate and build relationships with outside businesses and community-member entrepreneurs. Without that trust, having an efficient, accessible, culturally relevant system could not, on its own, lead to a thriving on-reserve economy (Starks et al. 2013).

Practicalities of Land Management for Business Development

The choice among land-management frameworks is an important foundational decision for First Nations. It is, however, only the first of a series of decisions necessary for structuring a land-management system supportive of business development on First Nations lands. An appropriately supportive Aboriginal community land-management system requires at least the following:

A *strategic vision* (determined by the community as a whole) of the First Nation's future that makes clear the desired role and nature of land in that future, and the desired role and nature of business development. What is the land situation that the community is trying to achieve? How does business development—by the First Nation, its citizens, and outsiders—fit into this vision?

A *comprehensive land inventory* that provides clear, accessible, usable information about the land base, including current land-tenure arrangements (Is the land held in common? Are parcels under CPs? Which parcels are leased by the nation, or by individuals?), parcel-by-parcel land-use data, parcel-by-parcel land-quality data (Is there road access to the parcel? Are there environmental contaminants on site?), the status of lands in dispute, etc. The idea is to provide adequate information for planners and decision-makers to engage in intelligent, informed land management, which will clarify the process of finding viable land for business development.

A *land-use plan* that links the strategic vision and land inventory, and provides a conception of the preferred uses of the First Nation's existing land base. It should indicate areas to be used for residential use, commercial development, and strictly public purposes. It should note areas of cultural or environmental significance, areas that are restricted from development, and any other land-use (or non-use) plans.

A *land code* that specifies community and individual rights—and responsibilities—in land. The code should specify how lands are to be held, registered, transferred, and used. It should specify where authority over land-related decisions rests, how that authority will be exercised, how disputes will be resolved, how additions to reserve will be handled, how regulations will be developed and enforced, and so on. The code also should include a clear process for amendments, in the event they become necessary. All of these elements should be designed in such a way that they meet both the community's land-related and business-related goals. For example, the land code should be clear enough in its assignments of rights and responsibilities that lenders have confidence in the value of leases and leasehold property (which helps business owners access financial capital).

The means of implementing and enforcing a code fairly and effectively. The community has to have the institutional and human capacity to do what the code requires (this is a matter both of governing structures and of necessary skills and resources) and the authority to enforce it. On the skills front, for example, staff tasked with implementing and enforcing the land code should understand the linkages between land policy and business development.

An institutionalized means of resolving disputes that is insulated from political interference and will be respected not only by the First Nation community, but also by the Canadian and relevant provincial government.

As this list[6] should make clear, creating a viable land-management system—a system that actually works to promote an Aboriginal community's goals (especially its business-development goals)—is a substantial undertaking. But business development is more likely to flow from this kind of careful planning and comprehensive thinking. Examples from Aboriginal communities across Canada underscore these points.

Aboriginal Land-Management Practices and Community Business Development: Brief Examples

Using First Nation Law to Increase the Development Value of Indigenous Lands

Westbank First Nation's self-governance agreement led to the creation of a Westbank First Nation constitution and a rule of Westbank law for the community (Coates and Morrison 2008). Since negotiating the agreement, the nation has worked consistently to improve its government, institute policies and procedures (particularly for land use and business development), address the challenge of rule enforcement, and become a transparent and accountable government (NCFNG [n.d.]). Residential and commercial real-estate development and management is a core business activity for this urban First Nation. To address federal government concerns that reserve residents who were not Westbank citizens might lack voice in government decisions that affected them (e.g., questions about leasing, taxation, budgets, and further land or commercial development), the First Nation established an advisory council under federal and Westbank law to represent these interests (Westbank n.d.). Westbank First Nation's strategic attention to the ways in which land use and business development go hand-in-hand, and to the development of law to maximize that connection, increased the development value of its lands by a factor of 120 over twenty years, from $100 million in 1991 to $1.2 billion in 2011 (Vogl 2013).

Providing Infrastructure and Services through an Intergovernmental Agreement

The Muskeg Lake First Nation opted into the *FNLMA* and has been operating under its own land code since 2005. As immediate neighbours to the municipality of Saskatoon, this urban First Nation chose to negotiate agreements with the Saskatoon municipal government for the provision of infrastructure and services such as water, sewer, roads, and schools (Dust 1995, 1997).

Municipal taxes typically cover the costs of infrastructure and service provision. Because reserve lands have a different tax status than non-reserve lands, the municipality was concerned that if it provided infrastructure and services to Muskeg Lake, businesses on reserve lands would realize an unfair advantage: their costs would be lower (AANDC 2014a). Muskeg Lake and Saskatoon addressed this concern by agreeing to a schedule of fees that the First Nation would pay in lieu of taxes (Dust 1995, 1997). As a result, Muskeg Lake gained access to infrastructure and services that make business operations possible.

Redefining the Terms of Land Ownership to Improve the Leverage Value of Assets

Nisga'a Lisims (First Nation) in northern British Columbia was the first to sign a treaty through the modern British Columbia treaty process. The 1998 treaty agreement, which acknowledged the First Nation's significant powers of self-government, went hand-in-hand with a land settlement that established full Nisga'a Nation title to 1,930 square kilometers of land. In 2013, after fifteen years of planning, the Nisga'a Lisims government also became the first to transfer land title in what is known as "fee simple" to a citizen of the nation (that is, ownership rests with the individual, not with the nation as a whole). The hope is that the new system will allow Nisga'a citizens more options to develop assets, because they will be able to use their land as collateral (CBC News 2013).

While many other First Nations do not support individual ownership—because, for example, they are wary of the implications of using reserve land as collateral (it can be seized by a lender in the case of default) or because there are strong cultural supports for communal ownership—the Nisga'a Nation implemented several legal and institutional safeguards to preserve the integrity of its land base. First, it made sure that land ownership expressed in the treaty, and other governments' interpretation of that land ownership, supported full Nisga'a Lisims government authority on the land. In other words, *underlying title* rests fully with the First Nation, and the Nisga'a Lisims government, not the Crown, has jurisdiction over all sales, estate transfers, land management, environmental codes, taxation, and land appropriation (a particularly important power in this context). Second, the Nisga'a use a Torrens system for land registry, in which the recorded information is itself evidence of the right to land. This contrasts with a deeds system, which requires registry of all historical instruments related to land title. The Torrens system keeps Nisga'a's underlying rights evident in all land transactions. This assertion of ultimate ownership and the system of supports for it are key innovations the nation is counting on to help it retain control as the Nisga'a land market develops (see Flanagan, Alcantara and Le Drassay 2010).

> **Fee simple** is a form of freehold land ownership. The ownership is absolute, without any conditions.

Complicating Business Development with a Bureaucratic Indigenous Governance Structure

Nunavut, an Inuit-controlled territory in the far north of Canada, provides a less positive example of land governance for business development.[7] Inuit living in Nunavut exchanged Aboriginal land title to all of their traditional land in the Nunavut Settlement Area for the specific rights and benefits in the Nunavut Land Claims Agreement (NLCA), which was signed in 1993. Nunavut Tunngavik Incorporated (NTI)—a quasi-governmental body—

ensures that promises made under the land-claims agreement are fulfilled. For example, the NTI Department of Lands and Resources "promotes and protects Inuit interests in the lands and resources of Nunavut" (NTI 2015). This means a territory-level department is essentially responsible for land management across this extensive territory—that is, for all matters relating to land administration, including land-use planning, environmental protection, water and marine management, minerals, oil and gas management, and geographic information systems and database technologies. The central department eliminates the possibility of conflicting policies, but also provides for only indirect community (hamlet-level) input into land policy and land-use decisions. Not surprisingly, commercial land-use decisions are decisions in which individual communities would like to participate, but the structure makes that difficult (though not impossible). At best, communities have input with one of the three regional Inuit associations, whose job it is to "work on behalf of Inuit in the regions to develop various businesses, [and] economic and career development opportunities" (NTI 2009, "Inuit Regional Development Corporations"). Ultimately, the experience of individual Inuit communities operating under the governing structures established by the NLCA has been similar to the experience of First Nation communities operating under the constraints of the *Indian Act*. Worse, Inuit communities lack the types of self-governing options that southern communities have to exercise greater local control (such as 53/60 authority or the *FNLMA*), as the Government of Canada already considers them to be self-governing (Ritsema et al. 2015).

> A **hamlet** is a small settlement or village.

Aboriginal Land-Management Practices and Community Business Development: Membertou Case Profile

The Membertou Mi'kmaw band in Unama'ki (Cape Breton, Nova Scotia) occupies a small reserve adjacent to the city of Sydney, Nova Scotia. Membertou is well known among Indigenous nations in Canada as a commercial success story. Membertou has pushed its governing bureaucracy to be efficient and reliable, and was the first International Standardization Organization (ISO)-certified Indigenous government in the world (Tattrie 2011; Kayseas, Hindle, and Anderson 2006).

Despite these advances, Membertou's leadership had long viewed land-related *Indian Act* requirements as unnecessary constraints on their economic development efforts—and by the late 2000s, the band's leaders decided the time was ripe to do something about them. According to Dan Christmas, a senior advisor to the band, "our leadership finds it offensive that the *Indian Act* forces us to go through a land designation process. We need to give legal contracts to businesses, and we need to have the power to develop our own laws around land allocation and use" (NCFNC 2010: par. 5). At the same time, exiting the *Indian Act* could have costs. For example,

Membertou Executive Director Trevor Bernard pointed out that without the "security" of *Indian Act* procedures, banks might be unwilling to offer long-term financing (Starks et al. 2013). So, while its leaders felt strongly that the band had progressed as far as was possible under the *Indian Act*, and that a new land-management system was needed, they also knew that any new system would need to provide investors with certainty. In other words, if Membertou developed its own land-management rules, they would need to be transparent, fair, consistent, and enforceable.

After weighing the options, Membertou First Nation became a signatory to the FAFNLM in April 2012. Soon thereafter, the band's administration began strategic visioning, held information sessions, interviewed Membertou citizens to better understand preferences for land use, consulted with the Kwilimu'kw Maw-klusuaqn (the Mi'kmaq Rights Initiative, an organization that negotiates land rights and priorities for Mi'kmaq across Nova Scotia),[8] and otherwise engaged in developing Membertou land law. Ultimately, the Membertou land code must be ratified by the band's voters and approved by INAC. When the process is complete, Canada will transfer land-management responsibilities to the band, and Membertou will have the flexibility and self-determination over land that it desires.

Measured against the practicalities of land management for business development discussed above, Membertou's process is appropriately comprehensive. Membertou has:

A strategic vision. Strategic visioning began with high-level chief and council discussions. Chief and council also tasked a governance committee (consisting of a council member, staff persons, and several community members) to lead a community-wide process. Among other things, the governance committee commissioned a study on Aboriginal land-management options and actively participated in the research process (Starks et al. 2013). Because a desire to improve the business climate motivated land-management reform, visioning paid attention to the impact that changes might have on commercial activity.

A comprehensive land inventory. Membertou has land holdings on four reserves: Membertou Indian Reserve 28B, Sydney Indian Reserve 28a, Caribou Marsh Indian Reserve, and Malagawatch Indian Reserve 4 (AANDC 2012b). Membertou holds the records pertaining to these land holdings, which serve as a base for a more comprehensive land inventory.

A land-use plan. Membertou initiated land-use planning discussions in concert with its visioning process. The community has worked to delineate commercial, residential, public-use, and protected areas.[9] Community members were especially in favour of protecting and sustaining the natural environment (Starks et al. 2013). A consulting firm has helped the community map this input, and facilitators have used the resultant land-use maps in an iterative process to clarify ideas and build consensus. Because the maps contain additional data relevant to current land use, they also are part of the land inventory. The community worked on visioning Membertou's future and on identifying ways to incorporate core values into a land code.

A land code, with processes for amendments. Creating and ratifying a land code is a core component of the FAFNLM process. When this chapter was written, Membertou had finished drafting a land code with community input. As directed by the community, code writers tried to craft a document that reflected Membertou's vision for the future and values concerning land and laid out clear land-management rules. A process for amendments was included. It must be ratified by the community through a referendum.

The means of implementing and enforcing a code, and resolving disputes. Membertou's research on land management included learning from other land managers across Aboriginal Canada. They found that having strong community involvement in code development increases compliance and aids in enforcement. When disputes arise, other communities have decided that some types of disputes (e.g., commercial contracts) will be settled in provincial court, while other conflicts will be addressed through alternative dispute resolution. Membertou used this research in its plans for land-code implementation, enforcement, and dispute resolution (Starks et al. 2013).

Land Control, Self-Determination, and the Future of Canadian Indigenous Nations

Canadian law creates many roadblocks to business-friendly land management in Indigenous communities. Self-governance over land can remove these barriers, giving a community greater control over the land-management processes, regulations, and financing issues that affect business development.

But achieving self-governance can be complicated. There are a variety of mechanisms for gaining control—each Aboriginal nation has different needs and different opportunities—and the choice of frameworks may not be straightforward. After a choice is made, the nation must attend to the detailed work of writing the statutes and regulations that will govern land management and land-related economic development within its territory—and gain Canada's approval of its work.

A goal shared by most Indigenous communities in Canada is for their lands to be places where community members—their own citizens—want to live. But even though an Aboriginal community is "home," and may be rich in cultural resources, if it offers only limited economic opportunity and few community amenities, it may not be an attractive place to live.

Certainly, some First Nation citizens choose to move off reserve or out of the region for reasons unrelated to local opportunities—but many choose to leave because of the limited options available to them if they stay. Off-reserve communities offer jobs and the chance to put marketable skills to work. They offer entertainment, education, healthcare, and family-support options. Much of this vitality is driven by a thriving local economy. If First Nations can replicate such opportunities on reserve (with the caveat that development should be driven by community preferences and occur under community control), "home" becomes an attractive place for Aboriginal community members to live, work, and stay.

This, then, is the point of self-determined land management for business development: to make it possible for an Indigenous nation to offer options in terms of work, services, and leisure that fulfill citizen and community aspirations. In other words, the ultimate goal of First Nation land management for business development isn't really economic development at all: it's managing the land for development that will preserve, enliven, and invigorate the nation as an Aboriginal nation on traditional lands for years to come.

This is Muskeg Lake First Nation's goal, and Westbank's, Membertou's, and that of every other Indigenous community in Canada that is working to increase control over land management and change the incentives for business formation: self-governed land management helps assure the well-being, vitality, and life of the nation and its people.

Key Points

- The Indian Act significantly affects business and economic development on First Nation reserves. Consequently, development is often more difficult.

- The rules governing ownership and control of treaty lands and reserve lands are not always clearly defined or easy to understand. Risk-adverse banks and other lending institutions have been less willing to provide financing through traditional means (discussed further in chapter 8).

- There are some initiatives that help to address issues of land ownership and management, such as the First Nations Land Management Act, by working with governing bodies to clarify and streamline land-management processes.

- The ability to set parameters around land use for many is central to a community's ability to be self-governing. Many Aboriginal communities across Canada are negotiating self-government agreements, often with varying scope depending on the goals of the particular community or groups of communities.

Questions for Review

1. Why does land, and how it is managed and regulated, matter in a business context?

2. What are some of the challenges associated with business development on reserve land?

3. What is the *Indian Act* and how does it specifically affect business development on reserve land?

4. What other models exist for land management in Aboriginal communities and what are the benefits and drawbacks of each?

5. What practical considerations are important in relation to land management?

Suggested Assignments

1. Conduct research on the Inuit model of land governance. Is it really less positive, as the authors suggest?

2. Explore the process of developing a business on a specific First Nation's lands:

   a. For any of the First Nations mentioned in this chapter, or another First Nation in which you are interested, search for available land-related documents regarding business development. For example, look for zoning laws; directions for obtaining a site lease; information about processes the nation uses to certify that businesses meet environmental or safety regulations; etc.

   b. Based on this documentation, how would you start the process of developing a small business in this community? If the information was difficult to find—or if you cannot find it at all—what does that imply about the process of business development within this First Nation?

3. Find the list of First Nations that have become signatories to the Framework Agreement on First Nation Land Management (FAFNLM). Choose one of these First Nations and examine

its land law or land code. Given this law, what do you now know—if anything—about the process of business development on the First Nation's lands?

Notes

1. See also Tsilhqot'in v. British Columbia (2014), which more broadly affirms Aboriginal nations' activities in defense of territorial boundaries.

2. See, for example, "Akwesasne Law Enactment Procedure," Mohawk Council of Akwesasne (2012), and "Community Decision Making Process," Mohawk Council of Kahnawà:ke (n.d.).

3. British slang meaning "free," a gift, or, interestingly, a bribe.

4. The original First Nation signatories were Westbank, Musqueam, Lheidlei T'enneh, N'quatqua, Squamish, Siksika, Muskoday, Cowessess, Opaskwayak Cree, Nipissing, Mississaugas of Scugog Island, Chippewas of Mnjikaning, Chippewas of Georgina Island, and Saint Mary's.

5. See, for example, Bigstone Cree Land Claim Settlement Agreement (2010), Fort William Boundary Claim Agreement (2011), and the Nunavut Land Claims Agreement (1993).

6. This discussion is adapted from a private community report co-written by one of the authors (Jorgensen) and Stephen Cornell.

7. There is debate over the benefits and drawbacks of centralized vs. decentralized governance and management of traditional territories.

8. For more information on Kwilimu'kw Maw-klusuqn, see www.mikmaqrights.com.

9. Generally, protected areas are sites with environmental and cultural resources valuable to the Mi'kmaw people.

References

AANDC (Aboriginal Affairs and Northern Development Canada). 2012a. First Nations Commercial and Industrial Development Act, March 31. http://www. aadnc- INAC.gc.ca/eng/1100100033561/1100100033562 (accessed February 13, 2014).

———. 2012b. Membertou Band, July 18. https://www.aadnc- INAC.gc.ca/ eng/1100100017130/1100100017131 (accessed March 30, 2014).

———. 2013a. Land Management, July 24. http://www.aadnc- INAC.gc.ca/ eng/1100100034737/1100100034738 (accessed January 10, 2014).

———. 2013b. Locatee Lease Policy and Directive, July 24. https://www.aadnc- INAC.gc.ca/eng/1374091139187/1374091182369 (accessed January 13, 2015).

———. 2014a. Fact Sheet: Taxation by Aboriginal Governments, March 31 https://www.aadnc- INAC.gc.ca/eng/1100100016434/1100100016435 (accessed April 11, 2015).

———. 2014b. Reserve Land and Environment Management Program (RLEMP), May. https://www.aadnc-INAC.gc.ca/eng/1399305895503/1399306034289 (accessed January 20, 2015).

Akee, R. K. Q. and M. Jorgensen. 2014. Property Institutions and Business Investment on American Indian Reservations. *Regional Science and Urban Economics* 46:116-25.

Auditor General of Canada. 2011. Programs for First Nations on Reserves. In *The 2011 Status Report of the Auditor General of Canada to the House of Commons*. Ottawa: Office of the Auditor General of Canada.

Ballentyne, B. and J. Dobbin. 2000. Options for Land Registration and Survey Systems on Aboriginal Lands in Canada. Prepared for Legal Surveys Division of Geomatics Canada. https://www.acls-aatc.ca/files/english/aboriginal/Ballantyne-Dobbin_report.pdf (accessed December 5, 2015).

Baxter, J. and M. Trebilcock. 2009. "Formalizing" Land Tenure in First Nations: Evaluating the Case for Reserve Tenure Reform. *Indigenous Law Journal* 7 (2): 45-122.

BC Treaty Commission. 2004. *Why Treaties? A Legal Perspective*. Vancouver: BC Treaty Commission.

Bigstone Cree Land Claim Settlement Agreement. 2010. An Agreement between the Bigstone Cree First Nation, the Government of Canada, and the Government of Alberta. http://www.specific-claims.ca/~specific/bigstone%20treaty%20land%20entitlement.

Campo, G. and H. Vear. 2011. Land Interests in Reserves. Paper presented at the Native Courtworker and Counselling Association of BC, Aboriginal People and the Law Programme, Vancouver, BC, April 15. http://www.woodwardandcompany.com/wp-content/uploads/pdfs/LandInterestsinReserves-April142011-FINAL.pdf (accessed Feb. 11, 2016).

CBC News. 2013. B.C.'s Nisga'a becomes only First Nation to privatize land. *CBC.ca*, November 4. http://www.cbc.ca/news/canada/british-columbia/b-c-s-nisga-a-becomes-only-first-nation-to-privatize-land-1.2355794. Accessed December 1, 2015.

Coates, K. 2008. *The Indian Act and the Future of Aboriginal Governance in Canada*. West Vancouver, BC: National Centre for First Nations Governance.

Coates, K. S. and W. R. Morrison. 2008. From Panacea to Reality: The Practicalities of Canadian Aboriginal Self-Government Agreements. In *Aboriginal Self-Government in Canada: Current Trends and Issues*, 3rd ed., ed. Y. D. Belanger. Saskatoon, SK: Purich Publishers.

Dust, T. M. 1995. *The Impact of Aboriginal Land Claims and Self-Government on Canadian Municipalities: The Local Government Perspective*. 1st ed. Toronto: ICURR Press.

———. 1997. The Impact of Aboriginal Land Claims and Self-Government on Canadian Municipalities. *Canadian Public Administration* 40 (3): 481-94. doi: 10.1111/j.1754-7121.1997.tb01520.x

First Nations Land Management Act. 1999. SC 1999, c 24. http://canlii.ca/t/5288m.

Fort William First Nation Boundary Claim Settlement. 2011. An Agreement between the Fort Williams First Nation, the Government of Canada, and the Government of Ontario. http://www.specific-claims.ca/~specific/fort%20william%20northern%20boundary%20settlement.

Flanagan, T., C. Alcantara and A. Le Dressay. 2010. *Beyond the Indian Act: Restoring Aboriginal Property Rights*. Montreal: McGill-Queen's University Press.

Hurley, M. C. 2009. The Indian Act. Parliamentary Information and Research Service, Library of Parliament, Ottawa. PRB 09-12E. http://www.parl.gc.ca/Content/LOP/ResearchPublications/prb0912-e.pdf (accessed December 5, 2015).

Imai, S. 2007. The Structure of the Indian Act: Accountability in Governance. Research paper for the National Centre for First Nations Governance, July 30. http://fngovernance.org/ncfng_research/shin_imai.pdf (accessed December 5, 2015).

Indian Act. 1985 [1876]. RSC 1985 c I-5, http://canlii.ca/t/52fln.

INAC (Indian and Northern Affairs Canada). 1996. *Framework Agreement on First Nation Land Management between the Following First Nations: Westbank, Musqueam, Lheit-Lit'en, N'quatqua, Squamish, Siksika, Muskoday, Cowessess, Opaskwayak Cree, Nipissing, Mississaugas of Scugog Island, Chippewas of Mnjikaning, Chippewas of Georgina Island and the Government of Canada*. Ottawa: Indian and Northern Affairs Canada.

Isaac, T. 2004. First Nations Land Management Act and Third Party Interests. *Alberta Law Review* 42: 1047-60.

Kayseas, B., K. Hindle and R. B. Anderson. 2006. Fostering Indigenous entrepreneurship: A case study of the Membertou First Nation, Nova Scotia, Canada. Paper presented at the IIBEC 2006: Proceedings of the 2006 International Indigenous Business and Entrepreneurship conference, Albuquerque, NM.

Kunst'aa guu–Kunst'aayah Reconciliation Protocol. 2009. Protocol Between the Haida Nation and Her Majesty the Queen in Right of the Province of British Columbia. http://bclaws.ca/civix/document/id/bcgaz1/bcgaz1/kunstaa%20guu%20kunstaayah.

Libin, K. 2008. Shackled by red tape. *National Post*. February 15. http://bit.ly/1DL70rd. (Accessed December 1, 2015).

Mackenzie, J. M. 2013. Environmental Laws on First Nations Reserves: Bridging the Regulatory Gap. Paper presented at Site Remediation in B.C.—From Policy to Practice, Vancouver, March 7-8.

Mohawk Council of Akwesasne. 2012. Akwesasne Law Enactment Procedural Regulation. 2012/2013-#061. Retrieved from http://www.akwesasne.ca/legislativedevelopment

Mohawk Council of Kahnawà:ke Legislative Coordinating Commission. [n.d.]. Community Decision-Making Process. *Mohawk Council of Kahnawá:ke.* http://www.kahnawake.com/council/laws.asp. (Accessed December 1, 2015).

NCFNG (National Centre for First Nations Governance). 2010. Making the Indian Act Irrelevant: Membertou's Journey Toward Self-Government. *Centre News*, March. http://fngovernance.org/news/news_article/making_the_indian_act_irrelevant. (accessed December 1, 2015).

———. [n.d.]. *Governance Toolkit: Best Practices. Principle: Transparency and Fairness. Government: Westbank First Nation.* West Vancouver, BC: National Centre on First Nations Governance.

Noda, A. 2004. Reserve Land Management as an Expression of Aboriginal Self-Determination. *The Scrivener* 13 (3): 32-33.

Nunavut Land Claims Agreement. 1993. An Agreement between the Inuit of the Nunavut Settlement Area and Her Majesty the Queen in Right of Canada. http://www.gov.nu.ca/sites/default/files/files/013%20-%20Nunavut-Land-Claims-Agreement-English.pdf.

NTI (Nunavut Tunngavik Incorporated). 2015. About NTI Lands. *Nunavut Tunngavik Incorporated.* http://ntilands.tunngavik.com (accessed April 11, 2015).

———. 2009. Inuit and Land Claims Organizations in Nunavut. *Nunavut Tunngavik Incorporated.* http://www.tunngavik.com/documents/NTIOrgChart/LandClaimChart/index.html (accessed April 11, 2015).

Provart, J. 2003. Reforming the Indian Act: First Nations Governance and Aboriginal Policy in Canada. *Indigenous Law Journal* 2 (Fall).

Richard, G., J. Calla and A. Le Dressay. 2008. The High Costs of Doing Business on First Nation Lands in Canada. *Journal of Academy of Business and Economics* 8 (4).

Ritsema, R., J. Dawson, M. Jorgensen and B. Macdougall. 2015. "Steering Our Own Ship?": An Assessment of Self-Determination and Self-Governance for Community Development in Nunavut. *The Northern Review* 41: 205-228.

Starks, R., J. E. Tulk, M. Jorgensen, T. Young, M. B. Doucette, T. Bernard and C. Knockwood. 2013. Managing Our Land, Governing for the Future: Finding the Path Forward for Membertou. Report prepared for Atlantic Aboriginal Economic Development Integrated Research Program. http://goo.gl/VzY1ro.

Tattrie, J. 2011. Native Uprising. *Atlantic Business Magazine.* September/October, 20-24.

Tsilhqot'in Nation v. British Columbia. 2014. 2 SCR 257, 2014 SCC 44 (CanLII), http://canlii.ca/t/g7mt9. (Accessed December 1, 2015).

Vogl, T. 2013. Self-Government at Westbank First Nation: Model or Anomaly? *Public Policy and Governance Review* 4 (2): 105-119.

Warkentin, C. 2014. Study of Land Management And Sustainable Economic Development On First Nations Reserve Lands: Report of the Standing Committee on Aboriginal Affairs and Northern Development. Ottawa: House of Commons Canada.

Westbank First Nation. [n.d.]. Frequently Asked Questions. [Web page]. http://www.wfn.ca/docs/faq.pdf. (accessed February 11, 2016).

Wilkins, K. 2000. "Still Crazy after All These Years": Section 88 of the Indian Act at Fifty. *Alberta Law Review* 38 (2): 458-503.

Chapter 3

A leader by personal traits, a leader by election, a leader by promotion, a leader by actions, a leader by wisdom and knowledge: These are all acceptable categorizations of an integral part of business—that is, leadership.

Formal leadership within an Aboriginal context differs little from other Canadian contexts in that such leaders are elected, governed by law, and subject to the views of the electorate. However, those wishing to do business with Aboriginal communities would be wise to acknowledge that their citizenry may have a greater say in how a community does or does not develop than in non-Indigenous communities. Additionally, Aboriginal informal leadership structures must be accepted and respected. Such informal leaders may not have formal authority, but nonetheless influence opinion, use moral and cultural suasion to guide elected officials and community members, and in many cases thus have "power" equal to elected officials.

For those wishing to do business with Indigenous communities, knowledge and respect for these leadership norms is imperative. While the specifics may differ from or within First Nation, Métis, and Inuit communities, respect and knowledge of traditional governance structures operating within an elected, formal matrix is key to any successful business venture, as is an understanding of a community's corporate governance structure and the relationship between the two.

Leadership and Management:
Competencies for Indigenous Community Economic Development
Brian Calliou

In order to be effective in their roles, leaders need to have certain knowledge and skills to direct positive change and economic success. While in some cases there are natural born leaders, there are many Indigenous leaders in positions of authority who do not have an adequate level of knowledge or skills to lead through the external challenges their communities face. As a result, in Canada there are still many Indigenous communities that continue to struggle with external pressures and find themselves on the lowest rung of the socioeconomic ladder. Among Canadians, they have the most health and social problems and have the least amount of education, employment, and wealth levels (King 2014).

Despite these substandard conditions, many Indigenous peoples also have opportunities to develop and grow since much of the industrial development of natural resources is taking place on their traditional territories (see chapter 12, for example). The Supreme Court of Canada stated in several cases that Indigenous peoples whose Aboriginal and treaty rights are affected by development must be consulted and their interests accommodated (Newman 2014). This has resulted in many Indigenous communities negotiating so-called impact and benefit agreements, business contracts, and employment opportunities for their members. There is an urgent need for effective leadership, governance, and project management so that Indigenous communities can set up businesses to take advantage of these opportunities and address and manage the changes that will come about as a result. Furthermore, there are some outstanding examples of successful Indigenous leadership where we find First Nations who run successful, sustainable businesses and have vastly improved social conditions, such as increased employment, and improved infrastructure, leading to happier, healthier lives.

This chapter will explore effective leadership and successful economic and community development in Indigenous contexts. It will do this first by stating the importance of both informal and formal leadership. It will focus, however, on formal leadership and highlight the multiple roles that Indigenous leaders play. Then it will explore Indigenous perspectives on the competencies that lead to such effective leadership in Indigenous community economic development. Finally, it will explore wise practices as a model for competency development for leaders.

The Study of Leadership

What is leadership? There is no easy definition of leadership as considered in this chapter. The root of leadership, "lead," has been defined as "to guide on a way ... to direct the operations, activity, or performance of ... to tend toward a definite result" (Merriam Webster Dictionary 1997: 423). Rost (1993: 102) defined leadership as "an influence relationship through which leaders and followers intend real change that is mutually acceptable and has individual commitment." Yukl (1998: 3) argues that the concept of "influence" underpins most leadership definitions, concluding that the majority of definitions of leadership reflect the assumption that "it involves a social influence process," whereby one person exerts their influence over others "to structure the activities and relationships" of the group. Thus, leadership

> **Leadership** is the act of inspiring and influencing others to work together to achieve a particular goal.

involves actions by a person (a leader) who guides, directs, or in some way moves people to work toward a goal or result. Leadership, therefore, involves the inspiring ideas and related actions of someone who can influence others to work together toward real change.

Leadership theory has broadened the scope of how we understand leadership, going beyond the traditional study of characteristics and behaviours into new areas of social leadership, transformational leadership, or neo-charismatic theory (Conger 1999; House and Shamir 1993; Hunt 1999). Traditional theories of leadership were marked by outdated command-and-control approaches, where someone in an authoritative position barked orders for others to follow, and the related practice of transactional leadership, where leaders cajoled, controlled, and threatened employees to perform. In contrast, transformational leadership sees leaders create meaning for a group with an inspirational vision and strategic direction, empowering employees to be all they can be, thereby mobilizing group energy to carry out goals (Burns 1978; Bass 1990; Rafferty and Griffen 2004). This new leadership theory also reflects studies on stewardship and servant leadership, where the leader serves the group to carry out their work by empowering them, finding the resources they need, and supporting their efforts (Block 1992; Greenleaf 1977; Coyhis 1993). This research has added much to the concept of leadership, especially recognizing some leaders' extraordinary influence on their followers.

One other interesting area of scholarship views leadership as shared or collective, rather than tied to one heroic leader (Waldersee and Eagleson 2002; Conger and Pearce 2003; Wood 2005; Carson, Tesluk and Marrone 2007). Indeed, given the complexity of contemporary life, it is increasingly challenging for a single leader to possess the core knowledge and skills required to competently lead an organization or community. Shared leadership can be defined as "a dynamic, collaborative process ... whereby influence is distributed" among a team of people for the purpose of achieving beneficial outcomes for an organization (Kocolowski 2010: 28). This form of leadership is sometimes referred to as "distributed leadership," "horizontal leadership," or "collective leadership" (Mehra et al. 2006). Katzenbach and Smith (1993) have argued that there is wisdom in teams that an individual leader cannot possess on their own. When team members come together around a common purpose and share an ethic to achieve outstanding results they are more effective than an individual. Ospina and Foldy (2005: 4) have argued that

> **Neo-charismatic** refers to a new approach to understanding leadership that focuses on the role of charisma in a leader's ability to inspire dramatic change in an organization and gain the support of its membership or workforce to achieve a vision or goal. It is closely related to transformational leadership.
>
> **Transformational leadership** is a style of leadership in which a leader has an inspirational vision that is achieved through strategic planning and implementation with the engagement and support of an organization's membership or workforce. This leadership produces results wherein people are inspired to follow.

research into social-change leadership allows for a broader way to think of leadership, one that sets out an "emergent, constructionist approach [which] offers alternative ways of theorizing a post-heroic perspective on leadership that heightens its relational and collective dimensions." By such a shift, we move from focusing on just the leader (or the leader and follower) to the "instances" of people's experiences in carrying out a collective purpose. This shared form of leadership fits well with many Indigenous cultures and their organizations, which also have forms of shared leadership.

Indigenous Leadership

The most effective and successful Indigenous communities today are being led by leaders who are entrepreneurial in their approach to community development, especially in relation to the development of their businesses. These new leaders are visionary risk takers, dreamers and doers, and, with the best interests of their community in mind, they look for opportunities for social entrepreneurship. They do not fear change, but instead are willing to embrace challenges and to turn threats into opportunities. They are proactive rather than reactive. Indigenous peoples are adamant about their rights to be self-determining, to have healthy and prosperous lives, and to preserve their culture and identity. Many of these successful Indigenous leaders have taken a business approach to self-government in meeting these needs and aspirations (Calliou 2008).

Community-development practitioners have noted that there are two levels of leadership in an Indigenous community: the "constituted leadership, the Band Council or the elected council" and "a level of leadership in a community that does not occupy any constituted position of authority or any official leadership role" (Langin and Ensign 1988: 142). What, then, is the distinction between formal and informal leadership?

Informal Leadership

In Indigenous communities there is plenty of leadership exhibited by informal leaders—that is, by people who do not have a formal role of authority. These individuals have significant presence in the community, and have the influence and ability to lead initiatives.

One example of this informal leadership is seen among community citizens to whom others go when they have problems or need something done. The people they turn to are often an auntie or grandma who just seem able to get things done. These regular citizens with no formal position of authority reflect this informal leadership when they take up a cause or an issue that drives them to take some form of action. They often influence oth-

Informal leadership is leadership by individuals who have significant presence in the community and hold powerful influence to lead change initiatives, but are not necessarily elected officials.

ers to join the cause. For example, the recent Idle No More social movement began when four Indigenous women responded to the federal government's passing of laws affecting Indigenous peoples rights with no consultation beforehand.[1] These examples illustrate what some scholars have already documented—that women are often the movers and shakers who exercise informal leadership in an Indigenous community (Kenny and Fraser 2012; Voyageur 2008).

Elders are an example of informal leadership in Indigenous communities (Couture 2011). They are sometimes utilized by formal leaders as advisors and they certainly play a significant role as knowledge keepers. Their experience, knowledge, and advice are sought after and used by many in the community. Similarly, traditional or hereditary chiefs are not formally recognized by Canadian governments, yet they play a significant role in Indigenous communities. Like Elders, they are very respected among community citizens. This has caused some tension and factionalism on occasion between the traditional chiefs and the formal chief-and-council system (as imposed by the *Indian Act*).

> **Elders** are influential community members who are recognized by their community as being knowledge holders and who exhibit qualities that are valued. Elder approval may be a requirement of development initiatives.
>
> A **hereditary chief** is one whose authority to lead comes from cultural protocols or traditional selection processes rather than an election process.

Formal Leadership

Indigenous communities in Canada are led by formal leaders, that is, elected officials. Thus, by formal leadership we mean the decisions and actions taken by someone in a defined position of authority. For example, in the majority of First Nations in Canada, an elected chief and council are viewed by government or industry as the only "legitimate" leaders with which they will enter contractual arrangements. Most First Nations are still governed under the *Indian Act* system, a delegated power from the federal government pursuant to section 91(24) of the constitution, which sets out the authority for the band and the chief and council (Crane, Mainville, and Mason 2006; Imai, Logan and Stein 1993). Chief and council exercise the authority on behalf of the band, that is, on behalf of the First Nation and its citizens. Chiefs and councillors are generally elected for two-year terms and have limited powers that they can exercise without having to get approval from the Minister of Indigenous and Northern Affairs Canada. Increasingly, however, communities are developing their own election codes, so this is changing across the country.

> **Formal leadership** is leadership by individuals who are in a position of authority, usually by virtue of being elected to those roles.

Some of these same relationships with governments and the business community can occur at broader levels through tribal councils, provincial organizations, and national organizations. For example, each national Indigenous organization in Canada—including the Assembly of First Nations, Inuit Tapirisat Kanatami, Métis National Council, Congress of Aboriginal Peoples, and the Native Women's Association of Canada—have elected officials and administrative staff, as do each of their provincial and regional arms (Calliou 2011). Formal arrangements, such as funding agreements, partnerships, joint ventures, and purchase or sales agreements, all require the approval of these formal leaders (partnerships and joint ventures are discussed in chapter 5).

Formal leadership in Indigenous communities is also practiced in corporations and not-for-profit organizations. A board of directors is often appointed, but on occasion may be elected for a set term. Formal leaders of these organizations or corporations, exercise powers as set out under legislation and bylaws to direct and guide the work done by these legal entities. They can bind the corporation or organization as agents of the entity for which they work. This formal leadership also exists at the management level of these Indigenous organizations. The president and chief executive officer (CEO), vice-presidents, and other senior officers of Indigenous-owned corporations also exercise formal leadership within their mandate and job descriptions, and, therefore, exercise a significant amount of power. Likewise, the executive director and senior program managers of not-for-profit organizations in Indigenous communities exercise specific authoritative powers. Economic development corporations and non-profits are discussed further in chapter 6.

Band is the legal term used to refer to a particular group of Indians, so-called under the *Indian Act*. Other terms such as "nation" or "community" may be used to refer to the same group of people.

Chief and council is the government of a band, elected by band members.

A **board of directors** oversees the activities of an organization or company. Its members may be appointed or elected. It is the management structure required for the formal establishment of a corporation.

Many Indigenous communities across Canada now have a variety of organizations and band-owned corporations. A 2013 report found that there were sixty-one Indigenous economic development corporations in Ontario alone, representing around one hundred communities (Canadian Council for Aboriginal Business 2013). The estimated size of the Indigenous market share in Canada in 2016 is approximately $32 billion of combined income from Indigenous households, businesses, and governments (TD Economics 2011). It is significant to note that there is a recent trend that sees more Indigenous women being elected, appointed, or hired into formal leadership roles (Voyageur 2008, 2011; Kenny and Fraser 2012).

Multiple Roles of Formal Leaders

Indigenous political leaders play many formal roles as they lead community economic development. They are often involved in band-owned business development and lead governance matters in their communities, including social programming, infrastructure development, and government-to-government relationships. They often assume many roles as formal leaders, exercising a variety of responsibilities that are similar to a mayor, a cabinet minister, or a CEO. Thus, most Indigenous political leaders have to wear many hats.

Formal leaders deal with many issues at the same time. What they actually do day-to-day in their work is varied and voluminous. Indigenous leaders often have many social issues to deal with and have to tackle these regularly, whether it relates to historical trauma, the effects of colonization, residential schools (see chapter 14), or healing (Wesley-Esquimaux and Smolewski 2004). Formal leaders are generally dealing with self-government issues, including the exercise of control over community services mentioned above. They are building their capacity at good governance and toward greater control over their own affairs, free from interference from federal or provincial governments. Many are involved in negotiations of self-government agreements where this jurisdictional space is formally recognized by other levels of government (Belanger 2008).

They are also leading the implementation of many programs to meet community needs, such as exercising authority over child and family services, unemployment, mental health, education, and training. They are often involved in negotiations, consultation, and sometimes even litigation regarding jurisdiction over or funding for these programs. Also, they are always fighting for the recognition of their Indigenous or treaty rights to be respected and honoured through these same methods (treaties are discussed in chapter 13). Indigenous leaders continue to face many challenges in their struggle to represent their communities' interests in their relationships with government, business, and other parties (Calliou 2011). They work very hard to protect and preserve their communities' cultures and associated rights. Whether they are working on social programs, economic development, or rights litigation, they generally are weaving in mechanisms that respect their identities and cultures as distinct, Indigenous peoples.

Entrepreneurship (discussed in chapter 4) and economic development are areas in which virtually all formal Indigenous community leaders are working. They seek to be less dependent on external government funding, which otherwise limits their capacity to do what they want to do when they want to do it (Helin 2006). Given these roles and responsibilities, Indigenous leaders need to have competency in a wide variety of knowledge and skills (Calliou 2005, 2008).

Competency Requirements for Formal Indigenous Leadership

Competency maps are used by organizations to clarify responsibilities and expectations, improve productivity, enhance the feedback/evaluation process, adapt to change, and align behaviour with organizational strategies and values (Lucia and Lepsinger 1999; Spencer and Spencer 1993; Dubois 1993; Mansfield 1996). Technical skills are not enough, and leaders must exhibit competencies that allow them to deal with the complexities of today's issues, including leading their organizations to do well, but also to do good in the world.

A competency has been defined as "a cluster of related knowledge, skills, and attitudes that affects a major part of one's job (a role or responsibility), that correlates with performance on the job, that can be measured against well-accepted standards, and that can be improved via training and development"

> A **competency map** identifies key characteristics or behaviours that are required for a particular position. It is then used in a variety of activities and processes within the organization, such as in recruitment, training, and succession planning.

(Parry 1996: 48). Others have defined a competency as "any motive, attitude, skill, knowledge, behavior or other personal characteristic that is essential to perform the job and that differentiates average from superior performers" (Alberta Public Service Managers 1995). Thus, competencies are a combination of the knowledge, skills, experience, and attitudes, as well as beliefs and values, that a leader exhibits in their work. In other words, the observable behaviour of a leader exhibits their competency in certain areas.

We all have natural strengths in some competency areas, while we may have to work harder to improve in other areas. Scholtes (1998) has argued that "new leadership" competencies include:

Table 1: Scholtes New Leadership Competencies
Competency Type
Ability to engage systems thinking and knowledge of how to lead systems
Ability to understand the variability of work in planning and problem solving
Understanding how we learn, develop, and improve
Leading true learning and improvement
Understanding people and why they behave as they do
Understanding the interdependence and interaction between systems, variation, learning, and human behaviour, and knowing how each affects the others
Giving vision, meaning, direction, and focus to the organization
Source: Scholtes (1998).

While it is recognized that Indigenous leaders also need to develop these leadership and management competencies, there is a growing recognition that they need to do this in concert with the development of their own cultural and traditional knowledge and skills (Ottmann 2005a; King 2008; Metoyer 2010; Calliou 2005; Warner and Grint 2006; Washington 2004; Cowan 2008; Kenny 2012). Indeed, as Ottmann (2005a) reported, Indigenous leaders she interviewed felt that any leadership-development program would have to take into account any specific Indigenous culture, needs, and issues, in tandem with current and innovative leadership practices.

The competencies that formal Indigenous leaders need to run their governments, organizations, and businesses have many similarities with competencies identified by Western scholars (such as Scholtes in table 1). However, an Indigenous perspective on competencies differs to some degree from mainstream competencies.

Table 2: Indigenous Leadership and Management Competencies
Competency Type
Knowledge of culture and history of community
Spiritual harmony and balanced lifestyle
Holistic and global worldview
Strategic thinker and planner
Responsible leader who is accountable to his or her followers
Team-builder
Visionary
Risk-taker
Implement plans and take action
Strong integrity
Delegates authority and shares power
Ability to resolve disputes
Strong communications skills
Business management skills
Objective and open minded
Strong Indigenous identity, yet understands both worlds
Problem-solving and decision-making skills
Source: Calliou (2005).

Differences include a strong belief that an Indigenous leader must be knowledgeable and proficient in their identity and culture, including speaking their language and involvement in ceremonial activities. Another important difference is the spirituality that Indigenous leaders carry within themselves. Their spiritual beliefs and worldview see them having a strong connection to the land and animals. They believe in the wisdom of their traditional knowledge. Furthermore, values and ethics may differ between Indigenous leaders and mainstream leaders, affecting their characteristics and behaviours. Formal Indigenous leaders often have a strong belief in the collectivity of their community. They believe in the shared ownership of their lands, rather than individual ownership. They have a passion for public-spirited leadership, that is, to work for the collective good of the entire community. They also practice shared decision-making, where a council of leaders works together, rather than one leader imposing their own perspective (Calliou 2005).

These differing values and ethics make up this Indigenous perspective on competencies and have a strong influence on the way formal leadership is carried out in Indigenous communities. Hofstede (1980, 1983) argued that the failure of many international development initiatives during the 1960s and 1970s was partly due to the lack of cultural sensitivities in the transfer of management ideas. He led a movement exploring cultural differences in leadership and management, arguing that culture is the mind's software, and that it programs the values and behaviours of leaders. The characteristics and competencies of Indigenous leaders tend to differ from those of non-Indigenous leaders, and apply to all the areas in which formal leaders work, including community economic development.

> **Traditional knowledge** refers to the information and practices that are handed down from one generation to the next within a community.

Indigenous Leadership in Economic Development

Indigenous leadership in economic development and social enterprise is an important area of growth and change in Indigenous communities across Canada. A relatively new phenomenon in Indigenous entrepreneurship is "the creation, management and development of new ventures by Indigenous peoples for the benefit of Indigenous people" (Hindle and Lansdowne 2005; see also Peredo and Anderson 2006; and Dana 2007). Like entrepreneurship in the mainstream, Indigenous entrepreneurship can be purely for profit or encompass broader social and economic benefits. Indigenous peoples are open to participating in economic enterprises, but they often do so in an attempt to improve their social and economic circumstances, while at the same time rebuilding their communities on a traditional and culturally grounded foundation (Vinje 1996; Lurie 1986). Anderson (1999) sets out a contingency theory for Indigenous economic development where he acknowledges that there are world systems at play, where the global affects the local, and that Indigenous peoples' role is contingent upon several factors, many of which are under the control of Indigenous people. In other words, contingency theory takes agency and social relations seriously, thus emphasizing community-driven approaches to development; it places much of the control in the hands of the community, where it ought to be, and allows community leaders to be active agents of change.

One important dimension that seems to recur is that many Indigenous businesses are collectively owned and thus more closely reflect a social enterprise, that is, an enterprise that makes a profit that is used for social purposes. This collective approach for social as well as economic goals has been described as "tribal capitalism" (Champagne 2004), and the foray into the business world with band-owned enterprises has been referred to as "capitalism with a red face" (Newhouse 2000). Some scholars view this approach as a community orientation, where the citizens view their membership as part of a living organism, where they have a reciprocal role to play for the smooth function of the whole (Peredo and Chrisman, 2006). In support of this notion is a view presented by Redpath and Nielsen, using the "cultural dimension" of individualism versus collectivism made famous by Hofstede, that Indigenous people differ from non-Indigenous cultures by their core belief in collectivism rather than individualism (Redpath and Nielsen 1997; Hofstede 1980, 1983). Although some scholars question whether this is a cultural characteristic or just a recent phenomenon resulting from the reserve system with its collective land tenure (Galbraith, Rodriguez and Stiles 2006; Galbraith and Stiles 2003), most scholars agree that Indigenous peoples economic enterprises reflect a collectivist ethos.

> A **social enterprise** is an organization that operates like other businesses with the goal of generating revenues; however, rather than creating profit for shareholders or owners, these businesses are developed around socially minded missions, such that any profit is re-invested for the purpose of improving some aspect of social well-being in a community.

Successful leadership in Indigenous-community economic development is carried out by formal leaders who practice entrepreneurial thinking. These successful Indigenous leaders took what has been described as the business approach to self-government and community economic development (Calliou 2008). Rather than wait for the slow self-government negotiating process, these leaders have decided to be pragmatic and get more immediate results by adopting the business approach.

Chief Darcy Bear, one of the formal leaders from Whitecap Dakota First Nation in Saskatchewan, is in his seventh consecutive term as the chief of his nation. He has focused his leadership on self-government, wealth creation through partnerships, and financial accountability (Whitecap Dakota 2015). Soon after being elected, Chief Bear and his council worked to improve their financial accountability, thereby correcting a 40 per cent annual deficit, followed by twenty consecutive unqualified audits, and consistent operating budget surpluses (ibid.). Chief Bear and his council set up good governance structures and processes along with laws and policies to create a stable investment environment. Then they sought out partners to develop business ventures incrementally. Chief Bear and his council's focus on "progress through partnerships" has led to many economic and social ventures.

In 1990, they established Whitecap Development Corporation, after which they partnered with Lac La Ronge First Nation and Muskeg Lake First Nation to develop the Dakota Dunes Golf Links in 2005, which was ranked fifteenth out of approximately 3,500 golf courses in Canada by *Golf Digest*. This was followed by the development of the Dakota Dunes Casino in 2007, the expansion of the Whitecap Trail Gas Bar Confectionary in 2010, and a hotel and convention centre that had been scheduled to open in 2015, but is experiencing delays. They are currently working on both a light industrial park and a home-ownership project around the golf course.

The economic success allowed chief and council the financial ability to increase services and amenities of the community, such as high-speed Internet and cellphone service, new water and sewer infrastructure, expansion of schools, a new health centre, new paved roads, and expanded natural-gas capacity, along with many other improvements. Their partnerships with surrounding communities has allowed them to enter into agreements on tourism, fire and protective services, and education, and led to the designation of Highway 219 that runs through their community as the Chief Whitecap Trail tourism corridor (Whitecap Dakota 2015).

Chief Darcy Bear is one example of an Indigenous leader who took a business approach to self-government by leading a team in a strategic direction to be self-determining, and no longer dependent upon transfer payments. He worked to establish the institutions, systems, structures, and processes needed to run a stable government, set up community-owned businesses and partnerships, and keep politics out of business. Other similar examples of communities whose Indigenous leaders embraced business approaches to self-government include Membertou (discussed in chapter 2) and Lac La Ronge.

Developing Leadership Skills

Training for leadership is an important element of successful community economic development. There is a growing interest by post-secondary institutions in Indigenous-community economic development and Indigenous entrepreneurial/leadership training. A variety of departments have developed courses or entire programs on Indigenous business management or community economic development, which includes topics such as leadership and good governance. Colleges and technical institutions have also developed programs in leadership development and management training (training is also discussed in chapter 4). Indigenous institutions have also been established to carry out some of this work, such as the Council for the Advancement of Native Development Officers, Aboriginal Financial Officers Association, Indigenous Leadership Development Institute, and the former National Centre for First Nations Governance (Oppenheimer, O'Connell and Weir 2010). There is, of course, also a plethora of private consultants doing much of this work.

Generally, it is understood that the required competencies include traditional Indigenous knowledge and values, and mainstream knowledge and capabilities. It may also include knowledge and skills related to nation rebuilding, community development, economic development, and good governance (Jorgensen 2007; Calliou 2008). Many different organizations have attempted to identify the exact competencies required for contemporary Indigenous leaders to advance their communities in the global market economy. Studies have been carried out by the Harvard Project on American Indian Economic Development, the Institute on Governance, the National Centre for First Nations Governance, the Conference Board of Canada, various federal government commissioned reports, the Royal Commission on Aboriginal Peoples (see chapter 14), and by others who documented which kinds of factors lead to successful Indigenous ventures. Each of these best-practices research reports identified certain elements believed to be instrumental in the success of Indigenous business, organizational, or community development, and, therefore, areas of knowledge and skills in which leaders need be competent. Reviewing the results of these studies, a wise-practices model emerges (Wesley-Esquimaux and Calliou 2010; Calliou and Wesley-Esquimaux 2014).

> The **Harvard Project on American Indian Economic Development** at Harvard University, was founded in 1987. Through applied research, it seeks to identify the factors that lead to successful Aboriginal economic development, primarily in the United States.

Wise Practices

Calliou and Wesley-Esquimaux (2014) developed a leadership model that sets out seven elements of success that leaders need to be knowledgeable and competent in. The term "wise practices" was adopted instead of the more commonly known "best practices" since there is a growing skepticism about the universality of best practices. Some commentators argue that we cannot assume that what is successful in one situation, context, or culture can automatically work in another (Krajewski and Silver [n.d]). Others argue that the supposed objective, universal standard of best practices may not be able to take into account the differing contexts, values, subjectivity, and plurality, and may not accommodate "multiple perspectives, with different groups in different places having different views of what quality was or different interpretations of criteria" (Dahlberg, Moss, and Pence 1999: 4).

Furthermore, what criteria do we use to determine what is "best" as a practice? It is often a mainstream corporate standard that reflects a certain ideological lens—that of the neoliberal marketplace. Cornell (1987) argued that Indigenous peoples in the United States have a different view of success than mainstream middleclass people. Material possessions and personal wealth are not necessarily the measure of what is best for Indigenous peoples. Some commentators have argued that best practices in adult education run the risk of eroding the traditional grounding in an ethic of the common good and of social justice (Bartlette 2008).

Our adoption of the term "wise practices" makes space for local Indigenous knowledge and experience and, therefore, resonates with Indigenous leaders. Wise practices can be defined as "locally-appropriate actions, tools, principles or decisions that contribute to the development of sustainable and equitable conditions" (Wesley-Esquimaux and Calliou 2010: 19). Wise practices do not aspire to be universal, but instead are "idiosyncratic, contextual, textured, and not standardized" (Davis 1997). Among leadership and organizational-studies theorists and practitioners, there is a growing interest in wisdom. They see there is a need for wisdom to be learned and practiced by current leaders, managers, and business persons who have to make important decisions in this period of rapid change, uncertainty, and paradox, while considering the welfare of others and the planet (Cooperrider and Srivastva 1998; Korac-Kakabadse, Korac-Kakabadse, and Kouzmin 2001; Weick 2006; Sternberg 2005). One commentator argued that wisdom requires a leader to respect "tradition and experience," and the issues a leader faces can be "considered reflexively from a cultural-historical perspective" (Kok 2009: 54). Local Indigenous knowledge and wisdom ought to be part of any leadership development, along with the knowledge and skills required of contemporary competencies. It is this blended approach of local traditional knowledge and best practices that informs the wise-practices model.

Identity and Culture

The first key factor is identity and culture, which Indigenous leaders and scholars have increasingly expressed as an important area of knowledge and skills in which a contemporary Indigenous leader needs to be competent. They must have a strong understanding and grounding in their culture, traditional knowledge, and values, and in their people's historical connection to their traditional territories (King 2008; Warner and Grint 2006; Cowan 2008). Our competency-map research also supports this proposition (Calliou 2005). Indigenous scholars have also argued that competency in identity and cultural knowledge is important for Indigenous leaders (Ottmann 2005a; Washington 2004; Metoyer 2010; Kenny 2012).

> A **best practice** is a method or technique that is preferred or considered to be standard in an industry. It is normally used because it is believed to produce superior results when compared with other options.

Leadership

The second key factor to success is leadership. Bennis and Nanus define leadership as that which "gives an organization its vision and its ability to translate the vision into reality" (Bennis and Nanus 1985: 19). In other words, leadership is a verb and refers to action taken by someone who leads others into action, and thus into results. Leaders must therefore be action-oriented in order to motivate others to bring ideas to action, lead change, and achieve results for the organization or community. More scholars are arguing that leadership is not about one great leader, but rather is about shared leadership, or collective approaches to leading social change and social justice (Ospina and Foldy 2005). In Indigenous communities, chiefs often practise shared leadership with their teams. They may also look to informal leaders, such as Elders, for guidance.

Strategic Vision and Planning

The third key factor is strategic vision and planning, which means that leaders need to be systems thinkers who take a holistic approach to setting out a long-term strategic vision and corresponding strategic plan. Leaders make meaning for their followers through their vision, thereby inspiring and motivating them to give maximum effort in implementing the ideas into action and results. Strategic plans also provide a mechanism for decision-making, where decisions made on the use of scarce resources and possible new initiatives must align with the vision and plan (Cornell 1998; Anderson and Smith 1998; Guyette 1996). It allows community leaders to be proactive rather than reactive.

Good Governance and Management

The fourth key success factor combines good governance and management. Leaders must establish structures, systems, and processes that provide for good governance and effective management if they want to achieve successful and sustainable organizations and businesses (Cornell and Kalt 1990; Cornell 2007; Cornell and Jorgensen 2007; Calliou 2008). Building effective governing institutions and management processes allows for leaders or managers to come and go, and the government, organization, or business can continue to operate effectively. Stable governance and management sends a strong message to potential external partners that they can rest assured that the Indigenous government, organization, or business operates professionally.

Accountability and Stewardship

The fifth factor for success is accountability and stewardship. Leaders and managers act as stewards of the community resources, making decisions that are in the best interests of the community members. Since they are in a powerful role with significant responsibilities, they are accountable to the community or organization for their decisions and actions (Block 1992; Davis, Schoorman and Donaldson 1997; Hernandez 2008; Fox 1992; Leithwood 2001). Leaders and managers are thus expected to meet a high standard of accountability. By being transparent in their decision-making and spending,

> A **steward** is an individual who has been entrusted with the responsibility for managing or administering the property or financial affairs of someone else. It is expected that a steward will act in a careful and responsible manner for long-term benefit. In an Indigenous context, these resources (whether land, finances, or other property) are often communally owned.

they build trust among their own staff as well as with the community. By openly reporting regularly on how their decisions are made, how scarce resources are used, and whether results were achieved, leaders and managers illustrate how they practice stewardship leadership in an accountable way.

Performance Evaluation

The sixth key factor is performance evaluation, and relates to leaders being accountable and practicing stewardship of community or organizational resources. Evaluation of performance is a method to track if the decisions made and dollars spent on specific initiatives achieved the desired results. Performance evaluation of the initiatives undertaken by leaders and managers ensures that they achieve the most value for every dollar spent (Martz 2013; Meier 2003). Evaluation of the performance of human resources is also an important part of performance management of any organization and ensures that staff performance is tied to strategic objectives, and that results are being achieved (Bacal 1990). There is now a growing literature critiquing evaluation

> **Performance evaluation** is a method of determining whether an investment achieves its desired results. This could be an investment of time, money, or other resources. When used in relation to employees, it is a method of comparing behaviour and outcomes to standards and expectations. Performance evaluation may be used to identify training needs, as well as promotion.

approaches and calling for an Indigenous framework that makes room for culturally appropriate evaluations (Chouinard and Cousins 2007; LaFrance and Nichols 2010; Kawakami et al. 2007).

Collaborations, Partnerships, and External Relationships

Finally, the seventh key factor to success of the wise-practices model is collaborations, partnerships, and external relationships. External relationships and partnerships are often necessary for an Indigenous community's success, since they require external financial and other support systems. They need trading partners, either suppliers or clients, for their business ventures. There is also a trend toward more Indigenous communities collaborating with each other, including forming co-operatives or entering into partnerships or joint ventures (Wuttunee 2002; Fraser 2002; Ketilson and MacPherson 2002; Thayer Scott 2006). This will be discussed further in chapter 5.

This wise-practices model can guide Indigenous leaders into the areas of knowledge and skills that they would have to develop in themselves, and in their followers, in order to achieve successful community economic development.

Table 3: Wise-Practices Model
Elements of Success
Identity and Culture
Leadership
Strategic Vision and Planning
Good Governance and Management
Accountability and Stewardship
Performance Evaluation
Collaboration, Partnerships, and External Relationships
Source: Wesley-Esquimaux and Calliou (2010).

Conclusion

As Indigenous communities continue to face rapid change from external forces they are in need of competent leadership to adapt to such change. The development and training of leaders is important in this respect. They must learn modern leadership, and management, and gather business knowledge and skills to operate effectively in the global market, but must also continue to learn and practise their own traditional knowledge and culture. Thus, they must learn to become competent as strategic thinkers who set long-term goals for the benefit of their community, take action and remain focused during the implementation of strategic initiatives, and evaluate for performance, all the while supporting and meeting community needs and aspirations, including preservation of their cultural identity.

Such leadership development prepares the community, its administrators, and its members to adapt to the external changes they face and to build the internal capacity required to operate their government, businesses, and organizations effectively. For leadership development and business development, Indigenous peoples are seeking a blended approach to their training, where traditional Indigenous knowledge is learned along with the knowledge and skills of the modern business world (Calliou 2005; Ottmann 2005b). Furthermore, successful Indigenous leaders use a business approach to self-government (Calliou 2008).

We use the concept of wise practices because it allows for Indigenous experience and knowledge to play a prominent role in community economic development. We make the assumption that others can learn from Indigenous case studies of success and that there is wisdom there to be shared. We also assume that the community leaders reading or learning about such Indigenous success stories will begin to realize that their own community has wisdom, assets, and strengths. In other words, each community can take the strengths-based approach to development, building upon the assets they already have available. They can be inspired by success stories and develop their knowledge and skills around the wise-practices model. The economic success that can be achieved through a wise-practices model is not merely for wealth accumulation, but also for the public good, for making the world a better place, and for preservation of the particular Indigenous culture. This quadruple bottom line has been described as tribal capitalism (Champagne 2004) and as capitalism with a red face (Newhouse 2000).

A **strengths-based approach** focuses on the strengths that individuals already possess and can draw upon to solve a problem or advance a cause.

A **triple bottom line** is a scorecard that is used to help a business evaluate its performance in three different realms, usually financial, social, and environmental (sometimes referred to as "profit, people, and planet"). A balance of the three is thought to indicate the sustainability of the business. A **quadruple bottom line** has a fourth realm added against which performance is evaluated, usually culture.

Key Points:

- There is a wide variety of people who take on different leadership roles in Aboriginal societies.

- Formal leaders have an official capacity and are often elected or appointed; however, traditional selection processes may be followed in some Aboriginal communities. There are differences among First Nation, Métis, and Inuit communities across Canada.

- Informal leaders have significant presence in the community and hold powerful influence to lead change initiatives, but are not elected officials.

- In Aboriginal communities, Elders are important informal leaders who may be consulted on business and other development initiatives.

- Aboriginal leaders often are oriented toward the collective rather than the individual, meaning their work is expected to benefit the community, and not just themselves.

- "Wise practice" is sometimes the preferred term in Aboriginal communities because it allows for Indigenous experience and knowledge to play a prominent role in community economic development.

- The wise-practices model identifies seven key elements of success: identity and culture; leadership; strategic vision and planning; good governance and management; accountability and stewardship; performance evaluation; and collaboration, partnerships, and external relationships.

Questions for Review:

1. Which leadership competencies are required to lead positive social and economic change in Indigenous communities?

2. How are the competencies required of Aboriginal leaders similar to or different from those of mainstream society?

3. How might the role of informal leaders affect business development and relations?

4. What are the key success factors for community economic development and how do they relate to leadership?

5. How might an orientation toward collectivism over individualism affect business development?

6. Why is "wise practices" suggested instead of "best practices"? Is there really a difference?

7. Can the wise practices identified be applied to non-Aboriginal communities and businesses as well?

8. Is there anything missing from the wise-practices model?

9. Identify leaders in your spheres. How are the wise practices described in this chapter reflected in their leadership style or approach?

Suggested Assignments:

1. Think of an informal leader in your community. What is his or her most important attribute? Can it be learned or developed, or was the person born with it? Compare this to the competencies in the chapter. Discuss your example in class or write a profile of this informal leader.

2. Research strengths-based approaches to economic development. How is this approach different from others that you are familiar with?

3. Discuss the differences between a board of directors and a chief and council in terms of an economic development corporation.

4. What are the risks of assuming there is only one best-practice approach to economic development?

Note

1. More on Idle No More can be found at http://www.idlenomore.ca.

References

Alberta Public Service Managers. 1995. *Core Competencies for Alberta Public Service Managers.* Edmonton, AB: Alberta Public Service Managers.

Anderson, J. S. and D. H. Smith. 1998. Managing Tribal Assets: Developing Long-Term Strategic Plans. *American Indian Culture and Research Journal* 22 (3): 139-56.

Anderson, Robert Brent. 1999. *Economic Development Among Aboriginal Peoples in Canada: The Hope for the Future.* North York, ON: Captus Press.

Bacal, Robert. 1990. *Performance Management.* New York: McGraw-Hill.

Bartlette, Deborah. 2008. Are "Best Practices" Hurting Adult Ed: McIntyre and the Globalization of Practice. Paper presented at Thinking Beyond Borders: Global Ideas, Global Values 27th National Conference––Online Proceedings of the Canadian Association for the Study of Adult Education, University of British Columbia, Vancouver.

Bass, B. M. 1990. From Transactional to Transformational Leadership: Learning to Share the Vision. 18:3 *Organizational Dynamics* 18 (3): 19-31.

Belanger, Yale, ed. 2008. *Aboriginal Self-Government in Canada: Current Trends and Issues.* Saskatoon, SK: Purich Publishing.

Bennis, W. and B. Nanus,. 1985. *Leaders: Strategies for Taking Charge.* New York: Harper and Row.

Block, Peter. 1992. *Stewardship: Choosing Service Over Self-Interest.* San Francisco: Berrett-Koehler.

Burns, J. M. 1978. *Leadership.* New York: Harper and Row.

Calliou, Brian. 2005. The Culture of Leadership: North American Indigenous Leadership in a Changing Economy. In *Indigenous Peoples and the Modern State*, ed. Duane Champagne, Karen Jo Torgesen and Susan Steiner. Walnut Creek, CA: AltaMira Press

Calliou, Brian. 2008. The Significance of Building Leadership and Community Capacity to Implement Self-Government. In *Aboriginal Self-Government in Canada: Current Trends and Issues*, 3rd ed., ed. by Yale Belanger. Saskatoon, SK: Purich Publishing.

———. 2011. From Paternalism to Partnership: The Challenges of Aboriginal Leadership. In *Visions of the Heart: Canadian Aboriginal Issues*, 3rd ed., ed. David Long and Olive Patricia Dickason. Toronto: Oxford University Press.

Calliou, Brian and Cynthia Wesley-Esquimaux. 2014. A Wise Practices Approach to Indigenous Community Development in Canada. In *Restorying Indigenous Leadership: Wise Practices in Community Development*, ed. Cora Voyageur, Laura Brearley and Brian Calliou. Banff, AB: The Banff Centre Press.

Canadian Council for Aboriginal Business. 2013. Community and Commerce: A Survey of Aboriginal Economic Development Corporations in Ontario. Research report by CCAB in partnership with Environics, Spring, Toronto, ON. https://www.ccab.com/community-and-commerce.

Carson, J. B., P. Tesluk and J. A. Marrone. 2007. Shared Leadership in Teams: An Investigation of Antecedent Conditions and Performance. *Academy of Management Journal* 50 (5): 1217-34.

Champagne, Duane. 2004. Tribal Capitalism and Native Capitalists: Multiple Pathways of Native Economy. In *Native Pathways: American Indian Culture and Economic Development in the Twentieth Century*, ed. Brian Hosmer and Colleen O'Neill. Boulder, CO: University Press of Colorado.

Chouinard, Jill A. and J. Bradley Cousins. 2007. Culturally Competent Evaluation for Aboriginal Communities: A Review of the Empirical Literature. *Journal of Multidisciplinary Evaluation* 4 (8): 40-57.

Conger, J. A. 1999. Charismatic and Transformational Leadership in Organizations: An Insider's Perspective on These Developing Streams of Research. *Leadership Quarterly* 10 (2): 145-69.

Conger, J. A. and C. L. Pearce. 2003. A Landscape of Opportunities: Future Research in Shared Leadership. In *Shared Leadership: Reframing the Hows and Whys of Leadership*, ed. C. L. Pearce and J. A. Conger. Thousand Oaks, CA: Sage Publishers.

Cooperrider, David L. and Shuresh Srivastva. 1998. *Organizational Wisdom and Executive Courage*. San Francisco: New Lexington Press.

Cornell, Stephen. 1987. American Indians, American Dreams, and the Meaning of Success. *American Indian Culture and Research Journal* 11 (2): 59-70.

———. 1998. Strategic Analysis: A Practical Tool for Building Indian Nations. Harvard Project Report No. 98-10. Cambridge: John F. Kennedy School of Government, Harvard University.

———. 2007. Remaking the Tools of Governance: Colonial Legacies, Indigenous Solutions. In *Rebuilding Native Nations: Strategies for Governance and Development*, ed. Miriam Jorgensen. Tucson: University of Arizona Press.

Cornell, Stephen and Miriam Jorgensen. 2007. Getting Things Done for the Nation: The Challenge of Tribal Administration. In *Rebuilding Native Nations: Strategies for Governance and Development*, ed. Miriam Jorgensen. Tucson: University of Arizona Press.

———. 1998. Sovereignty and Nation-Building: The Development Challenge in Indian Country Today. *American Indian Culture and Research Journal* 22:187-214

Couture, Joseph E. 2011. The Role of Native Elders: Emergent Issues. In *Visions of the Heart: Canadian Aboriginal Issues*, 3rd ed., ed. David Long and Olive Patricia Dickason. Toronto: Oxford University Press.

Cowan, David A. 2008. Profound Simplicity of Leadership Wisdom: Exemplary Insight From Miami Chief Floyd Leonard. *International Journal of Leadership Studies* 4 (1): 51-81.

Coyhis, D. 1993. Servant Leadership: The Elders Have Said Leadership is About Service – They Say We Are Really Here to Serve the People. *Winds of Change* 8 (3): 23-24.

Crane, Brian, Robert Mainville and Martin W. Mason. 2006. *First Nations Governance Law*. Markham, ON: LexisNexis Canada.

Dahlberg, Gunilla, Peter Moss and Alan Pence. 1999. *Beyond Quality in Early Childhood Education and Care: Postmodern Perspectives*. London: Routledge.

Dana, Leo-Paul. 2007. Toward a Multidisciplinary Definition of Indigenous Entrepreneurship. In *International Handbook of Research on Indigenous Entrepreneurship*, ed. Leo-Paul Dana and Robert B. Anderson. Cheltenham, UK: Edward Elgar Publishing.

Davis, O. L. 1997. Beyond "Best Practices" Toward Wise Practices. *Journal of Curriculum and Supervision* 13 (1): 1-5.

Davis, J. H., F. D. Schoorman and L. Donaldson. 1997. Toward a Stewardship Theory of Management. *Academy of Management Review* 22 (1): 20-47.

Dubois, D. 1993. *Competency-Based Performance Improvement: A Strategy for Organizational Change*. Amherst, MA: HRD Press.

Fox, Jonathan. 1992. Democratic Rural Development: Leadership Accountability in Regional Peasant Organizations. *Development and Change* 23 (1): 1-36.

Fraser, Sarah Jane. 2002. An Exploration of Joint Ventures as a Sustainable Development Tool for First Nations. *Journal of Aboriginal Economic Development* 3 (1): 40-44.

Galbraith, C., C. Rodriguez and C. Stiles. 2006. False Myths and Indigenous Entrepreneurial Strategies. *Journal of Small Business and Entrepreneurship* 8 (2): 1-20.

Galbraith C. and C. Stiles. 2003. Expectations of Indian Reservation Gaming: Entrepreneurial Activity Within a Context of Traditional Land Tenure and Wealth Acquisition. *Journal of Developmental Entrepreneurship* 8 (2): 93-112.

Greenleaf, R.K. 1997. *Servant Leadership: A Journey into the Nature of Legitimate Power and Greatness.* Mahwah, NJ: Paulist Press.

Guyette, Susan. 1996. *Planning for Balanced Development: A Guide for Native American and Rural Communities.* Santa Fe, NM: Clear Light Publishers.

Helin, Calvin. 2006. *Dances With Dependency: Indigenous Success Through Self-Reliance.* Vancouver: Orca Spirit Publishing.

Hernandez, Morela. 2008. Promoting Stewardship Behavior in Organizations: A Leadership Model. *Journal of Business Ethics* 80:121-28.

Hindle, K. and M. Landsdowne. 2005. Brave Spirits on New Paths: Toward a Globally Relevant Paradigm of Indigenous Entrepreneurship Research. *Journal of Small Business and Entrepreneurship* 18 (2): 131-41.

Hofstede, G. 1980. *Culture's Consequences: International Differences in Work Related Values.* Beverly Hills: Sage Publishers.

———. 1983. The Cultural Relativity of Organizational Practices and Theories. *Journal of International Business* 4:75-89.

House, R. J. and B. Shamir. 1993. Toward the Integration of Transformational, Charismatic and Visionary Theories. In *Leadership Theory and Research: Perspectives and Directions*, ed. M. M. Chemers and R. Ayman. New York: Academic.

Hunt, J. 1999. Transformational/Charismatic Leadership's Transformation of the Field: An Historical Essay. *Leadership Quarterly* 10 (2): 129-44.

Imai, Shin, Katherine Logan and Gary Stein. 1993. *Aboriginal Law Handbook.* Toronto: Thomson Canada Limited.

Jorgensen, Miriam, ed. 2007. *Rebuilding Native Nations: Strategies for Governance and Development.* Tucson: University of Arizona.

Katzenbach, Jon R. and Douglas K. Smith. 1993. *The Wisdom of Teams: Creating the High Performance Organization.* Boston: Harvard Business Press.

Kawakami, Alice J., Kanani Aton, Fiona Cram, Morris K. Lai and Laurie Porima. 2007. Improving the Practice of Evaluation Through Indigenous Values and Methods: Decolonizing Evaluation Practice – Returning the Gaze From Hawai'i and Aotearoa. *Hulili: Multidisciplinary Research on Hawaiian Well-Being* 4 (1): 319-48

Kenny, Carolyn. 2012. Liberating Leadership Theory. In *Living Indigenous Leadership: Native Narratives on Building Strong Leadership*, ed. Carolyn Kenny and Tina Ngaroimata Fraser. Vancouver: University of British Columbia Press.

Kenny, Carolyn and Tina Ngaroimata Fraser. 2012. *Living Indigenous Leadership: Native Narratives on Building Strong Leadership.* Vancouver: University of British Columbia Press.

Ketilson, L. Hammond and I. MacPherson. 2002. Aboriginal Cooperatives in Canada: A Sustainable Development Strategy Whose Time Has Come. *Journal of Aboriginal Economic Development* 3 (1): 45-57.

King, Malcolm. 2014. Addressing The Disparities in Aboriginal Health Through Social Determinants Research. In *Aboriginal Populations: Social, Demography and Epidemiological Perspectives*, ed. Frank Trovato and Anatole Romaniuk. Edmonton, AB: University of Alberta Press.

King, T, 2008. Fostering Aboriginal Leadership: Increasing Enrollment and Completion Rates in Canadian Post-Secondary Institutions. *College Quarterly* 11 (1): 1-16

Kocolowski, Michael D. 2010. Shared Leadership: Is It Time for a Change? *Emerging Leadership Journeys* 3 (1): 22-32.

Kok, Ayse. 2009. Realizing Wisdom Theory in Complex Learning Networks. *Electronic Journal of e-Learning* 7 (1): 53-60. http://www.ejel.org/volume7/issue1.

Korac-Kakabadse, A., N. Korac-Kakabadse and A. Kouzmin. 2001. Leadership Renewal: Towards the Philosophy of Wisdom. *International Review of Administrative Sciences* 67 (2): 207-27.

Krajewski, Henryk and Yvonne Silver. [n.d.] Announcing the Death of "Best Practices": Resurrecting "Best Principles" to Retain and Engage High Potentials. http://www.chba.ca/uploads/netac/2009-05_RightManagement_article.pdf (accessed December 1, 2015).

LaFrance, Joan and Richard Nichols. 2010. Reframing Evaluation: Defining an Indigenous Evaluation Framework. *Canadian Journal of Program Evaluation* 23 (2): 13-31.

Langin, F. Robert and Geneva Ensign. 1988. Ways of Working in a Community: Reflections of a Former Community Development Worker. *Canadian Journal of Native Studies* 8 (1): 131-46

Leithwood, Kenneth. 2001. School Leadership in the Context of Accountability Policies. *International Journal of Leadership in Education* 4 (3): 217-235.

Lucia, A. D. and R. Lepsinger. 1999. *The Art and Science of Competency Models: Pinpointing Critical Success Factors in Organizations*. San Francisco: Jossey-Bass Pfeiffer.

Lurie, N. 1986. Money, Semantics and Native American Leadership. *Native American Quarterly Journal of Native American Studies* 10:47-63.

Mansfield, R. S. 1996. Building Competency Models: Approaches for HR Professionals. *Human Resources Management* 35:7-18.

Martz, Wes. 2013. Evaluating Organizational Performance: Rational, Natural, and Open System Models. *American Journal of Evaluation* 34 (3): 385-401.

Mehra, Ajay, Brett Smith, Andrea L. Dixon and Bruce Robertson. 2006. Distributed Leadership in Teams: The Network of Leadership Perceptions and Team Performance. *Leadership Quarterly* 17:232-45.

Meier, Werner. 2003. Results-Based Management: Towards a Common Understanding Among Development Cooperation Agencies. Discussion paper prepared for the Canadian International Development Agency, Performance Review Branch, Ottawa.

Metoyer, Cheryl A. 2010. Leadership in American Indian Communities: Winter Lessons. *American Indian Culture and Research Journal* 34 (4): 1-12.

Newhouse, David. 2000. Modern Aboriginal Economies: Capitalism With a Red Face. *Journal of Aboriginal Economic Development* 1 (2): 55-61.

Newman, Dwight. 2014. The Rule and Role of Law: The Duty to Consult, Aboriginal Communities, and the Canadian Natural Resource Sector. Ottawa: Macdonald-Laurier Institute Publications.

Oppenheimer, Robert, Tom O'Connell and Warren Weir. 2010. Training Opportunities in Aboriginal Business, Community and Economic Development. *Journal of Aboriginal Economic Development* 7 (1): 19-25.

Ospina, Sonia and Erica Foldy. 2005. Toward a Framework of Social Change Leadership. Research Paper No. 2010-05, New York University Wagner, presented at Public Management Research Association annual meeting, Los Angeles.

Ottmann, Jacqueline. 2005a. First Nations Leadership Development Within a Saskatchewan Context. PhD dissertation, Department of Educational Administration, University of Saskatchewan.

———. 2005b. First Nations Leadership Development. Report for The Banff Centre, Indigenous Leadership and Management. Banff, AB: Banff Centre for the Arts.

Parry, S. R. 1996. The Quest for Competencies. *Training* (July): 48-56.

Peredo, Ana Maria and Robert W. Anderson 2006. Indigenous Entrepreneurship Research: Themes and Variations. In *Developmental Entrepreneurship: Adversity, Risk, and Isolation*, ed. C. S. Galbraith and C. H. Stiles. Oxford: Elsevier.

Peredo, Ana Maria and James J. Chrisman. 2006. Toward a Theory of Community-Based Enterprise. *Academy of Management Review* 31 (2): 309-28.

Rafferty, A. F. and M. A. Griffen. 2004. Dimensions of Transformational Leadership: Conceptual and Empirical Extensions. *Leadership Quarterly* 15:329-54.

Redpath, Lindsay and Marianne O. Nielsen. 1997. A Comparison of Native Culture, Non-Native Culture and New Management. *Canadian Journal of Administrative Sciences* 14 (3): 327-39.

Rost, J. C. 1993. *Leadership for the Twenty-First Century*. Westport, CT: Praeger.

Scholtes, P. R. 1998. *The Leader's Handbook: Making Things Happen, Getting Things Done*. New York: McGraw-Hill.

Spencer L. M. and S. M. Spencer. 1993. *Competence at Work: Models for Superior Performance*. New York: Wiley.

Sternberg, Robert J. 2005. A Model of Educational Leadership: Wisdom, Intelligence, and Creativity, Synthesized. *International Journal of Leadership in Education* 8 (4): 347-64

TD Economics. 2001. Special Report: Estimating the Size of the Aboriginal Market. TD Economics special report, Toronto, June 17. http://www.td.com/document/PDF/economics/special/sg0611_aboriginal.pdf

Thayer Scott, Jacqueline. 2006. "Doing Business with the Devil": Land, Sovereignty, and Corporate Partnerships in Membertou, Inc. In *Self-Determination: The Other Path for Native Americans*, ed. Terry L. Anderson, Bruce L. Benson, and Thomas E. Flanagan. Stanford, CA: Stanford University Press.

Vinje, D. 1996. Native American Economic Development on Selected Reservations: A Comparative Study. *American Journal of Economics and Sociology* 55:427-43.

Voyageur, Cora J. 2008. *Firekeepers of the 21st Century: Women Indian Chiefs*. Montreal: McGill-Queen's University Press.

———. 2011. Out in the Open: Elected Female Leadership in Canada's First Nation Community. *Canadian Review of Sociology* 48 (1): 67-85.

Waldersee, R. and G. Eagleson. 2002. Shared Leadership in the Implementation of Reorientations. *Leadership and Organization Development Journal* 23 (7): 400-407.

Warner, Linda Sue and Keith Grint. 2006. American Indian Ways of Leading and Knowing. *Leadership* 2 (2): 225-44.

Washington, Michele Siemthult. 2004. Bringing Traditional Teachings to Leadership. *American Indian Quarterly* 28 (2): 583-603

Weick, Karl E. 2006. Organizing for Mindfulness: Eastern Wisdom and Western Knowledge. *Journal of Management Inquiry* 15 (3): 275-287.

Wesley-Esquimaux, Cynthia and Brian Calliou. 2010. Best Practices in Aboriginal Community Development: A Literature Review and Wise Practices Approach. Report for The Banff Centre, Indigenous Leadership and Management, Banff, Alberta. http://www.banffcentre.ca/Indigenous-leadership/library/pdf/best_practices_in_aboriginal_community_development.pdf.

Wesley-Esquimaux, Cynthia and M. Smolewski. 2004. Historical Trauma and Aboriginal Healing. Report for the Aboriginal Healing Foundation, Ottawa.

Whitecap Dakota. 2015. *Economic Development*. http://www.whitecapdakota.com/programs-services/economic-development/ (accessed December 5, 2015).

Wood, M. 2005. Determinants of Shared Leadership in Management Teams. *International Journal of Leadership Studies* 1 (1): 64-85.

Wutunee, Wanda. 2002. Partnering Among Aboriginal Communities: Tribal Council Investment Group (TCIG). *Journal of Aboriginal Economic Development* 3 (1): 9-17.

Yukl, G. A. 1998. *Leadership in Organizations*. Upper Saddle River, NJ: Prentice-Hall International.

Chapter 4

While the term "entrepreneur" is used frequently, do we know what it really means? An entrepreneur is a person who develops or sets up a business, usually with considerable financial risk offset by potential of significant reward. There is much debate about whether entrepreneurs are "made" or "born," and there is a developing consensus that an entrepreneurial mindset can indeed be developed in people. "Entrepreneurship" more broadly refers to an approach used when developing new ventures or even projects in organizations.

The growth rate of Aboriginal entrepreneurs is increasing rapidly, outpacing that of non-Aboriginal Canada. Still, there are challenges faced in terms of obtaining financing to start a business, and of adequate training or capacity building to ensure its success. Mentorship in particular can be important for the success of new entrepreneurs. In an Aboriginal context, community support is essential. When these components are present, initiatives led by individual members of Aboriginal communities are often more able to succeed than community-lead initiatives.

Entrepreneurship
Teresa Callihoo and Derek Bruno

Derek's Story

Writing this chapter is a reflection of my own journey as an entrepreneur in my community. Partnering with my brother, Cody, we started our first two businesses twelve years ago, by opening Cree Convenience and Peace Hills Pure Water in our home community. This chapter takes into consideration our decision-making path and attempts to be as practical as possible in so doing.

Entrepreneurial thinking is what started our business. We looked around our community and noted its needs. Our first goal was to provide safe drinking water to our community members. However, after crunching the numbers we realized the bottled-water business would not be viable on its own. Instead of being deterred, we analyzed our community further and felt we could compete by opening a convenience store that better met community need. The success of our convenience store allowed us the cash flow to make our way into the water business. We faced many obstacles over the years, but we continue to have a vision for our businesses. Tenacity has kept our business going.

What is Entrepreneurship?

"'Regardless of the form, entrepreneurial enterprises remain at the heart of Indigenous economic development." (Peredo et. al. 2004: 3)

Aboriginal entrepreneurship is growing, from coast to coast to coast, as individuals and communities seek to reap the rewards of economic development. Whether the ventures spring up on or off the reserve, they provide Aboriginal entrepreneurs with the opportunity to play a significant role within their community. A growing business sector results in more dollars staying within the community as businesses provide essential services, employment opportunities, and revenue generation. As Anderson (2001: 37) states, Aboriginal people "are creating business in the global economy in order to generate the wealth necessary to support self-government and to improve socioeconomic conditions. At the same time, through business ownership Aboriginal people expect to exercise greater control over activities in their traditional territories."

> **Entrepreneurship** refers to the process of having an innovative idea or creative solution to a problem, and then developing that idea or solution into a viable business. Entrepreneurship requires initiative and tenacity, as well as a willingness to take on risk.

When looking at entrepreneurship it is important to first understand what we are talking about. Gartner (1989) discusses two approaches to understanding entrepreneurship as either trait or behaviour led. A trait-based approach looks at the traits possessed by entrepreneurs. Gartner (58) notes that "[e]ntrepreneurs often do seem like special people who achieve things that most of us do not achieve. These achievements, we think, must be based on some special inner quality." A behaviour-based approach looks at the entrepreneur as part of the new-venture-creation process and assumes that entrepreneurship is a process that can be taught (Rae 2007). This approach puts the organization as the primary level of analysis, while looking at the activities the individual undertakes in order to help the organization come into existence.

In addition, there is debate among practitioners regarding the true meaning of entrepreneurship. Many would argue that entrepreneurs are not merely business owners, delineating the difference between working "in" versus working "on" the business: a business owner primarily focused on working "in" their business spends time on tasks revolving around maintaining the business; an entrepreneur works "on" their business by looking for ways to innovate, grow, and expand.

While entrepreneurship scholars debate whether an entrepreneur is born (traits) or can be trained (behaviour), it is worthy to note that a major trend of the global economy is the prominent role of the entrepreneur as an innovator and creative force. According to Kuratko (2014: 3), "an entrepreneurial mindset can be developed in individuals. This mindset can be exhibited inside or outside an organization, in for-profit or not-for-profit enterprises, and in business or nonbusiness activities for the purpose of bringing forth creative ideas."

There is also discussion over whether there are specific qualities involved in Indigenous or Aboriginal entrepreneurial activities. Many of these qualities include ideas such as a collective versus individual focus; that is, businesses that provide communal benefit versus a benefit solely to the individual entrepreneur, as discussed in chapter 3. This idea is articulated by McBride and Gerow (2004: 2): "[i]deally a community minded entrepreneur is not solely interested in the bottom line but instead recognizes and supports community needs, hires local members, donates to community functions, attends community events and is willing to be a role model for the community." Although there are certainly traits necessary for entrepreneurship—such as tenacity, resolve, critical thinking, innovation, and vision—for our purposes, we will focus less on traits inherent to the individual and more on the action steps required to open and manage a business. This includes activities such as business planning, financing, and problem-solving.

In addition, while there are a number of First Nation communities that exhibit entrepreneurial thinking in their business- and economic-development activities, we will focus on individually owned enterprises. McBride and Gerow (2004) note that when comparing individual entrepreneurs to a band or nation, the individual is often able to capitalize on opportunities more quickly. Individuals do not have the same processes and bureaucracy to follow as chief and council does. Further, individuals will be more focused on success and will use less time and resources and take more risks in the development of the business. Individuals are also less burdened by communal factors, such as ensuring specific employment-level goals or the endeavour to provide profits back to the community. Individuals can thus run a much leaner operation, which may be especially important in the beginning stages of business development.

There may be thousands of Aboriginal-owned ventures spread across Canada, spanning every industry (more on the growth of entrepreneurship can be found in chapter 9). Some may be considered traditional, while others may straddle industries and ideas that reach far into new territory. It would be nearly impossible to profile all of the businesses owned by Aboriginal people and do each justice. Instead, we will narrow our focus to some of the commonalities among Indigenous entrepreneurs by focusing on the realities of opening a business. Although there are many hurdles to overcome, the sheer growth of entrepreneurs indicates that each of these challenges is being met and overcome.

Business Basics

Derek's Story

Our business is structured as a partnership. Incorporation would have meant losing the tax benefits of operating on the reserve. One aspect of partnership that is crucial is having an agreement on roles and responsibilities. Our business has evolved over the years; in the beginning, we both worked shifts in the business, taking on the role of cashier as well as manager on duty. However, as our business has grown, and as our personal interests have grown, we have taken a less hands-on approach and now rely on our team to keep things running day to day. A partnership agreement can provide a blueprint for navigating changes, disagreements, and growth.

One of the first decisions made in starting a new business is choosing the form of legal organization. The information service, Canada Business Network, provides information on the four types of business structures: sole proprietorships, partnerships, corporations, and co-operatives (http://www.canadabusiness.ca/eng/page/2853/). Sole proprietorship is considered one of the easiest legal structures for entering into business, as there is a sole owner for the business. As such, the owner can keep all profits and has all decision-making capabilities; however, it also means one individual is responsible for all debts and obligations related to the business. In addition, a creditor can make a claim against a proprietor's personal and business assets to pay off debts incurred by the business.

> A **sole proprietorship** is owned and run by one individual. That individual assumes liability for all debts and obligations of the business.

More complex business arrangements, such as partnerships and corporations, are also possible. A partnership is a legal entity formed by two or more co-owners to operate a business. Partnership enables individuals to combine financial resources into the business and share in the profits and the risks. A partnership should have a partnership agreement that protects the interests of both parties and clearly establishes roles and responsibilities, as well as addressing issues such as profit sharing and dissolving the partnership. Similar to a sole proprietorship, co-owners face unlimited liability. Alternatively, a limited-liability partnership can be established. This structure consists of one general partner and one limited partner. The general partner remains personally liable for the debts of the business, whereas the limited partner does not take part in the management of the business and has limited liability. Another type of business structure is a corporation, which is chartered under either federal or provincial law. An incorporated business is considered a legal entity separate from its shareholders. The shareholders of a corporation are not personally liable for the debts, obligations, or acts of the corporation. This structure is more expensive and there are more regulations and added reporting obligations. More information on partnerships, joint ventures, and corporations is found in chapter 5.

Aboriginal entrepreneurs, specifically First Nation individuals operating on-reserve, will want to consider their options. Sole proprietorship and partnerships operate at personal (self-employed) tax rates, meaning such individuals can operate the business at a tax-free rate; however, they also personally assume all liability. An incorporated company loses this tax advantage, but it also minimizes personal liability. Taxation is discussed in further detail in chapter 7.

According to Industry Canada, the term "small and medium-sized enterprise" (SME) is used to refer to all businesses with fewer than 500 employees. Firms with 500 or more employees are considered large businesses. More specifically, small goods-producing firms have fewer than 100 employees, according to the consideration, and small service-producing firms have up to 50 employees. Firms with between 50 and 499 employees are considered medium-sized. The smallest of small businesses are called "micro-enterprises," most often defined as having fewer than 5 employees.

Despite their small size, the employment opportunities provided by small businesses is significant. Industry Canada statistics point out that, in 2012, more than 7.7 million employees, or 69.7 per cent of the total private labour force, worked for small businesses. An additional 2.2 million employees, or 20.2 per cent of the labour force, worked for medium-sized businesses. In total, SMEs employed about 10 million individuals, or 89.9 per cent of private-sector employees (Industry Canada 2013).

> **Small and medium-sized enterprises** are businesses with fewer than 500 employees. They are important drivers in the economy, outnumbering large enterprises, and often leading innovation.
>
> A **micro-enterprise** is the smallest business enterprise, usually having no more than five employees.

Aside from employment, entrepreneurs provide many necessary services:

Entrepreneurs are the decision makers who help shape the free-enterprise economic system by discovering market needs and launching new firms to meet those needs. Much of the impetus for change, innovation and progress in our economy comes from entrepreneurs—energizers who take risks and spark economic growth (Longenecker et. al. 2003: 2)

Although SMEs may be considered small, given their employee numbers, the support they can offer big business is significant. Examples of entrepreneurs that rise up to meet the needs of larger businesses abound. Consider Alberta's oil sand development: in 2011 Shell Canada announced that in the previous six years it worked with more than seventy Aboriginal businesses on more than $1 billion in contracts. In addition, Imperial Oil has paid almost $140 million to twenty-five Aboriginal contractors on its Kearl project. Syncrude spends roughly $150 million every year with native suppliers (VanderKlippe 2012).

One Aboriginal-owned business that has benefited from such a contract is Birch Mountain Enterprises in Fort McMurray, Alberta (http://bmel.ca/). According to its website, Birch Mountain has more than 200 employees and has evolved from its early days as a maintenance company into a service-sector company. The company boasts a 58 per cent Aboriginal employment rate, utilizes Aboriginal contractors whenever possible, and makes regular financial contributions back to the community. Birch Mountain Enterprises is an excellent example of a company that benefited from the opportunities of big business, yet maintained the principles of entrepreneurship to remain competitive and grow.

Obstacles

Derek's Story

Our business faces a lot of challenges. In the beginning, we were told by the "professionals" that it was statistically impossible for our business to survive. We proved them wrong in our first year of operations and have been running for the past twelve years. Even our parents were unsure why we would want to start a business in the community. But we had a strong vision from the beginning. Entrepreneurship requires understanding the challenges and finding ways to navigate them.

Opening a business requires a significant commitment of time and re-sources. There is a preparatory phase articulating the goals, vision, and plan of the business, followed by the ability to open and maintain or expand operations. The challenges faced for any entrepreneur are considerable, while the challenges faced by Aboriginal entrepreneurs are often magnified.

Aboriginal entrepreneurs face greater obstacles than non-Aboriginal entrepreneurs when starting a business. Taken as a whole Aboriginal-owned businesses tend to have less access to capital and established business networks, incur higher costs of business due to their remote locations, do not have access to the necessary skills or training and encounter limited understanding of Aboriginal circumstances by non-Aboriginal firms and individuals. This may be especially true for First Nation entrepreneurs living on reserve, due to the provisions in the *Indian Act* that can impede business development. (National Aboriginal Economic Development Board 2012: 24)

Aboriginal entrepreneurs may also face additional challenges, such as "issues related to band governance (for band-owned businesses), and stereotyping" (Sisco and Stewart 2009). McBride and Gerow (2004) note that it is three times as complex to start a business on the reserve because of the involvement of Indigenous and Northern Affairs Canada (INAC) and the bureaucracy of band politics. Additional impediments include access to mentorship and community support for individually owned ventures.

Despite the obstacles faced, there are many Aboriginal businesses thriving across Canada. Entrepreneurs open doors for one another as they take advantage of opportunities and share their experiences. According to Anderson (2001: 43), entrepreneurial success for Aboriginal people requires three things:

- The ability to identify viable opportunities.

- The ability to apply management tools and techniques to convert opportunities into businesses, products, and services.

- The resources necessary to create viable business from the opportunities identified.

We now look at how advances in training, finance, mentorship, and community support can help entrepreneurs reach their goals.

Training

Derek's Story

The first concrete step I took in planning for the business was attending a twelve-week entrepreneurship course located in a neighbouring community. That course helped walk me through my first business plan and helped me solidify my ideas. After that, Cody and I would spend all of our spare time— outside of attending university classes and working—writing a business plan for Cree Convenience. Since then we have both balanced running our business with post-secondary education.

> A **business plan** is a detailed document that identifies the goal of the business and a plan for how this goal will be achieved. It will often include objectives and strategies from marketing, financial, and operational perspectives.

Compared with the non-Aboriginal population, the Aboriginal population in Canada is younger and faster growing. Aboriginal people experience lower rates of employment and education attainment when compared with non-Aboriginal people (see chapter 9 for details). The need for training, then, is twofold: to address the significant training and education gap between Aboriginal and non-Aboriginal people in Canada, and to develop the skill sets necessary for successful venture creation and maintenance.

Findings in the Standing Senate Committee on Aboriginal Peoples Report (2007) point out that capacity-building is one necessary step in supporting business development because many Aboriginal Canadians are first-generation business people. Further, the World Economic Forum (2009: 7) has indicated that "[e]ntrepreneurship education is essential for developing the human capital necessary for the society of the future." Leadership training for Aboriginal economic development is addressed in chapter 3.

A number of training initiatives have been developed in Canada to address the skills deficit related to Aboriginal business.

Kahnawake Youth Entrepreneur Training – Kahnawake, QC

Kahnawake Youth Entrepreneur Training was one of the first programs designed to help youth start or expand businesses in Kahnawake. Funding for the initiative was provided by a contribution from Industry Canada (Heidrick and Nicol 2002). Those running the program understood that "[a] critical component of the success of any project is determining who will be participants" (Oppenheimer, O'Connell, and Diabo 2001: 58). With this in mind, the project undertook an extensive recruitment campaign, screening and interviewing all participants to determine suitability for the program. Although the program was aimed at youth aged between fifteen and twenty-nine, there were concerns that the program might encourage some youth to drop out of school. Consequently, only participants aged twenty to twenty-nine were chosen to participate in the program. While no applicants were rejected, some were encouraged to work on their ideas further and wait for a second round of training. There were seventeen applicants chosen, out of twenty-three (Oppenheimer, O'Connell, and Diabo 2001).

The program covered marketing, market research, operations, and finance, as well as goal-setting, idea generation, entrepreneurial work habits, problem-solving, and basic management functions. It also profiled successful entrepreneurs within the community. Participants were expected to complete a business plan during the training. Over ten weeks, participants attended three-hour information sessions, where they were taught components of the business plan and were then expected to complete each portion before the next class. Completed business plans were presented to a committee for review.

A total of thirteen participants completed the program, with four participants dropping out after the first class. When the program concluded, six individuals presented their business plans to a

> **Capacity building** is a process of identifying knowledge and skill sets necessary to achieve objectives and goals, and developing them through training or other initiatives.

> The story of **Kahnawake Youth Entrepreneur Training** was published in the *Journal of Aboriginal Economic Development* (JAED). Published by the Council for the Advancement of Native Development Officers, JAED features lessons from research and experience.
>
> **Market** can refer to the place where business is done (where goods and services are sold) or to the group of consumers who might be interested in a particular good or service.

loan committee. The loan committee was made up of community members with backgrounds in business and community economic development. The committee approved five of the individuals for loans to start their businesses. One and a half years after the training, all five of the businesses that received loans were still in business, and the entrepreneurs were repaying their loans on schedule.

Change it Up Entrepreneur—Samson Cree Nation, AB

Change it Up Entrepreneur (CIU-E) is a six-month, full-time program that takes youth through skill-building activities and business planning aimed at helping them start their own business (http://www. changeitup.ca). The program includes one-on-one coaching; self-discovery; strength identification; social/emotional skill-building; hands-on experience in starting, financing, and running a community business; advice and assistance from successful entrepreneurs; and support in identifying business opportunities, creating a business plan, and business start-up.

Program participants are taken through a number of skill-building modules that aim to develop both personal and business skills. Participants run a group business for part of the program, where they take part in all components of the business, from planning to start up and shut down. During the first session of the program, a number of group businesses were run, including an automotive-detailing business and custom T-shirt design company. In session two, participants focused on a group business idea, running a local market that invited outside vendors to sell their goods—the idea was well received by the Samson Cree Nation (SCN). The main focus of the program is to ensure individuals have a completed business plan and can apply for a grant through the SCN Economic Development Office. Individuals who start their proposed business are provided with mentorship and after-care services. CIU-E aims to provide individuals with wrap-around services and training, giving them the best chances at success.

Fifty-two students successfully completed the first run of the program, with thirty-three new businesses started within the community. As an incentive to completing the training, SCN offers seed funding for individuals who complete the program. Similar to the Kahnawake program, entrepreneurs present their completed business plans to a committee, which provides feedback and decides on funding. After two sessions of the program, seven students received a total of $45,000, with four other submissions pending, based on additional requirements or individual circumstances (CIU Program Results 2015). The new companies thus started in the community include catering, beading supply, home fashion and décor, residential and commercial cleaning, transportation, bespoke fashion and merchandise, a hair salon, and a mobile aesthetics company.

Part of the program's success can be attributed to the rigorous selection process, which screens individuals based on their business ideas as well as personal suitability and readiness. Challenges that the program faced included the need for additional mentors, as there are few available locally. It was also noted that participants needed increased support after the program and while starting their business as they moved from the classroom component—which provided daily support by a facilitator and coach—to handling the demands of a business start-up.

Other Programs

In addition to programs run within First Nation communities, there are a number of programs run off-reserve. The Aboriginal Business and Entrepreneurship Skills Training program is provided in communities throughout British Columbia, for First Nation (regardless of status), Métis, and Inuit who are interested in becoming self-employed or starting their own business. The program provides job-creation and skills training aimed at developing entrepreneurial spirit in its participants. Participants take part in a twelve-week program, where they meet guest speakers, identify viable business ideas, determine their feasibility, and take steps to start or grow their own businesses by learning about topics such as market research, business planning, and financing. Success stories from the program include a fashion clothing brand, an artist, a spa, a marketing and communications firm, a furniture-design company, and a cleaning business.

While the majority of initiatives are aimed at helping individuals aged eighteen and over develop and run their own businesses, there are additional initiatives aimed at a younger group. The Young Entrepreneurs Symposium is a conference that connects Indigenous young people with business leaders and role models to help them build their skills, knowledge, and networks. Conference delegates are placed in teams that participate in a series of competitions designed to help build skills and acquire valuable business knowledge. Cash prizes are awarded to the top three teams. In addition to the competition, participants meet First Nation, Canadian, and international business leaders and role models. It is hoped that the combination of competition, fun, learning, and networking will result in an interest in entrepreneurship.

Another program directed at youth is the Aboriginal Youth Entrepreneurship Program (AYEP). As part of high-school curricula across Canada, AYEP, part of the Martin Aboriginal Education Initiative, aims to teach Indigenous youth about business and entrepreneurship while encouraging them to complete their high-school education and to go on to post-secondary studies. Participants gain skills in leadership, financial literacy, English, accounting, marketing, and information/communications. They also learn how to create a product- or service-based business, and funding is provided to qualified students to start a micro-business.

Entrepreneurial or business-development training is an important first step to helping individuals with business ideas to reach their goals. Training opportunities provided to high-school-age students help them to start to think about business development, introducing them to such ideas at an early age. Programs provide the support and knowledge essential to starting a business.

While they each take different approaches to reaching their goals—for example, a full-time program versus a shorter, part-time program—what is essential is that they continue to monitor progress, making changes as necessary, and ensuring they are meeting the needs of their target audience. Therefore, a program run on-reserve will differ from one in an urban setting. Maintaining a reflection of the community the program is serving will help to ensure program success.

Financing

Derek's Story

Financing was our biggest initial obstacle. We were denied grant financing because lenders considered our plan impossible. By their calculations, our market was saturated and there was no room for competition. We knew our community and we knew there was room for our company. Regular bank financing was not an option, but we pushed through until we found the Alberta Indian Investment Corporation, with a mandate to help Aboriginal entrepreneurs in the province of Alberta. They provided us our first loan and have since provided us with financing for expansion.

Next to writing a business plan, obtaining financing can be a significant initial challenge for entrepreneurs. Two of the programs discussed above helped participants overcome these challenges by providing access to funding if they were able to meet the criteria set out by the program. It is fundamental to have access to alternative financing, particularly because legislation such as the *Indian Act* provides some unique challenges for on-reserve businesses.

Many financial institutions are reluctant to finance on-reserve assets because of the *Indian Act*. Because property is considered an asset of the reserve (of the Crown, in fact), many individuals with on-reserve housing cannot use their home as collateral. Unless an individual has off-reserve holdings, they will likely face challenges in obtaining traditional methods of financing. Doing business on-reserve is a challenge for lenders due to the land-holding regime, restrictions on access, the taking of security, and the administrative regimes of bands, as described in chapters 2 and 8. All of these factors contribute to creating a complex situation where standard mainstream lending practices are not applicable (Heidrick and Nicol 2002).

> **Assets** are property or other resources that have economic value and can be used to meet debts.
>
> **Security** is a tradable asset that can be used as collateral for a loan. If the repayment terms of a loan are not met, creditors have the ability to take possession of tradable assets as an alternative form of repayment.

Although it creates considerable challenges, it does not mean that they are insurmountable. As indicated by the review of training programs, where start-up funds were provided by the reserve itself, such as Kahnawake Youth Entrepreneur Training and CIU-E, there are alternatives available. Many First Nation communities are taking steps to allocate funds toward business development by providing either loans or grants to aspiring entrepreneurs.

The Aboriginal Business Development Program, a program provided under INAC, provides a number of services to Indigenous entrepreneurs including financing. INAC partners with Aboriginal financial institutions, (AFIs) to deliver funding for business development. AFIs are located across Canada, serving status, non-status, on- and off-reserve First Nations, Métis, or Inuit clients. By working at the community level, this program is designed to meet the needs of individuals.

> A **loan** is money or property that is borrowed and must be paid back, often with interest.
>
> A **grant** is a financial award that normally does not have to be repaid.

There are also a number of Aboriginal-specific lending organizations, looking to fill the gap of service to entrepreneurs. For example, the Alberta Indian Investment Corporation (AIIC), formed in 1987, provides interest-bearing loans and equity financing to First Nation (status Indian) entrepreneurs, on- and off-reserve, aimed to help start and expand businesses. AIIC is owned by all the First Nation communities in Alberta and provides services across the province.

Created in 1982, with a mandate for promoting economic development and business initiatives for Yukon First Nations, däna Näye Ventures provides developmental-financing assistance and business services to SMEs, both Aboriginal and non-Aboriginal, in Yukon and northern British Columbia (http://www.dananaye.yk.net/financial.html). In addition to traditional lending services, the company has developed the Yukon Micro Loan Program. This program helps individuals who have limited credit history by providing micro loans to start, maintain, or expand a small business.

Loans are typically much smaller than traditional business loans, starting at $3,000 to a maximum of $12,000. It is one example of how the institution has responded to the specific needs of its community.

Kakivak Association is a community and economic-development organization serving Inuit in the Baffin region by providing business, employment, and training services (http://www.kakivak.ca/apps/authoring/dspPage.aspx?page=home). The organization provides a number of different loan and grant options to meet the needs of their target market. Some of the smallest loans are for artists and craftspeople. Aimed at providing funds to purchase tools and supplies, these loans go to a maximum of $2,500. However, larger loans are available to Inuit looking to start or expand businesses.

A **micro loan** is a small sum of money that is borrowed and must be paid back. Micro loans are often made to individuals who cannot otherwise obtain a traditional loan and have become particularly popular in relation to impoverished communities. One of the most popular micro-loan programs is Kiva.org.

Although financing can be a challenge for entrepreneurs, there are a number of examples of how communities and organizations have stepped up to find solutions to these challenges. Whether it is First Nation communities setting aside funds to help business start-ups, non-traditional sources of lending, or government programs, there is support for entrepreneurs. See chapter 8 for more financing options.

Mentorship

Derek's Story

Mentorship has been key in my life. In my first job, as a banker, I met a number of entrepreneurs, they talked to me about their lives and I could see their passion for business. Their stories inspired me to start reading about business. Since opening our business, I have found it important to find mentors that can help move my business to the next level. I also consider it important to give back and I spend some of my time mentoring young entrepreneurs and speaking at events that promote entrepreneurship. A mentor provides essential support.

As has been mentioned previously in the overview of CIU-E, one of the challenges facing the program was finding mentors to work with participants. The gap of knowledge between writing a business plan and actually opening and running a company is considerable. Even with the best plans, entrepreneurs inevitably run into a number of problems in day-to-day operations. The learning curve for a new business owner is steep and, without experience to fall back on, many navigate these challenges haphazardly, learning as they go. Having a mentor, someone who has established a business and knows the ropes of day-to-day operations, can be invaluable: "A mentor or advisor is an essential asset to a growing company. They can warn of problems on the horizon, help craft solutions to problems and be a sounding board for the entrepreneur. A mentor's many years of experience can save a business from major errors and costly mistakes with just a few words" (Cull 2006: 9). Some of the key components necessary in a mentor-entrepreneur relationship are open communication, honesty, support, being able to keep the client going, and being neutral, objective, and non-judgmental (Cull 2006).

The Canadian Council for Aboriginal Business (CCAB) has a mentorship program that pairs Indigenous entrepreneurs with experienced mentors, helping them to take their business to the next level. This initiative is likely related to the CCAB's own findings that "Aboriginal businesses tend to operate in isolation from other businesses and business organizations—there is need for more active support systems that offer mentorship and advice to help small businesses operate more effectively" (CCAB 2011: 8). The CCAB essentially provides a matching service, screening both the entrepreneur and mentor. This program, however, is not aimed at business start-ups, as individuals need to be in business for a minimum of two years before being eligible for the program.

Mentorship may be even more important for Indigenous women hoping to start their own businesses. The Aboriginal Business Survey found that 51 per cent of Aboriginal-owned SMEs belonged either entirely or partly to women, while the Canadian average stands at 47 per cent. Since 1981, the number of self-employed Aboriginal women has grown at a phenomenal rate (Statistics Canada 2002). A report by the Women's Economic Council found that Aboriginal women often required much greater support to successfully meet their aspirations for self-employment (Baxter 2011). Of the supports needed, mentorship was a key component.

Mentorship can be provided by an organization, such as the CCAB, or at the community level. The training programs previously mentioned aimed to profile local Aboriginal-owned businesses and link aspiring entrepreneurs to these individuals. Mentorship may be provided on smaller community-scale levels, such as chamber-of-commerce-style events or regularly scheduled networking events for entrepreneurs. With technology becoming more available in remote areas, instant messaging, email, and Internet calling can also link entrepreneurs with mentors outside of their immediate area.

A mentor is a key component, whether facing business start-up or growth, as they can draw on their knowledge to help entrepreneurs navigate the many obstacles they will undoubtedly face. Toren (2012: 1) notes:

You need a good idea. Startup cash can make a real difference. Business experience and savvy also help, of course. But to take advantage of the most powerful weapon an entrepreneur can have, find a mentor. A good mentor helps you think through a business idea, suggests ways to generate that startup capital and provides the experience and savvy you're missing.

Community Support

Derek's Story

Without the support of my community, my business would fail. However, I do not consider my community's support to be a sure thing. Our store strives to be competitive and we work diligently to ensure we are meeting customer needs. In my community, I advocate to my chief and council to make supporting local-owned businesses a priority, because it doesn't always happen. I often see non-local businesses providing services that my business can meet. But I see it as an opportunity to make sure our business is competitive. I also try to "walk my talk" by supporting Aboriginal business in my personal life. We support other Aboriginal business people because we understand the challenges. In addition, it is important for our business to support the community. We provide donations to many local groups and strive to give back.

Essential to the success of Aboriginal business is the ability to find and maintain community support. This will, of course, vary from community to community. Support for Indigenous entrepreneurs can take on many different forms. In the on-reserve setting, communities, governments, administration, and economic-development offices show support for their entrepreneurs by:

- designating funding for entrepreneur training;

- designating funding for business start-up grants or loans;

- designing policies that support local businesses by purchasing services and supplies from local individuals;

- leaving business opportunities open for individual entrepreneurs instead of band-owned entities; and

- providing needed infrastructure, such as office space and retail spaces, for entrepreneurs to set up their operations.

While many First Nations are touted for their entrepreneurial approach to nation-owned business development, the support of individual entrepreneurs at the community level is just as important. Individual entrepreneurs can provide services where gaps exist, and they can provide much needed employment and help the local economy to grow. It is, however, imperative that they are supported by the larger policies of the nation, which can increase their chances of success.

In urban settings, organizations such as the Northeastern Alberta Aboriginal Business Association (NAABA) help to promote Aboriginal business by linking Aboriginal business to industry (http://www.naaba.ca). This organization uses networking sessions, industry nights, and business showcases to strengthen relationships between industry and its members. These events help members to meet face to face with industry and promote business relationships. In addition, NAABA acts as a link to industry procurement opportunities, working directly with procurement managers and their members to help take advantage of opportunities. Overall, NAABA acts as an Aboriginal chamber of commerce in the region, providing positive public-relations opportunities by highlighting the work of Indigenous entrepreneurs in the region.

> **Procurement** is the process of acquiring goods and services. While it is often preferred that goods and services are purchased at the lowest available price, some companies also have procurement policies that can encourage the use of local and/or Aboriginal providers.

While there is a role for community (i.e., bands) and organizations (such as NAABA) in helping to secure support for entrepreneurs, there is also a role for individual business owners and individual community members. Aboriginal business owners, like all business owners, must take an active role in maintaining a positive presence in their community. In order to maintain relevancy, businesses must be competitive. Aboriginal entrepreneurs have to be flexible enough to stay on top of trends, managing their business and services in a manner that best meets the needs of their customers. Some entrepreneurs may face stereotypes that their business services are subpar; entrepreneurs need to be aware of these constraints and respond in a professional manner. In addition, Aboriginal entrepreneurs are setting the bar for the next wave of entrepreneurs. They are helping to put a face to the idea that Aboriginal people can be successful in business. They can give back to their communities by showing that planning, hard work, and determination can aid in the success of their business. They also give back to the community by providing employment and training opportunities to other local individuals, and, if they have the means, by choosing to give back to their community.

As consumers, each of us has a role in supporting Aboriginal business. Choosing products or services offered by Aboriginal companies helps to strengthen their position in the market. There are many provincial business directories that list Aboriginal-owned companies. There are also initiatives aimed at helping consumers easily identify authentic Aboriginal goods, which may be most pertinent in the arts-and-crafts sector. Consumer and community support for Aboriginal business are important and require more than simply recognizing and celebrating successful Aboriginal businesses. It also requires purchasing Aboriginal goods and services.

Conclusions

Aboriginal entrepreneurs have the potential to affect both Aboriginal and non-Aboriginal communities in profound ways. From products and services to jobs and community donations, there are few limits to the benefits that entrepreneurs can have in the communities they serve. For example, Neechie Gear, an apparel company aimed at empowering youth through sports, donates 5 per cent of its profits to help fund underprivileged youth, toward their participation in extracurricular sports. Its founder, Kendal Netmaker from Sweetgrass First Nation, was inspired to give back based on his own story; he had loved sports as a child and experienced barriers to access that included finances and transportation (Larson 2015).

While Neechie Gear donates profits to First Nation communities, there are Aboriginal businesses that have the potential to make a significant impact on a broader scale. Clearflow Enviro Systems Group Inc., one of *Alberta Ventures* "25 Most Innovative Organizations," has created wastewater-treatment microsystems that do not require a significant infrastructure setup. Under the leadership of Métis owner Jerry Hanna, Clearflow is working on development projects that recycle on-site storm water and grey water from bathrooms, reducing potable water usage by up to 35 per cent. For a company still in its infancy, they have completely changed the way environmental solutions are formed and implemented.

> **Sweat equity** refers to an investment of work or effort into a company, rather than a financial investment.

In communities that experience high levels of unemployment and limited infrastructure, entrepreneurs are finding ways to start businesses using their own sweat equity. These business owners add value to the mission of the local government by creating a better quality of life for the community using their own resources. Entrepreneurial thinking and action has been behind most of the Aboriginal community-development success stories.

In the broader community, Aboriginal entrepreneurs are paving the way for recognition of the impact a strong enterprise sector will have on the whole of Canada. As Indigenous entrepreneurs step forward and share their knowledge and passion—be it around traditional ventures, the use of traditional knowledge, or in sectors not considered to be traditional—the collective benefits from the growth of these businesses providing goods, services, and knowledge to the market.

For Indigenous entrepreneurs, it is indeed an exciting time as all of the components required for business success begin to materialize and fortify. Today's entrepreneurs benefit from the hard work of all of those who have blazed the trail. Also notable is how technology has revolutionized business development by providing access to unlimited amounts of information. Technology such as the Internet facilitates access to training, education, mentors, business-planning software, banking, suppliers, customers, and advertisers. In addition, businesses can be run from the comfort of home without having to spend money on the usual bricks and mortar, as long as there is access to the Internet. The opportunity for Aboriginal entrepreneurs is perhaps best summed up by the words of one of Canada's most successful Aboriginal entrepreneurs, Dave Tuccaro: "We've become an economic force. We're respected now, where in the past people would look at us and say, 'You don't know how to do this'" (VanderKlippe 2012).

> **Bricks and mortar** is an expression that refers to a building or physical storefront for business.

Key Points:

- Entrepreneurship refers to the process of having an innovative idea or creative solution to a problem, and then developing that idea or solution into a viable business.

- The simplest structure for a business is a sole proprietorship, but it comes with greater liability than with other structures, such as a corporation.

- Small and medium-sized enterprises are businesses and organizations with fewer than 500 employees. They make a significant contribution to the economy.

- Aboriginal entrepreneurs face several obstacles in engaging in entrepreneurship, including training, access to financing, and mentorship throughout the business-development process.

- Programs are being developed by communities and organizations to address the obstacles Aboriginal entrepreneurs face.

- Community and consumer support for Aboriginal business is critical for its success.

Questions for Discussion:

1. What is entrepreneurship?

2. Discuss the characteristics of an entrepreneur. Are entrepreneurs born or made?

3. What are some of the challenges Aboriginal entrepreneurs face and how do these compare to those faced by mainstream entrepreneurs?

4. Of the three obstacles presented in this chapter, which is the most important to address and why?

5. What types of programs have been developed to address obstacles encountered by Aboriginal entrepreneurs? Compare and contrast them.

6. What is the role of community in the development and success of Aboriginal business?

7. How do you test whether your idea for a business start-up is sound?

Suggested Assignments:

1. Research Aboriginal business-training and financing programs available in your community or province. How do they compare to those outlined in this chapter?

2. Why is youth entrepreneurship important? Is it more important than entrepreneurship at other stages in life?

3. Identify and discuss examples in which the principles of entrepreneurship apply in settings other than a new business venture owned by an individual entrepreneur.

References

AANDC (Aboriginal Affairs and Northern Development Canada). 2013. Aboriginal Business Development Program. http://www.aadnc-aandc.gc.ca/eng/1375201178602/1375202816581 (accessed August 5, 2013).

Anderson, Robert. 2001. Aboriginal people, economic development and entrepreneurship. *Journal of Aboriginal Economic Development. 2 (1): 33-42.*

Baxter, Patricia. 2011. Regional clustering model for Aboriginal women: Aboriginal women and economic development feasibility study report. Report prepared for Women's Economic Council, St. Catharines, ON, February.

CCAB (Canadian Council for Aboriginal Business). 2011. Promise and Prosperity: the Aboriginal Business Survey. https://www.ccab.com/uploads/File/Promise-and-Prosperity--The-Aboriginal-Business-Survey.pdf.

Cull, J. 2006. Mentoring young entrepreneurs: what leads to success. *International Journal of Evidence Based Coaching and Mentoring. 4 (2): 8-18.*

Gartner, W. B. 1989. Who is an entrepreneur is the wrong question. *Entrepreneurship Theory and Practice 13 (4): 47-67.*

Heidrick, Ted and Tracey Nicol. 2002. Financing SMEs in Canada: Barriers Faced by Women, Youth, Aboriginal and Minority Entrepreneurs in Accessing Capital — Phase 1: Literature Review. Research Paper prepared for the Small Business Branch as part of the SME Financing Data Initiative, Industry Canada. https://www.ic.gc.ca/eic/site/061.nsf/vwapj/FinancingSMEsinCanadaPhase1_e.pdf/$FILE/FinancingSMEsinCanadaPhase1_e.pdf

Industry Canada. 2013. Key small business statistics. Paper prepared for the Small Business Branch, Industry Canada. https://www.ic.gc.ca/eic/site/061.nsf/vwapj/KSBS-PSRPE_August-Aout2013_eng.pdf/$FILE/KSBS-PSRPE_August-Aout2013_eng.pdf

Kuratko, D. F. 2014. *Entrepreneurship: Theory, Process, Practice*. 9th ed. Mason, OH: South-Western Cengage Learning.

Larson, S. 2015. Neechi gear founder embraces being a role model. *StarPhoenix*, Jan 19. http://www.activecircle.ca/en/news-core/35-2015/2566-neechie-gear-founder-embraces-being-role-model.html (accessed December 2, 2015).

Longenecker, J., L. B. Donlevy, V. A. C. Calvert, C. W. Moore and J. W. Petty. 2003. *Small Business Management an Entrepreneurial Emphasis*. 2nd Canadian ed. Toronto: Thomson Nelson.

McBride, J. and R. Gerow. 2004. Minding Our Own Businesses: How to Create Support in First Nations Communities for Aboriginal Business. Report prepared for the Centre for Sustainable Development, Simon Fraser University. http://www.chnook.org/wp-content/uploads/2012/01/Minding-our-own-Businesses-Workbook.pdf

National Aboriginal Economic Development Board. 2012. The Aboriginal Economic Benchmarking Report. http://www.naedb-cndea.com/reports/the-aboriginal-economic-benchmarking-report.pdf (accessed December 2, 2015).

Oppenheimer, R. J., T. O'Connell and L. J. Diabo. 2001. Facilitating the development of successful entrepreneurs in kahnawake: a program that is working. *Journal of Aboriginal Economic Development*. 2 (1): 56-60.

Peredo, A. M., R. B. Anderson, C. S. Galbraith, B. Honig and L. P. Dana. 2004. Towards a theory of Indigenous entrepreneurship. *International Journal of Entrepreneurship and Small Business* 1 (1/2): 1-20.

Rae, D. 2007. Entrepreneurship: From opportunity to action. New York: Palgrave Macmillan.

Sisco, A. and N. Stewart. 2009. True to Their Vision: An Account of 10 Successful Aboriginal Businesses. Report prepared for the Conference Board of Canada, Ottawa. http://abdc.bc.ca/uploads/file/09%20Harvest/10-131_TrueToTheirVisions_WEB.pdf.

Standing Senate Committee on Aboriginal Peoples. 2007. Sharing Canada's Prosperity–A Hand Up, Not A Handout. Final Report. Special study on the involvement of Aboriginal communities and businesses in economic development activities in Canada. http://www.parl.gc.ca/Content/SEN/Committee/391/abor/rep/rep06-e.pdf_(accessed December 2, 2015).

Statistics Canada. 2002. Aboriginal Entrepreneurs Survey. Statistics Canada. http://www23.statcan.gc.ca/imdb/p2SV.pl?Function=getSurvey&SDDS=5048 (accessed December 2, 2015).

Toren, A. 2012. Mentors: a young entrepreneurs secret weapon. Entrepreneur, January 26. http://www.entrepreneur.com/article/222694 (accessed December 2, 2015).

VanderKlippe, Nathan. 2012. In oil sands, a native millionaire sees 'economic force' for first nations. Globe and Mail, Aug. 14. http://www.theglobeandmail.com/report-on-business/industry-news/energy-and-resources/in-oil-sands-a-native-millionaire-sees-economic-force-for-first-nations/article4479795/ (accessed December 2, 2015).

World Economic Forum. 2009. Educating the next wave of entrepreneurs. Unlocking the entrepreneurial capabilities to meet the global challenges of the 21st century. Report prepared for the World Economic Forum, Global Education Initiative, Geneva, Switzerland, April. http://www3.weforum.org/docs/WEF_GEI_EducatingNextEntrepreneurs_ExecutiveSummary_2009.pdf (accessed December 2, 2015).

Chapter 5

A strategic alliance may be defined as a long-term relationship between two or more parties for increased mutual benefit. It can take many forms, from informal arrangements and non-equity partnerships to equity partnerships and joint ventures. Clearly, to be workable, the entities must be stronger in the alliance than by operating individually. A strategic alliance may bring new markets, new technologies, new channels of distribution, product and market diversification, cost savings, and a competitive advantage.

Within an Indigenous context, there may be additional goals of cultural preservation, capacity development, assertion of Aboriginal and treaty rights, and the broadening of community-development options. Successful strategic alliances between Aboriginal and non-Aboriginal partners have recognized the need for extensive consultation and communication, an acceptance of cultural differences, support of mutual benefit, and recognition and understanding of communal ownership.

Strategic Alliances, Partnerships, and Joint Ventures
Peter Moroz, Bob Kayseas, Robert Anderson, and Léo-Paul Dana

The significance of strategic alliances to Aboriginal communities and institutions in Canada continues to rise. Alliances are viewed by many as an effective way to achieve the related goals of prosperity, autonomy, and cultural integrity (Anderson 1997). Partnerships involving Indigenous and non-Indigenous organizations are evidenced as increasing the socioeconomic health and status of Indigenous communities, particularly through the creation of jobs and the incomes derived from expanded employment. These partnerships often also provide Aboriginal peoples with access to training, education, and employment in return for non-Indigenous access to resources and labour. However, strategic alliances may also be leveraged to provide the resources and capacity for creating new ventures. These Indigenous-controlled and -operated businesses in turn provide opportunities for Canada's Aboriginal peoples to opt into the global economy on their own terms (Anderson et al. 2006). Entrepreneurship (discussed in

A **strategic alliance** is an agreement between two (or more) independent businesses or organizations to work together to achieve a particular common goal or set of objectives. The three most common forms of strategic alliance are non-equity alliances, equity alliances, and joint ventures.

chapter 4) and business development are widely accepted as the key to building economies and a strategy for Indigenous peoples to use in rebuilding their nations.

Perhaps most importantly, Indigenous peoples have also formed strategic alliances with non-Indigenous organizations to establish control over their traditional territory as a means to defend their natural rights (Usher et al. 1992; Coates et al. 2010). These natural rights extend to how, when, and even if the resources of the land should be developed. The forming of strategic alliances between Indigenous and non-Indigenous organizations is thus key to unlocking and sharing prosperity. It also is a potential source of legal, economic, and political conflict. This fact is punctuated by an estimated $500 billion dollars in resource and energy initiatives in Canada that involve the development of natural resources on Aboriginal peoples' traditional or reserve lands (CICS 2012). As in other areas of the world, many natural-resource corporations have moved to secure agreements with Indigenous peoples in order to preempt these problems (discussed further in chapter 12), taking the view that partnerships are a necessary foundation of their long-term success (Langton 2012; Sawyer and Gomez 2012). Therefore, determining the readiness of communities to participate in these types of long-term partnerships on equal footing is foundational to their success.

This chapter explores these three interrelated areas significant to Aboriginal peoples and organizations looking to develop successful strategic alliances in Canada:

- socioeconomic improvement through job creation;

- new venture creation and entry into the global economy in relation to Indigenous development objectives; and

- Indigenous defence of inherent rights and control of territorial lands.

Following an introduction to the types of strategic alliances and motivations for entering into such agreements, the chapter provides a framework for understanding strategic alliances in an Indigenous context, highlighting some of the key differences between Indigenous and mainstream contexts.

Defining Strategic Alliances

Organizations operating in a business environment continuously seek greater efficiency, better quality, and lower costs to maintain or improve their competitiveness. Strategic alliances are viewed by chief executive officers as one of the main tools that firms may employ to deal with a range of social, financial, regulatory, and cultural challenges, especially when their own size, capabilities, or the resources under their control are limited. But setting collective goals that directly benefit collaborators and stakeholders is no easy task and entering into a strategic alliance is often a process that requires a great deal of consideration.

Two ways of thinking about strategic alliances affect its definition, those being from the traditional perspective or the competitive perspective. From a traditional perspective, a strategic alliance may be defined as a long-term operative arrangement among two or more independent organizations that engage in business activities for mutual economic gain (Tsang 1998). This definition reflects the significance of creating value for participants. Scholars who view strategic alliances from a competitive perspective define them as formal or informal coalitions between two or more firms that share compatible goals, acknowledge interdependence, and involve partial or contractual obligations/ownership (Stiles 2001). For each perspective, though, the goals or objectives are often broadly defined as involving the exchange, sharing, or co-development of products, technologies, or services (Gulati 1998).

Although the types of alliances that exist in the business environment vary, to help understand the forms that they may take, five broad categories are identified: informal, non-equity, equity, joint ventures, and mergers and acquisitions (Barney 1991; Lorange and Roos 1992).

Informal alliances allow each organization to control its own activities without shared control, ownership, or risk. Therefore, no actual contracts or equity are involved. The organizations acknowledge and seek to coordinate activities to achieve joint or complementary objectives. An industry association is one example of this type of alliance. The Northeastern Alberta Aboriginal Business Association is a non-profit organization that seeks to promote businesses, jobs, and training for the betterment of all native people in the Wood Mountain region of northern Alberta. Full members must be businesses with at least 51 per cent Aboriginal ownership and must be located in the Wood Mountain region (NAABA 2014). In May 2014, the *Financial Post* reported there were more than a hundred member companies, earning over $1.5 billion annually (Cattaneo 2014).

> An **informal alliance** seeks to coordinate activities of two separate entities to achieve joint or complementary objectives. No contracts or equity are involved.
>
> An **industry association** is an organization with a mandate to support and promote businesses in a particular industry and often in a defined region.

A non-equity alliance develops a cooperative arrangement between organizations through contracts. These alliance types do not engage in the creation of independent organizations or cross-equity positions. The licensing of a good by one company for the sale or distribution by another is one example of a non-equity alliance; another is a service contract between two companies. Tatanka Boutique is a retail outlet based in Regina, Saskatchewan, that sells Indigenous-made clothing, jewellery, star blankets, toys, moccasins, books, music, artwork, and other specialty items (Tatanka Boutique 2015). Much of the goods offered for sale are procured from Indigenous artists and are sold on consignment—an agreement between the artist and the seller that allows the artist to maintain ownership until the goods are sold. Tatanka Boutique earns a percentage of sales as payment for its services.

> A **non-equity alliance** is a cooperative contract arrangement between two businesses or organizations. The contract outlines what resources each organization will contribute, such as time, knowledge, or expertise.

An equity alliance supplements cooperative contracts with equity investments by one organization in the other organization. The Ktunaxa Kinbasket Tribal Council is the home to St. Eugene Mission, which historically was an Indian residential school (see chapter 14). Instead of tearing down the almost hundred-year-old facility, the tribal council decided to convert it into a three-diamond hotel (managed by Delta Hotels), casino, and golf complex. The facility was made possible only through an equity investment from the Samson Cree Nation (Alberta) and Chippewas of Rama First Nation (Ontario). The legal form of this venture is a limited partnership (St. Eugene 2015).

A joint venture is developed when two or more organizations individually invest (typically at least a 5 per cent stake each) to create an independent organization. The investing partners are compensated by the profits of the independent organization. Casino Rama is a joint venture between the Ontario Lottery and Gaming Corporation, Penn National Gaming (based in the United States), and Ontario First Nations. The casino is located on the Chippewas of Rama First Nation, near Orillia, Ontario. It is the largest First Nation casino in Canada, with over 2,500 slot machines, 110 gaming tables, and a 5,000-seat entertainment facility (Casino Rama 2015).

> An **equity alliance** is a cooperative contract arrangement between two businesses or organizations that involves a financial investment by one business into the other.
>
> A **limited partnership** is a legal arrangement through which a new independent legal entity is created. It limits the liability of a partner to that partner's share or percentage of ownership.
>
> A **joint venture** is a form of strategic alliance that involves the creation of a new independent organization by investments from two or more pre-existing organizations. The original two organizations continue to operate, while, at the same time, the joint venture will produce a new product or offer a service.

Mergers and acquisitions occur when one organization buys another, and, therefore, the form of alliance is much less prominent than the process for establishing the new organization.

Motives for Entering Into Strategic Alliances

The motives for entering into a strategic alliance with one or multiple partners are moderated by the types of firm-specific characteristics that exist, the intensity of the competitive environment, and the nature of the industry. While the list below is highly informative when attempting to understand the motivations behind why firms may seek out collaborative solutions, it is far from conclusive (Khattab 2012):

> A **merger** occurs when two businesses or organizations combine into one new entity. The original entities cease to exist after the merger.
>
> **Acquisition** occurs when one business purchases the majority shares of another business or organization.

- entering new markets;
- adjust to environmental changes;
- gaining access to new technology;
- knowledge sharing; cooperative learning and embedded skills;
- achieving vertical integration, recreating and extending supply links;
- acquiring means of distribution;
- diversifying into new businesses;
- improving performance;
- cost sharing, pooling of resources;
- developing products, technologies, resources;
- reduce financial and political risk; and
- achieving competitive advantage.

Factors Significant to Strategic Alliance Formation and Performance

In general, the study of strategic alliances has been a strong area of research, providing valuable insights on the behaviour of firms in alliances and their performance. Despite the rising levels of strategic alliances formation, fewer than half can be said to have performed satisfactorily (Das and Teng 2000). Thus, researchers have spent a great deal of time on identifying the problems and performance issues facing strategic alliances from a wide range of perspectives, stages, and theories.

> **Vertical integration** refers to the diversification of an organization's value chain through the extension or expansion of activities by taking greater control of either operational inputs or outputs.
>
> **Competitive advantage** refers to an attribute or circumstance that puts a business or organization in a favourable position and allows it to perform better than its competitors.

Barriers to formation—Of these, perhaps the most significant and most difficult to understand is trust between partners in the selection process and throughout the alliance's operations; partner selection, cultural differences, prior relationships, and a thorough understanding of mutual goals and expectations are all factors that are important for the creation of inter-organizational trust.

Control—The ownership/control issue may be distilled into the question "Who is in charge?" and focuses on the systems for communication, responsibility, and decision-making. Some of the mechanisms that may be employed to deal with issues arising from control include: board meetings, key personnel appointments, and arrangements for resolving disagreements.

Bargaining power—Often, firms enter into cooperative agreements without establishing a proper balance of power, or, after entering into an agreement, a fundamental shift of bargaining power occurs. The latter often happens when one firm acquires sufficient knowledge, skills, or resources to eliminate dependency upon an alliance partner.

Instability—The reasons for alliance instability are numerous and often are linked with many of the factors identified above. Opportunistic behaviour, informational advantages, acting on the *anticipated* decisions of partners, share of risk and costs, and inter-alliance competition can contribute to alliance instability and performance problems. Although findings suggest that alliances are unstable and often unsuccessful, the termination of a strategic alliance does not necessarily signal failure. While liquidations, acquisitions, and reorganizations may suggest degrees of failure, they may actually result in positive returns.

> **Liquidation** is the process of converting assets into cash. When a business has terminated, the proceeds from the sale of assets are used to pay off debt before being distributed to shareholders.

Strategic Alliances in an Indigenous Context

Recognizing the challenges they face, many Aboriginal communities are looking to form strategic alliances in order to create jobs, develop viable businesses to strengthen socioeconomic conditions, and define and protect natural rights. Unlike mainstream organizations that seek to improve economic conditions and create profits, leaders of these communities are focusing on more than just wealth creation or socioeconomic conditions. The motivations for entering into strategic alliances are often framed through the overarching goals of respecting heritage and culture, achieving autonomy, and asserting Indigenous peoples' control over their traditional territories. However, more work needs to be done to determine how and when Aboriginal businesses ought best enter into partnerships, and what makes for a successful partnership. Questions that need to be considered include:

- What types of mainstream entities/organizations make the best partners?
- What processes and strategies are best suited to forming strategic alliances in Indigenous contexts as compared to the mainstream?
- When are strategic alliances likely to benefit Indigenous communities and when are they likely to result in exploitation?
- What are the necessary and sufficient conditions that must be present and functional within Indigenous organizations and communities?
- Where have strategic alliances in Indigenous contexts been successful, and why?

Unlike the formation of strategic alliances in the mainstream, where the focus is placed on the profit-seeking behaviours and strategies used in firm-to-firm cooperation, there are several important contextual differences that must be recognized when Indigenous peoples are involved. First, the common thread that unites all of the 634 First Nation communities in Canada is the paternalistic relationship imposed upon them by the *Indian Act*. The reality of this legislation is that much of the decision-making authority that occurs regarding First Nations and their interactions with actors in the mainstream economy is largely in the hands of federal government officials. Second, the disconnection from the mainstream economic system, resulting from a range of factors, including the *Indian Act*, has effectively led to First Nations' economic isolation. The resulting social issues prevalent within many communities translate directly into inadequate access to education, skills, and training. This has effectively confined First Nations peoples to the economic and societal margins, weakening their opportunities concerning the resources (both natural and human) that they seek to leverage. Third, this social exclusion has created disconnectedness between Indigenous and mainstream institutions that is further compounded by a consistent need to recognize, understand, and ameliorate the impact of differing world views. Dana (2015) has commented on the heterogeneity of the world views of Indigenous people, and while there may be commonalities throughout, there can also be stark differences between groups, both locally and internationally. The issues that arise from the intersection of mainstream institutions and Indigenous groups must be constantly evaluated by how history, culture, and values may shape the processes that lead to successful cooperation. This has a profound impact on the establishment of new relationships and the existence of parallel economies founded upon cultural and racial separateness.

From a constitutional or legislative perspective, many developments in governance policies also impact upon how strategic alli-

> **Policy** is the framework or set of guidelines that outline an organization's intentions and ideals. Policy is not, however, a set of procedures for how to execute decisions, proceed in a particular situation, or meet a particular goal.

ances are formed between Aboriginal and non-Aboriginal organizations. Of these, perhaps the most significant is the evolution of the "duty to consult" of both governments and corporations whenever potential impacts to Aboriginal peoples, or lands traditionally used by them, are in question (discussed further in chapter 12). While not fully understood or uniformly applied, the duty to consult opens up a much greater role to play in business- and resource-development questions that, at the very least, provides most Aboriginal communities a "seat at the table." New statutory regimes for dealing with development, such as the *First Nations Land Management Act*, may positively impact upon the establishment of strategic alliances. But due to the patchwork application and implementation of these regimes, often the result is greater uncertainty around property access and development rights. This uncertainty also extends to the covenants and contracts between Aboriginal and other nations seeking to access resources. As countries like China continue to seek out control of greater resources, questions regarding Indigenous businesses in Canada and elsewhere, and regarding the global marketplace, introduce an interesting set of political and economic conditions.

> A **covenant** is an agreement or contract.

Of the many positives, federal and provincial legislation that mandates procurement rights to Aboriginal businesses has offered a step forward. Access to supply-chain opportunities have created incentives and supported the creation and inclusion of hundreds of new ventures owned by Indigenous organizations and, in many cases, non-Aboriginal partners. Finally, the significance of treaties (or their exclusion) across all of Canada continuously impacts upon the partnerships formed. The agreements formed are significant and cannot be divorced from the establishment of greater meaning to these treaties.

Motivations of Aboriginal Organizations in Forming Strategic Alliances

In establishing the difference between mainstream and Indigenous contexts germane to the formation of strategic alliances, the many contextual factors stated above show why objectives can be divergent. There must still be a place for profit arrangements, yet profit objectives must be tempered with a diverging set of other considerations, such as the need of Aboriginal peoples to foster sustainable communities and environments as part of their desire for autonomy and as an expression of their heritage-based world views. These goals are often distinct from the typical corporate social-responsibility goals of large corporations, which are frequently related to the bottom-line interests of the corporation.

Although there are many reasons for entering into partnerships at a local level, there are typically three general conditions for understanding the motivations of Aboriginal communities in Canada to form strategic alliances with mainstream organizations:

- To address the socioeconomic disparities of Indigenous communities, particularly through the creation of jobs
and the incomes derived from employment. Partnerships with mainstream
organizations can help alleviate some
of the stresses within the community
through increased employment.

> **Corporate social responsibility** is the orienta-
> tion of a business toward operating in a manner
> that is financially, environmentally, and socially
> sustainable. It is related to the notion of a "triple
> bottom line," discussed in chapter 3.

- To provide the resources and capacity required for creating new ventures—both wholly owned and joint. Aboriginal
people are realizing that the creation of their own ventures not
only addresses the question of jobs and employment, but also
organizational capacity building, control of their resources,
and independent expression of their role within the global
economy.

- To establish control over their traditional territory as a means
to defend their rights. Strategic alliances provide opportunities
to empower Aboriginal governments who seek recognition for
nationhood and autonomy. Recent successes in the Canadian
court system that Aboriginal governments have enjoyed have
resulted in increased opportunities for input into resource-
extraction projects, for example.

At any time, one or several of these broad motivational perspectives
may be observed within the agreements, contracts, and partnerships entered into by Indigenous peoples. Alliances that do not meet the conditions
of the above may be viewed negatively and lead to the perception of unfair
treatment, violations of rights, and to the looming potential of legal means
for dispute resolution.

Factors Significant to Strategic Alliance Formation in an Indigenous Context

Two recent studies (CCAB 2010; Roness and Collier 2010) have focused
specifically on partnerships between Aboriginal and non-Aboriginal organizations in Canada, providing a set of general practices for businesses
seeking to partner with Aboriginal organizations, which include:

- the use of systematic communication processes;

- the existence of robust consultation mechanisms;

- a willingness to observe cultural differences; and

- an understanding of the importance of mutual benefit.

Specific factors or ingredients that mediate and/or moderate successful
partnerships from the corporate side were identified as:

- Providing mentoring at the outset of partnerships with Aboriginal businesses to ensure a stable and productive business relationship.

- Including the ability to house distinct objectives for Indigenous communities that align with economic and community development of differing degrees.

- Identifying the competitive-advantage differences that define each organization and making alignments that further serve to advance each organization's objectives.

- Policies, processes, and structures that align with basic principles of management while allowing for differing perspectives based in culture and world views.

- The establishment of trust, credibility, and consistency in leadership, while differing from the typical contexts in that cultural sensitivity and an awareness of the social return on investment must be accommodated.

- The sharing of authority, investment, risk, and responsibility in the operation of joint ventures by both parties.

- Non-Aboriginal and Aboriginal business leaders and executives must be engaged to convey the value of the partnerships to all levels of each partner organization.

Specific barriers to forming/maintaining partnerships from the Aboriginal side were identified as:
- a lack of bank-qualified collateral (particularly on-reserve), a lack of cash flow, and competition from others for limited funding;

- politics and factionalism;

- remoteness;

- misunderstandings about Aboriginal communities, cultures, or ability;

- a lack of business expertise, perceptions of non-Aboriginal indifference;

- less-than-honourable intentions by non-Aboriginal companies;

- a lack of community support, a fear of change;

- a lack of readiness or willingness on the part of the Aboriginal workforce to take advantage of opportunities;

- differing values, agendas, and visions;

- imbalances of power and resources;
- changes to traditional ways of life; and
- differing accountability structures and/or expectations.

While this list of general and specific factors is not authoritative, it does provide an understanding of some of the conditions, best practices, and barriers that may be significant to the formation and success of strategic alliances in an Indigenous context (CCAB 2010; Roness and Collier 2010).

Strategic Alliances: Reasons and Objectives

Canada is currently in a second wave of Indigenous development. The first wave consisted of top-down, state-directed efforts usually aimed at modernization. The second wave is one in which Indigenous peoples are striving to rebuild their nations and improve their lot through economic development "on their own terms." Two factors play a critical role in this process. The first is the pursuit by Indigenous people of the recognition of their rights to their traditional lands and resources by the nation state in which they are situated. The second is formation of mutually beneficial business alliances with non-Indigenous businesses, the major players in the new global economy. These two aspects are closely related in that the realization of the former gives Indigenous people control of key resources important to non-Indigenous business enabling the latter. This is not to say that all Indigenous communities in fact form alliances with multinational corporations, only that the potential for such alliances exists. Some communities outright reject the opportunity to enter into such alliances. And there are development strategies other than alliances based on access to and control over lands and resources being pursued by Aboriginal people in Canada and Indigenous people elsewhere.

A **multinational corporation** is a corporation that operates in two or more countries.

Aboriginal people in Canada have been pioneers in this second wave, adopting an approach in which reasserting control over lands and resources is a key objective, and strategic alliances play an important role. Recent comments made by Randy Moore, vice president of Bee-Clean, Canada's largest independently owned cleaning company, provide evidence of the use of strategic alliances to pursue goals and of the control that First Nations exert today. Moore stated, about a joint venture with the Athabasca Chipewyan First Nation, that "If you go into direct competition with First Nations on those projects, you're going to be at a disadvantage. Oil companies will do business with them, not you. We'd have beaten our heads and bloodied our knuckles against a brick wall forever, getting nowhere" (Financial Post 2013). He continued, "Isn't this the smart way to do business with anyone, anywhere? [...] They're there, they're going to be part of your future. The smart move is to make them a partner. The business community seems to just be waking up to that."

At the same time as the second wave of development was emerging among Aboriginal people, factors were influencing non-Aboriginal companies, making them more open to strategic alliances. Some of these forces were economy wide, while others specifically concerned relations with Aboriginal people. Anderson (1995) identified five mutually reinforcing factors that have increased the importance of Aboriginal people to their profitability and long-term survival (see table 1). These factors continue to be important today as the transition to the new economy continues. The first factor is the change in the global competitive environment that all corporations face and to which all must adjust. Among the characteristics of this new economy is the trend of increased alliances among business entities, meaning that companies are more likely to enter into alliances and partnerships now than they were in the past. Factors 2 through 5 relate to circumstances that make Aboriginal people attractive partners for corporations.

Table 1: Factors Influencing Corporate Aboriginal Alliances
A change in the global competitive environment from a "Fordist" (mass production) to a flexible regime of accumulation.
A broadening and deepening of society's expectations about what constitutes socially responsible corporate behaviour in general and toward Aboriginal people.
The large and growing number of legal and regulatory mechanisms that impose requirements and restrictions on business ventures impacting on Aboriginal lands and people.
The large and growing Aboriginal population, its increasing affluence, and increasing level of education.
The already enormous and rapidly growing pool of natural and financial resources (in addition to human resources) that aboriginal people control or will control in the near future.
Source: Adapted from Anderson (1997: 1487).[1]

Events during the final decade of the 20th century and the opening decade of the 21st have resulted in Indigenous people becoming even more important in the global economy. These include a succession of legal decisions (see table 2), international conventions, comprehensive land-claims agreements, and continuing demographic trends, especially those related to the growing significance of Aboriginal people in the labour force (see chapter 9). Three international conventions pertaining to the rights of Indigenous peoples have played an important role. They are the International Labour Organization Convention 169 (1989); the United Nations Declaration on the Rights of Indigenous People (2007); and the policy of the World Bank toward Indigenous people, which was revised in 2005. These conventions address four areas of rights for Indigenous peoples: the right of control over

Table 2. Recent Canadian Court Decisions—Aboriginal Rights and Title

Case Date	Outcome
Nowegijick, 1983	Treaties must be liberally interpreted
Guerin, 1984	Canada must recognize the existence of inherent Aboriginal title and a fiduciary (trust) relationship based on title
Mullin, 1985	Infringement on Aboriginal rights in clear-cutting on territorial lands; delayed or ignored past claims cannot be used as evidence to infringe upon Aboriginal title
Sioui, 1990	Provincial laws cannot overrule rights contained in nation-to-nation treaties
Sparrow, 1990	Section 35(1) of the *Constitution Act 1982* containing the term "existing rights" was defined as anything "unextinguished"
Badger, 1996	Aboriginal rights for hunting on territorial lands confirmed through treaty acknowledgements
Delgamukw, 1997	Oral history of Indian people must receive equal weight to historical evidence in land-claim cases
Union of Nova Scotia Indians, 1997	Lack of procedural fairness in environmental reviews pertaining to traditional lands that resulted in due-diligence definitions written into the *Environmental Assessment Act*
Marshall, 1999	Mi'kmaq have the right to catch and sell fish (incl. shell fish) to earn a "moderate living" under "logical evolution" interpretations
Sundown, 1999	Advanced concepts of rights over treaty lands and Aboriginal rights to traditional practices through explication of their standing outside of common-law concepts of title to land or the right to use another's land
Campbell, 2000	Challenge to Nisga'a treaty struck down
Apex, 2001	Aboriginal title cannot be extinguished or circumvented through dealings with the Crown
Powley, 2001	Métis rights to hunt for subsistence in territorial settlement areas trace back to establishment of colonial government
Athabasca Chipewyan First Nation, 2001	Established 1,000 km cause-and-effect factor pertaining to power-generation activities involving downstream impacts
Haida, 2004	British Columbia had duty to consult in transfer of timber harvesting licences that had direct bearing on the protection of old-growth forests
Mikisew First Nation, 2005	Defined procedural rights and substantive rights on Crown's duty to consult on the alignment of a winter road related to communities downstream from oil sands projects
Bernard, 2005	Logging rights and personal use and consumption upheld on traditional territories
Musqueam Indian Band, 2005	Transfer of land without duty to consult resulted in order for transaction to be undone
Dene Tha' First Nation, 2006	Crown must provide reasonable amount of time when consulting on environmental impact in order to allow stakeholders time to take part/respond (only 24 hours were provided); a reserve does not have to be affected to engage Treaty 8 right; establishment of Dene Tha' "test" for official standing
Kelly, 2007	Charge of hunting without licence impinges upon Métis right to hunt on territorial lands; Crown severely admonished

Labrador Metis Nation, 2007	The Crown has a duty to consult in the Trans-Labrador Highway project due to respondents' credible claims on jurisdictions owed to territorial lands
Tsilhqot'in Nation, 2007	Denied limitations to economic and commercial activities on territorial lands; distinction between bands and nations incorporated into ruling
Ardoch, Algonquin First Nation, 2008	The power for corporations to incarcerate native protesters struck down where Aboriginal interests in land and resource claims were ongoing
BrokenHead Ojibway First Nation, 2008	Duty to consult must pose unresolved, non-negligible impact arising from development of land for public purposes
Gooden, 2008	Métis rights on territorial lands through description of historic ties to lands involving Métis settlements
Carrier Sekani Tribal Council, 2010	Supreme Court recognizes the rights of native protesters to protect contested Aboriginal or treaty rights by halting corporate-development processes where a duty to consult is validated
Athabasca Chipewyan, Beaver Lake Cree, Enoch Cree Nations, 2011	Environment minister's decision set aside with respect to inadequacy of woodland Caribou-protection strategy

own land and resources; the right to economic benefit derived from traditional lands; the right to self-determination in development; and the right to maintain and strengthen institutions, cultures, and traditions. In addition, within Canada there have been a number of land-claims settlements and court decisions that have reaffirmed and strengthened Aboriginal rights over traditional lands and resources. Together these have increased pressure on companies to accommodate the development objectives of Indigenous people, often through strategic alliances (Mikkelsen, Camp, and Anderson 2008).

All of these factors have resulted in a growing number of corporations choosing to pursue a strategy of partnership with Aboriginal people in pursuit of competitive advantage and profitability. The case that follows demonstrates a strategic alliance between a corporation and a First Nation, and illustrates the impact of the combination of the Aboriginal approach to development and factors influencing corporate/Aboriginal strategic alliances. The Osoyoos Indian Band and Nk'Mip project case illustrates that these First Nations are clearly acting in a manner consistent with the approach to development described in table 1. They are using alliances as part of a larger strategy, which includes other forms of business ownership, the building of capacity, control over activities on traditional land, and the preservation and strengthening of culture, values, and practices.

Osoyoos Indian Band and Nk'Mip Project

The Osoyoos Indian Band (OIB) is one of 198 bands in British Columbia. It is located on the southern tip of the Okanagan Valley in south-central British Columbia. The southern extremity of the 32,000-acre reserve is approximately six kilometres from the U.S. border. In the closing years of the 20th century the OIB began a program of economic development in response to the unsatisfactory socioeconomic circumstances of its members.

The community accomplished a great deal in the 1990s and early 2000s. In 1994, the OIB had revenues from commercial activities of $1.3 million; by 2002, revenues increased to $14.3 million, a more than ten-fold increase. In 1994, the value of payments received from the federal government exceeded these self-generated commercial revenues. By 2002, self-generated revenues were seven times the amount of federal government payments received by the community. During this time period, employment increased significantly (Kayseas, Hindle, and Anderson 2006).

These efforts have continued under the leadership of Clarence Louie. For Chief Louie, economic development and the self-sufficiency it creates is the best way to secure the right of his people to be who they are, to take pride in their heritage, and to protect the fragile desert landscape in which a good part of their cultural identity is forever rooted. The motto of the Osoyoos Indian Band Development Corporation (OIBDC) is "working with business to preserve our past by strengthening our future." Two of the development objectives of the band and the OIBDC were to achieve full employment for its members and become economically self-sufficient by 2010. How did the community do in achieving these goals? A May 2014 article in the *Globe and Mail* reported the Osoyoos First Nation had "virtually no unemployment" and is "arguably the most prosperous First Nation in Canada" (MacDonald 2014).

Through the OIBDC, the band owns and operates a construction company, a gravel company, a forestry company, a campground and recreational-vehicle park, a golf course, two housing developments, and a grocery store. Along with the ownership of these businesses, the OIB has several strategic partnerships with outside interests, having part ownership of their businesses, for example, Nk'Mip Cellars (winery) in partnership with Vincor International Inc., and Spirit Ridge (hotel and spa) with Bellstar Hotels & Resorts.

Nk'Mip Cellars, opened in September 2002, is the culmination of almost thirty-five years of OIB involvement in the wine industry. The story begins in 1968. In that year, in association with Andres Wines Ltd., the OIB began planting its first vineyard. This has grown into the band-owned 230-acre Inkameep Vineyard, twenty kilometres north of Osoyoos. The vineyard provides high-quality vinifera grapes to many of the wineries in the Okanagan Valley, and some further afield. There are another thousand acres of vineyard on Osoyoos land, most in partnership with Vincor International. Vincor is Canada's largest wine producer and OIB's joint-venture partner in Nk'Mip Cellars. By the end of 2003, almost 25 per cent of the vineyard acreage in the Okanagan Valley was on Osoyoos land.

The next phase of the OIB's involvement in the wine business began in 1980. The band erected a building near the Inkameep Vineyard for T. G. Bright and Co. (now Vincor), which the company leased for twenty-five years and equipped it as a winery. The lease has since been extended and the winery is undergoing a $10 million renovation. Speaking of the company's ongoing relationship with the Osoyoos Indian Band, Donald Triggs, CEO of Vincor, says:

> We have a very long and important relationship with the Band. Two-thirds of the employees in the Oliver winery are from the band. Our relationship goes back 25 years. Our winery is on band land. We now have vineyards developed on band land of over 800 acres. Our future in the Okanagan is very much intertwined with the future of the band. (Schreiner 2002)

According to a wine writer, the relationship between Vincor and OIB is "a business partnership pure and simple. Vincor get access to vineyards in one of the hottest and richest growing climates in Canada. The Osoyoos Band gets the resources to develop their land and obtain a piece of an emerging industry" (Hayes 2002).

Nk'Mip Cellars opened on September 13, 2002. The $7 million project includes the 18,000-square-foot winery and a twenty-acre vineyard. It is North America's first Aboriginal winery, and the second in the world (a Maori-owned winery opened in New Zealand in 1998). The OIB contributed operating funding of almost $1 million and received $2-$3 million from various federal agencies, and, in return for this investment, it owns 51 per cent of the venture. Vincor invested about $3 million and owns the remaining 49 per cent. At least as important as the investment of money is the investment of Vincor's expertise. As Don Triggs reported, "We have shared with them everything that we know in design of the winery, in processing and in managing hospitality" (Schreiner 2002). With a capacity of 18,000 cases a year, the Nk'Mip winery is not large; rather, the objective "is to make small quantities of very high-end wine" (Schreiner 2002).

Another important strategic alliance is with Bellstar Hotels & Resorts. Bellstar manages a collection of boutique resorts and hotels in various vacation destinations throughout Alberta and British Columbia. As with Vincor, the OIB has entered into a strategic alliance that brings together important strengths from both parties; OIB's burgeoning presence in wine tourism and appealing geographic location, and Bellstar's expertise in operating high-end resorts. Bellstar entered into a long-term lease agreement with the OIB to build and operate the Spirit Ridge Vineyard Resort and Spa. The resort had opened thirty villas for operation by the fall of 2005. The villas have been rated as four star by Canada Select, which makes it one of only nine four-star resorts in British Columbia. Spirit Ridge, now fully operational, consists of thirty-four villas and sixty-four suites, along with a full-service spa, an outdoor pool, and equipment rentals.

More recently, the OIB was successful in a bid to build the first provincial jail on a reserve in Canada. The $200 million 378-cell facility will create 500 direct and 500 indirect jobs. The OIB will sign a sixty-year lease (a non-equity alliance) with the government of British Columbia (MacQueen 2013). The strategic alliances that Osoyoos and other successful communities form are only a small set of the economic activity that Indigenous groups across Canada are involved in that employs some form of alliance with other Indigenous and non-Indigenous corporations or groups.

Conclusion

Many Indigenous groups in Canada view strategic alliances as a way to achieve the related goals of prosperity, autonomy, and sustainable development. They also enable communities to build on partnerships to create other opportunities. The revenues and profits that are generated by Aboriginal groups are a means of funding programs and services to a level not possible by relying solely on government transfers. Profits allow them to pursue autonomy and independence, both in the economic sphere of Canadian society and as Indigenous governments. Profits are often used by Aboriginal governments to bolster health and education, and support cultural and language preservation. The entrepreneurial ventures created by these groups are clearly foundational to building economies and rebuilding nations.

There is also considerable evidence of the benefits that accrue to the non-Indigenous partners that gain access to resources—human, financial, and natural—through the creation of strategic alliances. The motivations that drive non-Indigenous groups to pursue strategic alliances are diverse. For example, corporations may benefit from partnering with Aboriginal people by gaining access to land for commercial development. Non-Indigenous corporations in British Columbia are producing some of the highest-quality grapes for wine production on reserve lands that, in the not-too-distant past, were thought of as useless desert. Mining operations involving some of the biggest uranium producers in the world are actively engaged in alliances with Indigenous groups across the North that allow corporations to gain the social licence they so desperately need to produce controversial products (see chapter 12).

Indigenous groups can no longer be expected to rubber-stamp the agreements of others when it pertains to their communities, lands, and resources. Presumptions by potential partners must be tempered by the fact that entering into a business partnership is a cultural learning process that demands understanding, tolerance, and respect from both sides. The new order of establishing successful partnerships must, first and foremost, strive for building solid foundations on the principles of understanding, equality, and respect.

Key Points:

- There are several different types of alliances that Aboriginal businesses and communities may enter into, ranging from informal alliances to equity alliances.

- The terms "alliances" and "partnerships" are sometimes used interchangeably; however, formal partnerships are legal agreements through which companies are created, while alliances can be much less formal.

- Second-wave Aboriginal economic development is directed by Aboriginal people. First-wave Aboriginal economic development largely involved programs created by non-Aboriginal governments to solve Aboriginal "problems."

- Alliances benefit both parties.

- Partnerships are sometimes formed in response to changes in government policy and legislation. Recently, partnerships between Aboriginals and non-Aboriginals have become increasingly appealing because of changes to government policies.

- There are many different reasons or motivations that lead to the development of partnerships.

Questions for Review:

1. What different types of strategic alliances might Aboriginal businesses and organizations enter into? Compare and contrast each.

2. What factors are significant for the formation of strategic alliances from an Indigenous perspective?

3. What factors are significant for the formation of strategic alliances from a mainstream perspective?

4. How does the Indigenous context affect strategic alliances?

5. How is first-wave Aboriginal economic development different from second wave?

6. How can Aboriginal communities build on and leverage their strengths through partnerships?

7. What did each partner contribute in the Osoyoos partnership?

Suggested Assignments:

1. When might a business or organization decide to terminate a partnership? For what reasons might a partnership be terminated?

2. Why might relationships that start out positive change and become controversial or less effective over time?

3. Can you prepare in advance for changes in relationships between partners? Why or why not?

4. Which four factors that influence the performance of strategic alliances do you think would be the most likely to be disruptive?

5. Discuss the value of diversification for Osoyoos development.

6. Construct a model for an Indigenous joint venture. Compare and contrast it with a non–Indigenous joint venture.

Note
1. These factors were initially distilled from a variety of sources including Thomas (1993), Sloan and Hill (1995), CANDO (1995), Brooks (1994), Jamieson (1994), and Newell (1994).

References
Aboriginal Affairs 2013. Fact Sheet – 2011 National Household Survey Aboriginal Demographics, Educational Attainment and Labour Market Outcomes. https://www.aadnc-aandc.gc.ca/eng/1376329205785/1376329233875 (accessed on March 12, 2015).

Anderson, R. B. 1995. The business economy of the first nations in Saskatchewan: A contingency perspective. *The Canadian Journal of Native Studies* 15 (2): 309-46.

———. 1997. Corporate/Indigenous partnerships in economic development: The first nations in Canada. *World Development* 25 (9): 1483-1503.

Anderson, R. B., L. P. Dana and T. E. Dana. 2006. Indigenous land rights, entrepreneurship, and economic development in Canada: "Opting-in" to the global economy. *Journal of world business* 41 (1): 45-55.

Barney, J. 1991. Firm resources and sustained competitive advantage. *Journal of Management* 17 (10): 99-120.

Beamish, P. W., ed. 2008. *Strategic Alliances.* Vol. 2. Edward Elgar Pub.

Beamish, P. W. and A. Delios. 1997. Incidence and propensity of alliance formation. In *Cooperative Strategies*, vol. 2, ed. P. W. Beamish and J. P. Killing. Asian Pacific Perspectives. San Francisco: New Lexington Press.

Brooks, C. 1994. A corporate policy on Aboriginal relations. *Canadian Business Review* 21 (2): 18-21.

CCAB (Canadian Council for Aboriginal Business). 2010. Partnerships and Prosperity: Key Findings from CCAB. Progressive Aboriginal Relations Research Series. Building Relationships, Sharing Knowledge. Issue 2. https://www.ccab.com/uploads/Image/PAR_Report_Jan2010D__2_.pdf

CANDO. 1995. Education: A Foundation for Economic and Community Development. Winnipeg: CANDO.

Cattaneo, Claudia. 2014. "This is your pipeline': Eagle Spirit plan is in Canada's best interests, Aboriginal leader says. *Financial Post.* May 14. http://business.financialpost.com/news/energy/this-is-your-pipeline-eagle-spirit-plan-is-in-canadas-best-interests-aboriginal-leader-says (accessed February 26, 2015).

Casino Rama. 2015. *About Us.* https://www.casinorama.com/About-Casino-Rama/About-Us.aspx (accessed December 5, 2015).

CICS (Canadian Intergovernmental Conference Secretariat). 2012. Defining the Opportunity: Assessing the economic impact of the natural resources sector. Report prepared for Energy and Mines Ministers' Conference, Charlottetown, PEI, September. http://www.scics.gc.ca/english/conferences.asp?a=viewdocument&id=1907 (accessed September 14, 2013).

Coates, K. and G. Poelzer. 2010. Defining Indigenous Space: The Constitutional Development of

Aboriginal Property and Resource Rights in Canada. *Georgetown Journal of International Law* 11 (1): 7-15.

Dana, L. 2015. Indigenous entrepreneurship: an emerging field of research. *International Journal of Business and Globalisation* 14 (2): 158-69.

Das, T. K. and B. Teng. 2000. Instabilities of strategic alliances: An internal tensions perspective. *Organization Science* 11 (1): 77-101.

Financial Post. 2013. Partnerships spur First Nations business growth. Special to *Financial Post.* June 11. http://business.financialpost.com/news/partnerships-spur-first-nations-business-growth. (accessed December 2, 2015)

Gulati, R. 1998. Alliances and networks. *Strategic Management Journal* 19 (4): 293-317.

Hayes, Julianna. 2002. Winery Makes North American History. *Okanagan Sunday.* September.

Hindle, K. and M. Lansdowne. 2005. Brave spirits on new paths: toward a globally relevant paradigm of Indigenous entrepreneurship research. *Journal of Small Business & Entrepreneurship* 18 (2): 131-41.

Jamieson, R. 1994. Mutual Opportunities Through Partnership. *Canadian Business Review* 21 (2): 14-17.

Kayseas, B., K. Hindle and R. B. Anderson. 2006. An empirically justified theory of successful Indigenous entrepreneurship: a case study of the Osoyoos Indian Band. In AGSE 2006: Regional frontiers of entrepreneurship research 2006: Proceedings of the 3rd Regional Frontiers of Entrepreneurship Research conference, 2006 (Auckland, New Zealand). Australian Graduate School of Entrepreneurship, Swinburne University of Technology.

Kayseas Bob. 2009. Understanding How Indigenous Community Factors Affect Indigenous Entrepreneurial Process. PhD dissertation, Swinburne University of Technology, Melbourne, Australia.

Khattab, S. A. A. 2012. Marketing Strategic Alliances: The Hotel Sector in Jordan. *International Journal of Business and Management* 7 (9): 222-32.

Light, I. and L. P. Dana. 2013. Boundaries of social capital in entrepreneurship. *Entrepreneurship Theory and Practice* 37 (3): 603-24.

Lorange, P. and J. Roos. 1992. Strategic Alliances: Formation, Implementation and Evolution. London: Basil Blackwell.

MacDonald, Jake. 2014. How a B.C. native band went from poverty to prosperity. *Globe and Mail.* May 29, Report on Business. http://www.theglobe-andmail.com/report-on-business/rob-magazine/clarence-louie-feature/article18913980/. (accessed December 2, 2015).

Macintyre, Ellen. 2012. Dream catcher: Membertou's turnaround. *Herald Magazine.* May 27. http://thechronicleherald.ca/heraldmagazine/99404-dream-catcher-membertous-turnaround (accessed November 15, 2013).

MacQueen, Ken. 2013. Osoyoos Indian Band wins bid for first provincial jail on reserve land. *Macleans,* September 19. http://www2.macleans.ca/2013/09/16/osoyoos-indian-band-wins-bid-for-first-provincial-jail-on-reserve-land/ (accessed November 15, 2013).

McKay, Raymond A. 2003. Kitsaki management Limited Partnership: An Aboriginal economic development Model. Report prepared for Sharing Voices: A Conference on Aboriginal Economic Development, University of Saskatchewan. http://iportal.usask.ca/docs/Journal%20of%20Aboriginal%20 Economic%20Development/JAED_v4no1/JAED_v4no1_Article%20pg3-5.pdf (accessed December 2, 2015).

Membertou. 2004. *Membertou Community Plan.* Halifax, NS: Membertou Geomatics Consultants.

Mikkelsen, Aslaug, Ronald Camp II and Robert B. Anderson. 2008. Managerial Implications. In *Social Issues and Sustainable Development in the Arctic: Challenges for the Emerging Oil and Gas Industry*, ed. Aslaug Mikkelsen and Oluf Langhelle. Net York: Routledge.

NAABA. 2014. About Us. *Northeastern Alberta Aboriginal Business Association.* https://www.naaba.ca/site/about_us (accessed February 20, 2015).

Newell, E. 1994. A New Spirit of Partnership. *Canadian Business Review* (Summer) 8-11.

OIBDC (2013) Mission & Vision. *Osoyoos Indian Band Development Corporation.* http://oibdc.ca/about-us/mission-vision/ (accessed December 1, 2013).

Peredo, A. M., R. B. Anderson, C. S. Galbraith and B. Honig, B. 2004. Towards a theory of Indigenous entrepreneurship. *International Journal of Entrepreneurship and Small Business* 1 (1): 1-20.

Sawyer, S. and E. T. Gomez, ed. 2012. *The Politics of Resource Extraction: Indigenous Peoples, Multinational Corporations and the State.* New York: Palgrave Macmillan.

Schreiner, John. 2002. Grape expectations: Osoyoos Indian Band thought to have first Aboriginal winery in North America. *National Post.* July 18, FP9.

Scott, J. T. 2004. Doing business with the devil: Land, sovereignty and corporate partnerships in Membertou Inc. Halifax, NS: Atlantic Institute for Market Studies.

St. Eugene. 2015. *About Us.* http://steugene.ca/?page_id=6 (accessed December 5, 2015)

Stiles, J. 2001. Managing Strategic Alliances' Success: Determining the Influencing Factors of Intent Within Partnerships. In *Effective Collaboration,* ed. J. Genefke J and F. McDonald New York: Palgrave.

Tatanka Boutique. 2015. About Us. *Tatanka Boutique.* http://www.tatankaboutique.ca/about-us-2/ (accessed February 26, 2015).

Thomas, K. 1994. The emergence of aboriginal business in Canada. *Canadian Business Review,* 21 (2): 12-17.

Tsang, E. W. 1998. Motives for strategic alliance: a resource-based perspective. *Scandinavian Journal of Management* 14 (3): 207-21.

Usher, P. J., F. J. Tough and R. M. Galois. 1992. Reclaiming the land: Aboriginal title, treaty rights and land claims in Canada. *Applied Geography* 12 (2): 109-32.

Wien, F. 2006. Economic development: a case study of the Membertou First Nation. Report submitted to the Conference Board of Canada, Ottawa, April.

PART TWO

Chapter 6

The British Crown's Royal Proclamation of 1763 established the guidelines for European settlement in North America, recognizing Aboriginal title to the land until ceded by treaty. In 1867, the *British North America Act* created Canada and recognized Canada's rights to make and enforce laws. The act did not recognize the same rights for Aboriginal governments. The Canadian government passed the *Indian Act,* which defined who the government would recognize as "Indian," and become a ward of the Crown, with limitations on their rights as citizens. In 1982, a Canadian constitutional amendment recognized Aboriginal and treaty rights, which has created new opportunities for Aboriginal governments to implement laws that are recognized by other governments in Canada.

As a result of the *Indian Act*, many First Nation businesses and governments find themselves dealing with regulatory gaps where provincial laws do not apply to reserve (i.e., federal) lands. Further, with gaps around the very definition of who is Aboriginal in Canada—and as such pertains to their respective rights—the implementation of policies is complicated. Increasingly, Aboriginal governments are exercising their right to the use of Aboriginal traditional and customary law, as well as bylaws, under the *Indian Act*, and to other legal mechanisms to address regulatory gaps and increase self-government powers. Aboriginal communities are increasingly building institutions and, where necessary, challenging laws to assert their Aboriginal rights and title. Because diverse Aboriginal groups have had very different experiences with governments and private industry, knowing the historical, business, and political climates, as well as legal precedents, of a region is important. It is critical that businesses and corporations realize that, in order to do business with Aboriginal peoples or within traditional territories, community engagement and involvement is necessary, and respectful.

Governance, Law, and Policy
Mary Beth Doucette and Jeanie Lanine

The Canadian Constitution and government was chiefly formed through an act of legislation known as the *British North America Act* (*BNA*) in 1867. Through this act, European governments officially recognized the authority of a new, Canadian government to make and enforce laws in the colonial territories that thus became the Dominion of Canada (Dawson and Ward 1970). At the same time, the act marked the point in history when the British government ceased to recognize, and began to ignore, the authority of Indigenous peoples as self-reliant, independently governing societies. Prior to the *BNA*, evidence in the form of treaties, signed documents, and other official alliances between the European nations and various Indigenous nations demonstrate that the rights of Indigenous societies were recognized (see discussion of treaties in chapter 13).

Canada's ability to write and enforce laws and policies stems from the Canadian Constitution, which sets out the powers and authorities of government and the basic law-making and structural principles of Canadian society. The Canadian Constitution is the supreme law of Canada and has been in constant evolution from colonial times until the present day. The *BNA* was eventually renamed the *Constitution Act, 1867*, with a further division of powers between federal and provincial legislatures, particularly in relation to natural resources. This then became the current *Constitution Act, 1982*, which includes the Charter of Rights and Freedoms.

Section 35 of the *Constitution Act, 1982*, specifically recognizes and affirms Aboriginal rights, referencing the Royal Proclamation of 1763, which set out guidelines for European settlement of Aboriginal territories in what is now North America (McNeil 1997). The Royal Proclamation states that Aboriginal title has existed and continues to exist, and that all land would thus be considered Aboriginal land until ceded by treaty. Despite this proclamation, Indigenous communities have struggled for recognition of their own customary laws. In recent times, Indigenous individuals and bands have challenged the application of Canada's statutory and common laws (described below) to Aboriginal peoples, often with reference to protections set out in historic treaties and the *Constitution Act, 1982* (Slattery 2015). For example, in *Tsilhqot'in Nation v. British Columbia* (2014), the Tsilhqot'in brought an action for Aboriginal title to 1,750 square kilometres of land in northern British Columbia. The Supreme Court of Canada granted the declaration and concluded that the guarantee of Aboriginal rights in section 35 of the *Constitution Act, 1982*, operates as a limit on both federal and provincial legislative powers, and that all legislative infringements by federal and provincial governments on Aboriginal rights and title must be justified. This decision, as well as others, has led to a very recent and remarkable evolution in the common law, which has forced government policy and procedure to change and to recognize the continuing existence of Aboriginal rights and title.

Law in Canada

Law is a set of rules and standards that a society agrees upon to govern the behaviour of its citizens (Griffin et al. 2011). Over time, laws are altered in response to changes in societies' norms and values. There are several different categories of Canadian law pertinent to the study of business, including common law, statutory law, and administrative law.

Common law is the written body of law developed by judges, through courts, based upon the application of past decisions that have interpreted and applied statutory law and the principles of equity (Glenn 1995). If a similar dispute has been decided in the past within a province or territory, courts usually follow and apply such reasoning in subsequent decisions. Provincial and territorial courts must follow the decisions of the Supreme Court of Canada. When a wholly new matter arises, courts must set new precedents. Canadian law is primarily based on the British common-law system in all provinces and territories except Québec, where law is based on the French civil code. This reflects the pattern and influences of the different colonial governments in Canada. The common practice in all provinces, except Québec, has been to first refer to recent leading Canadian case-law precedents. Where no provincial or territorial court precedent exists, higher-court case law from other provinces or territories is generally applied. In some instances, case law from other Commonwealth jurisdictions or decisions of the United States Supreme Court may be applied or used in argumentation.

Statutory law is written law developed by a legislative body. Unlike the court system, legislative bodies are comprised of elected officials. The largest legislative body is the federal government, followed by provincial and local legislative bodies. Statutes are drafted, debated, and enacted at an appropriate level of government, one with due authority. In situations where there is a dispute about the application or interpretation of these laws, it can be challenged in court. Although statutes may be struck down in whole or in part due to a violation of the constitution or a lack of constitutional authority,

> **Aboriginal title** refers to the inherent right of Aboriginal peoples to occupy and use traditional lands and territories.
>
> **Aboriginal rights** are those that are inherent, stemming from Aboriginal peoples' long standing occupation and use of particular areas of land.

> A **precedent** in law is a prior court decision that serves as a guide and/or may be binding for future cases with similar circumstances.
>
> **Case law** is part of common law. It refers to laws that are established by the outcome of earlier court cases.
>
> **Jurisdiction** is the official power to administer justice or make decisions regarding a legal question or geographic area.

judges must still follow statutory law (McGill Centre for Human Rights and Legal Pluralism 2015; Aboriginal Human Rights Project 2012).

Administrative law is the body of law that governs how courts review the decisions of administrative authorities that have been granted the power to interpret and implement statutory laws. A statute may also provide for a hearing before a board or tribunal in instances in which the entitlement to certain benefits depends on the interpretation of a statute or disputed facts (Bradley and Ewing 2007). The major purpose of administrative law is to ensure that the activities of government are authorized by the legislative branch, and that government statutes are implemented and administered in a fair and reasonable manner.

These three colonial legal systems have been the source of problems and debate for many Indigenous communities that want to be involved when decisions are made that affect their communities, and that believe those decisions should take into account the traditional laws of their societies, which existed prior to settlement and, of course, prior to Canadian confederation (McNeil 1989). Until recently, Canadian courts and governments gave little or no weight to Aboriginal legal traditions and customary laws when applying common-law standards (and civil law in Québec) to matters of particular importance to Aboriginal peoples, such as title and rights (Miller 2011). Regardless, it is important to realize that Aboriginal traditional and customary law exists and is practiced in some Aboriginal communities.

Aboriginal legal traditions and customary law, sometimes referred to as Aboriginal "traditional law," was not historically documented or recorded in the same way that colonial laws were. The rules or guidelines by which Indigenous societies managed and organized themselves were transmitted through the telling and re-telling, orally, of common knowledge and experiences (Secher 2014). Though unwritten, the shared beliefs and values of the people were understood, known, and enforced. The origin, transmission, and longevity of customary laws resulted in rules that constitute an integral part of Aboriginal traditional cultures. In order to understand customary law, one must also have an understanding of subtle and fundamental differences in cultural beliefs, languages, and traditions of various Indigenous communities (PLEA 2006).

Division of Authority and Regulatory Gaps

Under the Canadian Constitution, the power to legislate is divided between the provincial/territorial and federal governments. Generally, the federal list of powers in section 91 of the constitution is concerned with national matters, while the provincial list in section 92 is concerned with local matters (*Constitution Act, 1982*). For example, the federal government can regulate trade and commerce, criminal law and procedure, direct and indirect taxation, banking, currency, defence, navigation and shipping, copyrights, and statutes relating to peace, order and good government. The provinces and territories regulate direct taxation, municipal institutions, local works and undertakings, the administration of justice, property and civil rights, education, and matters of a local and private nature in the province (see chapter 7 for a discussion of taxation).

Despite these jurisdictional responsibilities, there is often overlap between jurisdictions and in some cases it is unclear as to whether a matter is provincially or federally regulated (Young 2013). This overlap may be physical and tangible. For example, the Trans-Canada Highway (federal) intersects with roads that are maintained by provinces and municipalities, and it isn't always clear where jurisdiction begins or ends. Another example is the location of national parks in provinces. Jurisdictional overlap may also be more abstract or intangible, and therefore more difficult to define (Gibson 1973). For example, if you sell or deliver goods in multiple provinces, in which province must you register your business and pay taxes? Laws affect some businesses more than others, depending on the primary industry, market segment, location, and number of employees, creating diverse challenges and opportunities for businesses.

The question of the division of powers becomes quite challenging when applied to lands reserved for Indians under the *Indian Act* (described in chapter 2). Indian reserves are federal lands; however, property and civil rights are normally regulated by the provinces. The general rule is that provincial and territorial laws of general application apply on reserve to the extent that they do not affect core aspects of "Indianness" or regulate reserve lands (McNeil 1998; Bankes 1998). In practical terms, this can create regulatory gaps. For example, residential tenancy laws and laws regarding the registration of lands, which are under provincial or territorial jurisdiction, do not apply on reserves. As there is no federal legislation regulating on-reserve landlord-tenant disputes, individuals must apply to court for dispute resolution of most landlord-tenant matters (Alcantara 2003). Some First Nation communities have developed their own landlord-tenant dispute resolution processes, which include an appeal body.

Another example is the division of property upon the breakdown of a marriage. This is regulated provincially, but provincial laws cannot address the use and possession of reserve lands, leaving local courts without the power to decide matrimonial interests in reserve land or issue emergency protection orders (Alcantara 2006). To deal with the regulatory gap, the federal government enacted the *Family Homes on Reserves and Matrimonial Interests or Rights Act* in 2013.

Other regulatory gaps, however, have not yet been addressed. When operating a business on reserve land, for example, it is important to be aware that building-code requirements shift from provincial to federal. During health inspections, provisions must be put in place so that provincial health inspectors are accompanied by federal (Indigenous and Northern Affairs Canada) health inspectors. Laws are enforced on reserves by the Royal Canadian Mounted Police (RCMP) instead of a local or municipality force. And these are only a few examples of how location on reserve land affects how things are done and who is responsible. In some cases, band councils have put bylaws and laws in place that adopt provincial standards instead.

After the *Indian Act* was adopted, the federal government developed policies to provide direction for the provision of Indian-aimed programs and services. These policies were often short on details about execution or enforcement, and are chronically underfunded. Programs are created with the goal of providing services to First Nations, or contribution agreements are established to fund the delivery of services on reserves; however, without a legislative or regulatory framework, programs are delivered inconsistently. A similar issue exists in relation to the *Constitution Act, 1982*, amended to include Métis, Inuit, and non-status Indians. Their rights have not yet been defined and there is no consistent structure in place that certifies citizenship, or confirms or denies self-identification as an Aboriginal person. Lack of clarity around citizenship creates confusion in the delivery of government services and the content of individual Aboriginal rights.

Registered Indians, those with Indian-status cards issued by the federal government, do not have to pay taxes on purchases made on reserves in most cases. However, some Aboriginal communities have negotiated with the federal and provincial governments to collect their own taxes, or to receive a portion of the taxes collected in their communities. As outlined in chapter 7, there are also income-tax exemptions that may be applicable to employees who are working and/or living on reserve land. Human-resources and payroll departments need to be aware of these complexities and have systems in place to address the multiple tax situations that may exist within a given organization.

Jurisdiction over decisions impacting Aboriginals living and working off-reserve belongs to the local, provincial, or territorial government. Provincial legislation does provide a basis of clarity for services delivered by provinces. A legislative base for programs specifies respective roles and responsibilities, eligibility, and other program elements. It constitutes an unambiguous commitment by government to deliver those services. The result is that accountability and funding are better defined and so each jurisdiction has clear, although often differing, definitions of Aboriginal status (McNeil 1998). For example, employment-equity programs and employment-stimulus programs were established with the intention

> **Employment equity** is a policy that requires employers to increase the number of employees from disadvantaged groups in their organization. In Canada, the *Employment Equity Act* includes Aboriginal people, women, visible minorities, and people with disabilities.

of increasing Aboriginal participation in the workforce (Howard, Edge, and Watt 2012). Clearly, the desire was to make it easier for Aboriginal peoples to gain employment and remove barriers such as systemic discrimination. But who is eligible to participate in these programs and what proof of eligibility is required? This is a significant concern. A self-identified Métis businessperson who wants to apply for Aboriginal funding grants must first prove his or her Aboriginal identity. Organizations have been formed to fill this gap (e.g., the Métis Nation of Ontario), but, still, each organization is responsible to determine what definitions they will apply and who they will represent.

Section 35 of the *Constitution Act, 1982*, provides constitutional protection of the Indigenous and treaty rights of Aboriginal peoples of Canada. The right to self-government was not specifically included, but since 1995 the federal government has had a policy of recognizing the inherent right of Aboriginal self-government under section 35 (Hogg and Turpel 1995). This means that First Nation communities may develop their own rules, subject to the limits set out in the Charter of Rights and Freedoms. Under the *Indian Act*, bands have had the power to regulate a number of matters through bylaws in a manner similar to municipalities—such as trespass, building permits, or nuisance. In these cases, bylaws apply to all reserve lands held by the band and everyone present on the reserve, whether or not they are a band member or live on the reserve.

The power to regulate granted to band councils under the *Indian Act*, however, is quite limited. First Nation governments do not have direct authority over the fundamental rights that provinces do, such as hunting and fishing, health care, child welfare, and education. Some First Nations have entered into delegation agreements with the federal and provincial governments that permit more local control over these matters, such as recent self-governing health policies in British Columbia (Lavoie et al. 2015).

The limited right to develop bylaws under the *Indian Act* does not meet the needs of many Aboriginal communities today (Imai 2012). Consequently, indigenous communities have been seeking legal recognition of customary laws and Aboriginal rights and title that federal and provincial governments had proscribed, attempted to assimilate, or failed to address for generations (Armitage 1995). The lack of clarity on the self-government powers of Indian bands yet to be recognized by the Canadian legal system—as well as the cost of implementation and enforcement—will pose additional challenges.

An **inherent right** is one that is fundamental and permanent.

A **bylaw** is a regulation, law, or rule set by a local or municipal authority.

Business, Law, and Policy

Business law encompasses rules, statutes, codes, and regulations that are established to provide a legal framework within which businesses operate. For tax purposes, the federal Canada Revenue Agency (CRA) defines business as an activity where there is a reasonable expectation of profit and where there is evidence to support that intention. However, for sales-tax (GST/HST) purposes, a business can also include any regular and continuous activity that involves leasing property, whether or not it is for profit (CRA 2015). In Canada, all businesses and individuals must file income-tax returns, even if there is no tax due and owing (*Income Tax Act* 1985). The *Income Tax Act* outlines how rates are set, as well as exemptions (see chapter 7 for more on taxation).

The structure of a business has a significant impact on the way that income is reported, the type of returns that are completed, and many other matters. The most common types of business structure in Canada are sole proprietorships, partnerships (including limited liability), joint ventures, and corporations (see chapters 4 and 5). There are two other, less-common, business structures that may also be used: Crown corporations and community co-operatives (Canada Business Network 2015; Anderson 2002). Crown corporations are businesses owned by federal or provincial governments. They are hybrid entities, somewhere between a government body and a private enterprise, and, though they are wholly owned by the state, they operate at arm's length from government. Crown corporations are created to advance certain policy objectives, and in this sense are "instruments of public policy" (Nelson 2015: 37). However, some of them also have to operate in a business capacity, meaning they have commercial interests and competitive pressures to contend with that can, at times, conflict with their policy mandates. They are generally created to fill a need a government feels is not being met by the private sector, which is either unable or unwilling to provide certain services the government deems necessary or in the public interest.

> A **Crown corporation** is one that is owned by the federal or provincial government.

There were 260 active Aboriginal economic-development corporations (EDCs) in 2011 (Canadian Council for Aboriginal Business 2011). This number is rising. Not unlike Crown corporations, EDCs are the economic and business development arm for First Nation, Métis, and Inuit governments. They are intended to operate at arm's length from governments and are tasked with evaluating new and existing business opportunities, creating community enterprises, managing development projects, increasing employment opportunities for community members, protecting the band from liability, and building relationships with local industry partners. They are registered as private corporations, with boards of directors, which may include members of council or people who have been appointed by chief and council as shareholders of the EDC (Stastna 2012).

The SaskMétis Economic Development Corporation (SMEDCO) is an example of an Aboriginal EDC, owned by the Métis Nation-Saskatchewan Secretariat Inc. (http://www.smedco.ca/). It finances the start-up, acquisition, and expansion of Métis-controlled small businesses in Saskatchewan. SMEDCO offers a variety of programs for Métis business such as loans, business-advisory services, youth programs, and other assistance programs.

Community-development organizations and community corporations are popular because they create administrative bodies that provide oversight to review community goals (as defined by political leaders or through a community-planning process), but then independently seek out partnership opportunities, initiate development projects, and create own-source revenues that can be re-invested in the community (Wesley-Esquimaux and Calliou 2010). Partnerships provide opportunities to pool and leverage community resources, primarily land and natural resources, to fill in the large federal-funding gaps, giving community administrators some additional financial resources to invest strategically in community priorities, such as education and health (Anderson 1997).

In the case of the Penticton Indian Band in Penticton, British Columbia, the Penticton Indian Band Development Corporation (PIBDC) is provincially incorporated. The band council serves as the shareholders in trust for PIBDC. The PIBDC is the shareholder of each subsidiary corporation, which also has a limited partnership (LP) agreement with the band. The LP structure is frequently used by First Nations for tax-planning purposes as it permits the band to receive its share of any profits tax-exempt, while retaining the limited-liability protection offered by a corporation provided it is operated in accordance with the rules governing the taxation of LPs (for more on strategic alliances, see chapter 5).

Addressing Governance Issues

As has been described above, Aboriginal communities and organizations often exist in a regulatory gap or overlap between federal, provincial, and municipal areas of control. These may be places where jurisdiction or decision-making authority is unclear or where there is an identified need to outline something that hasn't effectively been addressed by other governments. These gaps create confusion for stakeholders, so Aboriginal governments must step in and attempt to rectify the confusion.

There are two basic ways by which Aboriginal people can address the gaps identified: through policy development and institution building, or through legal challenges and court cases. Laws, policies, and procedures all have a place in management of organizations, regardless of whether they are Aboriginal organizations.

Aboriginal institutions (First Nation governments, Inuit governments, the Métis National Council, and other elected offices) operate as both businesses and public service providers with varying degrees of legal recognition and authority. They are attempting to identify operational compromises that allow them to maintain traditional governance structures and practices, while operating in conjunction with and adapting to changing national and international policies and standards (Wilson and Alcantara 2012).

Aboriginal governments can protect and assert Aboriginal rights through the creation of their own rules and these rules can match the real needs and wishes of the community. Despite the *Indian Act*, many communities have managed to maintain customary practices through oral history, and these are often accepted by community members as societal norms. Examples include the maintenance of complex governance and decision-making structures, use and management of traditional hunting and gathering areas, and continued family practices, such as customary adoption and marriage (Lavoie et al. 2015). Documentation of these customary practices creates opportunities for communities to discuss them before developing and passing laws that reflect their culture. Use of clear organization and policy-development processes helps communities define norms, values, and beliefs within the communities. Just implementing the process will add legitimacy to claims of distinctive community traits (Anderson and Denis 2003) and will be less costly in terms of money and time.

One example of customary governance is the Mi'kmaw Grand Council. Traditional Mi'kmaw territory spans the four Atlantic provinces (Nova Scotia, New Brunswick, Prince Edward Island, and Newfoundland and Labrador) and parts of Québec and Maine. The Mi'kmaw traditional governance structure included a system of traditional leaders from each of the seven districts of the traditional territory; however, as a result of legislated provincial boundaries, different communities must negotiate with different provincial governments and operate under their laws. Likewise, most provinces span multiple partial Aboriginal territories within their boundaries. New Brunswick has Mi'kmaq, Passamaquoddy, and Maliseet nations in different parts of the province. Consequently, an Aboriginal institution known as the Atlantic Policy Congress of First Nations Chiefs was established in 1995 specifically to study and address the policy issues that have been created as a result of Canada's structure and policies regarding Aboriginal rights in Atlantic Canada.

The National Aboriginal Lands Managers Association (http://www.nalma.ca) provides support and professional-development resources to communities who want to incorporate First Nation values and beliefs into their land-management processes and land codes. NALMA encourages community discussion of land use, land-use plans, traditional territories, and development of land codes. Community managers can use land codes as guidelines to strategically plan development, create supportive integrated policies and procedures, and consistently communicate actions or decisions. Land codes help private business owners by adding clarity around the services they can expect to receive when they build infrastructure on reserve land. Land-use plans and zoning create clarity for compatible future uses (Curry, Donker and Krehbiel 2014).

The First Nations Finance Authority, the First Nations Market Housing Fund, and others provide resources, training, guidelines, and templates to communities who want to create governance structures that focus on service standards and achievable results, but also can be modified to reflect each community's unique needs and situation.

As an alternative to the *First Nations Land Management Act* (1999), some communities have very publicly chosen to assert their jurisdiction on their own without the support of the federal government. Despite the lack of legal recognition, such communities are exercising their rights under what is referred to as an "assertion model" (http://www.fngovernance.org/). This goes beyond protesting resource-extraction development when it takes place without consent or negotiation. In some cases, this means that provincial and national borders, and the authority of their governing bodies, are not recognized. It may also mean that elected officials are recognized, but Aboriginal leaders want to meet and negotiate with all three levels of government as treaty signatories rather than wards of the state. It may also involve a community asserting itself as a nation in an international arena.

These processes are subject to challenge by other governments in Canada. Where their own rules for governance are not clear and easily accessible, they are particularly vulnerable to excessive cost and time spent on resolving matters in the courts. Others still have taken advantage of opportunities like comprehensive land-claim agreements, modern-day treaties, and self-government agreements.

In some cases, those who have attempted to maintain customary practices such as use of traditional hunting and gathering areas have met opposition when those practices were not recognized or accepted equally by every community member or other governments. As Canada evolved, the *Indian Act* outlawed traditional Indigenous practices, including hunting and fishing without a licence. A landmark example that changed that law is the Marshall decision, described in chapter 11, but there are others that are also significant. For example, in the 1996 case of *R. v. Gladstone*, William and Donald Gladstone were members of the Heiltsuk Band, in British Columbia, and were both charged with selling herring spawn contrary to the federal *Fisheries Act*. The Gladstone brothers asserted that they had a right to sell herring under section 35 of the *Constitution Act, 1982*, and they presented evidence showing that trade of herring spawn was a significant part of the Heiltsuk band's way of life prior to contact. The Supreme Court of Canada confirmed that the Heiltsuk had a pre-existing right to harvest herring roe, including for commercial purposes, subject to reasonable regulatory limits.

In Canada, when someone is charged with illegal activity under a law they go to trial court in their local area (province or territory). If unsatisfied with the decision, they have the option to appeal in higher courts, including the Superior Court (Ontario and Québec), the Federal Court of Appeal, and the Supreme Court of Canada. Supreme Court of Canada decisions are final until modified by a future decision of that court or taken to an international body for review. When decisions are made in court and escalated through the system, the discussion centres around interpretation of the original intent of the law. This means that decisions are more theoretical than practical; once decisions are made, they serve as a trigger for changes in legislative policy and enforcement. The Marshall decision, described in chapter 11, was significant for two reasons. It opened the door for individual Aboriginal fishers to fish for themselves, and to sell fish to maintain a moderate livelihood in their traditional territories without a licence. It also opened the door for the development of an Aboriginal commercial fishery in Atlantic Canada. But it would not have happened if Mi'kmaq and other communities had not acted litigiously. As a result of the court decision, various communities started formal discussions with Fisheries and Oceans Canada and developed policies and guidelines that created a structure in which they could all operate, including community-owned and managed fisheries (APCFNC 2014).

Métis and non-status Indians were legally recognized as Aboriginal peoples in section 35 of the *Constitution Act, 1982*; however, their rights haven't been clearly defined and do not necessarily apply consistently. For example, Métis descending from Louis Riel, the 19th-century spiritual and political leader, had more recognition of their rights than did Métis in other areas of Canada. Consequently, both Métis and non-status Indians have been challenging the federal and provincial governments in court to better establish and define their existing rights. In 1993, Steve Powley and his son, Roddy, set out hunting in Sault Ste. Marie, Ontario, where, unlicensed for such, they killed a moose. Moose hunting in Ontario is strictly regulated by the provincial Ministry of Natural Resources. They were charged with unlawfully hunting moose and knowingly possessing game hunted in contravention of the *Game and Fish Act*, R.S.O, 1990, c. G-1. They went to trial court, where they challenged provincial law that denied the existence of a distinct Métis right to hunt for food in the matter. The trial court, the Superior Court of Ontario, and the federal Court of Appeal all agreed with the Powleys. Finally, the Supreme Court of Canada, in 2003, delivered what is considered a landmark decision by the Métis Nation of Ontario, in *R. v. Powley*, which recognized and affirmed the existence of Métis as distinct Aboriginal people, with existing rights (MNC 2015). The process took thirteen years, and, while it appears on the surface to be simply a case of Métis ability to hunt without a licence, it did much more than that. This decision set a precedent that can be used to interpret/give rise to other Métis rights in Ontario and Canada. It has the potential to affect future business opportunities.

The Future of Aboriginal Business in Canada

Government laws and policies can influence businesses either directly or indirectly. Each business must be aware of the laws that will most directly impact them and their situation. A business owner looks at their product, industry, environments, and other internal and external factors to strategically manage their operations. Aboriginal businesses and those who work with them must do the same, but they also have additional factors that they must consider. Anyone who works with Aboriginal business must understand the industry, territory, and political climate in which they are working. It is also critical to identify the regulatory gaps that may exist and know when and how specific laws apply in a given situation.

The impacts of colonization, the laws that were put in place and enforced, and the subsequent misunderstandings have had devastating effects on traditional Aboriginal governance structures. For First Nations and Inuit, it has taken long series of court battles to have their treaties recognized, and the intent and meaning of such treaties is still open to interpretation (Leslie 2002: 23). It is up to those in leadership positions to work with their citizens to gain standing and determine how self-government rights will be exercised through the implementation of laws, codes, and areas of jurisdiction. As decision-making authority and areas of jurisdiction are clarified, more business opportunities will become available for communities that have stable leadership and well-defined organizational structures. Partnership opportunities will also become available as more organizations continue to diversify their resource base, market share, products, and services. Aboriginal communities who invest in governance and institution building will be well placed to critically evaluate these opportunities and negotiate terms of partnership with others.

Key Points:

- The three main types of law in Canada are common law, statutory law, and administrative law; however, Aboriginal legal traditions and customary law also exist and are still used in some communities.

- Laws need structures to support their implementation.

- When looking specifically at reserve lands in Canada, there are significant regulatory gaps.

Questions for Review:

1. How are Aboriginal legal traditions and customary law different from other types of law in Canada?

2. What is self-governance?

3. Why are economic development corporations and community cooperatives appealing to Aboriginal communities?

4. How do the complexities concerning law and regulatory regimes on a reserve impact business in practical terms?

5. How might Aboriginal communities address regulatory gaps?

Suggested Assignments:

1. Identify situations where there may be a gap created as a result of differing federal and provincial jurisdiction. Research how Aboriginal communities have addressed these gaps by putting bylaws in place or adopting provincial standards as a means of addressing those gaps. Discuss.

2. Locate current or recent news coverage about the inconsistent delivery of services to Aboriginal communities. Review the related public debate. Identify arguments that support each side of the debate and critically analyze them.

3. Read case commentary on one of the legal decisions referenced in this chapter and consider how section 35 of the Constitution has been used in these cases to advance Aboriginal rights and title in Canada.

References

Aboriginal Human Rights Project. 2012. First Nations Legal Traditions and Customary Laws and the Human Rights Complaint Process A Story, Reflections, Questions, Suggestions and an Offering. Paper presented for Mediate BC Aboriginal Human Rights Project. http://www.mediatebc.com/PDFs/LRG2046-Aboriginal-Human-Rights-Project---final-re.aspx.

Alcantara, C. 2003. Individual Property Rights on Canadian Indian Reserves: The Historical Emergence and Jurisprudence of Certificates of Possession. *Canadian Journal of Native Studies*, 23 (2): 391-424.

———. 2006. Indian women and the division of matrimonial real property on Canadian Indian reserves. *Canadian Journal of Women and the Law* 18 (2): 513-33.

Anderson, R. B. 2002. Entrepreneurship and aboriginal Canadians: a case study in economic development. *Journal of Developmental Entrepreneurship*, 7(1), 45.

Anderson, C. and C. Denis. 2003. Urban Natives and the Nation: Before and After the Royal Commission on Aboriginal Peoples. *Canadian Review of Sociology and Anthropology* 40 (4): 373-90.

Anderson, R. B. 1997. Corporate/Indigenous partnerships in economic development: The first nations in Canada. *World development* 25 (9), 1483-1503.

———. 2014. The business economy of the First Nations in Saskatchewan: a contingency perspective. *Canadian Journal of Native Studies* 15 (2): 309-46.

APCFNC (Atlantic Policy Congress of First Nations Chiefs Secretariat). 2014. About. *Atlantic Policy Congress of First Nations Chiefs Secretariat*. http://www.apcfnc.ca/about-apc/_(accessed December 2, 2015).

———. 2014. The Atlantic Integrated Commercial Fisheries Initiative. *Atlantic Policy Congress of First Nations Chiefs Secretariat*. http://www.apcfnc.ca/fisheries/projects-initiatives/_(accessed December 2, 2015).

Armitage, A. 1995. *Comparing the policy of aboriginal assimilation: Australia, Canada, and New Zealand*. Vancouver: UBC Press.

Bankes, N. 1998. Delgamuukw, Division of Powers and Provincial Land and Resource Laws: Some Implications for Provincial Resource Rights. *UBC Law Review* 32, 317-52.

Borrows, John. 2010. Canada's Indigenous constitution. Toronto: University of Toronto Press.

Bradley, A. W. and K. D. Ewing. 2007. *Constitutional and administrative law*. Vol. 1. Harlow, UK: Pearson Education.

Canada Business Network. 2015. Corporation, partnership, or sole proprietorship? *Canada Business Network-Government Services for Entrepreneurs*. http://www.canadabusiness.ca/eng/page/2853/ (accessed December 2, 2015).

Canadian Council for Aboriginal Business. 2011. Community and Commerce: A survey of Aboriginal Economic Development Corporations. https://www.ccab.com/uploads/File/Community-and-Commerce-Final-Report.pdf (accessed December 2, 2015).

Chambers, S. 1998. Contract or conversation? Theoretical lessons from the Canadian constitutional crisis. *Politics and Society* 26 (1): 143-72.

Chartrand, P. L. 2014. Understanding the Daniels Case on s.91(24) Constitution Act 1867. *Aboriginal Policy Studies* 3 (3): 115-31.

Chen, Y. 2015. *An Economic Analysis of Factors Influencing the Adoption of the First Nations Land Management Act and the Consequences of Adoption.* PhD dissertation, Guelph University.

Constitution Act, 1982. Constitution Acts, 1867 to 1982. *Justice Laws Website*: http://laws-lois.justice.gc.ca/eng/const/page-16.html (accessed December 2, 2015).

CRA (Canada Revenue Agency). 2015. Setting up your Business. *Canada Revenue Agency.* http://www.cra-arc.gc.ca/tx/bsnss/sm/sttng/menu-eng.html (accessed December 2, 2015).

Curry, J., H. Donker and R. Krehbiel. 2014. Land claim and treaty negotiations in British Columbia, Canada: Implications for First Nations land and self-governance. *The Canadian Geographer/Le Géographe canadien* 58 (3): 291-304.

Dawson, R. M. and N. Ward. 1970. *The Government of Canada*, Vol. 2. Toronto: University of Toronto Press.

Evans, A. B. 1998. *Frozen Fish Rights: A Socio-legal Analysis of RV Gladstone, RV Van Der Peet, & RVNTC Smokehouse (at the Supreme Court of Canada, 1995-96).* Simon Fraser University.

Fisheries and Oceans Canada (2013). Mission, Vision and Values. Retrieved from: http://www.dfo-mpo.gc.ca/about-notre-sujet/org/vision-eng.htm (accessed December 2, 2015).

Flanagan, T., A. Le Dressay and C. Alcantara. 2010. *Beyond the Indian Act: Restoring Aboriginal Property Rights.* Montréal: McGill-Queen's University Press.

Hernandez, G. (2013). Indigenous Perspectives on Community Economic Development: A North-South Conversation. *Canadian Journal of Nonprofit and Social Economy Research* 4 (1): 6-24.

Hoffman, R. and A. R. Robinson. 2010. Nisga'a Self-Government: A New Journey Has Begun. *Canadian Journal of Native Studies* 30 (2), 387-405.

Hogg, P. W. and M. E. Turpel. 1995. Implementing Aboriginal self-government: constitutional and jurisdictional issues. *Canadian Bar Review* 74 (2): 187-224.

Howard, A., J. Edge, and D. Watt. 2012. Understanding the value, challenges, and opportunities of engaging Metis, Inuit, and First Nations workers. Report prepared for the Conference Board of Canada. Conference Board of Canada.

Imai, S. 2012. The structure of the Indian Act: Accountability in governance. Comparative Research in Law & Political Economy. Research Paper No.

35/2012. Osgoode Hall Law School of York University. http://digitalcommons. osgoode.yorku.ca/cgi/viewcontent.cgi?article=1008&context=clpe (accessed December 2, 2015).

Income Tax Act. 1985. Income Tax Act. R.S.C., 1985, c. 1 (5th Supp.). *Justice Laws Website.* http://laws-lois.justice.gc.ca/eng/acts/I-3.3/page-1.html. (accessed December 2, 2015).

Gibson, D. 1973. Constitutional Jurisdiction over Environmental Management in Canada. *University of Toronto Law Review* 23:54-87.

Glenn, P. 1995. The Common Law in Canada. *Canadian Bar Review* 74: 261-92.

Griffin, R. W., R. J. Ebert, F.A. Stark, M. D. Lang, M. A. Hitt, S. Black and L. W. Porter, eds. 2011. *Introduction to Business Management.* Toronto: Pearson.

Lavoie, J. G., A. J. Browne, C. Varcoe, S. Wong, A. Fridkin, D. Littlejohn and D. Tu. 2015. Missing Pathways to Self-Governance: Aboriginal Health Policy in British Columbia. *The International Indigenous Policy Journal* 6 (1): article 2.

Leslie, J. F. 2002. Indian Act: an historical perspective. *Canadian Parliamentary Review* 25 (2): 23-7.

Maracle, C. 2014. Iroquois Nationals going for gold at 2014 World Lacrosse Championships. *CBC.ca.* July 15. http://www.cbc.ca/news/aboriginal/iroquois-nationals-going-for-gold-at-world-lacrosse-championships-1.2707456 (accessed December 2, 2015).

McGill Centre for Human Rights and Legal Pluralism. 2015. Aboriginal Human Rights Initiative. *McGill University.* http://www.mcgill.ca/humanrights/aboriginal-human-rights-initiatives (accessed December 2, 2015).

McNeil, K. 1989. *Common Law Aboriginal Title.* Oxford, U.K.: Clarendon Press.

———. 1997. Aboriginal Title and Aboriginal Rights: What's the Connection? *Alberta Law Review* 36 (1): 17-48.

———. 1998. Aboriginal Title and the Division of Powers: Rethinking Federal and Provincial Jurisdiction. *Saskatchewan Law Review* 61 (2): 431-65.

Miller, B. G. 2011. *Oral History on Trial: Recognizing Aboriginal Narratives in the Courts.* Vancouver: University of British Columbia Press.

MNC (Métis National Council). 2015. Métis Nation Rights. *Métis Nation.* http://www.metisnation.ca/index.php/who-are-the-metis/rights (accessed December 2, 2015).

Nelson, Rodney. 2015. Corporate Social Responsibility and Partnership Development. *Journal of Aboriginal Management* 16: 34-39.

PLEA (Public Legal Education System of Saskatchewan). 2006. Currents: Exploring Traditional Aboriginal Justice Concepts in Contemporary Canadian Society. http://docs.plea.org/pdf/Currents.pdf (accessed December 2, 2015).

Russell, P., R. Knopff and F. L. Morton. 1989. *Federalism and the Charter: Leading Constitutional Decisions.* Montréal: McGill-Queen's University Press.

Secher, U. 2014. Aboriginal Customary Law: A Source of Common Law Title to Land. Oxford, U.K.: Hart Publishing.

Stastna. 2012. What are Crown Corporations and Why do they Exist. *CBC.ca*. April 1. http://www.cbc.ca/news/canada/what-are-crown-corporations-and-why-do-they-exist-1.1135699 (accessed December 2, 2015).

Slattery, B. 2015. The Aboriginal Constitution. *Supreme Court Law Review* 67 (second series): 319-36.

Sosa, I. and K. Keenan. 2001. Impact benefit agreements between aboriginal communities and mining companies: Their use in Canada. Report prepared for Canadian Environmental Law Association. http://s.cela.ca/files/uploads/IBAeng.pdf.

Wilson, G. N. and C. Alcantara. 2012. Mixing politics and business in the Canadian arctic: Inuit corporate governance in Nunavik and the Inuvialuit settlement region. *Canadian Journal of Political Science* 45 (4): 781-804.

Wilson, J., M. Wilson, B. Urli and A. ben Hammouda. 2012. Changing Aboriginal Policy in Canada, and the Effects on Scale and Capacity Use in the Commercial Fisheries of Quebec. Paper prepared for Visible Possibilities: The Economics of Sustainable Fisheries, Aquaculture and Seafood Trade: Proceedings of the Sixteenth Biennial Conference of the International Institute of Fisheries Economics and Trade, Dar es Salaam, Tanzania. https://ir.library.oregonstate.edu/xmlui/bitstream/handle/1957/34918/Changing%20aboriginal%20policy%20in%20Canada%20IIFET%202012%20V3.pdf?sequence=1 (accessed December 2, 2015).

Webber, J. 2015. *The Constitution of Canada: A Contextual Analysis*. Oxford, UK: Bloomsbury Publishing.

Wesley-Esquimaux, C. and B. Calliou. 2010. Best Practices in Aboriginal Community Development: A Literature Review and Wise Practices Approach. Report for The Banff Centre, Indigenous Leadership and Management, Banff, Alberta. http://www.banffcentre.ca/Indigenous-leadership/library/pdf/best_practices_in_aboriginal_community_development.pdf.

Young, R. 2013. Multilevel Governance and Public Policy in Canadian Municipalities: Reflections on Research Results. Paper prepared for the Politics of Multilevel Governance, Canadian Political Science Association, Victoria, British Columbia. http://www.cpsa-acsp.ca/papers-2013/Young1.pdf.

Chapter 7

Perhaps one of the broadest misconceptions pertaining to Aboriginal peoples in Canada concerns taxation. Do Aboriginal peoples pay taxes? Yes. Are some Aboriginal peoples exempt from some taxation? Yes.

The Canadian constitution has defined who is legally "Aboriginal" in Canada, and section 87 of the *Indian Act* has defined who, as an Aboriginal, is eligible for exemption from income tax and under what circumstances—generally, status Indians working on-reserve. In other situations, Aboriginal peoples are usually subject to income tax.

Property tax is levied by municipal governments. First Nation peoples living off-reserve, and First Nation enterprises off-reserve, are subject to municipal taxation just like everyone else. First Nation property may also be subject to property tax levied by band councils.

Land on reserves is communally held (in trust by the Crown) and is not owned outright by individuals. Court decisions on taxation repeatedly state that certain tax exemptions are provided to protect the property of Indians on reserves, and that these are not intended to compensate nor remedy economically disadvantaged First Nations. It should be noted that Métis and Inuit are not included in the legal definition of Indian, and are therefore not eligible to tax exemptions noted in the *Indian Act*.

An Introduction to Taxation
Wendy Wadden

"Taxation is a cornerstone of an autonomous, responsible government."
Manny Jules[1]

Tax laws have been enacted at several governance levels in Canada, including federal, provincial, and municipal. First Nation bands and other reserve governing bodies have also enacted laws of taxation. Governments and governing bodies use tax revenues to fund public services, such as water, sewer, roads, garbage collection, education, and health care.

All individuals and businesses in Canada are subject to various types of taxation, including, but not limited to, property tax, income tax, and sales tax (Palacios and Lamman 2013). The Supreme Court of Canada, in the case of *Nowegijick v. The Queen*, determined that "Indians are citizens and, in affairs of life not governed by treaties or the *Indian Act*, they are subject to all of the responsibilities, including payment of taxes, of other Canadian citizens" (*Nowegijick* 1983: 36).

Some First Nation peoples in Canada have access to a general tax exemption under section 87 of the *Indian Act*. The extent of the tax exemption is subject to judicial interpretation of the *Act* (O'Brien 2002; Maclagan 2000). A review of related court cases shows that the tax exemptions included throughout the *Indian Act* have been linked to protecting the property of those living on reserves. Aboriginal peoples that have moved off a reserve often do not qualify for s. 87 tax exemptions (Newhouse and Peters 2003: 52-53; MacKinnon 1998).

> A **tax exemption** reduces or eliminates the requirement for an individual or organization to pay tax on either income or a purchase.

The cases and the literature reveal that the judiciary, scholars, and Indigenous peoples have concerns about the changing demographics of Aboriginal peoples and their access to the tax exemption in s. 87 of the *Act*. The number of cases involving Aboriginal peoples challenging the disallowance of tax exemption reveals that there has been uncertainty surrounding the applicable circumstances. In 2010, Judge Rowe, of the Tax Court of Canada,[2] recognized the need, in *R. v. Robinson*, for Parliament to develop a protocol that would respond to the changing demographics of Aboriginals (*Robinson* 2010: par. 107).[3] He suggested granting reserve status to institutions specifically mandated to provide necessary social services to Aboriginal people, or developing a partial tax exemption on the income of Indian employees of such institutions. Judge Rowe continued by suggesting that the Canada Revenue Agency (CRA) is "adept at calculating amounts to be attributed between personal and business expenses, use of assets, sources of income and so on" and that this "expertise could be put to good use in administering any ameliorative legislation passed by Parliament that put in place a system that was not dependent on the all-or-nothing approach" (Robinson 2010: 59).

Manny Jules, one of the originators of the First Nations Tax Commission, a shared governance institution, and others suggest that taxation is a mechanism to promote the economic independence and stability of Aboriginal communities (Graham and Bruhn 2008, 2009; Fiscal Realities 1997). Today, governing bodies have exercised options under provisions of the *Indian Act* to enact property-tax and sales-tax laws to raise funds required to provide services to those Indians living on reserves (*Indian Act* 1985: s. 83; *Canadian Pacific Ltd.* 1995; First Nations Tax Commission 2014).[4] The enactment of property and sales tax under s. 83 of the *Indian*

Act requires the council of a band to secure the approval of the minister of Indigenous and Northern Affairs Canada.

The federal and provincial income-tax obligations of all Canadian taxpayers are reported to and collected by a department of the federal government, the CRA. Canadian taxpayers are required to prepare their income-tax returns, report the amount of income tax they owe, and pay the amount of taxes owed to the CRA. The CRA has the authority to assess the income-tax payable as reported by a Canadian taxpayer.[5] In the event the CRA determines the taxpayer owes additional taxes or that the taxpayer has not filed an income-tax return, then the outstanding taxes, plus interest,[6] plus a penalty,[7] may be owing to the CRA by the taxpayer.[8] The violation of a tax law may result in a penalty; however, more serious violations may be punished by assets seizure and imprisonment.[9] It is easy to see why tax planning by individuals and business owners to ensure that tax laws are complied with and that tax liability is minimized is important.

This chapter introduces the taxation laws that apply to Aboriginal peoples in Canada. The tax exemption contained within s. 87 of the *Indian Act* is explored. Statutes such as the *First Nations Goods and Services Tax Act*,[10] which give governing bodies the power to enact tax laws on the supply of goods or services made on First Nation lands, despite section 87 of the *Indian Act*, are noted. *The New Brunswick Revenue Administration Act*,[11] which authorizes the province to enter into agreements with First Nation communities to allow for tax-revenue sharing and gaming-revenue sharing, is mentioned. These tax-revenue sharing and gaming-revenue-sharing agreements exist across Canada and relate to the sale of items such as alcohol, fuel, and tobacco. The movement of a band to self-government, the development and implementation of First Nation taxation systems, and the signing of tax-sharing agreements between provincial governments and First Nation communities all have an effect on the taxation of Aboriginals. It becomes clear in this chapter that the current taxation system does not adequately serve the needs of Aboriginal peoples, and that the steps to evolve the tax system require the cooperation of federal, provincial, municipal, and First Nation governing bodies.

Who Has the Authority To Make Tax Laws?

Constitution Act, 1867

The *Constitution Act, 1867* (formerly known as the *British North America Act*), identifies the power of the federal government and the provincial governments to make laws. Section 91 of the *Act* assigns to the federal government the general power to make laws for all of Canada. Section 92 outlines the law-making authority of the provincial governments. Provincial and territorial governments enact laws that deal with matters relating to their respective province or territory. The ability to enact laws to meet specific provincial needs results in variations in the law among the provinces. Provincial governments may assign some of their law-making authority to municipal governments there within. For example, under the terms of the *Nova Scotia Municipal Government Act*,[12] property assessment is assigned by a provincial department, and a municipality has the authority to set the tax rates for the land located within its municipal geographical boundaries. Since each of these government levels make tax laws, this leads to a complex and diverse system of taxation in Canada.

There are two types of tax laws: direct and indirect.[13] A direct tax is demanded from the person or company obliged to pay it; an example would be an income tax. An example of an indirect tax is a sales tax; sales tax is paid to the taxing body by the seller, who collects the tax from the buyer. Under the provisions of the *Constitution Act, 1867,* the federal government has the authority to use *any mode* of taxation, whereas the provincial governments were restricted to direct taxation methods. In particular, the federal government was given authority in s. 91(3) to raise "money by any mode or system of taxation." The provincial legislatures could, under s. 92(2), raise money by "direct taxation within the province," for example, retail sales taxes.

> A **direct tax** is tax paid by a person or organization directly to the entity that is imposing it.
>
> An **indirect tax** involves an intermediary that collects tax from a person or organization and remits it to the entity that is imposing it.

Indian Act and the *Constitution Act, 1982*

The term "Indian" is the legal term used in the *Indian Act.* Many pieces of legislation and court decisions concerning Indigenous and First Nation peoples also use the term "Indian." The specific authority to make laws relating to "Indians, and lands reserved for the Indians" was assigned to the federal government in s. 91(24) of the *Constitution Act, 1867.* It is important to note that this authority has been questioned by Aboriginal peoples, and it has been argued that the concept of "civil rule over aboriginals by the federal government has no foundation in the treaties" (Henderson 1994: 241). This raises questions about the authority of the federal government to enact the *Indian Act*, which, it has been argued, "compromised or ignored Aboriginal and treaty rights" (ibid.). It must be acknowledged that arguments have also been made that Indigenous nations had an "inherent right to self-define and set their own rules of membership," and, further, that the "operation of successive *Indian Acts* has not extinguished this right, but has clearly and unjustifiably infringed it" (Olthuis 2009).

An inherent Aboriginal right of self-government is recognized in s. 35 of the *Constitution Act, 1982,* the latter enacted to patriate the Canadian Constitution from Great Britain, and which contains the Canadian Charter of Rights and Freedoms (Rustand 2010; Wilkins 2011; Olthuis 2009). It has been suggested that the tax exemptions under the *Indian Act* have diminished in importance as more tax-exemption and treaty-rights arguments, based on s. 35 of the *Constitution Act, 1982*, have been raised by Indigenous peoples (Maclagan 2000; Gardner-O'Toole 1992).[14] As more Aboriginal communities move toward self-government, the *Indian Act* will become less relevant in defining the rights of the Aboriginal peoples, as will the use of the term "Indian" (Richards 2003).

Section 35 of the 1982 *Act* provides:

(1) The existing aboriginal and treaty rights of the aboriginal peoples of Canada are hereby recognized and affirmed.

(2) In this *Act*, "aboriginal peoples of Canada" includes the Indian, Inuit, and Métis peoples of Canada.

(3) For greater certainty, in subsection (1) "treaty rights" include rights that now exist by way of land-claims agreements, or may be so acquired.

The *Constitution Act, 1982*, provides protection of the recognized Aboriginal rights and freedoms in section 25, which states:

The guarantee in this Charter of certain rights and freedoms shall not be construed so as to abrogate or derogate from any aboriginal, treaty or other rights or freedoms that pertain to the aboriginal peoples of Canada including

(1) any rights or freedoms that have been recognized by the Royal Proclamation of October 7, 1763; and

(2) any rights or freedoms that now exist by way of land claims agreements or may be so acquired.

Section 88 of the *Indian Act* indicates that all provincial laws will apply to Indians unless specifically exempted or inconsistent with an act of Parliament or treaty or regulation.[15] It is recognized that s. 88 does not permit "infringement of Aboriginal title," and it "does not have the effect of making provincial laws in relation to land apply to lands reserved for Indians" or "Aboriginal title lands" (McNeil 2000: 193). So, provincial governments may provide broader exemptions for Indians, but cannot limit the exemptions that may exist for Indians under federal laws. More specifically, s. 88 states:

Subject to the terms of any treaty and any other *Act* of Parliament, all laws of general application from time to time in force in any province are applicable to and in respect of Indians in the province, except to the extent that those laws are inconsistent with this *Act* or the *First Nations Fiscal Management Act*, or with any order, rule, regulation or law of a band made under those *Act*s, and except to the extent that those provincial laws make provision for any matter for which provision is made by or under those *Act*s. (*Indian Act* 1985)

The *Indian Act* provides for the possibility of the taxation of Aboriginal peoples by a band council. Section 83 of the *Act* authorizes a band council to make bylaws, subject to the approval of the federal minister, to tax land, or interests in land, located on the reserve. As more Aboriginal communities move toward self-government, this provision takes on an important role in raising monies to support public services on the reserve.

Justice Dickson, in *Mitchell v. Peguis Indian Band*, confirmed the principle identified in *Nowegijick* "of resolving ambiguities in favour of Indians" (see *Mitchell* 1990: 113-14). Justice Kirkpatrick, in *R. v. Kapp*, suggested s. 25 be interpreted by referring to "the ordinary meaning of the words in the context of section 25 and the *Constitution* as a whole" (*Kapp* 2006: par. 123-24), and that "to be protected under section 25 these other rights and freedoms must be appropriate, applicable or related to a particular aboriginal nation, community or ethnic group" (par. 125). Justice Kirkpatrick suggested that "the phrase 'other rights or freedoms' in s. 25 includes benefits conferred on aboriginals by laws or agreements directed at their special status as aboriginals" (par. 151). The ambiguities that exist in the *Indian Act* tax exemptions are subject to challenge based on s. 25 of the Charter of Rights and Freedoms.

What Role Does the Judicial System Play in the Application of Tax Laws?

Courts have the task of interpreting the laws that all governing bodies make under their law-making authority. It must also be recognized that courts interpret tax laws; they do not make them. The statutory interpretation process by the court is intended to ensure that the law developed by the governing body is valid, and that it is applied fairly and justly. Challenges by Aboriginal taxpayers have been presented in the Tax Court of Canada, the Federal Court of Canada, and the Supreme Court of Canada.

In the event that an individual taxpayer and the CRA do not agree on a tax assessment, the taxpayer may appeal the assessment to the Tax Court of Canada. The Tax Court of Canada has jurisdiction under s. 12 of the *Tax Court of Canada Act* to hear appeals related to tax assessment.[16] The remedies available to the taxpayer via a Tax Court hearing are specifically identified in s. 171(1) of the *Income Tax Act*.[17] Some Aboriginal taxpayers have attempted to challenge the very process of taxation and tax assessment established under the provisions of the *Income Tax Act* and the *Tax Court of Canada Act* by making these arguments before the Tax Court of Canada.[18] Tax Court of Canada jurisdiction is restricted to the review of a tax assessment made by the minister and, as such, it does not have the authority to fashion a remedy for such complex jurisdictional claims. The Tax Court of

Canada has explained that "the scope of the exemption is a result of policy choices made by Parliament in drafting paragraph 87(1)(*b*) and it is not open to the Courts to expand the exemption beyond what was intended by Parliament" (*Roe* 2008: par. 109).

If the Aboriginal taxpayer challenges the payment of taxes as "a determination of a question of law under ... the Federal Court Rules" or "a declaration that their employment income falls within the tax exemption provided under section 87 of the *Indian Act*" rather than as an assessment issue, "then the Federal Court has jurisdiction to determine whether the exemption provided under section 87 of the *Indian Act* has been denied" (*Johnston* 2009: par. 53).[19] Aboriginal taxpayers, like any other taxpayer, usually begin their tax challenge as an assessment appeal in the Tax Court of Canada, and, through the judicial appeal process, that challenge may reach the Federal Court of Canada or the Supreme Court of Canada. Court challenges that progress to this high level of court are complex, time-consuming, and costly.

The Supreme Court of Canada is the highest court in the Canadian judicial system, and its decisions must be respected by all courts in Canada. In order to interpret and apply the law, Canadian courts use the "doctrine of precedent" and apply the existing jurisprudence to assist in interpreting the factors deemed relevant in a particular situation. Constance MacIntosh (2009: 399) draws attention to the oppressive nature of this practice when considering cases involving Aboriginal peoples, and suggests that "(w)e have created a common law concept of 'Indianness' that reflects the legislated and jurisdictional definitions that were once crafted to enable assimilation-era state goals" (MacIntosh 2009).

Obviously the courts play a very important role in determining whether or not a particular circumstance is eligible for a tax exemption. It is fair to say that court interpretation of tax statutes has greatly influenced the taxation of Aboriginal peoples.[20] The "common law concept of Indianness" may have contributed to the variation in the outcomes of the court decisions involving the Aboriginal peoples' access to tax exemptions.

> **Doctrine of precedent** is the way in which decisions are made and reasoned by judges, by referring to previous decisions in similar circumstances.
>
> **Jurisprudence** refers to the philosophy of the law.

The Supreme Court of Canada has directed that "treaties and statutes relating to Indians should be liberally construed and doubtful expressions resolved in favour of the Indians" (*Nowegijick* 1983: p. 36), and "aboriginal understandings of words and corresponding legal concepts in Indian treaties are to be preferred over more legalistic and technical constructions" (*Mitchell* 1990: 98). In other cases, the Supreme Court has expressed the opinion that taxpayers are "entitled to rely on the clear meaning of taxation provisions"; therefore, where the "words of a statute are precise and unequivocal, those words will play a dominant role in the interpretive process" (*Placer* 2006: 728). To apply a tax statute, the court has indicated that a "textual interpretation" is important (*Canada Trustco* 2005: par. 11). This means that when there is an ambiguity in a tax statute, a unified, textual, contextual, and purposive approach should be taken to the statutory interpretation (par. 47). The words used in the statute should be interpreted in the ordinary grammatical sense, and should be given a meaning that "harmonizes the wording, object, spirit and purpose of the provisions of the *Income Tax Act*" (*Stubart* 1984: 728).

It must be noted that the Canadian tax system has been described as a "murky tax system" that has developed as a result of "successive federal and provincial governments" adding layers of incremental tax-policy changes (Hodgson 2012: 2).[21] The volume of cases involving the general tax exemption under s. 87 of the *Indian Act* suggests that the harmonization of the provisions of the *Income Tax Act* with tax exemptions under the *Indian Act* is a complex process and has variable outcomes. Leslie J. Pinder (2000: 1502) suggests that:

> treating each case as if it were unique, without enabling the development of principles to be applied in future cases, leads to abuse. If each Judge (or Revenue Canada official) is able to assess the factors, according to his or her fancy—with the prejudice weighing in against applying the exemption—the system is discredited, and natives have to resort to the extraordinary costs of litigation, only to find that a successful outcome provides no relief for others.

It is understandable that this level of complexity makes it very difficult for Aboriginal taxpayers to make decisions that enable them to both exercise exemptions and to ensure that they are in compliance with tax legislation.

The Supreme Court has suggested that, when considering a provision of a tax statute, the interpretation given to the provision and adopted by the governing body are important factors to consider (*Placer* 2006: 722-23). It comes as no surprise that, where the evidence is clear that the transaction is legally ineffective or incomplete or a sham, the exemption in s. 87 will not apply (*Stubart* 1984: 545-46). The court has been clear in stating that "cases of improper manipulation by Indian taxpayers to avoid income tax may be addressed as they are in the case of non-Indian taxpayers" (*Bastien* 2011: par. 62). The Supreme Court has cautioned against the development of an interpretation approach that defeats the intention of s. 87 because of the improper manipulation by some taxpayers. For example, a review of cases from the Tax Court of Canada reveals that an employee-leasing operation (Native Leasing Services) relied on one or two factors as being controlling factors, and that led to the *Indian Act* tax exemption being both misinterpreted and potentially misused by taxpayers.[22]

What Types of Taxes may Canadians be Required to Pay?

Canadians may be required to pay a number of taxes, including property tax, income tax, and sales tax (Palacios and Veldhuis 2012). Tax laws in Canada apply to Aboriginal peoples, unless exempted (*Nowegijick* 1983: 36). Some First Nation communities have exercised their due authority and have implemented property tax and sales tax in their jurisdictions.

Property tax is a tax on land and structures attached to land. On non-First Nation property, this tax is levied by the municipal government under authority delegated to it by the provincial government. The tax provides a revenue source for municipal governments to provide services such as drinking water, roadways, and police and fire services. Generally, the value of the land and its attachments are used to determine an assessed value, which is thus applied to the tax rate to determine the amount of property taxes owing by the property owner. Certain properties may be exempt from property tax, such as publicly owned properties (schools, hospitals) or property used for religious purposes (churches, mosques). Property used for commercial purposes is often subject to an additional tax referred to as "business occupancy tax."

> **Property tax** is tax on land and structures attached to land.

First Nation property may be subject to property tax bylaws passed by band councils under the authority of either s. 83 of the *Indian Act* or the 2005 *First Nations Fiscal and Statistical Management Act*. Most First Nation property-tax bylaws exempt property occupied by band members from such property tax.

Income tax is a direct tax on the income of individuals and businesses. It is the chief source of revenue for the federal and provincial governments. The approach to income tax as a source of revenue earning is fundamental to political and economic ideologies and, as such, is often hotly debated among political parties. Both the federal and the provincial governments exercise their authority to collect income taxes (Rieksts 2010).

Most provinces initially exercised only their authority to impose income taxes on businesses. As the requirement for funds to provide the services required by residents grew, provinces began enacting personal income tax. The federal government, on the other hand, enacted legislation imposing personal and corporate income tax in 1917, known as the *Income War Tax Act*. This act was originally intended to assist with the costs of Canada participating in the First World War. The federal government collects income tax owing under the *Income Tax Act*, and has tax-collection agreements with most of the provinces to collect, on behalf of the provinces, all of the income taxes owing under provincial acts (Rieksts 2010).

Section 81 of the *Income Tax Act* directs that an amount declared to be exempt by another federal enactment is not to be included in the taxpayer's income. It reads as follows:

Amounts not included in income

81. (1) There shall not be included in computing the income of a taxpayer for a taxation year,

(a) an amount that is declared to be exempt from income tax by any other enactment of Parliament, other than an amount received or receivable by an individual that is exempt by virtue of a provision contained in a tax convention or agreement with another country that has the force of law in Canada. (*Income Tax Act* 1985)

A number of First Nations have entered, with the Government of Canada, into what is known as the First Nations Personal Income Tax Administration Agreements.[23] These agreements allow self-governing First Nation communities to exercise their power of direct taxation, to impose taxes on the income of individuals, and to enter into tax-collection agreements with Canada to permit Canada to collect taxes payable under the First Nation's tax act, and pay these taxes in accordance with the term of the tax-administration agreement to the applicable First Nation. However, "There is no national framework legislation allowing First Nations to opt into collecting income tax." It is relevant to note that the section 87 tax exemption in the *Indian Act* will not apply to the First Nations that have concluded self-government agreements (Graham and Bruhn 2009: 6).

> **Income tax** is tax on the income of individuals and businesses.
>
> **Sales tax** is a tax on the purchase of goods or services at the point of sale.

Sales Tax/Goods and Services Tax (GST)

The details of the Canadian goods-and-services sales tax (GST) are found under the provisions of the *Excise Tax Act*. It is important to note that the expression "Her Majesty in right of a province" includes the governments of Yukon, the Northwest Territories, and Nunavut, and the expression "legislature of any province" includes the council of the Northwest Territories and the legislative assembly of Yukon or Nunavut (*Excise Tax Act* 1985: s. 2[2]). The tax collected under the provisions of the *Excise Tax Act* is an example of an indirect tax.[24] In particular, under s. 165, the recipient of a taxable supply is responsible to pay the GST. Section 165 states:

165. (1) Subject to this Part, every recipient of a taxable supply made in Canada shall pay to Her Majesty in right of Canada tax in respect of the supply calculated at the rate of 5% on the value of the consideration for the supply.

(2) Subject to this Part, every recipient of a taxable supply made in a participating province shall pay to Her Majesty in right of Canada, in addition to the tax imposed by subsection (1), tax in respect of the supply calculated at the tax rate for that province on the value of the consideration for the supply. (*Excise Tax Act* 1985)

A recipient is specifically defined under s. 123(1) of the *Excise Tax Act* (1985), but generally includes a person liable to pay for the delivery or use of property or the supply of a service.[25]

First Nations have been able to pass bylaws imposing sales tax on taxable goods and services since 1997. The 2003 *First Nations Goods and Services Tax Act* (FNGST 2003) enables First Nations to impose, under the *Indian Act*, a consumption tax under sharing agreements, and the tax applies to both band members and non-Aboriginal consumers (*FNGST* 2003: 5-6).

> **Excise tax** is an indirect tax imposed on the sale of a particular product.
>
> **Liable** means legal responsibility to honour and act in accordance with relevant laws or regulations.

Where are the Tax Exemption(s)?

The tax exemptions most often used by Aboriginal peoples are found in s. 87 and 90 of the *Indian Act*. S. 87 provides that:

> 87. (1) Notwithstanding any other *Act* of Parliament or any *Act* of the legislature of a province, but subject to section 83 and section 5 of the *First Nations Fiscal Management Act*, the following property is exempt from taxation:
>
> (*a*) the interest of an Indian or a band in reserve lands or surrendered lands; and
>
> (*b*) the personal property of an Indian or a band situated on a reserve. (*Indian Act* 1985)

The reference in s. 87(1)(b) is to "personal property" of a single individual or a band; therefore, the wording of the provision indicates the tax exemption was not intended to apply and does not apply to corporations or other business entities.

Section 90 ensures that *certain* items of personal property are protected from taxation or seizure by deeming that the property is situated on the reserve. Section 90 provides as follows:

> 90. (1) For the purposes of sections 87 and 89, personal property that was
>
> (*a*) purchased by Her Majesty with Indian moneys or moneys appropriated by Parliament for the use and benefit of Indians or bands, or
>
> (*b*) given to Indians or to a band under a treaty or agreement between a band and Her Majesty,
>
> *shall be deemed* always to be situated on a reserve. (*Indian Act* 1985; emphasis added.)

To deem means "to hold, consider; adjudge; believe; condemn; determine; treat as if; construe."[26] The location of personal property purchased by the government for the use or benefit of Indians or given to an Indian or band is always determined to be situated on the reserve for taxation-exemption purposes under section 90 of the *Indian Act*.

What is the Purpose of Tax Exemption under the *Indian Act*?

In order to understand the circumstances in which the tax exemptions apply it is helpful to review the purpose of the tax exemptions under the *Indian Act*. Court decisions repeatedly state that the tax-exemption provisions of the *Indian Act* are intended to protect the property of Indians on reserves and to ensure that benefits and value intended for Indians or a band are not reduced by the payment of taxes to another governing body (*Mitchell* 1990). The stated purpose has played a major role in determining when the tax exemptions are available, and is often quoted by the judiciary in decisions rendered by a court.

Court decisions emphasize that the exemption was not intended to provide Aboriginal peoples with an advantage, but "to remedy the economically disadvantaged position of Indians" (*Bastien* 2011: 726), or to ensure "Indians may acquire, hold, and deal with property in the commercial mainstream on different terms than their fellow citizens" (748). Later in the chapter, we will see how the phrase "commercial mainstream" has played a major role in limiting the access of Aboriginal people to the s. 87 tax exemption. Pinder (2000: 1505) suggests that "commercial mainstream" has been equated "to living and working off the reserve" and that evidence showing participation in the commercial mainstream has been identified as a "disconnecting factor." Justice Cromwell cautioned against elevating the "commercial mainstream" consideration to one of determinant weight as it could "significantly undermine the exemption" (*Bastien* 2011: par. 40). He acknowledged that the "*Recalma* line of cases" placed determinant weight on the taxpayer's economic activity being in the commercial mainstream (ibid.).

Who Qualifies to be Registered as an Indian in the *Indian Act*?

Section 35 of the *Constitution Act, 1982*, recognized three Aboriginal groups, namely, Indians, Inuit, and Métis. (Alberta 2011: par. 13) The terms "Aboriginal" and "Indian" are sometimes used interchangeably, though it is important to distinguish between the terms as there are specific rights under the *Indian Act* that are attached to the term "Indian." In order to be entitled to the tax exemption, the individual must meet the definition of "Indian" under the *Indian Act*.[27]

Under section 2(1) of the *Indian Act*, an Indian is defined as "a person who pursuant to this *Act* is registered as an Indian or is entitled to be registered as an Indian." The *Gender Equity in Indian Registration Act* (cf. Guimond 2003; Norris 2003) came into effect on January 31, 2011, and individuals that meet the requirements may register as an Indian. An individual who has been omitted or deleted from the Indian Register, or from a band list, may make an application to the have their name added.[28]

The Métis, discussed in chapter 1, are the descendants of 18th-century unions between European men and Indian women (*Alberta* 2011: par. 5). The *Métis Betterment Act*[29] excluded anyone registered as an Indian, and anyone with the ability to be registered as an Indian, under the *Indian Act* from the definition of Métis.[30] The "Métis communities were not given a collective reservation or land base and they did not enjoy the protections of the *Indian Act* or any equivalent" (par. 7). The

> The **Indian Register** is the official record of the federal government that identifies who is an Indian in Canada. It records a variety of information about individuals, including date of birth, band affiliations, parents, and band number. Individuals on this register are considered "status Indians."
>
> A **band list** is the official record of the federal government that identifies Indians who are recognized as belonging to a particular band. It is a subcomponent of the Indian Register.

definition of who could register as an Indian under the federal *Indian Act* was amended in 1985,[31] reinstating the right to Indian status for many Métis settlement members who had been previously denied status. (par. 124)

To further clarify who qualifies to be registered as an Indian, s. 4(1) of the *Act* makes it clear that the term "Indian" does not include any person commonly referred to as "Inuit." A Supreme Court of Canada decision brought the Inuit within the meaning of Indians under subsections 91(24), thus recognizing a special federal role in relation to the Inuit.

In the western provinces, the Crown entered into treaties with Indian bands, whereby the Indians surrendered their traditional lands and, in return, were granted reserves and other benefits (see chapter 13). These Indians were referred to as "treaty Indians" (*Alberta* 2011: par. 6).

What is Meant by "Band" under the *Indian Act*?

Under section 2(1) of the *Indian Act*, a "band" means a body of Indians:

(*a*) for whose use and benefit in common, lands, the legal title to which is vested in Her Majesty, have been set apart before, on or after September 4, 1951,

(*b*) for whose use and benefit in common, moneys are held by Her Majesty, or

(*c*) declared by the Governor in Council to be a band for the purposes of this *Act*.

The courts have been engaged in the interpretation of the term "Aboriginal rights" as it is expressed in section 35 of the *Constitution Act, 1982*. It is important to note that Indigenous peoples have argued that the concept of bands as identified under the provisions of the *Indian Act* was created by the *Act*, and questions are raised by Aboriginals as to whether or not "bands are capable of exercising the Aboriginal rights" as expressed under s. 35. As this argument progresses, and as self-government advances the creation of Aboriginal communities, the designation of member rights will be determined by the Aboriginal peoples themselves, and thus the *Indian Act* definitions will not be significant. This will influence the interpretation of s. 87 and 90 of the *Act*.

What is Meant By "Reserve" and "Designated Lands" under the *Indian Act*?

Reserve is defined in the *Indian Act* as "a tract of land, the legal title to which is vested in Her Majesty, that has been set apart by Her Majesty for the use and benefit of a band," and may include designated lands. Reserves were developed as a result of treaties between the federal government and Canadian Indigenous peoples, whereby some of the those peoples agreed to settle "their lands in exchange for reservations of land and other promises" (*Manitoba* 2013: par. 3). Section 2(1) of the *Indian Act* defines designated lands "as a tract of land or any interest therein the legal title to which remains vested in Her Majesty and in which the band for whose use and benefit it was set apart as a reserve has, otherwise than absolutely, released or surrendered its rights or interests, whether before or after the coming into force of this definition." Land is discussed in detail in chapter 2.

Some authors have expressed the opinion that "under Aboriginal law, the treaties could not have amounted to a transfer of land to the Crown but instead involved a sharing of it." The Indigenous peoples who were living in the western territories, particularly the Red River settlement (now Winnipeg), included the population now known as Métis (*Manitoba* 2013: par. 21, 23, 25). The Canadian government entered into negotiations with representatives of the Métis-led provisional government of the territory and the result was the *Manitoba Act*, 1870, S.C. 1870, chapter 3, a constitutional document, which made Manitoba a province of Canada (*Manitoba* 2013: par. 4, 26, 28). It is important to note that there were no reserves set aside for either Inuit or Métis peoples, and, as such, this greatly affected the access of the Inuit and Métis population to the general exemption identified in s. 87 of the *Indian Act* (Hanselmann 2003).

The Supreme Court of Canada, in *Ross River Dena Council Band v. Canada* (2002), confirmed that "there must be an intention to create a reserve by a person given the authority to bind the Crown" for the establishment of a reserve under the *Indian Act* (*MacKay* 2007: par. 16).

Many reserves were located in more rural areas and, as such, the populations were dependent on fishing, hunting, trapping, and gathering activities to sustain their communities. Some reserves have become more urban in nature as a result of the growth of a nearby urban centre. Examples include the Musqueam Reserve in Vancouver; the Tsuu T'ina Reserve in Calgary; the Opaskwayak Cree Nation in The Pas, Manitoba; the Wendake Reserve in Québec City; and the Membertou Reserve in Sydney, Nova Scotia (cf. Peters 2007; Loxley and Wien 2003). The migration of Indigenous Canadians from reserves to urban centers has been linked to the increased opportunities for Aboriginal peoples to obtain employment, education, and economic independence in urban locations, and to the poverty that exists on reserves (Newhouse and Peters 2003). The courts have interpreted evidence of living and working in an urban center as the Aboriginal individual choosing to enter the "commercial mainstream" (see *Kelly* 2009: par. 54).[32]

There is much debate surrounding Aboriginal title to land and the effect of section 35(1) of the *Constitution Act, 1982*. Kent McNeil (1999: 776-800) argues that, in *Delgamuukw v. British Columbia*, the Supreme Court of Canada unfairly placed the onus of providing evidence of occupation on Aboriginal peoples. He argues that when European settlers arrived in what is now known as Canada, Aboriginal peoples were occupying the lands, and that unless their occupation was extinguished or surrendered, the Aboriginal peoples have rights to the lands they exclusively occupied at the time of the Crown's assertion of sovereignty (ibid.). Currently, the reserves and designated lands definitions under the *Indian Act* provide limitations on the access to tax exemption; however, s. 35(1) of the *Constitution Act, 1982*, may allow Aboriginal peoples to challenge the nexus with the *Indian Act* reserves as a requirement of the s. 87 tax exemption.

Court decisions have attempted to establish mechanisms to identify Aboriginal interest in lands. The Supreme Court has determined that the "interest (title or some other interest) must be distinctly Aboriginal: it must be a communal Aboriginal interest in the land that is integral to the nature of the Métis distinctive community and their relationship to the land: see *R. v. Powley*, 2003 SCC 43, [2003] 2 S.C.R. 207, at par. 37" (*Manitoba* 2013: par. 53).

What is Personal Property Under S. 87 of the *Indian Act*?

In order to determine what constitutes personal property under s. 87 of the *Indian Act*, it is helpful to review the court decisions that have identified what is personal property.

Personal property has been determined to include:

- Employment income, which is included within the meaning of personal property under s. 87(1)(*b*) of the *Indian Act* (*Nowegijick*).

- Unemployment insurance payments, which are included within the meaning of personal property (*Williams*).

- Business income, as it is intangible property, and, as such, it has been determined to be the personal property of an *Indian* (*Dickie*).

- Investment income earned from a term deposit, as it is personal property within the meaning of s. 87 of the *Indian Act* (*Bastien*).

What Factors Determine the Site of Personal Property?

Personal Property Located on a Reserve

The location of a property on a reserve is relevant when considering whether or not it is eligible for the s. 87 tax exemption. The exemption from taxation under s. 87 and 89 of the *Indian Act* will always apply to property that is physically situated on a reserve. Court decisions have confirmed that the words "situated on a reserve" should be interpreted consistently throughout the act to mean "within the boundaries of the reserve" (*Union* 1998: par. 13; *Lewis* 1996: 955-59). As more claims advance under s. 35, and as Aboriginal peoples move toward self-government, the importance of this connecting factor will be re-evaluated.

Personal Property Purchased by the Crown

Section 90 of the *Indian Act* provides that:

for the purposes of sections 87 and 89, personal property that was (a) purchased by Her Majesty with Indian moneys or moneys appropriated by Parliament for the use and benefit of Indians or bands, or (b) given to Indians or to a band under a treaty or agreement between a band and Her Majesty, shall be deemed always to be situated on a reserve.

This is the only provision of the *Indian Act* that indicates how the location of property is to be determined. Under s. 90, certain property is deemed to be situated on a reserve even though it may in fact be physically located elsewhere. The deeming provision applies, speaking generally, to personal property purchased for the use and benefit of Indians (with Indian funds or funds appropriated by Parliament therefor) and to personal property given to Indians under a treaty or agreement with the Crown.

The *Williams* Test

In *Williams v. Canada*, the Supreme Court of Canada established a series of connecting factors that could be used to determine the jurisdictional site (known as *situs*) of personal property for the purpose of the s. 87 exemption. The factors identified by the court included, but were not limited to,

- the location of the debtor,

- the location of the creditor,

- the location where the payment is made,

- the location of the employment which created the qualification for the receipt of income, and

- the location where the payment will be used.

> *Situs* refers to the location or site a property is considered as being for purposes of legal jurisdiction or taxation.

To begin the process, the court directed that it was necessary to identify the connecting factors that are relevant to a particular taxpayer's situation. Once the connecting factors are identified, a determination of what weight they should be given must be made. The weight assigned is determined by using three considerations: (1) the purpose of the exemption under the *Indian Act*, (2) the type of property in question, and (3) the nature of the taxation of that property (*Williams* 1992: 892). It is at this stage that the particular judge assigns the weight they attribute to a particular factor by "answering the question whether to tax that form of property in that manner would amount to the erosion of the entitlement of the Indian *qua* Indian on a reserve" (893). The phrase "erosion of the entitlement of the Indian *qua* Indian on a reserve" is not found in the tax-exemption provisions of the *Indian Act*.

> *Qua* means "in the capacity of."

Some have argued that the *Williams* test has provided little if any certainty to assist the taxpayer with tax planning (Maclagan 2000: 1511). Each case turns on its own facts and each situation is decided by the judge, who exercises discretion in identifying the connecting factors and assigning the weight to the factors, which results in variation in the case results, and thus numerous cases have to proceed to the courts for resolution.

Taxpayer Not Required to Live on Reserve Where Personal Property is Located

The court decisions are explicit in that the Indian taxpayer does not have to reside on the reserve where the property is located to be eligible for the tax exemption.[33] The legislation does not impose a requirement that the Indian claiming the exemption occupy the reserve where the property is situated (*Dubé* 2011: par. 17). The Supreme Court, in *Dubé v. Canada*, determined that "the expression 'situated on *a* reserve' means any reserve, not just a reserve where the Indian taxpayer resides or to which community he or she belongs" (par. 18). Residence on the reserve is not a connecting factor required under s. 87; however, a review of the cases reveals that numerous times the court has considered not only the taxpayer's residency on the reserve (*Verreault* 2012: par. 30), but has also examined the frequency and purpose of taxpayer's visits to a reserve when determining whether the tax exemption applies (*Davad* 2011: par. 31).

In *Dugan v. The Queen*, the court stated that "when the Indian lives off-reserve as in the case of Mr. Dugan who works entirely off-reserve in a mainstream off-reserve commercial operation, it is difficult to imagine the evidence that might be required to establish that the income is entitled to protection from diminution by taxation" (*Dugan* 2011: par. 107). The *Dugan* appeal was heard with five other appeals deemed similar in nature. One of the appeals was that of a man named Sault. Sault lived on a reserve and worked off-reserve, in a mainstream, off-reserve commercial operation, which did nothing to benefit life on the reserve (par. 108). The tax court determined that living on the reserve was of little weight in assessing the tax-exemption eligibility. The evidence that the income was earned from an off-reserve commercial operation was assigned enough weight to make it a disconnecting factor.

A Nexus Between Reserve and Work

The courts have also examined evidence tendered by taxpayers to determine if there are any benefits "accruing to a reserve from the employment relationship," if there was any working time on the reserve, the nature and circumstances of the work (*Googoo* 2008: par. 102, 106, 113-17), and if the taxation of the employment income would result in the erosion of the entitlement to property held as Indians *qua* (i.e., in the capacity of) Indians on a reserve (*Nahwegahbow* 2011: par. 29). In *Vincent v. The Queen*, the court held that the evidence did not establish a sufficient connection between Ms. Vincent's work (provide services at an off-reserve location to women living off-reserve) and a reserve to render her income tax exempt, even though "she and her employer were located on reserves."

In *McKay v. The Queen*, the Tax Court determined that the tax exemption applied to a taxpayer who did not live on a reserve, but had connections with a reserve and visited band members regularly for her work, which was integral to the land-claims process. The court determined the monies she earned were intimately connected with a reserve and that her work was not connected to the commercial mainstream. In *Davad v. The Queen*, the Tax Court made it known that visits to a reserve where the taxpayer was born or raised "to take part in family activities, renew acquaintances and re-immerse themselves in the communities that form part of their heritage" (*Davad* 2011: par. 31) will be assigned little weight as a connecting factor for the purpose of s. 87 tax exemption.

In many cases, the court was required to apply the factors identified in *Williams* to employment situations involving organizations located on a reserve with employees that performed their work off-reserve. In such cases, the court examined the employment relationship between the taxpayer and the stated employer. In cases where the employer's activities were more like an employment agency, with little actual management or direction of the employees on a daily basis (*Davad* 2011; Baptiste 2011[34]) or the employer appeared to have served solely as the vehicle through which payment for the employee's services was made, little weight was assigned to the fact that the employer was located on a reserve (*Verreault*). The court recognizes the need to provide certainty with respect to the s. 87 tax exemption for those employed in such agencies (*Hester* 2010: par. 31).

Business Income

The relevant factors to consider when determining whether business income is connected to a reserve were identified in *Southwind v. Canada*. The federal court identified the following as being some of the relevant factors:

- the type of business and the nature of the work;
- the location of the business activities;
- the location of the customers of the business;
- the place where payment was made;
- the residence of the business owner;
- the place where decisions affecting the business are made;
- the location of a fixed place of business and the place where the books for the business are kept; and
- the degree to which the business is in the commercial mainstream (*Southwind* 1998: par. 12)

Evidence in *Pelletier v. The Queen* revealed that the logging activities in question in the case occurred off-reserve, the business books were kept and the office work occurred on-reserve, the customers were located off-reserve, and the business decisions were made on- and off-reserve (*Pelletier* 2009: par.10-14). The Tax Court applied the relevant factors identified in *Southwind* to the facts in *Pelletier*, and determined that the income did not qualify as property situated on a reserve under the provisions of s. 87 of the *Indian Act.* The payment of income tax would not erode property held by Pelletier *qua* Indian, and the payment of income tax would place Pelletier on the same basis as those he competed with in the commercial mainstream. *Indian Act* tax exemption is not intended to give Aboriginal peoples an advantage over non-Aboriginals.

In *Ballantyne v. The Queen*, an Aboriginal taxpayer was engaged in fishing. The court found that the catching of the fish took place off-reserve, the customer did not reside on a reserve, the business decisions were made on and off the reserve, the decisions as to the placement of the fish nets was made off the reserve, the taxpayer resided on the reserve, and the fixed place of the business was on the reserve. The court determined the taxpayer earned his income in the commercial mainstream and that the taxpayer's income did not qualify for the exemption pursuant to s. 87 (*Ballantyne* 2009: par. 25, 50-51, 53-55, 77).

In *Kelly v. The Queen*, the court found that money earned by providing services to the reserve or individuals on the reserve still showed no nexus between said business income and reserve lands. The Court explained that when the payment was made by the reserve for the services provided by the Aboriginal taxpayer, the money left the reserve and entered the economy off the reserve, thereby ceasing "to have anything to do with a reserve" (*Kelly* 2009: par. 57). The money entering the commercial mainstream was a disconnecting factor that was worthy of recognition.

> **Nexus** means "connection" or "link."

The Federal Court of Appeal, in *Amos v. Canada*, permitted tax exemption for employment income earned from a pulp mill situated off-reserve, where it was determined that "the reserve lands were an integral component" of the pulp-mill operations. In *Amos*, the pulp-mill company leased reserve lands from the band on the condition that members of the band were to be employed in the mill operations. The court held that employment was directly related to the band members' entitlement to the reserve land (Amos 1999).

The judge in *Dale v. The Queen* held that the Indian taxpayer, who was an Aboriginal cultural adviser and who was described as being "clearly an honourable person," had found employment in the commercial mainstream so as to be able to "stand on her own two feet" and was not entitled to the tax exemption. The judge found that "to exempt her income from taxation would afford her an advantage over others working in the commercial mainstream, be they Indian or not" (*Dale* 2011: par. 14-15).

In *Bastien Estate v. Canada*, the Supreme Court of Canada attempted to remove the confusion surrounding the importance of the "commercial mainstream" factor, and clarified that, "even if an Indian acquired an asset through a purely commercial business agreement with a private concern, the exemption would nonetheless apply if the asset were situated on a reserve" (*Bastien* 2011: 740).

In *The Estate of Charles Pilfold v. The Queen*, the court acknowledged that courts "have had to readjust their analysis in these types of cases since *Bastien* and *Dubé*, and a case such as this is an important step in the evolution of the connecting factors test" (*Pilfold* 2013: par. 74). The Tax Court recognized that, since *Bastien*, there was a "belief the Supreme Court of Canada had broadened the parameters, de-emphasizing commercial mainstream, and leading to greater weight to be given to situs of head office" (ibid.). Taxpayers had relied on this belief and arranged their business activities to ensure they were in compliance with the s. 87 tax exemption by locating their head office on a reserve. The court determined that even though the head office of the business was located on the reserve, there was not a sufficient nexus with the reserve, and the exemption was not allowed.

Investment Income

In *Stigen v. Her Majesty the Queen*, the court provided a listing of the factors that were identified as being relevant when the *situs* of passive investment income for tax-exemption eligibility were being considered (*Stigen* 2008: par. 17). The listing included the following factors:

- the residence of the taxpayer;
- the origin or location of the capital invested;
- the location of the bank branch where the investment activities occurred;
- the location where the interest income is used;
- the location of the investment instruments;
- the location where the interest payment is made;
- the nature of the investment;
- the residence of the issuer;
- the location of the issuer's property in the event of default that could be subject to potential seizure; and
- the location of the issuer's income generating activity from which the interest derives.

The Supreme Court of Canada applied these connecting factors in *Bastien* and determined that the interest income earned on term deposits was clearly on the reserve where all the connecting factors—the location of the debtor, the location where payment was made, the residence of the payee,

> A **debtor** is a person or organization that owes money.
>
> A **payee** is a person or organization receiving a payment.

the location of the source of the capital, and the place where the contract was entered—were all on the reserve (*Bastien* 2011 par. 44-47, 60-62).

The court found that there was not a sufficient nexus in *Stigen* to enable the income to be tax-exempt, because the source of the investment was earned off the reserve, the taxpayer's residence was off-reserve, the dealings with the financial institution were primarily off-reserve, the money could not be linked to on-reserve investments, the financial corporate office was off-reserve, and the financial institution had off-reserve investments (*Stigen* 2008: par. 34-35).

The judge in *Marcinyshyn v. The Queen* (2011) confirmed that the "connecting factors" test identified in the *Williams* case remains important and will continue to play a role in the determination of whether the tax exemption is available.

What is the Relevance of the Rights of an "Indian *qua* Indian" in Mitchell?

Justice Cromwell of the Supreme Court of Canada made it clear in *Bastien* that "there is no requirement that the personal property be integral to the life of the reserve, or that it must, in order to be exempted from taxation, benefit what the court takes to be the traditional Indian way of life" (*Bastien* 2011: 729). He acknowledged that the relationship between the property and life on the reserve may in some cases be a connecting factor; however, the availability of the exemption does not depend on whether the property is integral to the life of the reserve or to the preservation of the traditional Indian way of life. Justice Cromwell indicated that *Mitchell* and *Williams* did not mandate that a court must perform an assessment of what does or does not constitute an "Indian way of life on a reserve" (729).

What is the Relevance of the "Commercial Mainstream"?

In cases involving business activities and access to the s. 87 *Indian Act* tax exemption, the court considers whether the business operated by an Indian is engaged in the "commercial mainstream." In *Robinson*, the court felt that the taxpayers employed by Native Leasing Services (NLS) provided their services to not-for-profit organizations established to assist Aboriginal peoples and as such the "commercial mainstream" factor was not relevant. Judge Rowe took notice of the fact that the funding for the organizations came from government, and that it was unlikely that the commercial mainstream would invest in providing competing services (*Robinson* 2010: par. 105).

In *Dickie v. The Queen*, a sole proprietor, who was a status Indian, operated his business from a location on an Indian reserve. He was a member of and resided on the same reserve. The majority of the management work was done on the reserve, the work (timber clearing) was done off the reserve, and the customers did not reside on the reserve. The court determined that the business income had a strong connection to the reserve and was thus property situated on a reserve, and thereby eligible for the s. 87 exemption under the *Indian Act*. The Court provided guidance for future business decisions by indicating that:

> it must be emphasized that just because a finding that a property is situated on a reserve may lead to a competitive advantage given an Indian over a non-Indian does not give reason to negate the finding it is situated on a reserve. Any advantage such finding may render is in my view the exact advantage that was contemplated by section 87 of the *Act*. (*Dickie* 2012: par. 68)

The wording of the *Indian Act* does not render a business involved in the commercial mainstream ineligible for the s. 87 tax exemption.

The taxpayers involved in the case of *McDonald v. The Queen* (2011) fished in the Newfoundland commercial fishery. After considering the evidence, the judge held that their fishing income was exempt from taxation because their work was "intimately connected" to the reserve. In the case, the evidence established that the Indian taxpayers lived on the reserve, they fished on fishing vessels owned by the band and, pursuant to licences owned by the band, they performed some of their work on the reserve, and they were paid on the reserve by a corporation controlled by the band. The nexus to the reserve was given more importance than the participation in the commercial fishery.

Section 87 of the *Indian Act* and Income Tax

The CRA has developed a form to assist with the determination of whether the employment income of an Aboriginal individual is exempt from taxation under s. 87.[35] The form collects the information identified in *Williams*. It requires the individual to provide the following information: name, address, whether the address is located on a reserve, whether the individual is registered or is entitled to be registered as an Indian under the *Indian Act*, and the proportion of the employment duties that are performed on the reserve.

Residence on a reserve is a factor to be considered when determining whether the exemption applies to employment income. A connection or nexus between the employment and a specific reserve seems to be important to ensure the employment income is exempt. In an appeal involving five taxpayers, the Tax Court of Canada referred to the case of *Shilling v. M.N.R* (*Shilling* 2001), and indicated that "where the "property" in question is employment income, the relevant connecting factors are: "the location or residence of the employer; the nature, location and surrounding circumstances of the work performed by the employee, including the nature of any benefit that accrued to the reserve from it; and the residence of the employee" (*McIvor* 2009: 16). In each of the appeals, the court was not persuaded that there was a sufficient connection between the "employment income and a reserve to render her employment income tax exempt" (par. 92). The decision deliberated that one individual contributed to the residential-school-survivor program, another worked as a problem-gambling coordinator focused on Indians and other Aboriginal people with gambling problems, another's duties required her to promote Aboriginal artists and music, while another worked to improve the lot of at-risk Aboriginal children; however, there was not a sufficient connection between the employment income and a reserve to render the employment income tax exempt (par. 89-108). Even though the work an individual performs contributes "to life on certain reserves," if there is "no evidence presented to show that the services provided are integral to the life of any reserve" or "connected to a particular reserve," the tax exemption does not apply (*Roe* 2008: par. 134-36).

Section 87 of the *Indian Act* and GST

The cases have held that "individuals who were Indians for the purposes of the *Indian Act* and who operated stores on a reserve were obligated to collect GST from their customers who were not Indians, as defined for the purposes of the *Indian Act*" (*Obonsawin* 2010: par. 37). Furthermore, the court has confirmed that the collection of GST from the non-Indian customers of an Indian owned business "does not thwart the purpose of s. 87 of the *Indian Act*" (par. 49).

In *Union of New Brunswick Indians v. New Brunswick (Minister of Finance)* (1998), the question was whether Indians living in New Brunswick were exempt from sales tax on purchases of goods made off-reserve to be used on-reserve. A majority of the Supreme Court applied the rule that tax is paid at the point of sale and concluded that the tax was not in respect of property situated on a reserve. Essentially the acceptance that this is merely a point of sale tax decision and has no relation to a tax exemption results in on-reserve sales to Indians living off-reserve being exempt from sales tax.

In *Tseshaht Indian Band* v. *British Columbia*, the British Columbia Court of Appeal considered the application of provincial taxes imposed on tobacco and gasoline. The Tseshaht Band operated a store on the reserve that served both Indian and non-Indian customers. At the time of purchase, the band had to pay to the seller an amount equal to the amount of tax that would be collected from consumers when tobacco and gasoline were sold at the band store. The B.C. Court of Appeal held that the requirement of the band to pay the monies that would be collected from customers did not result in the band paying a tax for the purposes of s. 87 of the *Indian Act* (*Obonsawin* 2010: par. 59).

The applicants in *Diome v. The Queen* "argued that their ancestral rights, which are protected by the Canadian and Quebec charters of rights, exempted them from liability under the *Quebec Fuel Tax Act*, Part IX of the *ETA* and the *Quebec Retail Sales Tax Act*." (*Diome* 2012: par. 14). The Supreme Court referred to the case of *Tseshaht* and confirmed that the collection and remittance of tax does not constitute the payment of tax, and, further, that:

> [S]ection 87 of the *Indian Act* does not release individuals with
> Indian status from the obligation to collect and remit the GST when
> they are selling goods in the commercial mainstream to non-Indian
> consumers. If they did supply goods and services to individuals with
> Indian status and collect tax from them, these same individuals could be
> entitled to claim a refund. (*Diome* 2012: par. 22)

Bands and governing bodies may, under the aforementioned *First Nations Goods and Services Tax Act*, enact sales tax with respect to taxable supply of goods or services made on the lands of the First Nation, or on tangible personal property brought onto the lands of the First Nation, or an imported taxable supply made on the land of the First Nation (*FNG-STA* 2003: s. 4[1]).[36] Section 3(1) of the *FNGSTA* (2003) makes it clear that the sales tax that is to be paid under a First Nation law applies despite the exemption under s. 87 of the *Indian Act* or any other exemption under any other *Act* of Parliament. It is relevant to note that the *FNGSTA* has the same basic operating rules as the GST/HST; that the same goods and services taxable under the GST/HST are taxable under the *FNGSTA*.[37] To discover which First Nations have implemented the First Nations Tax (FNT)[38] or the *FNGSTA*,[39] visit the CRA website (http://cra-arc.gc.ca/E/pub/tg/rc4365/rc4365-e.html).

Summary

A tax policy is intended to provide a governing body with the funds necessary to support the expenditures required to provide services to the citizens of a community while balancing economic activity with social concerns. As Aboriginal peoples move from reserves to urban centres, and become more involved in what is viewed as "commercial mainstream" occupations, fewer will qualify for the s. 87 tax exemption under the *Indian Act*. First Nations peoples are exercising their right to self-government and are developing tax policies, similar to non-Aboriginal communities, that enhance the right to self-government. The tax policies developed by federal, provincial, municipal, and First Nation governing bodies must address the short- and long-term changes in the demographics of Aboriginal peoples, as ultimately the tax burden will be borne by both Aboriginal and non-Aboriginal Canadians. Tax policies must incorporate plans for the role each governing body will play. The tax-exemption rights under the *Indian Act* do not and will not sufficiently address the needs of Aboriginal and non-Aboriginal communities in Canada.

Key Points:

- There are several different types of tax in Canada—income tax, property tax, and sales tax—and they are made and implemented at different governmental levels (municipal, provincial, and federal).
- Governments make tax laws, the Canada Revenue Agency enforces them, and courts interpret them.
- Tax exemptions may exist for First Nation individuals, but they are complicated and dependent on a number of factors.
- Location is an important factor in determining tax exemptions.
- Relationship to or entry into the "commercial mainstream" is also an important factor when determining tax exemptions, though the concept is not well defined.

Questions for Review:

1. Who has the authority to make tax laws, and how are they tested, interpreted, and enforced?
2. What are some of the different types of tax in Canada?
3. What is a tax exemption? What is its purpose? By what legislation might Aboriginal people be eligible for exemptions?
4. What types of factors might be considered when determining whether a tax exemption applies?
5. What is the definition of "commercial mainstream" and why is that relevant?

Suggested Assignments:

1. Consider the popular notion that "Indians don't pay taxes." Discuss how the information in this chapter challenges that myth.

2. Compare the idea of tax in Canada to traditional Aboriginal concepts of contributing whatever you can back to the community (such as potlatch, discussed in chapter 1). Are there similarities? How are they different?

3. Discuss the potential value of community-owned corporations as a revenue stream for First Nation governments who do not collect taxes from their citizenship.

4. Research examples of communities that have instituted First Nation tax laws and collect taxes in their communities. Compare and contrast these examples.

Notes

1. Gerson (2012).

2. "The Tax Court of Canada was formed by an Act of Parliament, the *Tax Court of Canada Act*, R.S.C. 1985, c. T-2. The Tax Court came into existence in 1983" (*Johnston* 2010: par. 7).

3. Rowe continued by suggesting, "The exemption could be linked to the particular percentage of the total clients/patients who were status Indians connected with a reserve. This would require the creation and implementation of an overall policy establishing guidelines for eligibility and sophisticated software could be utilized to record the origin of recipients of services, their circumstances, links to a reserve and to track the progress of those individuals should they choose to return to their own reserve following treatment or other improvement in their personal circumstances. In that way, the benefit flowing to a reserve would move from the category of intangible to that of tangible" (*Robinson* 2010: par. 107).

4. *Property Taxation By-Law Policy* First Nations Tax Commission *http://fntc. ca/proposed-property-taxation-by-law-policy/*. See also note 40.

5. *Income Tax Act* (1985), s. 151. The section indicates that every person required to file a return of income shall in the return estimate the amount of tax payable.

6. *Income Tax Act* (1985), s. 161. The taxpayer pays interest on the excess amount—the difference between the tax payable calculated and the amount the taxpayer has submitted to the CRA.

7. *Income Tax Act* (1985), s. 162. This section indicates that every person required to file a return and does not file a return or files it late or files in an inappropriate format is liable to a penalty.

8. *Income Tax Act* (1985), s. 152(1). The section indicates that the Minister shall, with all due dispatch, examine a taxpayer's return of income for a taxation year, assess the tax for the year, the interest and penalties, if any, payable and determine the amount of the refund or the amount of tax to be paid.

9. *Income Tax Act* (1985), ss. 162-163 and ss. 238-239.

10. *First Nations Goods and Services Tax Act*, S.C. 2003, c.15, s. 4(1). A specified governing body identified in the administration agreement the band entered into with the Federal Minister of Finance is authorized to enact tax laws.

11. *The New Brunswick Revenue Administration Act*, S.N.B. 1983, c.R-10.22, s. 11.1.

12. Nova Scotia Municipal Government Act, S.N.S. 1998, chapter 18, section 73.

13. For more information on direct and indirect taxation see Dahlby (2001), Saez (2004), and Martinez-Vazquez, Vulovic, and Liu (2009).

14. See also *Pigeon* (2010: par. 5): "I recognize that this act of law was not well thought out and still, to my knowledge, the issue of taxation has never been discussed with my leadership, and it abrogates and derogates my treaty rights as stated in section 25 of the Canadian Constitution."

15. See Wilkins (2011) for a discussion of the provincial capacity to restrict Aboriginal or treaty rights under s. 35 of the *Constitution Act, 1982.*

16. See *Tax Court of Canada Act* (1985: s. 12[1]): "The Court has exclusive original jurisdiction to hear and determine references and appeals to the Court on matters arising under the *Air Travellers Security Charge Act*, the Canada Pension Plan, the *Cultural Property Export and Import Act*, Part V.1 of the *Customs Act*, the *Employment Insurance Act*, the *Excise Act*, 2001, Part IX of the *Excise Tax Act*, the *Income Tax Act*, the *Old Age Security Act*, the *Petroleum and Gas Revenue Tax Act* and the *Softwood Lumber Products Export Charge Act*, 2006 when references or appeals to the Court are provided for in those Acts."

17. See *Tax Court of Canada Act* (1985: s. 171[1]), which reads:

The Tax Court of Canada may dispose of an appeal by

(a) dismissing it; or

(b) allowing it and

(i) vacating the assessment,

(ii) varying the assessment, or

(iii) referring the assessment back to the Minister for reconsideration and reassessment.

18. See *Lafontaine* (2010), *Johnston* (2010), and *Pigeon* (2010: par. 5).

19. The court continued to explain that it has "the exclusive jurisdiction to hear appeals from assessments (or reassessments) arising under the *Income Tax Act*, it would appear that the Federal Court has the jurisdiction to deal with determinations of questions of law or declarations related to whether an individual has been denied his or her exemption as provided by section 87 of the *Indian Act*. As a remedy of last resort, judicial review by the Federal Court of a decision by the Minister to reassess an individual pursuant to subsection 152(4) of the *Income Tax Act* based on a determination that the exemption under section 87 of the *Indian Act* does not apply, may also be available" (*Johnston* 2009: par. 56).

And the court noted that: "It must also be remembered that the *Indian Act* is not one of the statutes in relation to which jurisdiction has been granted to this Court pursuant to s. 12 of the *Tax Court of Canada Act* (1985). The jurisdiction of this Court to deal with s. 87 of the *Indian Act* arguably arises because paragraph 81(1)(*a*) of the *Income Tax Act* provides that income exempted by another *Act* of Parliament is not to be included in income as determined for the purposes of the *Income Tax Act*. Since this Court has jurisdiction to deal with appeals arising under the *Income Tax Act*, the determination of whether the exemption under the *Indian Act* is applicable is relevant to an appeal arising under the *Income Tax Act* from an assessment or reassessment based on a determination that the exemption is not available, as it is necessary to determine whether the income should not be included in determining income for the purposes of the *Income Tax Act* as a result of the provisions of paragraph 81(1)(*a*) of the *Income Tax Act* and section 87 of the *Indian Act*" (*Johnston* 2009: par. 57).

20. For additional information, see *Introduction to Aboriginal Law in Canada* available at www.treaty8.ca/documents/T8_info_Legal_Introduction.pdf.

21. See Hodgson (2012: 2): "Today, there are 190 tax exemptions (or 'tax expenditures' in technical language) at the federal level that are applied to personal income taxes, corporate income taxes, and the GST ... Provincial governments have provided exemptions within their own tax structure, adding to the layers of tax complexity."

22. See *Robinson* (2010: par. 75): "*Obonsawin* located NLS (Native Leasing Services) on Six Nations Reserve so employees could claim a tax exemption pursuant to section 87 of the *Indian Act*. Not that there is anything wrong with that. The contracts between NLS and each Appellant employed in the within appeals were genuine and legal rights and obligations were created."

23. See First Nations Goods and Services Tax Administration Agreements for a listing of some of the First Nations that have signed such agreements as of August 2013 at: http://www.fin.gc.ca/activity/firstnations/aapers_-eng.asp.

24. Subsection 221(1) of the *Excise Tax Act* (1985) provides that:

> Every person who makes a taxable supply shall, as agent of Her Majesty in right of Canada, collect the tax under Division II payable by the recipient in respect of the supply.

25. "Recipient" of a supply of property or a service means:

(*a*) where consideration for the supply is payable under an agreement for the supply, the person who is liable under the agreement to pay that consideration,

(*b*) where paragraph (*a*) does not apply and consideration is payable for the supply, the person who is liable to pay that consideration, and

(*c*) where no consideration is payable for the supply,

(i) in the case of a supply of property by way of sale, the person to whom the property is delivered or made available,

(ii) in the case of a supply of property otherwise than by way of sale, the person to whom possession or use of the property is given or made available, and

(iii) in the case of a supply of a service, the person to whom the service is rendered, and any reference to a person to whom a supply is made shall be read as a reference to the recipient of the supply. *Excise Tax Act* (1985L s. 123[1])

26. Black's Law Dictionary. 5th Edition. 1979. St. Paul, MN: West Publishing.

27. See Reynolds, James I. (2002) 18 B.F.L.R. 37 particularly at pp. 4-5.

28. In particular, see the *Indian Act* (1985: ss. 6-14).

29. *Registered Societies Act.* 1955, c. 202, as referenced in *Alberta v. Cunningham*, [2011] 2 S.C.R. 670, at. 11.

30. *RSA*. 1955, c. 202, as referenced in Alberta v. Cunningham, [2011] 2 S.C.R. 670, at par. 11.

31. *An Act to amend the Indian Act*, S.C. 1985, c. 27 (Bill C-31).

32. Kelly (2009: par. 54) reads: "Mr. Kelly carried on business from his residence in Winnipeg. His residence in Winnipeg was the centre or nucleus of his business operations. From Winnipeg he consulted with the many reserves and Indians who engaged his services to advance the preservation of their traditions. To this extent he carried on his business as any other consultant would: he had an expertise, he found a niche where he could exploit his expertise and offered and provided his services to persons who could make good and valued use of his expertise and he invoiced his clients for services performed. He was carrying on business as any other Canadian in a commercial mainstream."

33. See *Dubé* (2011: par.15), *Nowegijick* (1983: 41), *Lewis* (1996: 958), *Union* (1998: par. 13-14), *McDiarmid* (2006: par. 19), and *Verreault* (2012: par.30).

34. *Baptiste* (2011: par. 3) refers to the fact that the respondent's appeal was related to more than 1,000 other appeals before the Tax Court of Canada involving workers from the same placement agency, Native Leasing Services or its sister company, O.I. Employment Leasing Inc. In most of these cases, it was determined that the taxation of the employment income would not amount to

the erosion of the entitlement of an Indian *qua* Indian to property on a reserve and, as such, there was no justification or legitimate basis for exempting the employment income from taxation.

35. See the form titled "Determination of Exemption of an Indian's Employment Income," used to assist an Aboriginal employee with determining whether his/her income is taxable, at http://www.cra-arc.gc.ca/E/pbg/tf/td1-in/td1in-14e.pdf.

36. See note 23.

37. See First Nations Goods and Services Tax (FNGST), RC4365(E) Rev. 09/13, Canada Revenue Agency, http://www.cra-arc.gc.ca/E/pub/tg/rc4365/rc4365-e.html.

38. See note 4.

39. Canada Revenue Agency-First Nations that have implemented the *FNGST* 2013-03-28.

Yukon—Champagne and Aishihik First Nations,First Nation of Nacho Nyak Dun,Little Salmon/Carmacks First Nation, Selkirk First Nation, Ta'an Kwach'an Council, Teslin Tlingit Council, Tr'ondëk Hwech'in First Nation, Vuntut Gwitchin First Nation, Kluane First Nation, Kwanlin Dun First Nation, Carcross/Tagish First Nation.

Northwest Territories—Tlicho First Nation.

British Columbia—Tsawout First Nation, Akisqnuk First Nation, Lower Kootenay Indian Band, Shuswap First Nation, St. Mary's Indian Band, Tobacco Plains Indian Band, Nisga'a Nation, Tsleil-Waututh Nation (Burrard), Songhees First Nation.

Newfoundland and Labrador—Inuit, within the meaning assigned by the agreement, as defined in the *Labrador Inuit Land Claims Agreement Act*, S.C. 2005, c. 27.

Saskatchewan—Whitecap Dakota First Nation , Nekaneet First Nation.

Manitoba—Buffalo Point First Nation.

References

Alberta v. Cunningham. 2011. 2 S.C.R. 670, SCC 37 (CanLII). http://canlii.ca/t/fmd78.

Amos v. Canada. 1999. F.C.J. No. 873 (CanLII). http://canlii.ca/t/4lst.

An Act to Amend the Indian Act, S.C. 1985, c.27 (Bill C-31).

Ballantyne v. The Queen. 2009. TCC 325 (CanLII). http://canlii.ca/t/2421j.

Baptiste v. The Queen. 2011. TCC 295 (CanLII). http://canlii.ca/t/flvf3.

Bastien Estate v. Canada. 2011. 2 S.C.R. 710, SCC 38 (CanLII), http://canlii.ca/t/fmdps (accessed December 2, 2015).

CRA (Canada Revenue Agency). 2013. First Nations Goods and Services Tax (FNGST), *Canada Revenue Agency*. http://www.cra-arc.gc.ca/E/pub/tg/rc4365/rc4365-e.html.

Canada Trustco Mortgage Co. v. Canada. 2005. 2 S.C.R. 601, SCC 54 (CANLII), http://canlii.ca/t/1ls81.

Canadian Pacific Ltd. v. Matsqui Indian Band. 1995. 1 S.C.R. 3 CanLII 145 (SCC), http://canlii.ca/t/1frm3.

Constitution Act, 1867 (Constitution Acts, 1867 to 1982). 1867. 30 & 31 Vict. c. 3 (U.K.). *Justice Laws Website*. http://laws-lois.justice.gc.ca/eng/const/page-1.html.

Constitution Act, 1982 (Constitution Acts, 1867 to 1982). 1982. Enacted as Schedule B to the Canada Act 1982 (UK), 1982, c.11. *Justice Laws Website*. http://laws-lois.justice.gc.ca/eng/const/page-15.html#h-38.

Dahlby, Bev. 2001. *Restructuring the Canadian Tax System by Changing the Direct/Indirect Tax Mix*. In *Tax Reform in Canada: Our Path to Greater Prosperity*, ed. H. Grubel, 77-108. Vancouver: Fraser Institute.

Dale v. The Queen. 2011. TCC 206 (CanLII). http://canlii.ca/t/fl3h0.

Davad v. The Queen. 2011. TCC 162 (CanLII). http://canlii.ca/t/fkv7g.

Dickie v. The Queen. 2012. TCC 242 (CanLII). http://canlii.ca/t/fs1p1.

Diome v. The Queen. 2012. TCC 9 (CanLII). http://canlii.ca/t/fq6ft

Dubé v. Canada. 2011. 2 SCR 764, 2011, SCC 39 (CANLII). http://canlii.ca/t/fmdpp.

Dugan v. The Queen. 2011. TCC 269 (CanLII). http://canlii.ca/t/fllkb.

Excise Tax Act. 1985. R.S.C. 1985, c. E-15. *Justice Laws Website*. http://laws-lois.justice.gc.ca/eng/acts/e-15/.

First Nations Goods and Services Tax Act. 2003. SC 2003, c 15, s 67, http://canlii.ca/t/52drz.

First Nations Tax Commission. 2014. s.83 Toolkit, Taxpayer Relations Policy. *First Nations Tax Commission*. http://fntc.ca/s-83-toolkit/. (Full policy at http://sp.fng.ca/fngweb/taxpayer_relations_policy_web.pdf.)

First Nations Goods and Services Tax Act. 2003. S.C. 2003, c. 15, s. 67. *Justice Laws Website*. http://laws-lois.justice.gc.ca/eng/acts/F-11.7/FullText.html.

Fiscal Realities. 1997. First Nation Taxation and New Fiscal Relationships. Paper presented to the Indian Taxation Advisory Board, and the Research and Analysis Directorate Policy and Strategic Direction Branch of the Department of Indian Affairs and Northern Development. http://publications.gc.ca/collections/Collection/R32-228-1997E.pdf.

Gardner-O'Toole, E. 1992. *Aboriginal People and Taxation*. Law and Government Division. http://publications.gc.ca/Collection-R/LoPBdP/BP/bp309-e.htm (accessed June 24, 2013).

Gerson, Jen. 2012. Taxes the Key to Healthy Aboriginal Communities, Kamloops Band Chief Says. *National Post*. May 26. http://news.nationalpost.com/

news/canada/taxes-the-key-to-healthy-aboriginal-communities-kamloops-band-chief-says.

Googoo v. The Queen. 2008. TCC 589 (CanLII). http://canlii.ca/t/22dk6.

Graham, J. and J. Bruhn. 2008. In Praise of Taxes and Good Governance in a First Nation Context. Ottawa: Institute on Governance. http://iog.ca/wp-content/uploads/2012/12/2008_March_in_praise_taxes.pdf.

———. 2009. In Praise of Taxes: The Link Between Taxation and Good Governance for First Nations Communities. Policy Brief No. 32. Ottawa: Institute on Governance. http://iog.ca/wp-content/uploads/2012/12/2009_February_policybrief32.pdf.

Guimond, Eric. 2003. Fuzzy Definitions and Population Explosion: Changing Identities of Aboriginal Groups in Canada. In *Not Strangers in These Parts: Urban Aboriginal Peoples*, ed. D. Newhouse and E. J. Peters. Ottawa: Policy Research Initiative, Government of Canada.

Hanselmann, Calvin. 2003. Ensuring the Urban Dream: Shared Responsibility and Effective Urban Aboriginal Voices. In *Not Strangers in These Parts: Urban Aboriginal Peoples*, ed. D. Newhouse and E. J. Peters, 167-77. Ottawa: Policy Research Initiative, Government of Canada.

Henderson, J. Y. 1994. Empowering Treaty Federalism. *Saskatchewan Law Review* 58: 241-329.

Hester v. The Queen. 2010. TCC 647 (CanLII), http://canlii.ca/t/2f45m.

Hester v. The Queen. 2010. TCC 647 (CanLII), http://canlii.ca/t/2f45m.

Hodgson, Glen. 2012. Reinventing the Canadian Tax System: The Case for Comprehensive Tax Reform. Ottawa: Conference Board of Canada.

Income Tax Act. 1985. RSC 1985, C.1 (5th supp.). *Justice Laws Website*. http://laws-lois.justice.gc.ca/eng/acts/I-3.3/.

Indian Act. 1985. RSC 1985, c I-5. *Justice Laws Website*. http://laws-lois.justice.gc.ca/eng/acts/i-5/.

Johnston v. The Queen. 2009. TCC 327 (CanLII), http://canlii.ca/t/2655v.

Johnston v. The Queen. 2010. TCC 627 (CanLII). http://canlii.ca/t/2dx02.

R. v. Kapp. 2006. BCCA 277 (CanLII). http://canlii.ca/t/1nj7p.

Kelly v. The Queen. 2009 TCC 189 (CanLII). http://canlii.ca/t/232gw.

Lafontaine v. The Queen. 2010 TCC 433 (CanLII). http://canlii.ca/t/2c7kq.

R. v. Lewis. 1996. 1 SCR 921, 1996 CanLII 243 (SCC). http://canlii.ca/t/1frc5.

Loxley, John and Fred Wien. 2003. Urban Aboriginal Economic Development. In *Not Strangers in These Parts: Urban Aboriginal Peoples*, ed. D. Newhouse and E. J. Peters. Ottawa: Policy Research Initiative, Government of Canada.

MacIntosh, C. 2009. From Judging Culture to Taxing "Indians": Tracing the Legal Discourse of the "Indian Mode of Life." *Osgoode Hall Law Journal* 47 (3): 399-437.

MacKay v. The Queen. 2007. TCC 757 (CanLII). http://canlii.ca/t/1qqk0.

MacKinnon, D. 1998. *Review of Literature on Fiscal Relationships*. Research and Analysis Directorate, Indian and Northern Affairs Canada. http://publications. gc.ca/collections/collection_2012/ainc-inac/R2-222-2002-eng.pdf

Maclagan, B. 2000. Section 87 of the *Indian Act* Recent Developments in the Taxation of Investment Income. *Canadian Tax Journal* 48 (5): 1503-25.

Manitoba Metis Federation Inc. v. Canada (Attorney General). 2013. 1 SCR 623, 2013 SCC 14 (CanLII). http://canlii.ca/t/fwfft.

Marcinyshyn v. The Queen. 2011. TCC 516 (CanLII). http://canlii.ca/t/fnr6l.

Martinez-Vazquez, Jorge, Violeta Vulovic, and Yongzheng Liu. 2009. Direct verses Indirect Taxation: Trends, Theory and Economic Significance. International Studies Program Working Paper 09-11 Andrew Young School of Policy Studies, George State University. http://scholarworks.gsu.edu/cgi/viewcontent. cgi?article=1045&context=econ_facpub (accessed December 2, 2015).

McDiarmid Lumber Ltd. v. God's Lake First Nation. 2006. 2 SCR 846, 2006 SCC 58 (CanLII). http://canlii.ca/t/1q553.

McDonald v. The Queen. 2011. TCC 437 (CanLII). http://canlii.ca/t/fn5zc.

McIvor v. The Queen. 2009. TCC 469 (CanLII). http://canlii.ca/t/25q9n.

McNeil, K. 2002. Extinguishment of Aboriginal Title In Canada: Treaties Legilsation and Judicial Discretion. *Ottawa Law Review* 33 (2): 301-46.

McNeil, K. 2000. "Aboriginal Title and Section 88 of the Indian Act." *UBC Law Review* 34.1: 159-194.

McNeil, K. 1999. The Onus of Proof of Aboriginal Title. *Osgoode Hall Law Journal* 37 (4): 775-803.

Mitchell v. Peguis Indian Band. 1990. 2 S.C.R. 85, CanLII 117 (SCC). http:// canlii.ca/t/1fswd.

Nahwegahbow v. The Queen. 2011. TCC 296 (CanLII). http://canlii.ca/t/flvwd.

Newhouse, David and Evelyn Peters, eds. 2003. *Not Strangers in these Parts: Urban Aboriginal Peoples*. Ottawa: Policy Research Initiative, Government of Canada. http://publications.gc.ca/collections/Collection/CP22-71-2003E.pdf.

Norris, Mary Jane. 2003. Aboriginal Mobility and Migration Within Urban Canada: Outcomes, Factors and Implications. In *Not Strangers in These Parts: Urban Aboriginal Peoples*, ed. D. Newhouse and E. J. Peters. Ottawa: Policy Research Initiative, Government of Canada.

Nowegijick v. The Queen. 1983. 1 SCR 29, 1983 CanLII 18 (SCC). http://canlii. ca/t/1lpd4.

Obonsawin v. The Queen. 2010. TCC 222 (CanLII). http://canlii.ca/t/29hpw.

O'Brien, M. 2002. Income Tax, Investment Income, and the *Indian Act*: Getting Back on Track. *Canadian Tax Journal* 50 1570-96.

Olthuis, Brent. 2009. The Constitution's Peoples: Approaching Community in the Context of Section 35 of the *Constitution Act, 1982*. *McGill Law Journal* 54:1-44.

Palacios, M. and N. Veldhuis. 2012. Taxes versus the Necessities of Life: The Canadian Consumer Tax Index. 2012 Edition. Vancouver: *Fraser Institute*. https://www.fraserinstitute.org/sites/default/files/canadian-consumer-tax-index-2012.pdf.

Palacios, M. and C. Lamman. 2013. Canadians Celebrate Tax freedom Day on June 10, 2013. *Fraser Institute*. https://www.fraserinstitute.org/content/canadians-celebrate-tax-freedom-day-june-10-2013 (acessed August 2013).

Peters, Evelyn. 2007. Urban Reserves. Paper prepared for the National Centre for First Nations Governance, Ottawa.

Pelletier v. The Queen. 2009. TCC 358 (CanLII). http://canlii.ca/t/24gsc.

Pigeon v.The Queen. 2010 TCC 643 (CanLII). http://canlii.ca/t/2f3xs.

The Estate Of Charles Pilfold v. The Queen. 2013. TCC 181 (CanLII). http://canlii.ca/t/fz6nr.

Pinder, Leslie J. 2000. The *Indian Act* Taxation Exemption—Beguiling Simplicity. *Canadian Tax Journal* 48 (5): 1496-1502.

Placer Dome Canada Ltd. v. Ontario (Minister of Finance). 2006. 1 S.C.R. 715, 2006 SCC 20 (CanLII). http://canlii.ca/t/1nb6r.

Reynolds, J. I. 2002. Taking and Enforcing Security under the *Indian Act* and Self-Government Legislation. *Business and Finance Law Review* 18:37-65.

Richards, John. 2003. A New Agenda for Strengthening Canada's Aboriginal Population: Individual Treaty Benefits, Reduced Transfers to Bands and Own-Source Taxation. Backgrounder 66. Toronto: C.D. Howe Institute.

Rieksts, M. 2010. The History of Income Tax in Canada. *LawNow* 34 (6).

Robinson v. The Queen. 2010. TCC 649 (CanLII). http://canlii.ca/t/2f4w0.

Roe v. The Queen. 2008. TCC 667 (CanLII). http://canlii.ca/t/2f6fd.

Ross River Dena Council Band v. Canada. 2002. 2 SCR 816, 2002 SCC 54 (CanLII). http://canlii.ca/t/51r1.

Rustand, Jeffrey K. 2010. Is "Inherent Aboriginal Self-Government" Constitutional? Calgary, AB: Canadian Constitutional Foundation.

Saez, Emmanuel. 2004. *Direct or indirect tax instruments for redistribution: short-run versus long-run.* Journal of Public Economics 88:503-18.

Samji, H. and D. Wardman. 2009. First Nations Communities and Tobacco Taxation: A Commentary. *American Indian and Alaska Native Mental Health Research* 16 (2).

Shilling v. M.N.R. 2001. 4 FCR 364, 2001 FCA 178 (CanLII). http://canlii.ca/t/4k3x.

Southwind v. Canada. 1998. CanLII 7300 (FCA). http://canlii.ca/t/4ms5.

Stigen v. The Queen. 2008. TCC 405 (CanLII). http://canlii.ca/t/1zfvr.

Stubart Investments Ltd. v. The Queen. 1984. 1 SCR 536, 1984 CanLII 20 (SCC). http://canlii.ca/t/1lpfb.

Tax Court of Canada Act. 1985. RSC 1985, c T-2. http://canlii.ca/t/523m6.

Tseshaht Band v. British Columbia. 1992. (CanLII). 5970 (BC CA). http://canlii.ca/t/231p1.

Union of New Brunswick Indians v. New Brunswick (Minister of Finance). 1998. 1 S.C.R. 1161, 1998 CanLII 783 (SCC). http://canlii.ca/t/1fqsk.

Verreault v. The Queen. 2012. TCC 293 (CanLII). http://canlii.ca/t/ft2fm.

Vincent v. The Queen. 2011. TCC 430 (CanLII). http://canlii.ca/t/fn4t3.

Wilkins, K. (2011). Dancing in the Dark: Of Provinces and Section 35 Rights After 2010. *54 Supreme Court Law Review (S.C.L.R.),* 530.

Williams v. Canada. 1992. 1 S.C.R. 877, 1992 CanLII 98 (SCC). http://canlii.ca/t/1fscq.

Chapter 8

A study by TD Economics estimates that the total combined income of First Nation households, businesses, and governments in 2016 will reach $32 billion. This represents a rapidly growing market in Canada for financial services. Surveys indicate that the majority of Aboriginal entrepreneurs have inadequate access to capital, and there is a perception towards financial risk from lending vehicles which is overstated. Consequently, Aboriginal entrepreneurs rely heavily on personal and family support, and there is growing need for "angel investors" and more readily available access to banking products. The inadequate access to capital also impacts Aboriginal governments and community-owned businesses.

Mainstream banks are recognizing the need for broadened banking services and have been diversifying services and products in response, but demand outstrips supply. First Nation banks and credit unions are also developing, and a network of Aboriginal financial institutions continues to grow.

Finance and Banking
Tom Cooper

Aboriginal peoples in Canada have witnessed many challenges in starting and maintaining a business venture and engaging in community development. For example, the proceedings of the Canadian Standing Senate Committee on Aboriginal Peoples identified the following barriers to economic development: building human capital, infrastructure deficits, lack of governance capacity, fragmented federal approach to economic development, and limited funding. This limited funding is closely aligned to access to capital, as well as legislative and regulatory barriers, which are among the most significant challenges (Standing Senate Committee on Aboriginal Peoples 2007). There have also been successes, such as the emergence of the Aboriginal Financial Officers Association of Canada (AFOA), an organization that helps develop capacity and expertise in the financial-services sector for Aboriginal businesses and communities.

> **Capital** refers to money and other assets that are used to start and finance a business.

Readily available capital for economic development is a challenge for government, business organizations, and individuals in both affluent and indigent, developing countries. Efficient capital markets allocate capital to earn the highest possible return for a given level of risk transferred from saving units to borrowing units at the lowest transactions cost, while reflecting all available relevant information. The legal and regulatory system should complement these capital-allocation decisions to provide lenders and other investors with comfort to protect the integrity of their depositors and shareholders. This ideal set of circumstances has seldom been witnessed in capital transactions anywhere in the world. In Aboriginal business, the challenges are even greater. Understanding the barriers and opportunities to Aboriginal banking and finance in Canada is an important element in furthering Aboriginal peoples' business, economic, and social development.

> **Shareholders** are individuals or organizations that own shares in a corporation.

The Importance of Finance and Banking to Aboriginal Business

Banking and finance is an important part of business. Canadian financial institutions are paying greater attention to the nation's more than 1.4 million Aboriginal peoples (Statistics Canada 2011). With help from billions of dollars in land-claim settlements and from joint ventures with established corporations, Aboriginal communities and entrepreneurs are starting more businesses. The reasons for starting new businesses are plentiful. For instance: Aboriginal people own and control 20 per cent of the Canadian land mass. That's expected to rise to 30 per cent in the next fifteen years.[1] A study by TD Economics estimated the total combined income of Aboriginal households, businesses, and governments to be close to $24 billion in 2011; by 2016, it is estimated that this total combined income could eclipse $32 billion (TD Economics 2011). According to Charles Coffey (2002), executive vice-president, government and community affairs with RBC Financial Group, the business benefits of providing financial services in the Aboriginal community are clear:

> We see a major and expanding market opportunity. The rapid increases in the Aboriginal population represent new customers. Land claims represent increased economic and financial clout. The aboriginal business sector, which has grown at a dramatic rate in recent years and is steadily moving the aboriginal population toward economic self-sufficiency, is generating wealth and creating jobs.

Significant barriers exist, however, to obtaining and accessing capital for Aboriginal communities and businesses. A study for Industry Canada (Caldwell and Hunt 2002: 17-19) found that 56 per cent of Aboriginal entrepreneurs had inadequate access to debt financing. They cited the following reasons: lack of collateral (40 per cent); inability to use on-reserve assets as collateral (30 per cent); no local financial institutions (27 per cent); and lack of profitability (22 per cent). Reasons for inadequate access to equity included: lack of personal resources (58 per cent); unavailability of venture capital (36 per cent); inadequate retained earnings (32 per cent); absence of community investment funds (31 per cent); and inability of family/friends to invest (16 per cent). A more recent study by Ulnooweg Development Group (2008) similarly outlined that there has been a clear lack of access to capital through mainstream banking and financial institutions for Aboriginal entrepreneurs and communities. Finally, a study by the Canadian Council for Aboriginal Business (CCAB 2011) indicated that Aboriginal entrepreneurs rely primarily on their own resources for both start-up and ongoing financing, and for access to financing. To start a business, Aboriginal entrepreneurs rely most heavily on personal savings (55 per cent), compared with business loans or bank credit (17 per cent), credit from government programs (17 per cent), or loans from Aboriginal lending institutions (15 per cent). The council also concluded that Aboriginal small-business owners consider access to financing, and access to equity or capital, to be obstacles to their growth plans (CCAB 2011, 2013) (see also chapter 4).

> **Collateral** refers to property or other assets that are offered to lenders by borrowers to secure a loan. In the event of default, the property or assets may be seized.

Barriers are not only limited to access issues. In Aboriginal businesses and communities there is a perception that financing risk is higher than it actually is (Cooper and Ulnooweg Development Group 2010: 197-217). There is also a lack of understanding by mainstream financial institutions with regard to cultural and regulatory challenges facing Aboriginal communities and businesses. Contributing to these perceptions and lack of understanding is the relative absence of regulatory frameworks, institutions, and services in Aboriginal communities to deal with banking and finance issues. For example, a 2004 study examined some of the barriers to obtaining capital through banks and other financial institutions for Aboriginal peoples (NARCA 2004: 4). Some of the barriers include:

Security issues—it is difficult for Aboriginal entrepreneurs to get access to capital because on-reserve properties are normally owned by the community. Certificates of possession (CPs) may be issued, which can be sold to other members of that community. "CP'd" land can be used as collateral; however, this still results in lower market values and certainly lower levels of financing (more on land ownership and CPs is found in chapter 2).

Lack of familiarity with Aboriginal cultures—it is important to recognize that mainstream financial intermediaries have limited amounts of capital with which to finance. As a result, they prefer to deal with organizations and communities they know and understand. Aboriginal businesses and communities can be problematic for financiers because of a lack of cultural understanding.

Perception of Aboriginal governments as unstable—the election process in Aboriginal communities is often misunderstood and the frequency of elections (for First Nations, mandated by the Indian Act) sometimes results in a higher turnover rate than in municipal government. This is interpreted as instability and, because banks see instability as risk, communities struggle to access capital on competitive terms because of this perception.

Isolation—geographic distance and limited technical/communications infrastructure make it difficult for mainstream financial institutions to engage with Aboriginal business and communities.

Limited managerial/financial capacity—although this is increasingly changing, training and attracting high-level managers with financial and management capacity into Aboriginal communities has proved problematic. AFOA's work, as well as other training efforts, are increasing managerial and financial capacity through building human capital.

Perceived risk underlies most of these issues. In many cases this perception is shaped by a lack of accurate information about the governance and fiscal capacity of Aboriginal communities. Many of the media images associated with Aboriginal people highlight the gap in living standards between Aboriginal communities and mainstream society (see chapter 9). While these images may be true, they do not accurately represent the full picture of the progress made by many communities. As a result, Aboriginal individuals and communities in Canada have been placed at a disadvantage to the rest of Canadian society. In order to catch up with the Canadian economy, First Nation and Aboriginal individuals, businesses, and governments require large amounts of financed capital for (Ulnooweg Development Group 2008):

- Community and economic infrastructure
- Private and government institutions
- Social and private housing
- Resource development
- Business development

One solution would be to go to capital markets directly. This can be done through developing financial products, such as bonds and other financial instruments, that are sold directly to investors and financial intermediaries. However, capital markets are best suited to the large capital requirements of mature and established governments and businesses operating in regulated environments. They are not are not well-suited to the needs of small business and developing economies, such as those seen in the Aboriginal world, due to the following reasons (Ulnooweg Development Group 2008):

- Higher transaction costs
- Lower volumes of capital
- Less certainty
- Lower short-term expectations

Instead of going to capital markets (through bonds and other large loans), Aboriginal entrepreneurs, businesses, and governments rely more on financial institutions, such as banks, credit unions, and other structures, to access capital. In Canada, there are also specific financial institutions aimed at Aboriginal peoples that address this problem of going directly to the market. The potential to go to the capital markets directly, such as through initial public offerings (IPOs), develop bonds, or other forms of financial securities that may be bought and sold, is minimal.

There is a unique opportunity, then, that can be filled by Aboriginal banking and financial institutions. Reflecting the true capacity of communities in a transparent and industry-accepted manner provides an entry point for external capital and the opportunity to form relationships with financial-service providers. Aboriginal banks and financial institutions can assist in this reflection of the true capacity of Aboriginal entrepreneurs and communities.

Since the 1960s, the Government of Canada has introduced a number of programs and initiatives to close the capital gap that exists between Aboriginal and mainstream communities. These included:

- Indian Economic Development Fund, which provided loan guarantees and contributions to First Nation communities
- National economic-development programs
- Aboriginal capital corporations
- Aboriginal Business Canada
- Community economic-development strategies

Apart from these Aboriginal-specific initiatives, there is still a reliance on mainstream financial institutions, such as banks and credit unions, to fund Aboriginal business and economic development. In order to understand how and why Aboriginal entrepreneurs and communities access and deal with financial and banking issues, it is vital to recognize the structure of Canada's regulated financial-services industry.

> A **credit union** is a non-profit, co-operative financial institution that is owned by its members. They often provide general banking services (chequing and savings accounts), as well as loans.

Canada's Regulated Financial Services Industry

The Canadian financial-services sector is made up of banks, trust and loan companies, credit unions and caisse populaires, life- and health-insurance companies, property/casualty-insurance companies, securities dealers and exchanges, mutual-fund companies and distributors, and financing and leasing companies, as well as independent financial advisers, pension-fund managers, and independent insurance agents and brokers (Department of Finance Canada 2003). The most applicable financial institutions for Aboriginal business are chartered banks and credit unions/caisse populaires.

> A **chartered bank** is a privately owned financial institution that is authorized to operate by the federal government.

In Canada, a chartered bank is a federally regulated financial institution that engages in the business of taking deposits, lending, and providing other financial services. There are three distinct types of banks that transact business, Schedule I (domestic banks), Schedule II (largely Canadian subsidiaries of foreign banks) and Schedule III (foreign banks with branches in Canada) (see OSFI 2011). Schedule I banks are Canada's major, domestic chartered banks. To prevent a concentration of ownership in a Schedule I bank, no single interest is permitted to own more than 10 per cent of a bank's outstanding common shares. The six major Schedule I banks in Canada are Bank of Montreal (BMO), Bank of Nova Scotia (BNS), Canadian Imperial Bank of Commerce (CIBC), National Bank of Canada, Royal Bank of Canada Financial Group (RBC), and Toronto-Dominion Bank (TD). Schedule II banks include all foreign- and Canadian-owned banks where a single interest is allowed to hold more than 10 per cent of the outstanding shares. There are special restrictions on Schedule II and III banks on the number and size of their branches. Schedule I, II, and III banks offer banking services to customers, including establishing personal and corporate accounts, providing loans and mortgages for commercial and personal use, and handling transactions involving foreign exchange (Department of Finance Canada 2003).

> A **mortgage** is a loan for the purchase of property. The property is pledged as collateral for the monetary loan. When the loan is repaid in full, the title of the property returns to the debtor.

Credit Unions and trust companies also provide personal and business financial services including personal and commercial mortgages, loans, and accounts. Canada has a strong cooperative financial-services sector, comprised of credit unions and caisse populaires (as credit unions are known in French-speaking Canada), with the world's highest per-capita membership in the credit-union movement, more than 10 million members, just under a third of the population (Department of Finance Canada 2003). As of 2015, there were 694 credit unions and caisse populaires in Canada, with almost 3,000 branches. They hold combined assets of $328 billion (Central1 [n.d.]). While being prevalent throughout the country, the sector captures the largest percentage of population in western provinces (60 per cent) and Québec (70 per cent). According to the Office of the Superintendent of Financial Institutions, Canada's banking regulator, there are 148 regulated deposit-taking institutions. Seventy-one of these institutions are banks, and the rest are trust companies (OSFI 2012).

Aboriginal Banking Services

The six Schedule I (domestic) banks in Canada have made efforts to develop banking solutions that are more responsive to the needs of Aboriginal communities. In a number of communities, banks have established full-service branches. In other, more rural and remote communities, banks have established agency-banking outlets (ABOs). Each chartered bank has branches or ABOs in most of the Canadian provinces, except in the Atlantic Provinces. Additionally, TD has specifically partnered with First Nations in Saskatchewan to establish a stand-alone entity, the First Nations Bank of Canada.

First Nations Bank of Canada

In 1993, the Saskatchewan Indian Equity Foundation (SIEF) submitted a proposal to the Federation of Saskatchewan Indian Nations (FSIN) calling for the creation of a First Nations bank. Based on the approval of this proposal, SIEF began an initiative to reach out to financial institutions for support in the creation of such a bank. On November 19, 1996, TD, SIEF, and FSIN officially launched the First Nations Bank of Canada with an investment of $2 million from SIEF and an investment of $8 million from TD.

> **Equity** is excess of the value of an asset or piece of property over any financial liabilities.

The bank's shareholders as of October 31, 2006, included significant Aboriginal organizations from the principal regions in which it operates, including: FSIN; SIEF and sixty-two Saskatchewan First Nations and tribal councils; the Cree Regional Authority's Board of Compensation, Québec; the James Bay Eeyou Corporation, Québec; the Tribal Councils Investment Group of Manitoba, Manitoba; the Champagne Aishihik Trust, Yukon; däna Näye Ventures, Yukon (discussed in chapter 4); the Yukon Indian Development Corporation, Yukon; and TD Bank.

First Nations Bank of Canada produced its sixth straight year of profitability in fiscal 2006, reporting a net income of $1,390,000—an increase of $1,014,000 over the prior year, eliminating the remaining shareholders deficit and contributing $865,000 to retained earnings at year-end. First Nations Bank of Canada announced in 2007 that it had closed a private-placement share offering to Aboriginal investors of 6,222,240 shares, at an issue price of $2.25 per

> A **private-placement share offering** is a means of raising capital by selling shares or stock to select investors in small numbers rather than employing a public offering, where anyone can purchase shares or stock.

share, for gross proceeds of $14 million. The bank headquarters are located in Saskatoon, Saskatchewan. Following the success of the bank, there has been a separation from TD; they now operate as competitors.

Business Development Bank of Canada

The Business Development Bank of Canada (BDC) also serves an important role in Aboriginal business. BDC is wholly owned by the government of Canada and plays a leadership role in delivering financial, investment, and consulting services to Canadian small and medium-sized businesses. These services complement those of private-sector financial institutions.

Credit Unions / Caisse populaires

Legally, a credit union is a bank and must operate as such, but because it is set up as a co-operative its mission is more community-oriented and can incorporate values such as mutual self-help. The main operational difference between banks and credit unions is that banks are federally regulated and credit unions are provincially regulated, through specific legislative acts. In each act, there are rules governing liquidity, capital maintenance, and asset and risk management. There are also credit-union deposit-insurance corporations set up in each jurisdiction to protect depositors. In most respects, these mirror the protections offered to depositors in banks by the Canada Deposit Insurance Corporation. Legislation is designed to provide a secure environment to conduct financial transactions in a highly provincially regulated environment with a view toward protecting the depositors of the credit unions. There are also a number of Aboriginal-owned-and-controlled credit unions in Canada.

> **Liquidity** is a financial ratio that measures the ability of a business to convert an asset to cash.

The Anishinabek Nation Credit Union officially received its charter from the Ontario Ministry of Finance, Credit Unions and Co-operatives Services Branch, on May 31, 2000. There are forty-three First Nation communities who are member communities of the Anishinabek Nation. The Anishinabek Nation incorporated the Union of Ontario Indians (UOI) as its secretariat in 1949. The UOI acted as the secretariat in the development of the credit union and provided leadership to member communities. A bond of association already existed among the First Nation communities of the Anishabek Nation (also a requirement in the formation of any credit union).

The Caisse Populaire Kahnawake is in a unique geographic location, situated only about twenty kilometres from Montréal. In the mid-1980s, the community of Kahnawake wanted their own source of capital for economic development, not wanting to rely on outside government. They chose the credit-union model so they could tailor products and services to meet their members' needs. The caisse populaire is headquartered on the reserve, so there is no question of taxability on interest earned. In 2004, 5,288 people from a reserve of 8,000 were members of the caisse. This is a significant accomplishment given that in such a small geographical area there were concerns among residents about confidentiality, about "everyone knowing my business." In its first year of operation, the caisse was able to reach half of the community and realized a net profit of $47,000. It projected $20 million in assets in five years and achieved it in two years. These profits have continued to grow. In 2004, the Caisse Populaire Kahnawake had profits of $1,879,665 on an asset base of $113,545,899. Kahnawake was a pioneer by being the first banking institution to introduce a system of guarantees adapted specifically to an Aboriginal community. The model is known as a "trustee agreement," under which trustees are used as third parties when loans are guaranteed. Because the trustees are members of the community, they may receive land as security and sell it in the event that the borrower is unable to repay. The trustees can then reimburse the caisse. The Kahnawake Caisse Populaire held $130,370,871 in assets at end of its 2006 fiscal year. In 2006, the caisse achieved earnings of $1,977,511 and distributed patronage allocations totalling $950,000. Over the past five years, patronage allocations have amounted to $3,043,340 (Ulnooweg Development Group 2008).

Overall, the positive aspects of the credit-union movement in Aboriginal banking and finance in Canada include:

> **Patronage allocations** are dividends that are paid to investors or members of a co-operative.

- The ultimate control and management of the credit union is vested in the members of the Aboriginal communities.

- There is increased pride in knowing that Aboriginal people own a financial institution.

- Business and other loans are secured through a collection process, which at the same time respects the exemption from seizure of assets.

- The flexibility to respond to the lending needs of persons who may not otherwise be adept in proposal writing is beneficial.

- Credit unions can become, over time, a vital contributor to the self-government practices and independence of Aboriginals.

Apart from the banks and credit unions, there are a number of specific Aboriginal financial institutions that provide banking and financial services in Canada. This is manifested through a network of Aboriginal financial institutions (AFIs) in Canada.

The Network of Aboriginal Financial Institutions in Canada

The current AFI network had its beginnings in the mid-1980s with the creation of Aboriginal capital corporations (ACCs) (see NARCA 2004). In 1996, the National Aboriginal Capital Corporations Association (NACCA) was formed as an association of eighteen ACCs to develop and deliver business products and services to Aboriginal entrepreneurs. By 1998, all thirty-one of the ACCs were NACCA members. In 1998, NACCA opened its membership to Aboriginal Community Futures Development Corporations (ACFDCs). Since then, the ACCs and ACFDCs have been collectively referred to as AFIs. The NACCA membership now includes fifty-nine AFIs: thirty-three ACCs, twenty ACFDCs, and five other financial institutions.

Since the inception of the ACC network, the Canadian government has advanced $163 million for capitalization. In addition, the ACCs have sourced an additional $17 million in capital through mainstream sources. Collectively, the ACCs and the ACFDCs across Canada reached the $1 billion loan threshold in October 2004. Three of the most successful AFIs in Canada are Peace Hills Trust, Ulnooweg Development Group, and Me-Dian Credit Union.

Peace Hills Trust (PHT) is wholly owned by the Samson Cree Nation of Hobbema, Alberta. It was established in 1980 to deliver financial services throughout Canada to First Nations and their members, corporations, institutions, and associations, both on- and off-reserve. Since 1981, PHT has been offering deposit and lending services, personal savings and chequing accounts, residential and commercial mortgages, term loans, and consumer loans. They have also managed First Nation trust funds, including land-claim-settlement trusts, First Nation-owned retirement-savings and pension plans, and individual and education trusts. It also now provides services to non-Native clientele. PHT employs more than 120 people in a network of eight regional offices throughout Canada.

Ulnooweg Development Group (UDG) is a non-profit ACC that has been serving status-Indian clients in Atlantic Canada since 1985. The initial client base was inclusive of all status Indians resident in Nova Scotia. The client base was later expanded to include status Indians living in New Brunswick and Prince Edward Island. UDG now has a presence across the Atlantic region, with offices located in Nova Scotia, New Brunswick, and Newfoundland and Labrador. UDG provides business loans to Aboriginal entrepreneurs and government entities throughout Atlantic Canada. Since its inception, Ulnooweg Development Group has cycled the initial capital investment of $7 million nearly 600 per cent, making loans of more than $40 million in Atlantic Canada. UDG is discussed in detail in chapter 11.

Me-Dian Credit Union (formerly Métis Credit Union of Manitoba) was founded in 1978 as a "closed bond" credit union. Members of closed-bond credit unions share a distinct association based on religion, profession, culture, or some other criteria, and nearly every credit union in the province has been closed bond (not open to public membership) at one time or another (Me-Dian Credit Union n.d.). The driving force behind the founding of this credit union was the Manitoba Métis Federation and its members, but the credit union later changed its name to the Me-Dian Credit Union of Manitoba when the board opened up the bond of association to include First Nations and Inuit along with Métis. In 2009, Me-Dian opened its doors even wider, welcoming those who are not of Aboriginal heritage as associate members of the credit union.

Other Aboriginal Banking and Finance Institutions

In circumstances where market capital falls short, governments and civil society can help through provision of assisted-market sources of capital— instruments that lower the risk or transaction costs to facilitate flow of market capital. They can also assist through non-market sources of capital concessionary funding (no or very low interest), contributions, and subsidies, where risks exceed market tolerance and where there is a public-policy rationale. Most recently, Canada's First Nations and the Government of Canada have engaged in an institution-building exercise designed to provide First Nation communities with the tools to access capital markets available to other levels of governments within Canada. On March 23, 2005, the *First Nations Fiscal and Statistical Management Act* (*FSMA*) became law. This resulted in the creation of a finance authority, a tax commission, and a financial-management board.[2]

> A **concessionary loan** has no or below-average interest.
>
> **Risk tolerance** refers to the amount of risk or degree of uncertainty that an investor is willing to tolerate.

First Nations Finance Authority (FNFA)

The FNFA is a not-for-profit finance authority formed in 1995 to provide member First Nations with the opportunity to use debentures to access long-term affordable financing. Its primary purpose is to raise capital by issuing bonds on behalf of its member First Nation governments. This provides its members with the opportunity to raise long-term private capital at preferred rates for public works, such as roads, water and sewer, and buildings. First Nations provide security to these debentures through securitizing a portion of their property-tax revenues or similar long-term revenues.[3] More on the FNFA can be found in chapter 6.

Regulations published in the *Canada Gazette* (the official newspaper of the Government of Canada) on December 26, 2007, officially enable thirty-three First Nations to participate in the property-tax

> A **bond** is a written agreement between a lender and a borrower to pay a specified sum (value of the bond plus interest) on a set date.
>
> A **debenture** is an unsecured bond. It is issued without collateral, usually on the basis of a company or government's reputation and likelihood of repayment.

provisions of the FNSMA. As a result, these First Nations have access to additional fiscal tools not otherwise available under the *Indian Act*.[4]

First Nations Financial Management Board (FNFMB)

The FNFMB is an institution whose purpose is to provide independent and professional management services to First Nations seeking access to the FNFA borrowing pool. It assists First Nations in building stronger community management and accountability frameworks, as well as practices, standard-setting, and capacity-building required to participate in raising capital through the FNFA.

First Nations Tax Commission (FNTC)

Since 1988, First Nations have had the power to levy property taxes on their lands. In 1989, the forerunner of the FNTC, the Indian Taxation Advisory Board (ITAB) was formed. In its first ten years of operation, eighty-three First Nations implemented property-tax laws and generated $168 million in revenues. The FNTC officially began operations July 1, 2007, and continues the work of the ITAB. It provides services that allow First Nations to securitize property-tax revenues and oversee the bylaw approval process. It also provides greater investor certainty, serves as a level of appeal and authority to balance community and rate payers' interest in rate setting, and provides timely and professional dispute resolution.

The ability to successfully provide transparent, risk-rated investment opportunities to private capital providers requires that First Nation communities undertake initiatives to enhance their ability to borrow. The practices and processes of the FNFA and the FNFMB are tools which can be of immediate assistance to the First Nation communities as they proceed to prepare themselves for dealing with private capital providers. Even then, there will be areas of borrowing that may not be readily accepted by private capital providers.

> **Securitize** refers to a process through which sound financial principles can consistently be applied to calculate the value of an asset that banks would not value otherwise.

Summary

In examining Aboriginal banking and finance, it is important to clarify the contextual reasons that Aboriginal entrepreneurs and communities need to access financing. When deciding to venture into a new business, many motives exist for the owner, whether internally focused (i.e., personal drive) or externally focused (i.e., profit driven). Aboriginal entrepreneurs and managers are no different, with the exception that one of their fundamental motives may be to satisfy the socioeconomic needs of their communities. Community-owned enterprises are also numerous, and the role of the social entrepreneur is especially important (Graham and Edwards 2003).

Economic development is seen as part of the larger agenda of rebuilding Aboriginal peoples' communities and nations and reasserting control over their traditional territories (Anderson et al. 2005). Aboriginal entrepreneurs create businesses to compete in the global economy for the purpose of wealth generation to help support self-government and socioeconomic conditions (Anderson et al. 2005). Many First Nation leaders see the solution to these conditions in having greater access to capital in order to stimulate economic growth. In a speech, Chief Terry Paul of the Membertou First Nation in Nova Scotia outlined:

> Capital, and access to it, is a key ingredient in economic activity. As we look to future economic development it is imperative that First Nations have ownership and control over such an essential lever of the economy. Alternatively, a nation which does not control the essential levers of its economy will always be subject to the influence of the external forces which do control these levers. The financial services industry which provides capital to our communities is an essential element for our future growth and development. (Ulnooweg Development Group 2008)

> A **rate buy-down** is a technique in which a lower interest rate for a specified period is secured by paying a sum of money upfront.

First Nation borrowing markets are comprised of debt that usually falls within the risk profile of private capital providers and debt that falls outside that risk profile. Attracting private capital to that aspect of the market requires incentives. These incentives could take the form of loan guarantees, insurance, rate buy-downs, investment tax credits, or special grants and contributions to make that aspect of the market more acceptable to private capital providers.

> **Crowdfunding** is a fund-raising practice in which small sums of money are collected from a large number of supporters, usually through social media and other Internet platforms.

There is a role for provincial and federal governments to play in creating incentives for private capital to address the borrowing needs of First Nation communities. Also, in the future, communities and entrepreneurs may be able to use innovative funding models, such as crowdfunding, to further address capital and funding needs.

Key Points:

- Capital is necessary for a business, a community organization, or a government to achieve its goals and grow in size and scope.

- There are many different barriers to obtaining financing for Aboriginal entrepreneurs, businesses, organizations, and governments, but a variety of solutions have been created in relation to financing.

- Banks are changing to recognize and accommodate the specific needs of Aboriginal businesses and communities.

- More Aboriginal communities are becoming engaged in banking directly by running institutions.

- Credit unions and caisse populaires are popular with Aboriginal communities.

- Aboriginal financial institutions are emerging to help address the borrowing needs of Aboriginals.

- Some communities are exercising taxation powers on their lands to provide a revenue stream for development.

Questions for Review:

1. What barriers exist to obtaining financing for Aboriginal entrepreneurs, businesses, and communities?

2. What Aboriginal banking services and institutions have been created to address financing issues? How are they different from traditional bank lending or financing?

3. How is taxation being used to finance on-reserve development?

4. Could crowdfunding provide a non-traditional financing stream? What sorts of business ventures might it be suited to?

5. Why is the credit-union model of banking of more interest to Aboriginal communities?

Suggested Assignments:

1. Discuss reasons the risk tolerance of credit unions may be different than those of other banks. Analyze whether their tolerance for risk should be higher or lower.

2. Explain the securitization process. Propose the examples of the processes and calculations you would apply. Who would you have to convince of your process accuracy?

Notes

1. Canadian Council for Aboriginal Business (http://www.ccab.com).

2. The Statistical Institute was eliminated in 2012. Additional information on the institutions can be accessed at the First Nations Finance Authority Website, http://fnfa.ca/en/.

3. See http://fnfa.ca/en/fnfa/.

4. Ibid.

References

Anderson, R. B., R. D. Camp II, L.-P. Dana, B. Honig, J.-M. Nkongolo-Bakenda, and A. M. Peredo. 2005. Indigenous land rights in Canada: the foundation for development. International Journal of Entrepreneurship and Small Business 2 (2): 104-33.

Caldwell, D. and P. Hunt. 2002. Financing SMEs in Canada: Barriers—Faced by Women, Youth, Aboriginal and Minority Entrepreneurs in Accessing CapitalPhase 1: Literature Review. https://www.ic.gc.ca/eic/site/061.nsf/vwapj/FinancingSMEsinCanadaPhase1_e.pdf/$FILE/FinancingSMEsinCanadaPhase1_e.pdf (accessed December 2, 2015).

CCAB (Canadian Council for Aboriginal Business). 2011. Promise and Prosperity: The Aboriginal Business Survey. https://www.ccab.com/uploads/File/Promise-and-Prosperity--The-Aboriginal-Business-Survey.pdf.

———. 2013. Community and Commerce. A Survey of Aboriginal Economic Development Corporations. https://www.ccab.com/uploads/File/Community-and-Commerce-Final-Report.pdf.

Central1. N.d. About Us. Central1. http://www.central1.com/about-us/credit-union-system (accessed December 2, 2015).

Coffey, C. 2002. Building Aboriginal/Corporate Relationships Our call to action. Speech delivered at JEDI Luncheon and Roundtable, Fredericton, NB, March 25. http://www.rbc.com/newsroom/20020325coffey.html.

Cooper, T. and Ulnooweg Development Group. 2010. Risks and Opportunities for Aboriginal Financial Services Organizations. In Aboriginal Policy Research Volume 10: Research Methods, Justice, Governance and Politics, ed. Jerry P. White at al. Toronto: Thompson Publishing.

Department of Finance Canada. 2003. Canada's Financial Services Sector—Canada's Credit Unions and Caisses Populaires. https://www.fin.gc.ca/activty/factsheets/ccu_e.pdf (accessed December 2, 2015).

Graham, J., and H. Edwards. 2003. Options for Commercial Enterprises in First Nations. Institute of Governance, Ottawa. http://iog.ca/wpcontent/uploads/2012/12/2003_February_FNenterprises.pdf (accessed December 2, 2015).

Me-Dian Credit Union. N.d. About Us. Me-Dian Credit Union. http://www.me-diancu.mb.ca/_aboutUs/index.aspx (accessed December 2, 2015).

National Aboriginal Risk Capital Association. 2004. Equity Capital and First Nation Business Development. Ottawa, Ontario.

OSFI (Office of the Superintendent of Financial Institutions). 2011. Federally Regulated Financial Institutions. http://www.osfi-bsif.gc.ca/eng/docs/arra/1112/eng/p10-eng.html

Standing Senate Committee on Aboriginal Peoples. 2007. Sharing Canada's Prosperity—A Hand Up, Not A Handout. Final Report. Special study on the involvement of aboriginal communities and businesses in economic development activities in Canada. http://www.parl.gc.ca/Content/SEN/Committee/391/abor/rep/rep06-e.pdf (accessed December 2, 2015).

Statistics Canada. 2011. Aboriginal Peoples in Canada: First Nations People, Métis and Inuit. National Household Survey. http://www12.statcan.gc.ca/nhs-enm/2011/as-sa/99-011-x/99-011-x2011001-eng.cfm (accessed December 2, 2015).

TD Economics. 2011. Estimating the Size of the Aboriginal Market in Canada. Special Report, June 17. https://www.ccab.com/uploads/File/Promise-and-Prosperity--The-Aboriginal-Business-Survey.pdf (accessed December 2, 2015).

Ulnooweg Development Group Inc. 2008. Atlantic Aboriginal Financial Services Market Demand Study. Truro, NS: Virtual Ink Ltd.

Chapter 9

A tremendous tool for any business venture, demographics refers to the size and composition of a population. Age, gender, educational attainment, and income levels are just some of the segments which can be analyzed for business entry or expansion. Canada's population, like in most developed countries, is aging rapidly, with declining birth rates. This trend colours all aspects of investment in the Canadian economy. The largest segment of the Canadian population, the "baby boomers," is quickly approaching retirement age en masse, which will impact the housing market, and the related construction industry, as well as consumer goods, health care, travel, recreation, and investment planning.

The Indigenous population of Canada, representing approximately 4.3 per cent of the Canadian population, is growing rapidly and is much younger than the non-Aboriginal population. It is also important to analyze regional norms, as some Western provinces have Aboriginal populations that exceed 15 per cent of the total population and may exceed 20 per cent of the total by the 2020s. This significant cohort of the Canadian population is young and poised to enter the work force in ever-increasing numbers. Some authors opine this young population will be one of the most important factors to address Canada's forecast labour shortages as baby boomers retire in the millions.

This is Canada's second "baby boom." While arguably much smaller than the first, it can impact regional economies significantly. As older boomers leave larger houses and require greater health care, this young cohort will need more schools, daycares, housing, and services and consumer products tailored to their needs.

Demographics
Lori Ann Roness

Demography assists in understanding present and potential trends. Governments often rely on demographic data to anticipate the types of services the populace might require or demand and to better plan for the delivery of such services. Non-profit agencies use demographic data to identify community needs and interests, identify gaps in their own services, tailor programs to specific audiences, and understand potential donors. Similarly, businesses also use demographics to better comprehend who potential customers are, their location, and what their needs, desires, and interests are so they can better design, package, market, and sell their wares.

To get the most out of demographic data, it should be grounded within socioeconomic contexts that relay information about broader society, commercial interests, the economy, and social issues. Accordingly, the goal of this chapter is to not only talk about what demographics are, but also to discuss what "the numbers" tell us about society, particularly in reference to Aboriginal business and employment. Thus, the chapter will (a) explain what demographic information is and the purposes it serves; (b) provide an overview of current Aboriginal demographics; (c) discuss the impacts and implications of these demographics, particularly in terms of Canada's aging workforce; and (d) present possibilities in terms of the potential roles of Aboriginal and non-Aboriginal business, governments, and Aboriginal people in addressing gaps.

> **Demographics** refers to the characteristics of a particular population.

An Explanation of What Demographic Information Is and the Purpose it Serves

What are Demography and Demographics?

The sociologists Hauser and Duncan notably defined demography as "the study of the size, territorial distribution and composition of population, changes ... and the components of such change, which may be identified as natality, mortality, territorial movement (migration), and social mobility (change of status)." (qtd. in Wargon 2001: 311). Types of demographic information include:

- Total population – the number of people that comprise a particular population.

- Population change or events – population growth or decline; patterns of population change; births and deaths; marriages and divorces; or vertical or social mobility.

- Population movement – internal or external migration.

- Population density – the number of people who reside in a given area, per square kilometre.

- Population composition or characteristics – for example, age, sex, (un)employment, income, household size, education, disability, occupation, language, religion, ethnicity.

- Geographic distribution – where people are living, or how they are spread across a particular geographic area.

At the same time, demography is more than the sum of its numbers; it connects raw data to the social fabric of our lives and tells "the human story [through a series of] ... vital events," like births, deaths, movement, and economic, social, and cultural change (Tuljapurkar 2011: 166). From a business perspective, such demographic data can then be used to create a narrative about who its target population is in order to communicate with it as effectively as possible.

Sources of Demographic Information

Numerous agencies collect demographic information, including governments, industry, the private sector, educational institutions, healthcare-delivery agents, social-policy agencies, and non-profit organizations. General sources of demographic information include the census, vital statistics, databases, departmental and administrative records and research, business and company records, annual reports, survey results, land records, crime statistics, and industry-sector councils and associations. Such sources may also reveal demographic characteristics for specific subpopulations, depending on how the information was collected. The type of information one is seeking and the population under study will influence where one looks for information.

> A **target population** is a specific group of people who share particular characteristics and are intended to be the recipient of a message, advertisement, promotion, and so on.

There are several key (though not exhaustive) sources of demographic information to consider when seeking demographic information about Aboriginal people. Statistics Canada conducts the Canadian census every five years and uses it to develop federal programs and to help determine federal transfer payments to provinces and territories. As part of the census, Statistics Canada collects a range of Aboriginal data, such as Aboriginal identity, Indian status, area of residence, age, sex, labour-force participation, educational attainment, literacy, income, language, housing, health, and life expectancy.

> A **census** is an official enumeration of a population that collects demographic information, such as age, gender, residence, and occupation.

Conducted in 2011, the National Household Survey (NHS) is a voluntary survey completed by more than four million Canadian households every five years. It addresses a variety of topics, including immigration, citizenship, place of birth, ethnicity, visible minorities, religion, labour and employment, education, mobility, migration, language, income, and housing (Statistics Canada 2011). There is an Aboriginal-specific component that reports on Aboriginal identity, population growth, population distribution, age, and living arrangements.[1]

In Canada, the **mandatory long-form census** was replaced by a voluntary National Household Survey (NHS) in 2010. The short-form census and NHS are conducted every five years.

Conducted by Statistics Canada, the Aboriginal Peoples Survey is a national survey that reports on the social and economic conditions that Aboriginal people experience in Canada. It was last conducted in 2012 and surveyed First Nations people who live off-reserve, Métis, and Inuit people who are six years of age or older. It covers a range of topics like education, language, employment, income, health and well-being, housing, and mobility (Statistics Canada 2013c).

Overseen by the First Nations Information Governance Centre, the First Nations Regional Health Survey is a First Nations-governed national health survey. It was first conducted in 1997 (as a pilot) and included First Nations and Inuit adult and youth respondents. Subsequent surveys conducted in 2002/03 (phase 1; included 238 First Nation communities) and 2008/10 (phase 2; included 10 regions and 216 First Nations) focused only on First Nations. The survey collects information about people living on-reserve and in northern First Nations. It considers demographics and migration; employment and income; education; language; housing; living conditions; access to healthcare; chronic illness; HIV/AIDS; suicide; mental and emotional health; physical activity; nutrition; residential schools; substance abuse; prenatal, oral, and sexual health; health status and quality of life; injury; disability; wellness; and traditional culture (First Nations Information Governance Centre 2012: 1).

In 2011, the Canadian Council for Aboriginal Business conducted the Aboriginal Business Survey, which surveys the size, growth, and key characteristics of Aboriginal small businesses.

Nationally and provincially, there are multiple organizations that represent the interests of Aboriginal people; they sometimes conduct research and collect demographic data regarding their constituents. Nationally, the Assembly of First Nations represents First Nations' priorities; the Congress of Aboriginal People represents off-reserve and non-registered First Nations and Métis people; the Métis National Council represents the interests of Métis people; the Inuit Tapiriit Kanatami represents the interests of Inuit people living in Inuit Nunangat (the Inuvialuit settlement region in the Northwest Territories, Nunavut, Nunavik [Northern Québec], and Nunatsiavut [Northern Labrador]); and the Native Women's Association of Canada represents and advocates for Aboriginal women in Canada. Provincial and territorial organizations (PTOs) are organizations that represent the collective interests of First Nations that are located within the boundaries of a particular province or region. For example, in the Atlantic region, the PTO is the Atlantic Policy Congress of First Nation Chiefs, which represents the interests of First Nations in Atlantic Canada at the Assembly of First Nations.

The Importance of Demography in the Context of Aboriginal Business

Demographic information is useful in multiple ways when talking specifically about Aboriginal people, business, and economic development. At the governmental level, policy-makers and analysts can use demographic data to develop and ensure policies reflect current needs, service responsiveness, and the creation of funding programs and development support for Aboriginal entrepreneurs.

Demographic data is helpful for Aboriginal business owners seeking start-up or business-development funding. Most funders want to know about the population or socioeconomic characteristics of the people a venture is targeting. Having demographic information allows one to relay that information clearly and succinctly, to explain the intended use of the money applied for, and who it will ultimately benefit.

Demographic data is also important for business modelling and planning. It can assist in identifying one's potential client base and determining the best business model in taking advantage of opportunities to respond to the needs and demands of that client base. In addition, demography can be used to evaluate potential business initiatives, conduct cost-benefit analyses, and develop long-range business, marketing, and communication plans.

Demography can also be used to better understand the workforce and one's target market, which could, in turn, help determine where to set up one's business, and ensure one has the proper staffing, with the right skills and expertise, to best serve one's customer base. It can also help both Aboriginal and non-Aboriginal business owners identify staff-training and professional-development needs.

> **Business modelling** refers to the process of creating multiple, often complex, scenarios as a means of considering a variety of possible outcomes of a decision where the future state cannot be known. Analysis of various models created using different assumptions helps decision-makers assess risk given uncontrollable forces, often in finance and operations.
>
> **Cost-benefit analysis** (CBA) is a process by which decisions and outcomes are evaluated in terms of the cost and the benefits derived. Generally, the goal is to have benefits outweigh the costs.

Current Aboriginal Demographics

Population Growth

The NHS reveals that the Aboriginal population was 1,400,685 people in 2011, or 4.3 per cent of the Canadian population of 33,476,688. This is an increase of 0.5 per cent since 2006, when the Aboriginal population was 3.8 per cent (1,172,790 individuals) of the Canadian population (Statistics Canada 2012a: 3, 2013a: 6).

Of the people who self-identified as Aboriginal in the 2011 NHS, 60.8 per cent identified as being First Nation (registered or non-registered Indians[2]); 32.3 per cent identified as being Métis and 4.2 per cent identified as being Inuit; 1.8 per cent reported having "other" Aboriginal identities, having reported belonging to more than one identity group, and/or belonging to a First Nation but not indicating having an Aboriginal identity or being registered Indians. A quarter (25.5 per cent) of the First Nations population is made up of people who are not registered Indians (Statistics Canada 2013a: 6-11). Table 1 depicts the breakdown of the Aboriginal population (Statistics Canada 2013a: 7).

Self-identification is the attribution of particular qualities to oneself. For Indigenous peoples, this means self-identifying as an Aboriginal person, regardless of whether one is officially registered as a status Indian on the federal government's Indian registry or a band list.

Between 2006 and 2011, the Aboriginal population increased by 20.1 per cent (232,385 people). This compares to a population growth of only 5.2 per cent for non-Aboriginal Canadians. Therefore, the Aboriginal population grew four times faster than the non-Aboriginal Canadian population.

Table 1: Aboriginal Identity Population, 2011		
Aboriginal Identity	Number	Per Cent
Total Aboriginal identity population	1,400,685	100.0
First Nations single identity	851,560	60.8
First Nations single identity (registered or treaty Indian)	637,660	45.5
First Nations single identity (not a registered or treaty Indian)	213,900	15.3
Métis single identity	451,795	32.3
Inuit single identity	59,445	4.2
Multiple Aboriginal identities	11,415	0.8
Aboriginal identities not included elsewhere	26,475	1.9
Source: Statistics Canada 2013a: 7		

When one considers population growth among different types of Aboriginal people, one can see that the First Nation population grew at the fastest rate. The population of First Nation people grew by 22.9 per cent, the Inuit population grew by 18.1 per cent, and the Métis population grew by 16.3 per cent. Among First Nation people, the number that were registered Indians increased by 13.7 per cent, while the number that were not registered increased by 61.3 per cent (Statistics Canada 2013a: 8). This suggests that the non-registered First Nation population is growing faster than the registered population. The overall growth of the Aboriginal population stands in stark contrast to the general Canadian population, which is not growing as quickly.

Age

The Aboriginal population is considerably younger than the general Canadian population. Almost half (46 per cent) of Aboriginal people were under twenty-five years of age in 2011, compared with 29 per cent for the rest of the Canadian population. Only 5.9 per cent of the total Aboriginal population are aged sixty-five or older. In contrast, 14.2 per cent of the non-Aboriginal population are older than sixty-five. At the other end of the age spectrum, 28 per cent of the total Aboriginal population (or 7 per cent of all Canadian children) are under fourteen. In contrast, 16.5 per cent of the non-Aboriginal population in Canada are under fourteen. Just under a fifth (18.2 per cent) of Aboriginal people are between fifteen and twenty-four years old; they represent 5.9 per cent of all youth in Canada. Non-Aboriginal youth between fifteen and twenty-four years of age represent 12.9 per cent of the population (Statistics Canada 2013a: 15).

The median age of the Aboriginal population in Canada is twenty-eight. Among Aboriginal people, Inuit are the youngest. The median age for Inuit is twenty-three. The median age for First Nation people is twenty-six, and the median age for Métis is thirty-one. In contrast, the median age for the non-Aboriginal population was forty-one by 2011. By 2056, it is anticipated that the median age in Canada will be 46.9 (Statistics Canada 2013a: 16).

> The **median** is the middle number or midpoint in a particular range of numbers.

Distribution of the Aboriginal Population in the Provinces and Territories

Table 2 depicts the number and distribution of people that identify as Aboriginal across Canada, by province and territory. The bulk of Aboriginal people are concentrated in Québec, Ontario, Manitoba, Saskatchewan, Alberta, and British Columbia. However, Aboriginal people comprise a significant proportion of the total population in Manitoba, Saskatchewan, and the northern territories.

In terms of Aboriginal-identity populations, the registered-Indian population represents the highest proportion of Aboriginal people in each province and territory, with the exception of Nunavut, where Inuit people are the clear majority (AANDC 2013: 7). Winnipeg, Edmonton, and Vancouver are the census metropolitan areas (CMAs)3 with the largest registered-Indian populations. In those cities, registered First Nations represent 3.6 per cent, 1.6 per cent, and 0.7 per cent of the population, respectively. The CMAs with the largest non-registered Indian population is Toronto, with 0.3 per cent of the population, Vancouver, with 0.6 per cent of the population, and Montréal, with 0.3 per cent of the non-registered Indian population (Statistics Canada 2013a: 11).

Table 2: Number and Distribution of Aboriginal Identity Population and Percentage of Aboriginal People in the Population by Province/Territory

Provinces and Territories	Total Canadian Population	Aboriginal Identity Population	Per Cent Distribution	Aboriginal Identity Population as a Percentage of the Total
Canada	34,342,800	1,400,685	100.0	4.3
Newfoundland and Labrador	535,000	35,800	2.6	7.1
Prince Edward Island	144,00	2,230	0.2	1.6
Nova Scotia	944,500	33,845	2.4	3.7
New Brunswick	755,500	22,615	1.6	3.1
Québec	8,007,700	141,915	10.1	1.8
Ontario	13,263,500	301,425	21.5	2.4
Manitoba	1,233,700	195,900	14.0	16.7
Saskatchewan	1,066,300	157,740	11.3	15.6
Alberta	3,790,200	220,695	15.8	6.2
British Columbia	4,499,100	232,290	16.6	5.4
Yukon	35,400	7,705	0.6	23.1
Northwest Territories	43,500	21,160	1.5	51.9
Nunavut	34,200	27,360	2.0	86.3

Source: Statistics Canada (2013a: 9, 2013d).

The vast majority of Inuit (73.1 per cent) live in Inuit Nunangat, which is the Inuit homeland that encompasses the regions of Nunatsiavut (northern Labrador), Nunavik (northern Québec), Nunavut, and Inuvialuit (Northwest Territories). In Inuit Nunangat, 3.9 per cent of Inuit live in Nunatsiavut, 18.1 per cent live in Nunavik, 45.4 per cent live in Nunavut, and 5.6 per cent live in the Inuvialuit region. The vast majority (84.9 per cent) of people who self-identify as Métis live in the western provinces. Just more than 21 per cent (21.4 per cent) of those who report being Métis live in Alberta. Almost 20 per cent (19 per cent) of Métis live in Ontario, 17.4

per cent live in Manitoba, 15.4 per cent live in British Columbia, and 11.6 per cent reside in Saskatchewan. Conversely, only 5.1 per cent of those who report being Métis live in the Atlantic Provinces combined. One-quarter of the Métis population lives in the four western CMAs of Winnipeg (46,325 individuals), Edmonton (31,780), Vancouver (18,485), and Calgary (17,040). Saskatoon has a Métis population of 11,520, while Toronto has a population of 9,980 Métis (Statistics Canada 2013a: 12-13).

Urban versus Rural Distribution

The majority of non-registered and Métis people tend to live in urban areas. However, Inuit people are primarily rural. Almost half (49.3 per cent) of the registered-Indian population lives on-reserve with a significant number of reserves being semi-remote or remote. In contrast, non-Aboriginal Canada is primarily urban. As of 2011, almost seven in ten Canadians (69.1 per cent, or 23.1 million people) lived in one of thirty-three CMAs. Moreover, more than one in three Canadians was living in Toronto, Montréal, or Vancouver (Statistics Canada 2012a: 12, 2013a:11).

The rural nature of many Aboriginal communities is due to the fact that the traditional territories of many Aboriginal peoples are in remote regions of Canada, and present-day Aboriginal communities may still be located in or nearby. Furthermore, for a significant number of First Nations, the federal government expropriated land and relocated reserves to remote areas to make room for a growing Canadian population and for urban expansion.

> **Non-registered Indians** are those who are not registered as Indians on the federal government's Indian registry and, therefore, are not officially recognized by the federal government.

Educational Attainment

In 2011, almost half (48.4 per cent) of Aboriginal people between twenty-five and sixty-four who responded to the NHS had a post-secondary education, 14.4 per cent had a trades certificate, 20.6 per cent had a college diploma, and 9.8 per cent had a university degree. In contrast, 64.7 per cent of the non-Aboriginal population had a post-secondary education. Among non-Aboriginal Canadians, 12 per cent had a trades certificate, 21.3 per cent had a college diploma, and 26.5 per cent possessed a university degree. Therefore, a greater proportion of non-Aboriginal Canadians are university educated as compared with Aboriginal Canadians. As well, the proportion of Aboriginal people without a degree, diploma, or certificate was 28.9 per cent, whereas the proportion among non-Aboriginal people was only 12.1 per cent. Younger Aboriginal people also tend to be more educated than older ones. For example, 68 per cent of Aboriginal people between age thirty-five and forty-four had at least a high-school diploma as compared with 58.7 per cent for Aboriginal people aged between fifty-five and sixty-four. This is considerably lower than among the general Canadian population; more than two-thirds (88.7 per cent) of non-Aboriginal people aged between thirty-five and forty-four had a high-school diploma, as had 79.5 per cent of those between fifty-five and sixty-four (Statistics Canada 2013e: 4-5).

Employment

In 2009, the average employment rate for Aboriginal people was 57 per cent, as compared with 61.8 per cent for non-Aboriginal Canadians. Likewise, the unemployment rate was 13.9 per cent for Aboriginal people and 8.1 per cent for non-Aboriginal people (Statistics Canada 2012b: 2). Employment is an important indicator of poverty. Lack of employment can lead to less access to nutritious food, and greater risk of obesity, diabetes, and heart, lung, and renal disease. Poverty also contributes to greater mental illness, stress, and anxiety, which can be connected to increased risk of violence and addiction (Reading and Wien 2009: 9-10).

Health

On average, Aboriginal people have greater health problems than do non-Aboriginal people. For example, heart disease is 1.5 times higher than it is among Canadians as a whole. The diabetes (type 2) rate is three to five times higher among First Nations than among non-Aboriginal Canadians and the rate of tuberculosis is eight to ten times higher. Fifteen per cent of people who are newly diagnosed with HIV or have AIDS infection are Aboriginal. Suicide and self-injury are the main causes of death for First Nation youth and adults, and First Nation youth are five to six times more likely to commit suicide than their non-Aboriginal counterparts. The rate of injury and poisoning-related deaths is 6.5 times higher for First Nation and Inuit people than the general Canadian population (Health Canada 2014a, 2014b; Standing Senate Committee on Social Affairs, Science and Technology 2001: 130).

Aboriginal people, except Métis, are also more likely to live in over-crowded houses than non-Aboriginal people are; 31 per cent of Inuit, 3 per cent of Métis, and 15 per cent of First Nation people live in crowded homes as compared with just 3 per cent of non-Aboriginal people. Related to this, 28 per cent of Inuit, 14 per cent of Métis, and 28 per cent of First Nation people live in homes that need major repairs. In contrast, 7 per cent of non-

Aboriginal people do. Poor housing has been linked to increased risk of infectious diseases, respiratory infections, injury, poor mental health, and family discord (Reading and Wien 2009: 9).

Aboriginal Business

There is not a lot of research regarding Aboriginal entrepreneurs. The Canadian Council for Aboriginal Business (CCAB), in the aforementioned Aboriginal Business Survey (ABS), found that self-employment among Aboriginal people increased by 37.6 per cent between 2001 and 2006, and by 85.4 per cent between 1996 and 2006. Self-employment among Canadians in general grew by only 7.2 per cent, showing that the rate of self-employment growth among Aboriginal people was five times that of general Canadians overall (CCAB 2011: 9).

Almost half, 49.3 per cent, of Aboriginal people who reported being self-employed were Métis. Forty-five per cent reported being First Nation and 1.9 per cent identified as Inuit. Looking at Aboriginal entrepreneurship in another way, 6.6 per cent of the Aboriginal labour force older than fifteen years of age in 2006 was self-employed. Of Canadians in general, 11.6 per cent reported being self-employed in 2006. Aboriginal people were half as likely to be self-employed as other Canadians. However, the proportion of Aboriginal people who were self-employed did not grow between 2001 and 2006, largely because the Aboriginal labour force grew overall (by 29.7 per cent as compared with 8 per cent among general Canadians). Therefore, the growth of Aboriginal entrepreneurship has been relatively flat and represents an ongoing gap when compared to the non-Aboriginal Canadian population (CCAB 2011: 9-10).

Aboriginal entrepreneurs are concentrated in Ontario, British Columbia, and Alberta; respectively, 23 per cent, 22 per cent, and 18 per cent are located there. Self-employed Aboriginal people are underrepresented in Manitoba and Saskatchewan, which is interesting given that those two provinces have the fastest-growing Aboriginal population in the country. The majority of Aboriginal businesses are off-reserve and home-based. However, when one considers different types of Aboriginal people, one can see that 72 per cent of First Nation businesses are located on-reserve, and that 97 per cent of Métis and 81 per cent of Inuit businesses are located off-reserve. Thus, 63 per cent of Aboriginal businesses are located off-reserve. The majority of Aboriginal entrepreneurs (72 per cent) were operating as sole proprietorships (61 per cent) or partnerships (11 per cent). Just over a quarter (26 per cent) were federally or provincially incorporated (CCAB 2011: 11-14).

Aboriginal business seems to be concentrated in construction (18 per cent) and in primary sectors, such as agriculture, forestry, fishing and hunting, mining, and oil and gas (13 per cent). Twenty-eight per cent of Aboriginal businesses operate in knowledge-based sectors, such as science and technology, education, and health. However, there is still a gap in the sense that 37 per cent of Canadian entrepreneurs operate in the knowledge-based sector (CCAB 2011: 11).

More than one third (37 per cent) of self-employed Aboriginal businesses employed at least one other employee. The remainder reported having no employees. Businesses operating in the service sector are least likely to have employees (27 per cent), and businesses operating in the agricultural and construction services are the most likely to have employees (CCAB 2011: 14).

Most markets for Aboriginal businesses are local. Eighty-five per cent of Aboriginal businesses surveyed in the ABS reported having customers within their own community or province/territory. However, a significant portion of Aboriginal entrepreneurs also conduct business elsewhere. For example, 48 per cent have clients in other parts of Canada, 26 per cent have clients in the United States, and 18 per cent have clients beyond Canada and the United States (CCAB 2011: 15).

The ABS also found that there are a number of factors of success. These include having stability, having a high-quality product or service, having a business plan, embarking on product or service innovations, being active more widely across Canada beyond the local community, having a more diverse client base, and accessing start-up funds and taking advantage of non-personal sources of capital (CCAB 2011: 39-41) (see also chapters 4 and 8).

Implications

The demographics presented above suggest a number of implications and possibilities. Over the last thirty years, 70 per cent of the general Canadian population was of working age, largely because of the post-war baby boom. However, it is estimated that the proportion of working Canadians will drop 10 per cent by 2030, when it is anticipated that only 60 per cent of the Canadian population will be of working age. Labour shortages are anticipated, and a lower proportion of the Canadian population will be responsible for generating the income, goods, and services that Canadian citizens require and expect. This may affect national productivity as there may be a decline in the gross domestic product (GDP), that is, the value of all

Baby boom is the expression used to identify a period of time during which there is a significant increase in the birthrate. In Canada, the expression "baby boomers" usually refers to the children born in the twenty years following the Second World War.

INDIGENOUS BUSINESS IN CANADA

the goods and services produced within a country in a specific time period. Between 1972 and 2011, real GDP growth (the rate of growth adjusted for inflation) averaged 2.9 per cent per year. Over half of this growth was due to increases in the labour supply. However, Canada's decreasing labour supply could slow GDP growth significantly, which could result in less per capita income, fewer job opportunities, and hiring slowdowns or freezes. In turn, less tax revenue would likely be generated and could ultimately result in less money for social programs and services, including business and entrepreneurship support. Lower productivity growth may also lead to a decline in the Canadian standard of living (Department of Finance Canada 2012: 22-29; Sharpe, Arsenault and Lapointe 2007: 18). To maintain the standard of living as it is today, the labour force has to be as productive as it currently is, regardless of whether its size remains constant or declines.

> **Gross domestic product** (GDP) measures the size of an economy by totalling the market value of all goods and services produced and provided in a country in a year.

Added to this, businesses are finding it increasingly difficult to recruit and retain skilled employees. While not necessarily specifically related to our aging population, that skilled workers with decades of experience are retiring and not being replaced does not bode well for businesses that require skilled personnel. Such businesses, when faced with the inability of filling their vacancies domestically, look beyond Canada's borders to satisfy their labour needs. Business owners may also face succession challenges, as they may not have children or other successors to take over their business when they retire. This may translate into a closing of Canadian businesses and lead to a tapering in terms of manufacturers and service providers.

> **Inflation** refers to the increase in the prices of goods and services or a decrease in the purchasing power of money.

In contrast, Aboriginal people are in the midst of a baby boom and could help fill Canada's anticipated labour shortage by increasing the national labour-force participation rate, boosting the economy, and assisting Canada in achieving greater productivity (Department of Finance Canada 2012: 34). This would be mutually beneficial, good for Aboriginal prosperity and economic development, and for Canada more generally. If the status quo remains, however, Aboriginal people will continue to represent an untapped human-resource potential, and there is the risk of continuing to underutilize domestic human resources.

> **Labour supply** is the availability of human resources to work in a particular industry.

Aboriginal business can be individual or communal. The former refers to initiatives that are privately owned by one person or a collective of people; the latter to business ventures that are embarked on by an Aboriginal community in order to generate revenue for the community itself, or for own-source revenue. Regardless, both types of Aboriginal entrepreneurship can fulfill multiple roles by creating innovative products and services, refreshing existing sectors with new ventures and Aboriginal philosophies and approaches, and increasing market competitiveness. Indigenous businesses can also create employment opportunities and jobs for Aboriginal people (and others), help foster independence and self-reliance, and create Indigenous leaders and mentors. In terms of the Canadian economy in general, Aboriginal business also has the potential to fill product and service gaps as other entrepreneurs retire or cease production, and to contribute to economic growth, locally, regionally, and nationally.

The distribution of Aboriginal people is predominantly in central and western Canada. Therefore, their potential contribution to the economy is perhaps the greatest there. For example, in Manitoba, 28 per cent of the youth population (aged fifteen to twenty-nine) will be Aboriginal by 2026, and they are expected to comprise half of labour force and employment growth until then. In Saskatchewan, it is anticipated that 36 per cent of the provincial population will be Aboriginal by 2026 and will be responsible for all labour-force and employment growth there (Elgersma and Simeone 2012: 10). For business, this could translate into Aboriginal people being a significant proportion of one's target market in these regions or a significant number of business owners and employers. Recognizing Aboriginal people as both consumers and producers of goods and services, therefore, becomes imperative, especially when one considers that non-Aboriginal customers and suppliers may be in decline.

In order to do that, a number of challenges, as illustrated by the demographic information, need to be addressed. A significant number of Aboriginal people are rural or remote. Some communities are only accessible by winter ice roads, when lakes and rivers freeze, leaving only air transport as the main, consistent method of transportation. This makes travel difficult, expensive, and sometimes unsafe. This also makes it difficult and expensive to transport goods or deliver services. While there is the potential for e-commerce, the lack of consistent Internet or even phone service could seriously affect one's ability to communicate with suppliers or customers.

E-commerce refers to sales of products and services electronically via the Internet.

Because Aboriginal businesses are largely home-based, they may face marketing challenges in terms of promoting their businesses and making their commercial presence known. Because the majority of Aboriginal businesses focus on local markets, advertising locally becomes even more critical. At the same time, since having a more diverse client base is a factor of success, learning how to market to a wider audience, particularly a non-Aboriginal one, is also integral.

Increasing human capital by means of education results in productivity growth in the form of more or better goods and services without using much more in the way of other resources. Therefore, increasing the educational attainment of Aboriginal people may boost productivity growth. Aboriginal skills and intellectual ability become assets (human capital) that can be used to create products and services, which, in turn, can be sold. Educated employees also tend to require less management and supervision, which ultimately saves money and boosts productivity. Educated workers are also more likely to be employed and, therefore, more likely to be productive. Unemployed workers are not productive by definition.

In terms of Aboriginal entrepreneurship, business success ultimately depends on long-term sustainability and profitability, as well as internal stability. Understanding business concepts and entrepreneurship, identifying potential opportunities, assessing the viability of business opportunities, transforming concepts into viable businesses, and managing daily operations become critical. Therefore, there is also a need to train more Indigenous people in business management to enhance Aboriginal capacity to do this.

> **Human capital** refers to the combination of knowledge, skills, and experience held by an individual that can be used to create financial value for businesses.

If Indigenous employment levels increase, the profile of the consumer base may also shift; as their purchasing power increases, Aboriginal people will become an important target market, particularly in areas with a burgeoning Indigenous population.

Projected skills shortages may allow Aboriginal communities to target education and training programs so that Aboriginal people are positioned to fill employment gaps. This could also assist employers who currently experience shortages of qualified people to develop targeted recruitment strategies and employee-retention strategies to encourage the employment and retention of Aboriginal employees in particular. This could be most immediately beneficial to Aboriginal people living in urban centres, where employment opportunities are more plentiful. However, targeted training and employment could also benefit more rural Aboriginal people. The vast majority of natural-resource development, for example, occurs in areas largely inhabited by Aboriginal people. A trained, local workforce may reduce the need for companies to bring in workers from the south, reducing their costs and, ultimately, the cost of production.

It is important to recognize, however, that even if every Aboriginal person of working age were gainfully employed, Canada would still face a labour shortage because the anticipated labour shortage is greater than our national capacity. Employing Indigenous people would assist in reducing Canada's need to look abroad for labour and would play an important social role in reducing the high unemployment rate that Aboriginal people currently face.

Because Aboriginal people generally experience greater socioeconomic pressures than the average Canadian, they tend to place more demands on social and health systems. This ultimately translates into increased healthcare and social services costs. Moreover, people who are in poor health are less likely to be able to succeed academically, be as productive, maintain ongoing employment, or operate a business consistently and successfully. Poor health can contribute to increased rates of poverty and unemployment (and vice versa). Therefore, addressing Aboriginal health and wellness is important to addressing poverty and, ultimately, improving Aboriginal attainment of education, employment, and entrepreneurship.

There is also a legal basis for increasing Aboriginal representation in business and the workforce. Section 15 of the Charter of Rights and Freedoms guarantees that "(1) [e]very individual is equal before and under the law and has the right to the equal protection and equal benefit of the law without discrimination and, in particular, without discrimination based on race, national or ethnic origin, colour, religion, sex, age or mental or physical disability."[4] The *Employment Equity Act*, which came into force in 1995, is premised upon the principle that all Canadians should be able to participate in the workforce and advance according to their ability, regardless of their race, ethnicity, or heritage.[5] The *Act* is meant to advance the employment status of segments of the Canadian population that have been traditionally excluded from, or underemployed in, the workforce. It primarily focuses on four designated groups, namely women, people with disabilities, visible minorities, and Aboriginal people. While the *Act* applies to federally regulated businesses that employ 100 people or more, nothing precludes other businesses from applying the principles of employment equity and more equitable labour-force participation strategies in order to help them reach a more representative workforce.

From an ethics perspective, Aboriginal people should have the opportunity to choose whether to participate fully and meaningfully in society and the economy, simply because it is their right as Canadians. Aboriginal people have been disenfranchised and discriminated against, their land appropriated, and marginalized from their land and traditional economies. Supporting Indigenous people to more fully and meaningfully participate in the economy would be a step in righting past wrongs.

Employment equity aims to advance the employment status of segments of the Canadian population that have been traditionally excluded from or underemployed in the workforce. Such programs generally focus on four groups: women, Aboriginal peoples, people with disabilities, and members of visible minorities.

Possibilities

The Role of the Business Sector

Future income growth, productivity growth, and labour-force participation growth will be impacted significantly by decisions made by the business sector. In other words, how businesses choose to address their labour-force challenges, support their employees and their skills-development needs, and/or prepare for an aging workforce will be vital to determining how the Canadian economy performs at large. How businesses engage with the Aboriginal workforce could help fill Canada's human-resource needs. Consequently, it will be crucial to support the business sector in improving or building its human-resource skills, training, capacity, business performance, business-investment strategies, and creativity and innovation (Department of Finance Canada 2012: 35).

Starting with a stronger organizational commitment to employing Indigenous people, the corporate sector could take a more active role in soliciting Aboriginal employees in order to eliminate barriers to employment. It could, for example, be more active in developing targeted recruitment strategies and labour-force participation strategies geared specifically toward Aboriginal people. Revising job descriptions, monitoring staff performance (e.g., training and development, performance evaluations, promotions, terminations, job parameters, etc.), training interviewers, and adopting more valid and representative methods of screening potential employees to ensure they do not have prejudices would help (Thomas and Jain 2004). Having members of employment-equity groups on hiring committees, establishing mentorships, and adding innovations such as flex time may also help create a more hospitable work environment. So, too, would job orientation and mentorship pairings once people are hired. It will be important for businesses and corporations to adapt the work environment to be more inclusive of cultural norms and practices, not only to attract Aboriginal talent, but also to retain it.

Strong organizational leadership is key to such activities, not only at the upper echelons of a corporation, but at the managerial level as well. This is especially important when one considers that many corporate suppliers follow the lead of their clients. This could imply that corporate role-modelling demonstrating excellence and influence may have significant weight in terms of whether or not efforts are undertaken to employ Aboriginal people (Roness and Collier 2010: 40).

In addition, it is important to tap into the existing pool of Aboriginal entrepreneurs who can help address Canada's productivity needs. They may provide Aboriginal-friendly places of employment that offer culturally relevant working environments for Aboriginal people. They can also act as a gateway for other businesses, or even the public at large, to gain access to and better understand the role Aboriginal people and businesses play contemporarily. They may also introduce new business perspectives, approaches, products, and services.

The Role of Government and the Public Sector

At the same time, there is a role for governments as regulators at all levels (municipal, provincial/territorial, federal) and the public sector (i.e., as employers) to play in nurturing Aboriginal labour-force and business participation.[6] Establishing policies and ensuring their enforcement could set the foundation for more equitable hiring practices, and to ensuring that Aboriginal people are able to fill the employment gap, at least in part. This would be coupled with improving resources (financial and otherwise) to improve Aboriginal skills development, education, and training, to building corporate understanding of and openness to hiring and retaining Aboriginal people, and to building entrepreneurship skills.

Governments could adopt measures to create tax incentives, offer education and training opportunities, create trade and investment opportunities across the provinces, nationally, and internally, and focus on Aboriginal people and other underrepresented Canadians to fill employment gaps (Department of Finance Canada 2012: 36). As noted earlier, this could involve using legislation, such as the *Employment Equity Act*, to increase Aboriginal representation.

Governments could also support businesses to develop human-resources strategies designed to recruit and retain Aboriginal people and to engage Aboriginal entrepreneurs as corporate partners. Part of this should involve (re)educating the private sector about the business case for increasing the employment of Indigenous people, and helping employers to become more aware of the history of Aboriginal people in Canada, their contribution to Canada's growth, and the foundation on which the current relationship between Aboriginal people and Canada is built, such as treaties. Government-supported work-readiness and mentoring programs could help train Aboriginal people to acquire the required knowledge, skills, experience, and confidence to compete for mainstream workforce jobs (Roness and Collier 2010: 42). Government could also build its support of Aboriginal business owners by facilitating greater access to start-up funding to assist Aboriginal entrepreneurs in generating sufficient capital to begin and stabilize their business ventures. Government, perhaps in partnership with educational or training institutes, could provide opportunities to Aboriginal entrepreneurs to build their skills regarding access to financing, accounting, business management, marketing, and sourcing materials or resources.

Government could also assist the private sector, Aboriginal communities and organizations, and Aboriginal individuals in overcoming barriers to employment. Barriers that are external to the Indigenous community may include: systemic discrimination; hidden barriers that preclude equitable representation; negative stereotyping; a poor grasp of Aboriginal-Canadian history; a lack of understanding about Aboriginal people, cultures, and communities; a poor understanding of the business case for hiring Aboriginal people; a biased interview process; and/or an absence of Aboriginal people or visible minorities on interview panels and among staff. There are also barriers that are more internal to the Indigenous community, such as a preference to work with Aboriginal colleagues, few Aboriginal role models, poor cooperation among Aboriginal communities and/or agencies, lack of family and community support when living in an urban environment, living in a rural environment and being distant from employment opportunities, low levels of education, insufficient or irrelevant training, limited exposure to the mainstream workforce, a lack of employment experience, and not being "job ready."[7]

As noted above, Aboriginal people also face socioeconomic and health-related barriers that underlie or influence low employment, retention, and workforce readiness. Thus, there is an important role for governments to play in helping to ameliorate the living conditions of Aboriginal people so that their overall quality of life and chances of success improve.

Government, employers, and educational institutions could collaborate in designing education-to-employment or entrepreneurship programs specifically for Aboriginal people. These could include actively recruiting Aboriginal students, providing added mental and social supports during their studies to increase rates of completion, earmarking funding specifically for Aboriginal students who are pursuing postsecondary education and training, and providing pre-employment training to help ensure that Aboriginal people are employment- or business-ready and understand the corporate environment (Sexsmith 2006: 2-3). See also chapter 4.

Creating cultural-sensitivity and cultural-competency training programs could also be important in paving the way for greater Aboriginal employment and business development: "Cultural competence is a set of congruent behaviours, attitudes, and policies that come together in a system, agency, or among professionals and enable that system, agency or those professionals to work effectively in cross-cultural situations" (Cross et al. 1989: 13). Cultural competence is no doubt affected by one's own personal understanding or lack of understanding of a person, group of people, or situation; how we are trained; where we live and work; our social environment, including the legislative and policy environment; and political will. Cultural competence considers how to integrate conceptions about people and groups into standards of practice that are culturally appropriate and which are designed to increase service quality and improve outcomes, how to behave in a manner that respects diversity and allows it to flourish, and how to acknowledge culture and alternative forms of knowledge. Such programs may have the added benefit of increasing corporate awareness of Aboriginal people as a potential source of labour, as business partners, or as suppliers. In this regard, governments, educational institutions, the corporate sector, Aboriginal communities, and even independent consultants experienced with Aboriginal community development could play a role in supporting, developing, and delivering such programs or brokering partnerships to increase corporate Canada's awareness of Aboriginal people as labour and to enhance corporate Canada's outreach to the Aboriginal labour force, so that businesses can better hire and retain Aboriginal workers. There may also be government support for businesses seeking to develop or enhance their internal policies around equitable and more representative hiring (Roness and Collier 2010: 89-90).

> **Cultural competency** is the ability to understand and respectfully interact with other cultures through the acquisition of knowledge, adjustment of behaviour and attitude, and the development of supporting policies.

The Role of Aboriginal People and Communities

Though the Indigenous population is young and could be available to fill Canada's labour shortages and create new businesses that respond to local, regional, and national needs, they must have the requisite training, skills, and orientation to the job and business market. Therefore, there are a number of steps that Aboriginal people, with the support of their communities and the public and private sectors, could take.

Improvements in educational attainment may increase Aboriginal rates of labour-force and business participation and help offset some of the projected employment gaps. Expanding stay-in-school programs, education incentives, and programs that are geared toward building positive self-esteem could ultimately boost educational accomplishments, and, in turn, raise employability, employment, and productivity levels, as well as entrepreneurship (Roness and Collier 2010: 19-20; Sharpe, Arsenault, and Lapointe 2007: 19-20).

Relationship building with the business sector could also help Indigenous people overcome barriers to employment, build Aboriginal/non-Aboriginal business partnerships, and demonstrate a mutual openness to working together to meet both Aboriginal and corporate employment needs. There is room for Indigenous communities and organizations and business to work together to develop labour-force participation strategies geared to attracting and retaining more Aboriginal workers, and for encouraging Aboriginal entrepreneurship and business-concept development (Roness and Collier 2010: 53-54).

Numerous steps could be undertaken in order to prepare Aboriginal people for entering the non-Aboriginal labour force or corporate world. These could include (a) offering pre-employment workshops that address issues like career development, dressing for success, résumé writing, identifying job vacancies, completing the application process, and networking; (b) offering life-skills training to ensure that people are job-ready, are oriented toward working in a non-Aboriginal environment, and can cope with living in a non-Aboriginal community and overcome feelings of isolation or lack of support; (c) coaching, mentoring, and pairing Aboriginal people with others who are employed and/or who understand an external (non-Aboriginal) hiring process and company expectations, and/or who are self-employed; (d) orienting Aboriginal workers or business owners toward working or operating in a non-Aboriginal employment or business environment; and (e) providing industry-approved training so that certification and training will be on par with or exceed industry standards.

Equally important is creating a supportive family and community environment. Similarly, Aboriginal communities and agencies concerned with employment and economic development could take steps to build relationships and partnerships with the corporate sector and potential employers and businesses. Steps could include: (i) establishing relationships between Aboriginal communities/agencies and sector councils, industry associations, unions; (ii) co-developing plans to identify anticipated corporate human-resource needs and community-based strategies for training Aboriginal individuals and entrepreneurs to fill those anticipated gaps; (iii) identifying companies that have developed or who are open to developing targeted Aboriginal labour-force and corporate-participation strategies or building corporate partnerships with Aboriginal businesses; and/or (iv) holding networking events that would allow the business sector, Aboriginal agencies, and even individual Aboriginal people and entrepreneurs to interact, share best practices, and build dialogue and relationships (Roness and Collier 2010: 85-94).

Final Thoughts

This chapter began with a discussion of what demographics are and discussed the linkage between the demographics and trends and opportunities for Aboriginal business. The demographics tell us that that Canada's baby boom is over and the country's general population growth is slowing. Furthermore, the general Canadian population is getting older and retiring, leaving labour-force and production gaps that will need to be filled. There are opportunities for Aboriginal people and entrepreneurs to fill those gaps. Yet addressing them is neither simple nor straightforward. As discussed above, there is a role for the corporate, government, and public sectors, and for Aboriginal individuals, businesses, and communities to work together toward this common aim.

Much work is required to improve awareness of Aboriginal people as potential business owners, suppliers, employees, corporate partners, and competitors. A shift in thinking is required to be more open to Aboriginal employment and entrepreneurship, build communications with Aboriginal people, businesses, and communities, and develop improved mutual understanding, respect, and cultural sensitivity. This shift includes the need to reorient how Aboriginal businesses are perceived and fit within the corporate sector, and to expand the focus of Aboriginal businesses beyond the Aboriginal community to servicing the general population at large.

Government can support efforts by ensuring legislation supports the advancement of Aboriginal people in Canada's labour force and corporate sector by supporting education and training initiatives designed to increase Aboriginal competitiveness. Government can also support the (re)education of corporate Canada so it is has a better understanding of the barriers that Aboriginal people and businesses face, and how it can amend its own way of doing business to better interact with Aboriginal people and entrepreneurs.

Working-age Aboriginal people can also be proactive about pursuing training and education, and about actively looking for employment or developing their own business. There is an integral role for Aboriginal communities and organizations to support Indigenous individuals and businesses, and to better equip them with the skills they will need to succeed. This will help shift the Aboriginal collective toward greater long-term employment, business viability, self-esteem, and positive role models for current and future generations.

A more holistic approach—one that brings together Aboriginal people and entrepreneurs with the corporate, government, and education sectors, and which is planned and integrated—is required. Such an approach must not only consider immediate employment or business-related needs. It must be cast wider and consider how poor mental and physical health, and generations of poverty, isolation, and colonialism affect contemporary employability, and how business and employment-related issues can be better addressed. Such an integrated approach is more likely to result in success in addressing Aboriginal employment and Canada's growing labour and business needs.

Key Points:

- Demographic information defines the characteristics of a particular population, which can be used in a variety of ways, such as the development of programs or new products and services.

- Communities and governments do not always take the same approach to identifying and defining "Aboriginal." Consequently, reports that look similar may not be reporting the same information. When reviewing and comparing data sets, it is important to understand the assumptions that were made.

- The Aboriginal population in Canada is young and growing.

- There is a growing labour-force shortage in Canada, which the Aboriginal population can help to address in a variety of ways, such as via business creation.

- While there is a capacity deficit that needs to be addressed for Aboriginal people to fully participate in the Canadian workforce, there is also a need for corporate Canada and other businesses to be respectful and ready to change so that Aboriginal people are welcome in their organizations.

Questions for Review:

1. What are some sources of demographic information about Aboriginal people in Canada?

2. What types of information can demography reveal, and why are such types of information valuable? How are they used, and for what purpose?

3. How does the *Indian Act* influence demographic reports regarding Aboriginal identity? What might this mean for decision-makers using multiple data sets from various sources?

4. Why are demographics important for understanding Aboriginal people and Aboriginal business and economic development?

5. What can demographics tell us about Canada's future?

6. How might Aboriginal Canadians and businesses help solve the problem of Canada's growing labour-force shortage and anticipated productivity challenges?

7. What is the potential role of business, government, the public sector, and Aboriginal communities and entrepreneurs in in-

creasing productivity and Aboriginal labour-force and business participation?

8. What challenges do Aboriginals in remote areas face in relation to business development?

9. What can be done to adapt the mainstream work environment for Aboriginal peoples?

Suggested Assignments:

1. As baby boomers leave the workforce and young Aboriginal people enter it, the rate of demographic change is compounded. At what point will the workforce become majority Aboriginal?

2. Look at the data provided by each of the data sets provided and discussed. What are the challenges with different sources of data and changing procedures for the collection of data? Consider, for example, that there is a gap in census data between 2011 and 2016, during which time the Canadian government eliminated the long-form census.

3. What benefits and opportunities might be created through improved cultural competence? What might change? Why are people reluctant to change?

Notes

The author thanks Dr. Stephen Law, associate professor, Department of Economics, Mount Allison University, for the clarification he provided. Any errors, omissions, or inaccuracies are the author's alone.

1. The Aboriginal component of the survey is not without its challenges. People living in First Nation communities and who participated in the National Household Survey were not asked questions about citizenship or immigration status. Terms such as "Aboriginal identity" can be vague and are understood differently by different people. Who qualifies for Indian status has changed as a result of changes to the *Indian Act* in 1985 and with Bill C-3 in 2011. Some people also reported their Aboriginal identity or ancestry differently from one survey period to another. Thirty-six out of 863 Aboriginal communities were not enumerated completely. See Statistics Canada (2013a: 6-7, 2013b: 8).

2. Note that registered Indians, or status Indians, are Aboriginal people who are entitled to be registered as Indians under the *Indian Act*.

3. A census metropolitan area (CMA) is "an area consisting of one or more neighbouring municipalities situated around a core." The total population of

the CMA must have at least 100,000 people, with at least 50,000 living in the core (AANDC 2013: 8).

4. *The Constitution Act*, 1982, Schedule B to the *Canada Act, 1982* (U.K.), 1982, c 11, (http://canlii.ca/t/ldsx).

5. *Employment Equity Act*, SC 1995, c 44 (http://canlii.ca/t/52c3h).

6. Governments are regulators that create policy, deliver services, and look after the social and economic interests of the country. Governments also constitute the public service, which delivers services and programs. As such, governments are employers, too.

7. For a more detailed discussion of these barriers, please refer to Roness and Collier (2010: section 3).

References

AANDC (Aboriginal Affairs and Northern Development Canada). 2013. Aboriginal Demographics From the 2011 National Household Survey. Planning, Research, and Statistics Branch. https://www.aadnc-aandc.gc.ca/DAM/DAM-INTER-HQ-AI/STAGING/texte-text/abo_demo2013_1370443844970_eng.pdf.

CCAB (Canadian Council for Aboriginal Business). 2011. *Promise and Prosperity The Aboriginal Business Survey.* Toronto: Canadian Council for Aboriginal Business.

Cross, T. L., B. J. Bazron, K. W. Dennis and M. R. Isaacs. 1989. Towards A Culturally Competent System of Care: A Monograph on Effective Services for Minority Children Who Are Severely Emotionally Disturbed. Volume I. Washington, DC: Georgetown University Child Development Center.

Department of Finance Canada. 2012. Economic and Fiscal Implications of Canada's Aging Population. Ottawa: Department of Finance. http://www.fin.gc.ca/pub/eficap-rebvpc/eficap-rebvpc-eng.pdf.

Elgersma, Sandra and Tonina Simeone. 2012. Canada's Aging Population and Public Policy: 5. The Effects on Employers and Employees. Background Paper, February 20. Publication No. 2012-07-E. Ottawa: Library of Parliament. http://www.parl.gc.ca/Content/LOP/ResearchPublications/2012-07-e.pdf.

First Nations Information Governance Centre. 2012. First Nations Regional Health Survey (RHS) 2008/10: National report on adults, youth and children living in First Nations communities. Ottawa: First Nations Information Governance Centre. http://fnigc.ca/sites/default/files/First_Nations_Regional_Health_Survey_2008-10_National_Report.pdf.

Health Canada. 2014a. First Nations and Inuit Health. Mental Health and Wellness. *Health Canada.* http://www.hc-sc.gc.ca/fniah-spnia/promotion/mental/index-eng.php (accessed December 28, 2014).

———. 2014b. First Nations and Inuit Health. Diseases and Health Conditions. *Health Canada*. http://www.hc-sc.gc.ca/fniah-spnia/diseases-maladies/index-eng.php (accessed December 28, 2014).

Reading, Charlotte Loppie and Fred Wien. 2009. *Health Inequalities and Social Determinants of Aboriginal Peoples' Health*. Prince George, BC: National Collaborating Centre for Aboriginal Health.

Roness, Lori Ann and Mary Collier. 2010. Assessing the Effectiveness of Labour Force Participation Strategies. Dartmouth, NS: The Atlantic Policy Congress of First Nations Chiefs Secretariat. http://www.apcfnc.ca/images/uploads/FinalReport-AssessingtheEffectivenessofLabourForceParticipationStrategies.pdf.

Sexsmith, Kathleen. 2006. Aboriginal Employment in the Banking Sector in Manitoba. Ottawa: Canadian Centre for Policy Alternatives. https://www.policyalternatives.ca/sites/default/files/uploads/publications/Manitoba_Pubs/2006/Aboriginal_Employment_in_Banking.pdf.

Sharpe, Andrew, Jean-Francois Arsenault and Simon Lapointe. 2007. The Potential Contribution of Aboriginal Canadians to Labour Force, Employment, Productivity and Output Growth in Canada, 2001-2017. CSLS Research Report No. 2007-04. Ottawa: Centre for the Study of Living Standards. http://www.csls.ca/reports/csls2007-04.pdf.

Standing Senate Committee on Social Affairs, Science and Technology. 2001. *The Health of Canadians – The Federal Role. Volume Four – Issues and Options*. Ottawa: The Senate.

Statistics Canada. 2011. NHS Profile, 2011–About the data. *Statistics Canada*. http://www12.statcan.gc.ca/nhs-enm/2011/dp-pd/prof/help-aide/aboutdata-aproposdonnees.cfm?Lang=E (accessed December 22, 2014).

Statistics Canada. 2012a. The Canadian Population in 2011: Population Counts and Growth. Catalogue no. 98-310-X2011001. Ottawa: Minister of Industry. http://www12.statcan.gc.ca/census-recensement/2011/as-sa/98-310-x/98-310-x2011001-eng.pdf.

Statistics Canada 2012b. *Canada Year Book 2011*. Catalogue no. 11-402–X, Ottawa: Minister of Industry.

———. 2013a. Aboriginal Peoples in Canada: First Nations People, Métis, and Inuit. National Household Survey, 2011. Catalogue no. 99-011-X2011001). Ottawa: Minister of Industry. http://www12.statcan.gc.ca/nhs-enm/2011/as-sa/99-011-x/99-011-x2011001-eng.pdf.

———. 2013b. *Reference Guide. Aboriginal Peoples Reference Guide. National Household Survey, 2011*. Catalogue no. 99-011-X2011006). Ottawa: Minister of Industry.

———. 2013c. Aboriginal Peoples Survey (APS). *Statistics Canada*. http://www23.statcan.gc.ca/imdb/p2SV.pl?Function=getSurvey&SDDS=3250&lang=en&db=imdb&adm=8&dis=2 (accessed December 22, 2014).

———. 2013d. Population by Year, by Province and Territory. *Statistics Canada.*
http://www.statcan.gc.ca/tables-tableaux/sum-som/l01/cst01/demo02a-eng.htm (accessed December 27, 2014).

———. 2013e. The Educational Attainment of Aboriginal Peoples in Canada. Catalogue no. 99-012-X0211003, Ottawa: Minister of Industry. http://www12.statcan.gc.ca/nhs-enm/2011/as-sa/99-012-x/99-012-x2011003_3-eng.pdf.

Thomas, Adele and Harish C Jain. 2004. Employment equity in Canada and South Africa: Progress and Propositions. *International Journal of Human Resource Management* 15 (1): 36-55.

Tuljapurkar, S. 2011. Demography as the Human Story. *Population and Development Review* 37 (1): 166-71.

Wargon, Sylvia T. 2001. Connections: Demography and Sociology in Twentieth Century Canada. *Canadian Journal of Sociology* 26 (3): 309-32.

PART THREE

Chapter 10

It could be said that there is no difference between mainstream marketing and marketing in an Aboriginal context. Only to a degree, is that true. Principles such as the "four Ps" of marketing—product, price, promotion, place—as well as customer demographics and market segmentation are universal. In a time of increased social media, information is shared more quickly and more easily, and with broader audiences, than it ever has been. In an Aboriginal context, however, there are additional considerations. The informed marketer will be aware of research-ethics protocols that must be followed in Aboriginal territories. Further, when specifically marketing Aboriginal cultural tourism, the notion of authenticity of product and experience becomes particularly important for consideration.

Marketing in Indigenous Contexts
Keith G. Brown and Joanne Pyke

In the Province of Nova Scotia, tourism is a thriving sector and major economic force. In 2010, tourism revenue in the province totaled $2.02 billion and contributed $722 million to the provincial gross domestic product, while employing 34,400 people (McNutt 2013: 1). In 2014, the total number of visitors to Nova Scotia was 1,958,900 (Tourism Nova Scotia 2015). In a report prepared by Saint Mary's University Business Development Centre for the Mi'kmaq Association of Cultural Studies in 2008, it was noted that the primary target market for the province's Indigenous cultural tourism is North American heritage tourism enthusiasts (HTEs). By 2026, the number of Canadian HTEs visiting Atlantic Canada is projected to grow to one million; by 2025, it is anticipated that the number of American HTEs visiting this region will reach 1.8 million (Business Development Centre 2008: 20). There is significant opportunity, then, for the development of Aboriginal tourism products in this context.

Nova Scotia is home to thirteen Mi'kmaw communities: Millbrook, Acadia, Bear River, Annapolis Valley, Glooscap, Indian Brook, Pictou Landing, Paq'tnkek, Chapel Island, Eskasoni, Membertou, Wagmatcook, and We'koqma'q (Waycobah) with a total population of 16,245 (Aboriginal

Affairs 2015). Mi'kmaw tourism is at varying levels of development within these First Nation communities. In 2008, three cultural sites were identified as being "market ready": the Glooscap Heritage Centre, Bear River First Nation Heritage and Cultural Centre, and the Wagmatcook Culture and Heritage Centre (Business Development Centre 2008). Since then, the Membertou Heritage Park (MHP) has opened, Eskasoni Cultural Journeys has been established, and efforts are underway to open the Mi'kmawey Debert Cultural Centre.

Cultural Tourism Products and Marketing Strategies

Eskasoni First Nation has embarked upon a marketing strategy that may be unique in the country, in both its deep and broad involvement of community. Eskasoni First Nation is the largest Mi'kmaw community in Canada. Over the past several years, the community has restructured its finances, retired its debt, and looked for opportunities to broaden its economic base. One of the areas the community has turned to is cultural tourism, following a classic approach to brand identification and product development while being true to its culture.

The community developed the brand "Our Eskasoni" to support local businesses and to instill a pride in the community and its offerings. Specifically in the realm of cultural tourism, strategists developed a series of long-term goals, which included personnel training, employment, experiential-product development, and tourism-development knowledge, all wrapped within a foundational principle of "an appropriate tourism offering for Eskasoni." Eskasoni Cultural Journeys was the first phase of product development.[1] The Our Eskasoni brand, which expresses a pride in Mi'kmaw history and culture, is prevalent in the Eskasoni Cultural Journeys product. Located on Goat Island, Eskasoni Cultural Journeys features interpretative panels within a village concept which is principally targeting cruise ship visitors. The longer-term vision for the site includes a large cultural demonstration site, a performance area, a seafood restaurant, and eventually a full conference site, all on the shores of Bras d'Or Lake.

Extensive community consultation was done for both the brand and product development. Elders participated as valuable cultural resources and also work on the site. The Eskasoni approach came from the community, on its own terms, which is perhaps its single biggest strength. It is anchored in an authentic Mi'kmaw experience, while its vision provides for the expectations of the 21st-century visitor.

Market ready means that a product or service is developed sufficiently to be brought to market (for sale) and delivered repeatedly and with consistency to customers.

A **brand** refers to a name, logo, design, or other distinguishable feature of a product or service that identifies it as being produced by a particular company.

The Glooscap Heritage Centre

Another Aboriginal cultural tourism product in Nova Scotia is targeting a niche market—bus tours—which are already in the province. Open year-round and located in the First Nation community of Millbrook, near Truro, the Glooscap Heritage Centre[2] provides visitors with a unique Mi'kmaw cultural experience. It houses a visitor information centre, a gift shop, a museum with Mi'kmaw exhibits, a seventy-five-seat movie theatre, and an outdoor area with a twelve-metre statue of Kluskap at its centre. Kluskap is the Mi'kmaw legendary figure at the centre of Mi'kmaw world view and central to many Mi'kmaw tales.

> **A niche market** is a small market segment with a very particular want or need to be satisfied on which a product or service is focused.

Tours at the centre commence with a seventeen-minute video depicting the history and plight of Mi'kmaq. Local interpreters escort visitors around the museum explaining the different artifacts and exhibits. The gift shop provides authentic Mi'kmaw handicrafts. On occasion, visitors are exposed to Mi'kmaw dancing, drumming, and storytelling, as well as the opportunity to learn some Mi'kmaw words. An information area is equipped with brochures and information about tourist sites in the region.

The centre has a competitive advantage due to its location near the Trans-Canada Highway, the busiest highway in Nova Scotia carrying traffic to and from Halifax, the provincial capital. The twelve-metre statue of Glooscap is visible from the highway and attracts the attention of motorists.

Capitalizing on the pre-packaged motorcoach travel industry already existing in the province, the Glooscap Heritage Centre has been able to secure visits during the prime tourist season with tour operators, including Atlantic Tours, Grand Circle Tours, and Caravan Tours. Tourists travelling from the eastern seaboard of the United States and various parts of Canada by way of motorcoach have been the primary target audience for the centre. During peak season (July to October) in 2011, for example, 72 buses carrying 3,170 passengers visited the Glooscap Heritage Centre.

The Glooscap Heritage Centre has employed several communication tools to reach its intended audience. Information about the centre and its offerings is provided by tour guides, tour operators, travel agents, brochures, the centre's website, online newsletter, social media channels, and educators who may have attended workshops at the centre related to Mi'kmaw history and culture. The efficacy of some of these methods, as well as their roles in destination image formation, can be judged by the results of a tourist questionnaire.

Current research suggests that if formal information sources appeal to travellers' motivations (benefits sought), then positive feelings and a positive image of the destination will be formed. Promotion may be designed around those benefits so that it appeals to the target market. To examine whether the promotional sources encountered by tourists visiting the Glooscap

Heritage Centre had a positive impact on image formation, respondents were asked to indicate if (based on promotional information) they expected that the centre would provide certain experiences (benefits) and to rate the importance of each element in forming their impression of the destination. Though the questionnaire queried all eight marketing sources employed by the centre, due to the low exposure rate of some promotional tools, only four sources are discussed in the analysis that follows: tour guide, tour operator, brochure, and travel agent.

Approximately 17 per cent of tourists were exposed to a travel agent's message. Fewer tourists arranged their pre-packaged travel plans using this source; however, they might consider interacting with this intermediary to obtain additional information about a motorcoach tour. The travel agent affected destination image development the least, among study participants. More tourists make direct contact with tour operators, who arrange the coach-tour travel package. This information source was received by 46.3 per cent of respondents and was rated second in impact of impression development.

A tour guide is present on all motorcoaches and provides verbal information about the centre and its offerings. Even though all tourists in this study were exposed to a tour guide's message, not all respondents (approximately 82 per cent) self-identified in this way. According to survey results, tour guides were rated third in influence to image formation among first-time visitors. Print material is also made available to tourists in the information area located outside the centre's main entrance. Travellers are encouraged to browse and examine any of the promotional information. This marketing source was received by 30 per cent of the respondents, and was ranked first in impact on image formation.

Tourists, like all consumers, make product choices based on psychological factors that equate to measure of motivation. In tourism, a significant task is to influence tourist behaviour based on images held in travellers' minds. If a traveller has never visited a destination, they must rely on various information sources to form their initial impression. Image formation can be examined through research tools, such as surveys conducted with first-time visitors, as just described in the example above. In that way, the influence of promotional sources on image formation and pre-visit impression development can be determined. Once tourists have experienced the product first hand, their comparison of the pre-visit impression to their experience will influence their degree of satisfaction. If they are satisfied, they are more likely to positively promote the product to other, future customers. Pre-visit image formation can be particularly important for Aboriginal tourism offerings, since sometimes a tourist's expectations for a product and the actual product do not align.

The Issue of Authenticity

Much has been written in scholarly literature critiquing "authentic" Aboriginal products, services, or experiences. Boniface and Fowler (1993) note that authenticity, or the perception of authenticity, is one of the key attributes in cultural tourism. Perception is the key word.

Notzke (2004) did pioneering work on Aboriginal cultural tourism, and her data on authenticity suggests that tourists do not want products or services which are not true to history and culture, and that presenters and producers must be knowledgeable, genuine, and of Aboriginal descent. Of course, the consumers of Aboriginal products and services may have a different view of what is authentic. Notzke tells of her research with German tourists coming to southern Alberta for an authentic Plains Indians experience. Did they expect a handsome young Blackfoot dressed in jeans and a T-shirt telling them the story of the Blackfoot at Head-Smashed-in Buffalo Jump?[3] Because their perception of the "noble brave" on horseback gazing over the prairie may have been formed through Hollywood movies, and through lack of preparation on their part, they may have been thoroughly disappointed by the knowledgeable, modern young man who could be equally at home on the Blood Reserve or in Munich. Their perception did not match reality.

Another topic of much discussion in the literature is the role of pow-wows in Aboriginal cultural tourism, and of their authenticity. The pow-wow revival of the 1970s swept across the country and hundreds are now hosted every year. Now Mi'kmaq do traditional dances of the Plains Cree and jingle dances[4] of the Anishinaabe during such events. The tourist, fascinated by the spectacular regalia and dance, may believe they are witnessing authentic Mi'kmaw dances—they are witnessing an authentic Aboriginal experience, but not one which is historically correct to the Mi'kmaq. These lines become more blurred if you have a young Mi'kmaw dancer who tells you she has been doing these dances all of her life at powwows and they are part of her culture. She is, of course, correct. Here we speak of borrowed culture, which happens among all peoples around the world. In this case, a young Mi'kmaw—or more correctly, her community and Elders—has borrowed from the Plains peoples to celebrate her Aboriginal heritage. In doing so, she has made it part of her current culture. Her grandmother, who says she didn't do those dances or wear that regalia when she was a girl, may not agree. As long as the marketer makes it clear what the tourist is witnessing, and they understand it is authentic pan-Aboriginal, with perhaps a Mi'kmaw interpretation, most likely they will nonetheless be satisfied and enriched by an "authentic" experience.

If a Québécois, Acadian, or tourist from Louisiana hears something in the music of the Métis of the Red River Valley that reminds them of the

> **Authenticity**
> refers to the quality of being real or genuine.

traditional music they heard as a child, this may in fact be true. The Métis of Manitoba were literally born of two cultures—First Nations and early French explorers. As these two cultures merged, borrowed, and learned from each other, a distinct culture emerged, which mingled language, customs, spirituality, and a sense of connection to the land. The tourist may at times identify with something they see as French, First Nation, or, more likely, uniquely Métis.

Tourists often categorize their authentic experiences as tangible or intangible. Observing a wood carver on Haida Gwaii in British Columbia may satisfy both attributes; as the carver tells tales of the raven and how he is integral to northwest coastal peoples,[5] the tourist learns of history and culture, and perhaps of a spiritual connection to the land, sky, and sea. When the tourist purchases the carving (a tangible artifact) and places it in a prominent place in their home, the intangible feelings of connection, exploration, and cultural learning may recur time and again.

> **Tangible** means that something has a physical form and is perceptible by touch. **Intangible** means that something does not have a physical form and cannot be touched or held.

Intercultural Marketing

Beyond issues surrounding authenticity, the urban Aboriginal marketer living in her condominium in Saskatoon and the non-Aboriginal marketer in corporate head office in Calgary equally must be aware of the cultural differences between Aboriginal communities from coast to coast to coast and notions of communal ownership.

As has been demonstrated elsewhere in this book, First Nation, Métis, and Inuit peoples have unique histories, languages, spiritual beliefs, and cultures. Hundreds of definitions for culture exist in the literature, and the ones we (the authors) as marketers most commonly use consider knowledge that is "learned, shared, and transmitted from one generation to the next," "common [ways] of thinking and behaving," and "customs, language, material artifacts, and shared systems of attitudes and feelings" (Czinkota and Ronkainen 2013: 61).

> **Artifacts** are objects made by humans that have historical or cultural significance.

If you are Swampy Cree, living in Oxford House, northern Manitoba, and your grandmother tells you stories of Wesakechak, the trickster and shape shifter,[6] of growing up on the trap line, and of her experiences in residential schools (see chapter 14), she is teaching you your culture, from one generation to another. Sitting in Cambridge Bay with your dad as he tells of shifting weather patterns, changes in animal migrations, and how his life has changed dramatically in forty years, he is imparting his cultural knowledge. When your grandfather tells tales told to him by his grandfather, of Métis charting the rivers of the west and northwest of Canada, and of the mixing of cultures of French and First Nation, he is "transmitting" his generational cultural knowledge.

When western First Nations speak of giving forward seven generations, it is a cultural philosophy that says you are accountable to protect and provide for your grandchildren's, grandchildren's, grandchildren. This principle[7] is first noted in the Great Law of Peace of the Iroquois Confederacy. This philosophy or cultural trait may baffle non-Aboriginal business people who may have their own cultural trait of signing a contract that is good for their company in the present. Imagine the confusion which may result in a business negotiation to develop a mine in the Northwest Territories when one side is focused on immediate profitability and the other focuses on what is best for the entire community in the present, the near future, and seven generations hence. The notion of collective versus individual oftentimes creates confusion when these two groups come together (see discussion in chapters 3 and 12).

Much of non-Aboriginal Canada, allowing of course for broad cultural differences in a multicultural country, is founded on the notion of individual rights, freedoms, endeavours, and ownership. Individuals, if they choose, buy their own land, own their own home, and finance these purchases through bank financing. The pronoun "I" is most commonly used.

For hundreds of thousands of First Nation peoples who live on one of the 614 reserves in Canada (AANDC 2014), however, and for many Inuit who have negotiated land settlements, land is owned collectively and the community—the group—makes decisions over these lands. Land ownership and property ownership is intrinsically different than in the broader Canadian society, is often widely misunderstood, and can pose huge hurdles in business negotiations (see chapter 2 for a discussion of land and chapter 13 for discussion of the types of treaties in Canada). The role of Elders and their pre-eminent positions in communities as living cultural "databases," protectors of language and traditional knowledge, and their role in governance are key to a broad swatch of Aboriginal Canada.

Many Aboriginal communities are fiercely protective of spiritual traditions and resist their marketing to the outside. Additionally, many Aboriginal jurisdictions have ethics councils who determine if research can be done in their nation, what type of research, and by whom. For example, Mi'kmaw Ethics Watch is a council of Mi'kmaw scholars, Elders, and community members who review each application for research to be done within Mi'kma'ki—the traditional lands of the Mi'kmaq encompassing the Atlantic provinces, Maine, and the Gaspé region of Québec. The role of a market researcher in Aboriginal communities is to ask what research protocols are in place and what procedures must be followed.

Marketing in an Aboriginal context, then, requires that the marketer be attuned to specific issues, such as that of authenticity and *perceived* authenticity. Given the role of marketing materials in image formation for tourists—as well as their satisfaction rates—it is important to take special

Ethics refers to moral principles which guide behaviour.

care in their production and use. Indigenous contexts also require acknowledgement of the diversity between different groups, as well as perspectives related to communal ownership and decision-making. Each community will have a different understanding of what is and is not appropriate for sharing (and marketing) outside a community. There may be community-specific protocols to follow when conducting research. Finally, ongoing assessment of the impact and efficacy of marketing activities is important and may require ongoing community consultation. While these concerns are specific to Indigenous marketing contexts, other marketing concepts—such as the "four Ps" and segmentation—are considered to be more universal.[8]

The Pathway to Marketing

Marketing is a core business function which identifies the needs and wants of the consumer, determines which target market is most suitable for a particular product or service, and then designs methods to best bring the message of that product or service to a group of consumers. On a daily basis we are all subjected to numerous marketing messages while viewing videos on YouTube, checking out photos of friends on Facebook, glancing at the financial pages of a newspaper, or listening to the radio while driving to university. North American society is consumer-based and everyone is a target for mass marketing. Those who choose to study marketing at more advanced levels will learn about consumer behaviour, advertising, social media marketing, intercultural marketing, and marketing research. Such knowledge equips one with the skills and knowledge to be the professional who designs the messages and refines the market segments, whether for an Aboriginal market within Canada or the launch of a broad-based, global marketing plan.

> A **consumer** is an individual who buys products or services.
>
> **Consumer behaviour** is the study of how consumers select, obtain, use, and dispose of products and services.

The Four Ps

Many think marketing is the act of selling a product and service and nothing more. That perception is not accurate. Marketers focus on what are referred to as the "four Ps": product, price, promotion, and place.

Product (or Service)

What are you providing to your customer that your customer is willing to pay for? This may be a highly crafted product, such as footwear from Manitobah Mukluks,[9] or a service, such as airport transportation by Air Creebec.[10] A marketer must know who the customers are and why they want a particular product. This concept will be explored further as we discuss target markets. The first-time marketer may be confused to see product and service used synonymously. However, the end result is that a customer has purchased something they need or want. They may not differentiate their purchase of traditional footwear or a plane ticket which allows them to travel to the site to make the footwear purchase; in both instances, a purchase has been made.

> **A service** is an intangible product, such as cleaning or transportation.

Promotion

It is common to hear or read references toward "advertising" and "promotion" as if these two tools of marketing are one and the same. These terms are linked, but differentiated. Advertising may take the form of traditional print-based ads in newspapers or magazines, or Web-based promotional videos on YouTube or digital ads on Facebook. Advertising is purchased.

> **Advertising** is bringing attention to a product or service through paid notices or announcements.

Promotion, on the other hand, is unpaid. When Wab Kinew, an Anishinaabe recording artist, blogs and tweets his messages of Aboriginal youth staying drug- and alcohol-free, he is promoting a lifestyle choice as well as his music.[11] Nathalie Bertin is an independent Métis artist from Ontario. Nathalie notes the importance of authenticity of her product and how she has few funds to do targeted marketing and promotion. However, she is making effective use of social media outlets and blogs. Nathalie says she "flies by the seat of her pants" when it comes to advertising, but does note the importance of her website in promoting her product (personal communication, July 10, 2013). This demonstrates how an unpaid promotion can have the same desired effect as a paid advertisement. In fact, many may argue the use of social media in this instance is far more effective than any form of paid advertisement. Other forms of promotion may include a flash mob, a celebrity speaking at an event to promote a cause or product, or text "blasts." The goal of this type of promotion is to raise awareness of the product or service, resulting in increased sales.

In these types of examples, it is important to measure the time and resources devoted to promoting the artist and their product and the actual return. If the artist's time, which should be devoted to producing the product, is disproportionately devoted to "free" promotion, production may suffer and profitability may be compromised.

Place

Where are you making your product or providing your service, and where are you selling it? Place may impact distribution costs, time and accessibility to market, and the overall profitability of a business. These considerations are key to the development of a marketing plan and must be addressed pragmatically. The use of online purchasing has changed the marketplace for many small businesses, giving them access to much broader markets with individualized distribution systems through the use of parcel post or courier services.

What methods (channels) are you using to get your product or service to market? The Squamish Lil'wat Cultural Centre has substantially increased its market penetration in the British Columbia tourist market segment by working directly with the travel industry (channel). Both trade shows and travel websites have boosted revenues in the past five years (Casey Heuvel, personal communication, July 2, 2013). Donna Light, the Métis owner of Cedar Points Soaps[12] in Ontario, learned her baking process of soap production from her grandmother, and draws upon her culture for inspiration. She has found that approximately 90 per cent of her production is sold through wholesale outlets, so this channel is of prime importance to her (personal communication, July 12, 2013). She categorizes the channel further by segmenting into four groups: health-food stores, Aboriginal stores, tourist stores, and gift/new age stores.

Distribution refers to the way that a product or service reaches the end consumer, and may involve supplying goods to other businesses that sell them.

A **marketing plan** is a document that identifies the current market position of a business and identifies marketing objectives, as well as specific actions for how they will be met.

Price

Price may appear to be straight forward, but on closer examination complexities arise. As a business person, what is the total cost of your production and what profit margin do you require? How much are you going to pay yourself? Do you provide volume discounts? Do you provide credit? Can customers use credit or debit for purchase? If your customers use credit cards for purchase, are you going to charge them for the credit-card costs that the banks pass on to you, or build these costs into your final price? Are your prices within a competitive range? Are you establishing your price point as a luxury good or at bargain discount? Are you competitive in the marketplace? Do you have a one-of-a-kind product or service?

Channel refers to the supply chain through which a product or service flows before reaching the consumer. Often, other businesses, such as distributors and retailers, serve as intermediaries between the producer and the consumer.

Market penetration refers to the amount of market share for a particular product or service in relation to the total market possible. It helps to measure popularity and success.

The principles of marketing hold valid whether or not the product or target market is Aboriginal. A marketer must know the product or service, as well as who the customers are and why they purchase it. Pricing should be established through a vigorous budget-based process, and all viable avenues of promotion and advertising should be explored to provide maximum reach into customer groups. Finally, a marketer must establish where production should occur, and where and how products will be sold.

Profit margin, expressed as a percentage, refers to the revenue that remains after all expenses are paid. It is often used to assess the health of a business.

Customers

In its simplest form, those who buy your product or service are your customers. You need to know as much detail about them as possible. Who are they? How old are they? What are their income levels (personal as well as household)? What is their educational attainment? Do they have children? Where do they live? This type of data is referred to as demographics and is vital to the success of a marketing strategy (see chapter 9 for more on demography).

Why people do what they do is equally important for a marketer to understand, along with consumer tastes, lifestyles, hobbies, and interests. This data, referred to as psychographics, allows one to tailor products and services to match consumer needs and wants.

> **Psychographics** involves the use of demographic information and analysis of psychological variables such as values or attitudes to develop a customer profile.

Imagine that you are at the earliest stages of preparing a business plan to establish a soft-adventure tourism enterprise in Nunavut. While there are varying degrees of the definition, most agree that soft adventure (e.g., cycling, canoeing, arts walks, culinary excursions) is about interactive experiences through which one has the chance to meet new people, learn new cultures, and perhaps acquire new skills. What might this mean for your business? Perhaps you establish a "menu" of selections for your customers that allows them to tailor their learning experiences. Your menu may include Elder storytelling, a presentation on the effect of global warming on the Arctic, a snowmobile trek, a visit to a stone carver, a lesson in throat singing, language instruction, wildlife excursions, traditional food preparation and consumption, and so on. If this is the business idea, the next question is: Is there a market for this experience, for this service or product? Answering this will require research to determine if the size of the market is sufficient to be profitable, and if the target market can sustain the price needed to be profitable.

There are several sources of data available from various organizations and associations, such as the Canadian Tourism Association, provincial and territorial departments of tourism, and tourism associations. There are Aboriginal tourism associations as well, such as the Aboriginal Tourism Association of British Columbia.[13] These organizations gather data on tourists and tourism trends, and such information can be used to tailor a profile of a potential market. Generally speaking, for the soft-adventure tourism idea here, you will be searching for high-income, university-educated "empty nesters" (those whose children have grown and left home) aged fifty plus, or "DINKs" (double income, no kids) aged thirty-five plus. How do we know this? Travel to the Arctic is expensive, with no cheap charters available, and with few flights and gateway cities. In fact, if our entrepreneur is located in

Iqaluit, the capital of Nunavut, there are only a few flights per day, which operate through Ottawa as the gateway city, making for an expensive flight.

Once you establish the age, education, and income demographics of this market segment, referenced with those of that segment who are interested in experiential travel (psychographics), this data allows us to establish programming and offerings to suit these interests.

Segmentation

Perhaps one of the most important lessons to learn in marketing is the need to segment the market. As mentioned in the example of Nunavut Soft Adventures, the entrepreneur is refining the population by using similar characteristics or traits. We first begin with the population at large, represented by **N**. For illustrative purposes only, we will assume the entire population of the country is 10,000 (**N**). Our entrepreneur is equally interested in attracting males and females, so **N** remains 10,000. They are only interested in those with a university degree, which in Canada is approximately 20 per cent of the population, so the potential population which we now refer to as "**N1**" has shrunk to 2,000. They further refine the search to two age categories—50-plus **N2** male, 50-plus **N3** female; and 35-plus **N4** male, no children, 35-plus **N5** female, no children—to reach a new potential target of 300 males and 200 females (this is an estimate only for illustrative purposes). Finally, using psychographic profiles of **N2**, **N3** and **N4**, **N5**, the entrepreneur seeks the percentage of these profiles which may be interested in experiential, soft-adventure tourism: surveys indicate 30 per cent of this target are potential clients representing a final target market of **N6**, that is, 246 people, 156 male and 90 female. Remember our entrepreneur began their business plan with a population of **N=10,000**, 50 per cent male and 50 per cent female. Now they must determine if the potential market is large enough to proceed and, of course, how to reach the market with the appropriate message.

> A **segment** is a group of potential customers who share certain characteristics and are thus likely to respond to marketing in a similar way.

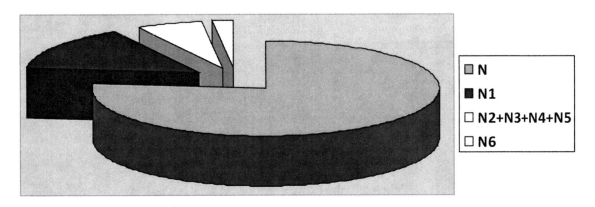

▨	**N**
■	**N1**
☐	**N2+N3+N4+N5**
☐	**N6**

This simplistic example of an idea to promote experiential tourism in the Arctic quickly became complex. The core of this example is twofold: know your customer and research the market. This example shows how quickly a potential market can shrink; in this case, this hypothetical target market represents only 2.5 per cent of the original population.

This example is one of a business-to-customer focus; however, business-to-business, community-to-business, and community-to-government relationships are all important Aboriginal target markets. We have focused on the Aboriginal-to-non-Aboriginal market to this point. However, the opportunities for Aboriginal-to-Aboriginal and non-Aboriginal-to-Aboriginal marketing are substantial.

Implications for Practice

Some marketing concepts are generally accepted throughout the industry and will apply in Aboriginal contexts. The four Ps—price, product, placement, and promotion—is one example. This chapter highlights additional considerations. It is critical to understand the market and customers by conducting research, but in an Aboriginal context this often moves beyond understanding individuals and their expectations, to the broader community and its relationship to the product or service being offered. A marketer or entrepreneur must understand what information is culturally appropriate to share, be attuned to any misconceptions or biases that may cause harm if they are perpetuated, and take care to avoid exploitation of the community. This type of knowledge often can only be obtained by asking the right questions of the right people in respectful ways. Finally, the astute marketer will identify community-specific protocols and follow them.

The success of both Eskasoni Cultural Journeys and the Glooscap Heritage Centre can be attributed to the developers' attention to issues of cultural authenticity and consumer demand for Indigenous tourism products, as well as their implementation of marketing strategies grounded in traditional marketing principles.

Key Points:

- The four Ps of marketing are product, price, promotion, and place.

- Demographic information is critical for business, both in the development of products and services, and the marketing of them.

- Segmentation is a process by which you can identify the size of the potential market for your product or service.

- A niche market is a small or very specific audience for your product or service.
- Authenticity is particularly important to the marketing of Aboriginal tourism products.
- Marketing plans and strategies must be evaluated to ensure that activities are producing the desired results and achieving the identified goals.

Questions for Review:

1. What are the "four Ps" of marketing?
2. What is "segmentation" and what is its purpose?
3. What challenges in marketing might be unique to Aboriginal products and services?
4. What is "authenticity," and why does it matter in relation to tourism specifically? Is authenticity only a concern for Aboriginal products and services?
5. How might a marketer evaluate their work?
6. Why does the Glooscap Heritage Centre attract only a tiny percentage of the highway traffic that passes just meters from its entrance? What could be done to capture a larger target segment? What tools would be effective for marketing to a larger segment?

Suggested Assignments:

1. Imagine a new product or service. Determine the target market and its potential size using demographics and segmentation.
2. Debate: Does it matter if products are authentic?
3. Identify your own customer traits. Define your own personal brand.

Notes

The authors thank Tracy Menge and Kurt Boone for their assistance with this chapter.

1. For more on Eskasoni Cultural Journeys, http://www.eskasoniculturaljourneys.ca/.

2. For more on the Glooscap Heritage Centre, www.glooscapheritagecentre. com.

3. For more on Head-Smashed-in Buffalo Jump, see Brink 2008 or http://history.alberta.ca/headsmashedin/.

4. For more on jingle dress dancing, see Thiel 2007.

5. See, for example, Squamish Lil'wat Cultural Centre (n.d.).

6. For more on this trickster, see *Native Languages* (n.d.).

7. For more on the seventh generation principle, see Clarkson, Morrissette, and Regallet (1992).

8. Such "universal" marketing principles are commonly found in introductory marketing texts, such as Solomon, Zaichkowsky, and Polegato (2005), Armstrong, Kotler, Cunningham, and Mitchell (2004), and Sommers, Barnes, and Stanton (1991).

9. For more on Manitobah Mukluks, http://www.manitobah.ca/.

10. For more on Air Creebec, http://www.aircreebec.ca.

11. For more on Wab Kinew, http://wabkinew.ca/.

12. For more on Cedar Point Soaps, http://www.cedarpointsoaps.com/.

13. For more on Aboriginal Tourism Association of British Columbia, https://www.aboriginalbc.com.

References

Aboriginal Affairs, Province of Nova Scotia. 2015. Mi'kmaq in Nova Scotia Summary as of December 31, 2014. Halifax: Office of Aboriginal Affairs. http://novascotia.ca/abor/aboriginal-people/demographics/ (accessed February 3, 2016).

AANDC. 2014. *First Nation People in Canada*. http://www.aadnc-aandc.gc.ca/eng/1303134042666/1303134337338 (accessed December 4, 2015).

Armstrong, G., Kotler, P., Cunningham, P., Mitchell, P. 2004. *Marketing: An Introduction*. Toronto, Canada: Pearson.

Brink, J. 2008. *Imagining Head-Smashed-In: Aboriginal buffalo hunting on the northern plains*. Athabasca University Press.

Business Development Centre. 2008. Mi'kmaq Cultural Tourism Network: Market Analysis. Report prepared for Mi'kmaq Association of Cultural Studies. Halifax: Saint Mary's University.

Clarkson, L., Morrissette, V., & Regallet, G. (1992). *Our responsibility to the seventh generation: Indigenous peoples and sustainable development*. Winnipeg: International Institute for Sustainable Development. http://www.ces.iisc.ernet.in/biodiversity/sdev/seventh_gen.pdf (accessed December 4, 2015).

Czinkota, Michael and Ilkka Ronkainen. 2013. *International Marketing*. 10th ed. Mason: South-Western, Cengage Learning.

McNutt, Karen. 2013. Nova Scotia's Visitor Economy – 2010. Nova Scotia Economic and Rural Development and Tourism.

Mi'kmaw Ethnics Watch. n.d. *Mi'kmaw research principles and protocols, conducting research with and/or among Mi'kmaw people.* http://www.cbu.ca/aboriginal-affairs/unamaki-college/mikmaq-ethics-watch/ (accessed December 4, 2015)

Native Languages of the Americas: Cree Legends, Myths, and Stories. n.d. http://www.native-languages.org/cree-legends.htm (accessed December 4, 2015).

Notzke, Claudia. 2004. Indigenous Tourism Development in Southern Alberta, Canada: Tentative Engagement. *Journal of Sustainable Tourism.* 12 (1): 29-52.

Solomon, M., Zaichkowsky, J., Polegato, R. 2005. *Consumer Behaviour.* Upper Saddle River, USA: Pearson.

Sommers, M., Barnes, J., Stanton, W. 1991. *Fundamentals of Marketing.* Toronto, Canada: McGraw-Hill Ryerson Limited.

Squamish Lilwat Cultural Centre. n.d. *Animal Symbology.* http://shop.slcc.ca/node/5 (accessed December 4, 2015).

Thiel, M. G. 2007. Origins of the Jingle Dress Dance. *Whispering Wind.* 36(5), 14-18.

Tourism Nova Scotia. 2015. 2005-2014 Visits by Origin. *Tourism Nova Scotia.* https://tourismns.ca/historical-tourism-activity-0 (accessed February 1, 2016).

Usunier, J., Lee, J. (2005). *Marketing Across Cultures.* Harlow, England: Pearson Education Limited.

Chapter 11

A 1999 decision of the Supreme Court of Canada affirmed the treaty right of the thirty-four Mi'kmaw and Maliseet First Nations in Nova Scotia, New Brunswick, Prince Edward Island, and the Gaspé region of Québec to fish in "pursuit of a moderate livelihood." This decision occurred as the Atlantic fishery was undergoing substantial restructuring, downsizing, and stock depletion. Tensions escalated over the management and regulation of the fishery. The federal government provided funds (in a buyback) to purchase fishing licenses and equipment (1,400 licenses and 300 boats) from fishers interested in retiring, thus allowing Aboriginal access to the fishery without increasing stresses on fish stocks.

The fishery is highly competitive and complex, and the new entrants recognized the needs surrounding governance, commercial performance, technical expertise, and business strategies. The federal Atlantic Integrated Commercial Fisheries Initiative addressed human capital development in these areas. By 2011, the value of fishery resources landed by First Nations in the region had surpassed $75 million, and an industry was created.

Overcoming Barriers to Entry in the Commercial Fishery: Ulnooweg Development Group and the Mi'kmaw Fishery
Harvey Johnstone

Ulnooweg Development Group Inc. (Ulnooweg) has been providing loans and business services to Aboriginal entrepreneurs in Atlantic Canada since 1986. Its business-development team (BDT) was established under the Atlantic Integrated Commercial Fisheries Initiative and operates through a partnership relationship between the Atlantic Policy Congress of First Nations Chiefs and Ulnooweg. For those familiar with its context, the BDT is widely regarded as an innovative and successful service provider. Its clients are First Nation communities (FNCs) who are attempting to establish sustainable enterprises in the Atlantic commercial fishery. This chapter examines features of the BDT that help to explain its uniqueness and account for its success.

The BDT has its roots in the First Nations struggle to gain access to the Atlantic fishery. In 1999, that struggle gave rise to a Supreme Court of Canada ruling referred to as "the Marshall decision." That decision affirmed the treaty right of Mi'kmaw and Maliseet First Nations (MMFNs) in Nova Scotia, New Brunswick, Prince Edward Island, and the Gaspé region of Québec to hunt, fish, and gather in pursuit of a moderate livelihood. The decision affected thirty-four MMFNs. Some of the implications of the Marshall decision have prompted responses from the federal Department of Fisheries and Oceans (DFO; officially, Fisheries and Oceans Canada). Among the earliest of these is the Marshall Response Initiative (MRI). This and other DFO initiatives that followed are discussed and provide a context for the business-development team.

The Atlantic fishery is an industry that has undergone dramatic changes over its long history; however, particularly over the last fifty years, changes to the fishery have been exceptionally numerous and transformative. A brief review of some of these industry changes is included here to provide you with some sense of the dynamic nature of the current fishery. As you read this chapter, you should develop a sense of the growing complexity and continuing turbulence of this modern industry. Certainly, the modern fishery is now global. One effective way to understand a global industry like this one is to view it in terms of its value chains. Fishery value chains trace activity along a series of stages, including production (either wild capture or aquaculture), primary processing, secondary processing, and distribution. Today, within any given fishery's value chain, individual stages may occur in different countries; that is, the value chain may be multinational, and many are.

So the fishery is global, competitive, dynamic, and very complex. Furthermore, over time, much as other mature industries have done, the fishery has developed barriers to entry. Industry barriers are of great relevance in the present context because they impact prospective entrants. First Nation communities

> A **value chain** refers to the series of activities through which a company adds value to a product or service. It might be thought of as a product's life cycle. The stages in a value chain are often specific to a particular industry.

(FNCs) hoping to establish themselves in the fishery must recognize and overcome these barriers if they are to succeed. Overcoming each barrier is a necessary, but not a sufficient, condition of success in the fishery. These are complex challenges. Entrants must develop tools that will also allow them to effectively overcome each hurdle. Designing those tools requires considerable thought, insight, resources, and commitment. Furthermore, the development phase also requires a realistic assessment of prospective entrants' strengths and weaknesses. These ideas are developed in this chapter and help to shape the BDT.

This chapter identifies some of the challenges faced by the business-development team, as well as the BDT's approach to addressing them. It describes some of the methods used by the BDT to engage FNCs. The chapter concludes with a reflection on the lessons learned from the BDT initiative. It is hoped that these innovations,[1] as well as the benefits of good design, may be transferrable to other contexts with good effect.

An Ancient Practice

Seafood harvesting and consumption are ancient practices. Shell middens[2] and cave paintings provide evidence that our early ancestors, who were hunter-gathers and on the move, consumed significant quantities of seafood. The first examples of more permanent settlements also provide evidence of our continued reliance on seafood. As societies developed and advanced, new tools for harvesting, new techniques for preserving, and new methods of distributing seafood were introduced. With these advances larger quantities could be harvested and an industry was born. Even these commercial developments are thousands of years old.[3] Centuries later, as the industry continued to spread, the waters of Atlantic Canada became multinational fishing grounds for fleets largely of European origin. Those adventurers exerted a profound influence on the Atlantic region as we know it today. As the Atlantic fishery has matured, the pace of change within it has quickened.

Changes Shaping the Atlantic Fishery

Particularly over the last fifty years, the Atlantic fishery has seen changes along a wide range of fronts including:

1. A tendency for greater regulation accompanied by recognition of the need for relevant data and scientific studies. "In the Atlantic Canadian fisheries, limited entry was first introduced in 1967, for the inshore lobster fishery. Four years later, in 1971 it was extended to offshore lobster and scallop fisheries as well as to herring purse seiners. In the Atlantic ground fish fishery movement toward limited entry began in 1973 when the Minister of Fisheries announced a new fishing fleet development policy for Canada's Atlantic coast aiming to match fleet size to fish stocks by instituting a more selective subsidy program for vessel construction and establishing a new license control program. In accordance with this program a freeze was introduced on off-shore trawl licences from 1973-74. From then on new vessels were only allowed as replacements of existing vessels. In the inshore sector, barriers to entry were gradually raised starting

in 1976.... By 1982 all Atlantic fisheries had been placed under limited entry." (Apostle 1998: 93)

2.   Ongoing technological advances in vessels and gear, with concomitant concerns about sustainability of fish stocks and impacts on fish processing. In 1983, the Kirby Task Force released its report, "Navigating Troubled Waters, A New Policy for the Atlantic Fisheries," to the public. The task force recommended changes to the organization of companies harvesting fishery resources and to other companies involved in processing such resources. These changes led to improvements in the deep-sea fishery and associated declines in the coastal fishery. In fact, the importance of government policies in shaping this industry would be difficult to overstate. Reporting in 2003 on fish processing in Newfoundland, Commissioner Eric Dunne had this to say: "The major processing operations are now less labour-intensive and utilize the latest technology to compete in today's global marketplace. Employment levels in processing facilities are now only 58 percent of what they were in 1990" (Dunne 2003: 1). It should be noted that in addition to automation, the collapse of the ground fishery (i.e., of halibut, sole, cod: groundfish) was another major factor contributing to this drop in employment.

3.   Concentrations of commercial activity and subsequent reconfigurations of these corporations. High Liner Foods Inc., a seafood-processing company, illustrates the extent of change necessary for survival in a highly competitive multinational industry. "High Liner, a leading producer of value-added frozen seafood products in North America, is headquartered in Lunenburg where it also operates a processing plant. Once an enormous fishing company that caught and processed 300 million pounds of fish a year, High Liner saw Atlantic fishing quotas fall to 5% of what they were in the early 1990s. This prompted them to explore the possibility of sourcing raw materials internationally. The cost savings and complexity of managing these international procurement activities were so great that they decided to sell off their struggling fishing assets and focus on becoming the North American leader in value-added frozen seafood. Today, High Liner procures 30 species of fish from 20 different countries. Primary processing is done in China, but High Liner maintains four secondary processing plants in North America which handle the more complex processing and packaging tasks. These facilities, located close to their final markets, allow for closer attention to quality and a buffer against supply disruptions." (Chaundy 2011: 50)

4.   Changes in the locations and methods of fish processing.[4] Fish processing has felt the full impact of restructuring within the Atlantic fishery. For example, by the mid-1980s there was significant overcapacity in fish processing (Parsons 1993). More recently, a

study undertaken by Gardner Pinfold, an economics consultancy, identified two major trends that have dominated seafood markets over the past decade: first, the internationalization of trade and the resulting shift in production to low-cost nations in the Far East, and, second, the growing significance of aquaculture. "Major fish processing companies in North America and Europe face an increasing challenge in competing for raw material as low cost producers have entered the market and bid up prices with the knowledge that raw material costs will be more than offset by substantially lower wage and production costs. These same processing companies then face the equally difficult challenge of competing with these low cost products in their own traditional North American and European markets. Most have found the challenge impossible to meet so are responding by shifting production to these same low cost producing nations. In Atlantic Canada, we have seen examples of this with ground fish and crab. To understand the overall magnitude of the trend, we only need to look in the frozen fish section in any supermarket to note that virtually every package, no matter which brand, is labeled product of China, Viet Nam or Thailand." (Gardiner Pinfold and Rogers Consulting 2007: 26)

5. Continued growth in consumer demand for seafood, along with occasional shifts in consumer preferences. World demand for seafood continues to be strong; in fact, consumption has been growing at a rate of 3.6 per cent per year since 1961 (FAO 2012). This can be partly explained by their being more mouths to feed, but growth in demand is even greater than the rate of population increase. Global per capita consumption (round weight) is expected to increase 8 per cent over the decade, from 19 kg to 20.6 kg per person (OECD 2013). Globally, fish provides about 3 billion people with almost 20 per cent of their intake of animal protein, and 4.3 billion people with about 15 per cent of such protein (FAO 2012).

6. The inclusion of new species in the harvest, as well as significant and ongoing increases in the importance of aquaculture. Offshore clams are an example of a newer harvest, while growth in the relative importance of shellfish such as lobster and crab has helped to offset the diminishing importance of groundfish to the Atlantic Fishery. For instance, in Eastern Canada, Shellfish accounted for 72 per cent of the $1.4 billion landed value in 2009; this distribution has remained stable for several years (Department of Fisheries and Oceans 2011). At the same time, rapid advances in the share of world production coming from aquaculture are expected to continue. This trend combined with the dominant role of Asia as a source of aquaculture production will continue to shift global supply.

Today's Atlantic fishery, forged in part by these changes, has become a sophisticated, competitive, dynamic, and highly complex industry. Among other things, these changes have contributed to a series of barriers to entry to the fishery that now form part of its character.

> **Aquaculture** is the cultivation and/or farming of aquatic plants and animals under controlled conditions. It may occur in freshwater or saltwater environments and can include species of fish, crustaceans, molluscs, or plants, like seaweed. It is contrasted with fishing, which is the commercial harvesting of wild stocks.

Harvard Business School Professor Michael Porter identifies seven different barriers to entry that are common among mature industries. Included in Porter's list are three barriers of particular relevance to the Atlantic fishery: (a) restrictive government policies, (b) capital costs, and (c) incumbency advantages (Porter 2008).

For any group aspiring to become part of the current Atlantic fishery, success will hinge critically on their ability to recognize and to effectively overcome each of these three barriers. Overcoming each barrier is a necessary, but not a sufficient condition of success. Part of the significance of the Marshall decision, and, in particular, the ongoing relevance of the BDT, can be understood by examining each in relation to these three barriers to entry.

Overcoming Industry Barriers

Barrier One—Restrictive Government Policies: The Fishery, First Nations Communities,[5] and the Significance of the Marshall Decision

In 1993, Donald Marshall Jr. was charged with fishing eels out of season, fishing without a licence, and fishing with an illegal net. Six years later, the Supreme Court of Canada rendered the Marshall decision,[6] which gave[7] MMFNs in Nova Scotia, New Brunswick, Prince Edward Island, and the Gaspé region of Québec the right to fish commercially for "a moderate living." Rights to fish for food and for ceremonial reasons—had already been guaranteed by the Sparrow decision.[8] As we saw earlier, "By 1982 all Atlantic fisheries had been placed under limited entry" (Apostle 1998: 93). By providing access (in principle) to the Atlantic fishery, the Marshall decision overcame a formidable barrier to entry associated with this industry. But there were practical barriers to overcome as well. The decision placed the DFO under considerable pressure to respond in order to ensure timely access:

> The Supreme Court made it clear that its judgment should be implemented with speed—and that's what happened, on both the Mi'kmaq and Maliseet First Nations and the DFO sides. For their part, the Mi'kmaq and Maliseet First Nations began fishing commercially right away, and indicated they would fish in the 2000 spring fishery whether

or not they had licences from DFO. DFO, however, was still legislatively and administratively responsible for management and regulation of the fishery. Tensions quickly escalated at dockside and on the water, as DFO scrambled to negotiate Contribution Agreements with the MMFNs, so licences and money could flow to them. The government allocated $159.6 million in the initial phase of the Marshall Response Initiative, and within a month of the decision had appointed a chief federal representative to oversee the process of negotiating interim fisheries agreements to give Mi'kmaq and Maliseet First Nations immediate access. (Thayer-Scott 2012: 3)

At the time of the Marshall decision, all available fishing licences were already in use. To overcome this barrier, part of the funding allocated by government for the MRI was used to buy back licences and equipment from current fishers who were interested in retiring. The repurchased licences could then be reissued without increasing the total number of licences, thereby providing First Nations access to the regulated fishery. By these means, a significant barrier to entry (i.e., restrictive government policies) into the Atlantic fishery was overcome.

Barrier Two—Capital Costs: The Fishery, First Nation Communities, and the Significance of the Marshall Response Initiative (MRI)

According to Porter, the need to invest large financial resources in order to compete can deter new entrants into an industry. In industries with high-capital-cost barriers, funds may be needed not only to acquire fixed assets but to provide working capital (Porter 2008). Capital barriers to entry associated with the Atlantic fishery are significant. They include the necessity of acquiring specialized equipment (especially vessels, traps, and gear), assets that are expensive to purchase and costly to maintain. Between 1999 and 2007, a total of $589.8 million was invested through the MRI (phases I and II); part of this money was used to purchase 295 new and used vessels (Thayer-Scott 2012).

Fixed assets are items that are owned by a company that have significant value and will be used over an extended period, usually spanning more than one reporting period. Examples are property, buildings, and equipment.

Working capital refers to the amount of money available for the day-to-day operations of a business, and is calculated by subtracting current liabilities from current assets.

The MRI provided approximately 1,400 licences and 300 vessels to groups, through fisheries agreements negotiated with thirty-two of the thirty-four eligible First Nation groups. Since then, the quantity and value of landings associated with FNCs have increased significantly; by 2011, the landed value had reached $75 million (BDTUDG 2013). Here again a significant barrier to entry (i.e., capital costs) into the Atlantic fishery had been overcome.

Barrier Three—Incumbency Advantages: The Fishery, First Nation Communities, and the Significance of the Atlantic Integrated Commercial Fisheries Initiative

Porter argues, no matter what their size, incumbents may have cost or quality advantages not available to new entrants. These advantages may stem from such sources as proprietary technology, preferential access to the best raw-material sources, pre-emption of the best geographic locations, established brand identities (brand is discussed in chapter 10), or cumulative experience that has allowed incumbents to learn how to produce more efficiently (Porter 2008). Whatever their origin, incumbency advantages are a significant barrier to new entrants—and represent a threat to their survival.

Threats of this nature are greater when prospective entrants are inexperienced. Certainly, that would be the case for First Nations hoping to enter and succeed in the Atlantic fishery. Speaking about the early days of the MRI, Jacquelyn Thayer-Scott has this to say about their preparedness:

> The Mi'kmaq and Maliseet First Nations never having been in this business before, for the most part didn't have the training or skill sets in the early years to assess and manage equipment. Similarly, Mi'kmaq and Maliseet First Nations fishers needed skills in a hurry, and through much of the succeeding decade have had to hire non-native captains and first mates (and, sometimes, their boats) for their higher end marine skills. There were no administrative or human resource (HR) systems in place for hiring and managing the new commercial fishing enterprises (CFEs) and governance issues and policies at the Mi'kmaq and Maliseet First Nations level had to be put in place—which would be a long term investment in people and systems. (Thayer-Scott 2012: 6)

Proprietary refers to ownership. If technology or knowledge is called "proprietary," it is owned by an individual or company and/or an individual or company has exclusive rights to it.

Incumbency advantage refers to the idea that companies already in an industry will have an advantage over those trying to enter the same industry.

Furthermore, the disadvantage of inexperience is amplified because the Atlantic fishery is a sophisticated, competitive, dynamic, and highly complex industry. Clearly, further program support would be needed to address these issues and to nurture the significant investments already made during the MRI. But the challenges here go well beyond providing additional funding. In addition to financial resources, innovative policy and program design are needed; these non-financial responses represent the greatest challenge to overcoming the barrier of incumbency advantage.

That new policy and program approach was the Atlantic Integrated Commercial Fisheries Initiative (AICFI). Introduced in 2007, AICFI represented a new response incorporating a number of lessons learned from the Marshall Response Initiative. Among other things, the AICFI would undertake to:

- build capacity to improve corporate governance of the commercial fishing enterprises;
- improve performance in the commercial sector;
- focus on growth support that would create high levels of technical expertise for the MMFNs and their commercial fishing enterprises; and
- recognize that a focus on business management strategies is critical (Thayer-Scott 2012).

Further insights into policy design may be derived from the Harvard Project on American Indian Economic Development (Taylor 2008).[9]

Commenting on the significance of this policy initiative, Jacquelyn Thayer Scott noted:

> AICFI represents a distinctive and positive case in major policy change and, more particularly, in its program implementation, conception, and delivery. Its lessons have high potential applicability in FN issues at a range of social and economic levels. Its lessons also reach farther afield and offer promise for improved policy and practice in a large country with widely differing inter-and intra-provincial differences and characteristics. (Thayer-Scott 2012: ii)

Compared to the other industry barriers (restrictive government policies and capital costs), incumbency advantage is not so easily delineated. Nevertheless, it poses a genuine threat to the survival of new entrants and must be dealt with effectively. Overcoming this particular barrier requires a deep understanding of the way the fishery is organized and its current best practices. That is, industry expertise and industry experience are needed. There are no substitutes. Furthermore, in this particular context there are additional challenges. First, a mechanism must be developed that effectively shares this expert knowledge with First Nation clients, who ultimately are the decision-makers. Second, the mechanism must also help those clients to identify and execute appropriate courses of action given their choices and given the competitive forces at play. Within the design of the AICFI, these challenges have been assigned to the business-development team. That is, the BDT is a frontline unit providing critical support to First Nation entrants. The primary goal of the team is to provide business facilitating support that will help FNCs enhance the operation and the long-term sustainability of their commercial fisheries enterprises (BDTUDG 2013).

The challenges faced by the BDT include:

1. Finding effective ways to build trust with their First Nations clients. Part of this is structural in nature, but human interaction is also critical. Here, structural refers to organizational hierarchies and reporting lines.

2. Ensuring that each FNC has a system of governance in place to formalize decisions taken in relation to the fishery.

3. Finding systematic ways of building each FNCs capacity to recognize opportunities and develop plans to pursue them. The BDT must also encourage the propensity of its clients to do both.

4. Coincident with these challenges is the need to ensure that effective systems of management are in place. This, in turn, implies the need for human resources with the capacity to implement these systems and assume responsibility for their continued use. The BDT is expected to provide support for this. (Capacity building is discussed further in chapters 3 and 4.)

5. A management system is made more effective when it includes measurable goals and a data-collection system that is used to monitor progress toward those stated goals. Again, in addition to these features, the propensity to use these tools needs to be encouraged and supported.

To address these challenges, the BDT has been equipped with two kinds of expertise: industry expertise and expertise in the processes of community (place-based) development.

Personnel for the BDT were recruited by an executive-search firm. The firm knew the fishing industry, and could identify people with the appropriate expertise. The search firm also provided independent assessments of candidates and advised on appropriate salary ranges. The first three individuals hired included an accountant, a former director of fisheries for a First Nation community in Québec, and a former fish-marketing manager who had also managed an offshore fishing fleet for a large seafood company. They worked for the BDT from their home communities across the Maritimes, each handling about nine communities. Their team leader, David Simms, came to that position with nearly thirty years of fisheries and community economic-development experience (Thayer-Scott 2012). Within the BDT, the team leader is the "glue"; Simms uses weekly reports and "virtual" meetings to keep a geographically separated staff informed of each other's activities.

In 2010, a new support framework, the Atlantic Commercial Fisheries Diversification Initiative (ACFDI) was launched and, with it, the role of the BDT was broadened. Since 2010, the business-development team also helps FNCs to undertake business-development activities that lead to the realization of new fisheries-related diversification opportunities (BDTUDG 2013). Two additional advisers were added to the BDT through the ACFDI;

Vertical supply chain refers to all the inputs and outputs (processes and products) involved in the production and distribution of products or services. Vertical integration means that a company owns or takes control of more input and output processes.

Horizontal diversification refers to the process through which a company expands operations into similar markets with related products or processes either through acquisition or creation of additional businesses.

one a specialist with experience in fish processing and marketing, the other a specialist in aquaculture. Their roles are to advise those MMFNs now starting to branch into vertical supply-chain businesses (such as ice-making, fish processing, and retail sales) or to diversify horizontally into aquaculture. Although the ACFDI wound down in March 2013, the BDT has been able to maintain and even expand its capacity to support aquaculture. The BDT now has two aquaculture adviser positions, which are supported under the Aboriginal Aquaculture in Canada Initiative (AACI). The BDT has expertise and depth of experience—they know what they were talking about and have a broad mandate. Now widely believed to be one of the "jewels in the crown" of the AICFI (Thayer-Scott 2012), the BDT has the ability to add value to commercial fishery enterprises at the conceptual development stage, through the financing stage, and all the way through execution and rollout.

Just as important as their expertise, is a shared understanding among the team members of their role. Accurate perceptions and trust are essential. This is where David Simms's expertise comes into play. Simms is a perceptive communicator with a wealth of experience in community engagement. He knows when to talk and when to listen. He also understands organizational structure and is able to recognize the possibilities created by innovative structures. For example, the organizational chart of AICFI shows that the BDT has a reporting relationship to Ulnooweg Development Corporation, the capital corporation for the MMFNs (Thayer-Scott 2012: 12). Ulnooweg was formed in 1984, with headquarters based in Eskasoni (McAllister 1993). Ulnooweg was set up as a province-wide economic-development organization supporting new and existing First Nation development projects in Nova Scotia (Wien 1986). Today, Ulnooweg serves Aboriginal entrepreneurs across Atlantic Canada and has representatives in Nova Scotia, New Brunswick, and Newfoundland and Labrador (Ulnooweg Development Group 2015). Ulnooweg provides a full set of business services, along with loans, to ensure Aboriginal business owners can run their businesses professionally and profitably (Ulnooweg Development Group 2015).

Ulnooweg is well known to FNCs; the corporation has dealt with those communities for thirty-one years. BDT's relationship with Ulnooweg is recognized as a key source of credibility. From the beginning, Simms has emphasized to the FNCs (BDT's clients) that he and his team are not employees of DFO, nor are they employees of the Atlantic Policy Congress; rather, they are employees of Ulnooweg. Furthermore, because of its reporting lines, the BDT is able to maintain client confidentiality. This is another key feature of the business-development team that enables its staff to cultivate relationships with FNCs that are based on trust. One indicator that the BDT has been accepted as a trusted and reliable adviser is the degree to which it has been engaged by its clients. By 2013, thirty of thirty-four MMFNs had joined the AICFI. Because they are mandated to share their expertise, BDT members have also worked with the Nova Scotia Community College in designing a fisheries-enterprise management training program, which is aimed at MMFN fishery managers. Over the longer term, it is expected that First Nation advisers will develop and will assume BDT roles. Given the high value placed on industry experience, this will take some time.

Structurally, the operation of the BDT has been carried out under the direction of the Atlantic Commercial Fisheries Diversification Initiative management committee. This committee meets regularly with representation from DFO, APC, and Ulnooweg. The primary responsibility of the committee is to direct and to guide the BDT in assisting the communities to make the best use of the AICFI program and, where appropriate, other sources of support (BDTUDG 2013).

As we have characterized it here, the work of the BDT supports FNCs in their ongoing efforts to enter into and to remain competitive in a mature industry—the Atlantic fishery. That is, the BDT helps them to overcome a barrier to entry. This is what the BDT does. In the next section we will try to get clearer on how this is done.

Barriers to Entry—the BDT and the Link to Value Chains

To be effective, the business-development team must be seen to "add value" to the decision-making processes engaged in by FNCs (i.e., their clients). The decision process is "structured" because each community and its commercial fishing enterprise must produce a business development plan, the basic document from which all funding proceeds, and against which all outcomes are measured. So, it is a crucial document and communities are motivated to produce one. As those communities explore possibilities and plan their commercial fisheries enterprises, the BDT members add value by providing their clients with value-chain analysis of the fishery.

Value chains describe the full range of activities that are required to bring a product or service from conception, through the different phases of production (involving a combination of physical transformation and the input of

> A **value chain** is the series of activities (processes and products) required to produce and distribute an end product or service.
>
> **Value-chain analysis** is the process of identifying, describing, and reviewing the series of activities required to produce and distribute a final product or service and how they relate to one another. Such analysis may identify opportunities to expand into complementary areas and improve products or services for customers and lead to improved competitive advantage.

various producer services), delivery to final consumers, and final disposal after use (Kaplinsky, Morris, and Redmon 2002). Value-chain analysis seeks to characterize how chain activities are performed and to explain how value is created and shared among chain participants (ibid.).

A recent study reports the growing importance to Atlantic Canada of global value chains where parts of the production process for a good or service are located in different countries. These arrangements take advantage of lower costs, local expertise or proximity to markets, or key suppliers. Firms within global value chains increasingly focus on what they do best and outsource the provision of other inputs to specialized suppliers operating in their home country or abroad (Chaundy 2011).

We have seen that the Atlantic fishery is part of a global commercial system that is subject to forces of competition from all over the world. Furthermore, the cacophony of changes occurring over the past fifty years is premised on a single, unalterable fact—the waters of Atlantic Canada hold a resource of immense value. One of the keys, therefore, to understanding the current Atlantic fishery and its best practices lies in knowing and being able to analyze its value chains. Value-chain analysis is thought to be particularly useful for new producers entering both domestic and global markets. It ensures sustainable income growth, based on an understanding of the value chain, from the time the fish is caught until it reaches the final customer (Russell and Hanoomanjee 2012: 6). One of the unique qualities of the Ulnooweg's BDT is that its members have been recruited from fishery value chains, and they know how they operate. On a global scale, today's fishery is of great importance to the economies of many countries; it represents a significant source of GDP[10] and employment,[11] and also provides a critical source of food to much of the world.[12] But it is also dynamic. Fish has become among the most highly traded food commodities, with nearly 40 per cent of all production now exported (FAO 2012). And the future is bright. World demand for seafood continues to be strong. A broad-brush representation of the global seafood value chain is provided below, in figure 1. Each activity along the chain contributes to the overall value of the industry, which was estimated to be worth $400 billion in 2007.

Figure 1: Seafood Industry Value Chain
Source: Davidsson (2007).

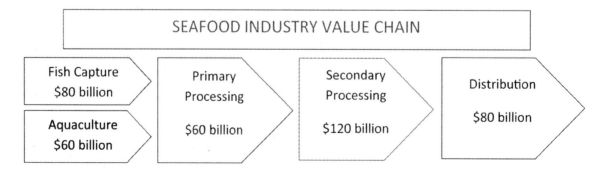

In terms of supplying this growing demand, world production comes from two sources: wild capture and aquaculture. In 2010, wild-capture production was estimated to provide about 90 million tonnes, with an additional 64 million tonnes produced through aquaculture. Not only is aquaculture an important part of current world production (accounting for about 40 per cent), it is also growing at a rate of 7 per cent per year (FAO 2010). In contrast, production through wild capture is a mature part of the industry. At present, the overall maximum potential of wild-capture fisheries from the world's oceans appears to have been nearly reached. Economists expect continuing strong growth in fisheries; however, capture fisheries output is projected to rise by only 5 per cent by 2022, while aquaculture should increase by 35 per cent. World fisheries production is projected to reach 181 million metric tons by 2022. Based on these projections, aquaculture was projected to surpass capture fisheries as the main source for human consumption by 2015 (OECD 2013). The convergence of these factors had led Peter Drucker, a Nobel Prize laureate and management author, to suggest that aquaculture, not the Internet, represents the most promising investment opportunity of the 21st century (Drucker 1999). Of course, these changes will alter the underlying value chains of the fishery. In fact, in a dynamic industry, value chains are constantly evolving.

Value chains can be used as a way to highlight the impacts of globalization on industries like fishing. They also can be used to provide a means of identifying areas of opportunity. As countries like China enter world markets, primary economic returns within the value chain are shifting and are increasingly found in areas outside of production, such as design, branding, and marketing. Figure 2 shows the astonishing importance of China (61 per cent) and of Asia (81 per cent) as current sources of aquaculture production. As Kaplinsky, Morris, and Redmon (2002: 4) note, "Value chain analysis provides not just a method of understanding these developments, but also a way of identifying key challenges in the promotion of upgrading." Global value chain (GVC) analysis has emerged since the early 1990s as a preferred methodological tool for understanding the dynamics of economic globalization and international trade. The GVC approach is based on the analysis of discrete 'value chains' where input supply, production, trade, and consumption or disposal are explicitly and (at least to some extent) coherently linked. Much of the discussion of global value chains has revolved around two analytical issues:

- how global value chains are governed (in the context of a larger institutional framework); and

- how upgrading or downgrading takes place along global value chains?

> **Globalization** refers to the process of the market-economy system spreading throughout the world, or the international flow of goods, communication, and money.

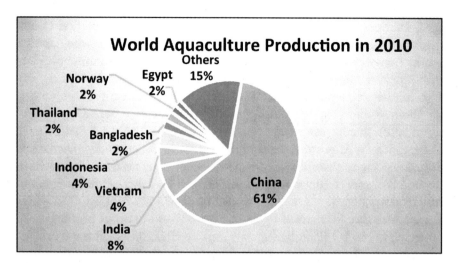

Figure 2: World Aquaculture Production in 2010
Source: FAO (2012: 28).

These discussions have been carried out with an interest in how power and rewards are embodied and distributed along global value chains, what entry barriers characterize global value chains, and how unequal distributions of rewards can be challenged in favour of labour and/or developing countries (Ponte 2008). Governance can have a profound effect on profitability.

Comparisons of value chains among countries engaged in the fishery show that the same industry looks quite different from one country to another. In a study for the Food and Agriculture Organization of the United Nations (Gudmundsson, Asche, and Nielsen 2006), value chains were compared. The objective of the study was to demonstrate how the revenues from seafood trade are distributed over the entire seafood value chain. Figure 3 compares Denmark and Iceland. We can see that the results are quite different.

Figure 3: Comparison of Fishery Value Chains of Iceland and Denmark
Source: Gudmundsson, Asche, and Nielsen (2006).

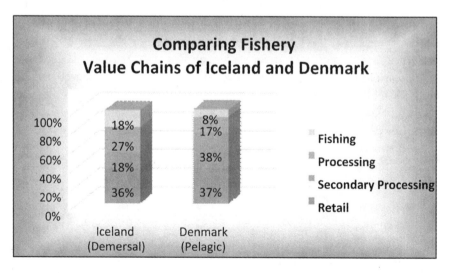

The concept of "governance" is central to the global value-chain approach. Governance here refers to the inter-firm relationships and institutional mechanisms through which non-market coordination of activities in the chain takes place. This coordination is achieved through the setting and enforcement of product and process parameters to be met by actors in the chain. In global value chains in which developing-country producers typically operate, buyers play an important role in setting and enforcing these parameters. They set these parameters because of the (perceived) risk of producer failure. Product and process parameters may also be set by government agencies and international organizations concerned with quality standards or labour and environmental standards (Humphrey and Schmitz 2001: 1). The BDT adds value because its highly specialized staff understand fishery value chains and the threats and opportunities that lie along them. There are no substitutes for this kind of knowledge, and its availability makes the BDT unique and indispensable. The types of services provided by the BDT are illustrated by this list:

> **Governance** refers to the rules, policies, and processes that guide or influence a business, company, industry, or government.

1. Assisting in the preparation of business plans and harvesting/operational plans;

2. Providing advisory and hands-on analysis to help determine the feasibility of new project ideas;

3. Assisting in the evaluation of proposals and reports pertaining to business-planning studies and assessments;

4. Assisting with adopting best management practices and strategies for improving the communities' commercial fisheries operations and business enterprises;

5. Assisting in preparation of proposals to secure funds for new project-development initiatives from sources other than AICFI and ACFDI;

6. Assisting with implementation of project-management action plans for more effective project management; and

7. Assisting with establishing a project-management action-team structure to help monitor progress of projects and to provide measurable aftercare (BDTUDG 2013).

In part, the success of the business-development team is explained by the supporting policy framework within which it operates. The original framework, the AICFI, was initially funded for five years, from 2007 to 2012; it was extended to March 2014, and renewed until March 2016. The AICFI provides an architecture of due diligence, but has other innovative features as well. The program is entirely voluntary: MMFNs are not obliged to participate. However, those who do participate must agree to compre-

> **Due diligence** refers to the prudence that should be exercised prior to entering into an agreement or transaction.

hensive project transparency and accountability. The program requires the development and implementation of band-approved business plans, training, and other capacity-building activities. These are areas where the BDT provides significant support to FNCs. Bands are also making financial contributions to projects from their own resources. The program also has bottom-line accountability: if there is no satisfactory performance, then there is no funding. Finally, the program has transparent, objective project-assessment criteria that ensure detailed information is obtained for program-evaluation purposes (Cook 2013). One key feature of the AICFI is that its delivery is undertaken through the Atlantic Policy Congress of First Nations Chiefs. Before approval, AICFI-supported projects undergo an independent third-party evaluation and are also assessed by an application review board. Given these expectations, the kind of support the BDT provides is highly relevant to FNCs engaged in the AICFI.

> **Transparency** refers to operating in an open fashion, such that it is clear what actions have been taken.
>
> **Accountability** is the ability to take responsibility for actions and decisions. Bottom-line accountability refers to the responsibility to explain a company's overall financial performance (the level of profit or loss found on the bottom line of an income statement) to stakeholders (owners or investors).

The results of these efforts have been significant. Looking at the earliest stage of the Atlantic fishery value chain (i.e., production), First Nation communities have managed to establish a presence. Between 2008 and 2011, FNCs registered significant increases in the value of their landings of lobster, crab, shrimp and scallops;[13] in addition to these achievements, the BDT has contributed importantly both to diversification and to capacity building among its FNC clients.

The BDT has helped to identify the shortfalls and weaknesses of existing governance systems, particularly as they relate to new projects, and has worked with each community in strengthening those systems before project proposals are prepared. The BDT has discussed and advised on the importance of enterprise governance and project management. For example, processes have been developed whereby financial management of fisheries projects has been separated from band finances to ensure more effective project delivery. To this end, the BDT helped to introduce a new model for project management, comprised of an Excel-based matrix that captures all necessary information to track project progress on a weekly basis. To strengthen the value of the matrix, the management model is complemented with the implementation of a project-management action team and a project-management action plan.

As we have seen, for those who are able to recognize them, the fishery provides numerous opportunities along its value chain. In terms of diversification, FNC initiatives involving BDT support now include spin-off businesses in fish processing, marine supply, tourist-vessel charters, seafood marketing, fish transportation, and aquaculture. Since 2010, the BDT has assisted with the start-up or expansion of twenty-seven fisheries diversification businesses, accounting for 250 new jobs (BDTUDG 2013). Major advances in aquaculture participation and growth have been made, with the ACFDI supporting eight development initiatives (APCFNC 2012).

The BDT provided an invaluable level of service to help address certain identified shortfalls within the communities that wished to undertake fisheries diversification activities. This includes BDT assistance to access outside expert advice and other relevant resources, and assistance for accessing project funds. Overall, the ongoing support activities of the BDT have been critically important to help facilitate fisheries diversification business planning and development processes and to assist with successful business implementation.

All of these initiatives are positive, adding value and stability. The activities in aquaculture are particularly interesting because they mirror an established trend that is evident within the wider industry, namely, the increasing importance of aquaculture as a source of fish production. Given the worldwide significance of this transformative change, it is reassuring that FNCs are part of it. Some of the opportunities associated with ACFDI, and the roles played by the BDT in relation to these, are described here.

1. When the ACFDI was put in place, communities interested in aquaculture saw a unique opportunity. For the first time, a program offered the necessary elements through a dedicated BDT to get their aquaculture initiatives on the way to sustainability.

2. The ACFDI and the BDT provided the vital pieces for a solid foundation in the form of technical expertise, professional advice, business-plan development, and project funding.

3. The ACFDI and the BDT have been instrumental in helping FNCs increase their participation and growth in the aquaculture industry.

4. In the aquaculture sector alone, the ACFDI has supported the development of eight new or expansionary initiatives by contributing some $2 million to leverage over $6.5 million from other funding sources.

5. The aquaculture-development initiatives have included mussel-, oyster-, trout-, salmon-, and Arctic-char-farming activities, and they have generated or maintained around thirty jobs for FNCs, and the potential exists to generate many more jobs as the operations grow.

6. The BDT provided the necessary assistance to adopt innovative technologies, sound project- and business-management

practices, and continuous aftercare to help the FNCS achieve total sustainability in their aquaculture operations.

7. Unlike other industries, the products in aquaculture are living organisms (as in agriculture) and the risks associated with a production failure are high. The BDT support has been crucial to assist in minimizing the risk and obtaining the positive results expected.

8. Success in aquaculture comes with time, and any program whose objective is to support aquaculture development needs to be implemented over a number of years. The three-year timeframe for ACFDI has been critically important for sustaining the capital and operational investment, and in providing the tools for building capacity within the communities that have chosen to pursue aquaculture.

9. The ACFDI and the BDT have been instrumental in giving some communities the option to invest in aquaculture, whether for improving the performance of existing operations or to create new business ventures (BDTUDG 2013: 18).

The importance of aquaculture as a stable source of opportunities within the fishery is recognized by the BDT, which has, with the ongoing support of the AACI, strengthened its own capacity to support aquaculture initiatives by FNCs. Also of considerable importance are other contributions the BDT has made to capacity building (discussed in chapters 3 and 4). Along these lines, the BDT has worked with the Nova Scotia Community College to develop a series of specific fisheries enterprise management-training courses, addressing topics such as: informed decision-making using the fisheries management system; introduction to financial management for fisheries managers; fisheries operational management; strategic business planning; project management for fisheries managers; and human-resource management.

On a related front, the BDT has been instrumental in promoting the adoption of an automated fisheries management system (FMS), which has been made available to FNCs at no cost. As a software management tool, FMS helps fisheries managers to track and monitor operational results of their fisheries enterprises, and to make comparisons to historical data. A fully utilized system can contribute significantly to improving management efficiencies, better strategic and operational planning, and overall increased profitability. The BDT has also worked with FNCs to help ensure that FMS reporting is reconciled with financial accounting systems. The FMS can be used to complement fisheries accounting data, as the FMS reporting system generally offers a greater depth of analysis compared with basic financial accounting. As an example, with the assistance of FMS, vessel-by-vessel performance comparisons can be made within fishing areas and within specified periods of operation. Also, the crew-, vessel-, fishing licence-, and quota-tracking capabilities of FMS are unique and are not generally found within financial accounting. (BDTUDG 2013). These enriched forms of integrated information help to build management capacity for FNCs.

Clearly, if perceived relevance is measured by participation, then from the perspective of FNCs, the BDT is relevant. In 2012-2013, twenty-nine FNCs submitted applications under AICFI component 2.3, and twenty-seven submitted applications/business cases under AICFI component 4 (Thayer-Scott 2012: 35).

Lessons Learned

While the business-development team is importantly different, it is certainly not the first service provider dedicated to assisting clients who aspire to start and grow commercial ventures. Therefore, we should expect that in many ways the BDT will (and should) resemble other conventional service providers. There is no need for every aspect of the BDT to be unique. But there are differences between the BDT and most service providers. Here are some.

In many situations, where demand conditions are weak, a service provider may require government support. Often, in cases where services are supported by government departments, staff expertise may be "program related," and clients are primarily advised about the "fit" of their proposed projects with the program guidelines. The BDT does not fit this profile. BDT members have been recruited from the commercial fishery value chain. Team expertise is, therefore, rooted in industrial experience and tacit knowledge of the fishery. Tacit knowledge includes scientific expertise, operational know-how, industry insight, business judgement, and technological expertise (Hansen, Norhia and Tierney 1999). This kind of knowledge is critical; "a firm's ability to produce, access and control tacit knowledge is most important to its competitive success" (Gertler 2001: 9).

> **Tacit knowledge** is that which is not easily learned or shared through writing or speech. It is often skills-based.

Composition of the team is a key issue and the choices made at the outset account for much of the uniqueness of the BDT. Furthermore, the strategy adopted by the BDT relies heavily on interpersonal communication; each BDT expert deals directly with members of FNCs. The appropriateness of this methodology is supported by research, which suggests that when people use tacit knowledge to solve problems, most often a person-to-person approach works best; established consulting firms such as Bain and Co., Boston Consulting Group, and McKinsey and Co. have used these methods successfully (Hansen, Norhia and Tierney 1999).

Because of their backgrounds, team members understand the nature of contracts that represent linkages along the fishery value chain; they know who the actors are and what those actors expect. BDT members also know what costs should be and the margins required to operate along various stages of the value chain. It is unusual to provide such services to third-party clients in the fishery—most people who need them, couldn't afford them. As a result, the market for such services is weak. Therefore, the BDT is not replicating an existing private-sector service. This implies that the BDT is innovative because it is doing what would otherwise not be done. Typically, people who have this kind of knowledge work in the industry—not outside. In larger commercial fishing operations, for instance, this knowledge is available "in house" in the form of experienced personnel who "add value" and contribute significantly to the competitiveness of those large firms. In part, the BDT is unique because some of the information it shares with its clients, who are new entrants, is tacit knowledge about the fishery; this uniquely assists the clients of BDT in their efforts to overcome industry barriers, like incumbency advantage. BDT "adds value" because it undertakes the difficult task of tacit-knowledge transfer (Gertler 2001: 14).

Another unique feature of the business-development team is its arm's-length relationship with government departments like DFO. The BDT reports to, and is accountable to, Ulnooweg. As mentioned, BDT team members are employees of Ulnooweg. This organizational structure allows the BDT to maintain a confidential relationship with each of its First Nation clients. Furthermore, in the long run, the BDT and its clients' commercial fishery enterprises are assessed on the same outcome—sustainable success in the commercial fishery. So, there is a common interest between client and provider. This, along with BDTs relationship to Ulnooweg, builds trust. The BDT's ability to build trust complements its industry expertise because trust is essential for effective tacit-knowledge transfer.

The BDT is recognized as a vital source of support that is not easily replaced; praise for it has come from several quarters. A review of the AICFI, completed in May of 2010, recognized, among other things, the value added by the BDT and recommended that more resources be directed to it. In light of the ongoing challenges FNCs face, the BDT remains an effective and relevant form of support.

In terms of demonstrating success in meeting the broader objective, which is to have FNCs establish sustainable enterprises in the Atlantic commercial fishery, it may be too early to declare success. According to the International Labour Organization, a sustainable enterprise operates a business that is viable, grows, and earns a profit (Ehnert, Harry, and Zink 2014). Only in the fullness of time will sustainability be demonstrable. Of course, in addition to allowing time for these enterprises to prove themselves, it is critically important to have systems of performance measurement in place. It is also critically important for those performance-measurement systems to be used effectively. The BDT has worked hard to ensure that FNC's have these systems, and the BDT has encouraged their use. In the near future, those systems will make it possible to assess whether FNC enterprises are viable, profitable, and growing. It would be an interesting exercise to propose a design for such an assessment. For now, we can say with confidence that the BDT has benefitted from thoughtful design. We also know that the BDT continues to be utilized by FNCs, which is a good measure of its perceived relevance.

> **Sustainability** refers to the ability of something to endure or be maintained at a particular rate. Sustainability may be evaluated in terms of several different, but overlapping areas of concern, including economic sustainability, environmental sustainability, and social sustainability. Increasingly, cultural sustainability is also of interest to businesses.
>
> **Performance measurement** is the practice of assessing a particular practice, process, system, component, individual, or group to determine whether and how closely they meet expectations and/or objectives and goals.

Implications for Practice

The Mi'kmaw experience of entering the fishing industry following a Supreme Court decision contains lessons that are applicable to other industries and contexts. Opportunity alone is not enough to bring Aboriginal peoples into a particular industry, as every industry will have its own unique barriers to entry. Administrative structures must be modified or created so that they meet the needs of the Aboriginal community, as well as the existing industry standard. Barriers to entry must be addressed by modifying structures (perhaps by adapting or incorporating traditional governance models), negotiating community benefits, and creating training pathways that help make up for lost time. Entry into an industry may additionally require consideration of new product development opportunities, changes to licencing protocols, and the creation of partnerships that ensure community engagement. As Aboriginal rights and governance structures are increasingly validated through court rulings, the lessons from this chapter will become relevant across a variety of industries and contexts.

Key Points:

- The Marshall decision had a significant impact, effectively enabling the rapid growth of a commercial fishery for Aboriginal peoples of the east coast of Canada.

- There is space for traditional economies and practices to work together with modern businesses.

- Different industries have different barriers to entry that must be overcome. Working with teams of people who have significant industrial experience makes those barriers easier to navigate.

- To maintain competitive advantage, it is important to consider horizontal and vertical value-chain integration.

- A holistic approach is necessary when entering new industries; in particular, capacity building and appropriate resources must not be overlooked when attempting to access a new opportunity.

- Organizational structures and governance systems can have significant impact on business and community relationships, and, therefore, the success or failure of projects.

Questions for Review:

1. How did the Marshall decision create a new industry opportunity for Mi'kmaq and Maliseet on the east coast of Canada?

2. What primary barriers to entry were present? How were these barriers addressed?

3. What is the BDT and what does it do?

4. What is a value chain? What is vertical and horizontal value-chain integration, and why are they important?

5. How is the launching of AICFL similar to other entrepreneurial processes?

Suggested Assignments:

1. Discuss assets and capital as they relate to the fisheries, and compare this to other industries or investment opportunities.

2. What was the most innovative decision that impacted the growth of the Atlantic fishery?

3. Was this experience in the Atlantic fishery different because it involved DFO, a federal ministry? How might it have been different if working with a provincial ministry?

4. Research other industries to determine the barriers to entry a start-up might face.

Notes

1. The BDT and other components of the AICFI are referred to as "innovations" in the DFO's "Evaluation of the Atlantic Integrated Commercial Fisheries Initiative" (http://www.dfo-mpo.gc.ca/ae-ve/evaluations/10-11/6b118-eng.htm).

2. Although shell middens are found around the world, the Canadian Museum of History is involved in the E'se'get Archaeology Project, which has identified shell middens associated with the Mi'kmaq, in Port Joli, Nova Scotia. E'se'get is a Mi'kmaw word meaning "to dig for clams." Ancient people in Atlantic Canada knew when and where various fish species would be available and they had independently developed methods of capture such as fish weirs, nets, harpoons and hooks.

3. Fresh and dried fish were staple foods for much of the population in ancient Egypt. Egyptian implements and methods for fishing are illustrated in tomb scenes, drawings, and papyrus documents.

4. For example, in the mid-1980s there was significant overcapacity in fish processing (see Parsons 1993).

5. In Atlantic Canada, there are thirty-four First Nation communities, with a combined population of approximately 61,000 people, either living on- or off-reserve. See Indigenous and Northern Affairs Canada, http://www.aadnc-aandc.gc.ca/eng/1100100016942/1100100016946.

6. See R. v Marshall decision at http://csc.lexum.org/decisia-scc-csc/scc-csc/scc-csc/en/item/1740/index.do.

7. Some of those who are close to these issues would consider this characterization to be an over simplification, one that ignores the legal and political nuances, but which are beyond the scope of this chapter.

8. See R. v Sparrow decision at http://scc.lexum.org/decisia-scc-csc/scc-csc/scc-csc/en/item/609/index.do.

9. The Harvard Project on American Indian Economic Development is influential and worth exploring. See http://hpaied.org/publications-and-research.

10. The estimated value of world fishery activity in 2007 was $400 billion.

11. There are nearly 55 million people employed in the worldwide fishery.

12. Not only do fisheries generate employment for millions, but fish provides vital nutrition to billions, and is often essential to the diet of the poor (World Bank 2010).

13. During the same interval, the value of FNCs' groundfish landings dropped.

References

Apostle, R. 1998. *Community, State, and Market on the North Atlantic Rim: Challenges to Modernity in the Fisheries.* Toronto: University of Toronto Press.

APCFNC (Atlantic Policy Congress of First Nations Chiefs Secretariat). 2012. *Importance of AICFI and ACFDI Business Development Support to Atlantic First Nations Communities.*

BDTUDG (Business Development Team, Ulnooweg Development Group). 2013. *Annual Progress Report 2012-2013, AICFI/ACFDI Business Development Support Services.*

Chaundy, David. 2011. *Taking on the World: Atlantic Canada's Role In Global Value Chains.* Report prepared for the Atlantic Provinces Economic Council. https://www.apec-econ.ca/private-files/publications/194/file/%7B86133CAE-F3EA-46DF-8EB1-FD12E9DCE8E0%7D.pdf.

Cook, D. 2013. *The Atlantic Integrated Commercial Fisheries Initiative Growth and Opportunity.* Atlantic Policy Congress of First Nations Secretariat.

Davidsson, K. 2007. *Globalisation and Fisheries: Proceedings of an OECD-FAO Workshop.* Paris: OECD.

Drucker, P. 1999. Beyond the Information Revolution. *Atlantic Monthly.* October, 47-57.

Dunne, E. 2003. Final Report: Fish Processing Policy Review. Report prepared for the Fish Processing Policy Review Commission, Newfoundland Department of Fisheries and Aquaculture. http://www.fishaq.gov.nl.ca/publications/dunne_report.pdf (accessed December 8, 2015).

Department of Fisheries and Oceans. 2011. Canadian Fisheries Statistics 2008. http://www.dfo-mpo.gc.ca/stats/commercial/cfs/2008/CFS2008_e.pdf (accessed December 7, 2015).

Ehnert, I., W. Harry and K. Zink. 2014. *Sustainability and Human Resource Management: Developing Sustainable Business Organizations.* Berlin: Springer Verlag.

FAO (Fisheries and Aquaculture Organization). 2010. *The state of world fisheries and aquaculture. Rome.* Rome: Fisheries and Aquaculture Organization, OECD.

———. 2012. *The state of world fisheries and aquaculture. Rome.* Rome: Fisheries and Aquaculture Organization, OECD.

Gardiner Pinfold and Rogers Consulting. 2007. Nova Scotia Seafood Processing Sector State of the industry and competitiveness assessment / for Nova Scotia Department of Fisheries and Aquaculture. Halifax, NS: Gardiner Pinfold. E-Book.

Gertler, M. 2001. Tacit Knowledge and the Economic Geography of Context. Paper prepared for the Nelson and Winter DRUID Summer Conference, Aalborg, Denmark. http://homes.chass.utoronto.ca/~trefler/workshop/Gertler.pdf (accessed December 8, 2015).

Gudmundsson, E., F. Asche, and M. Nielsen. 2006. Revenue distribution through the seafood value chain. FAO Fisheries Circular No. 1019. Rome: Food and Agriculture Organization of the United Nations.

Hansen, M., N. Norhia and T. Tierney. 1999. What's your strategy for Managing Knowledge. *Harvard Business Review* 77 (2): 106-16.

Humphrey, J. and H. Schmitz. 2001. Governance in Global Value Chains. IDS Bulletin 32.3, Institute of Development Studies, Brighton, UK. https://www.ids.ac.uk/files/dmfile/humphreyschmitz32.3.pdf (accessed December 8, 2015).

Kaplinsky, R. M. Morris and J. Redmon. 2002. Understanding Upgrading Using Value Chain Analysis. University of Brighton. http://eprints.brighton.ac.uk/876/1/Understanding_Upgrading_Using_Value_Chain_Analysis.pdf (accessed December 8, 2015).

McAllister, I. 1993. *Windows on the world: university partnerships, international cooperation, sustainable development.* Halifax, NS: Lester Pearson Institute for International Development, Dalhousie University.

OECD (Organisation for Economic Co-operation and Development). 2013. *OECD-FAO Agricultural Outlook 2013-2022 Highlights.* Paris: OECD. http://www.oecd.org/berlin/OECD-FAO%20Highlights_FINAL_with_Covers%20(3).pdf (accessed December 8, 2015).

Parsons, L. 1993. *Management of Marine Fisheries in Canada.* Ottawa: NRC Research Press.

Ponte, S. 2008. Developing a 'Vertical' Dimension to Chronic Poverty Research: Some Lessons from Global Value Chain Analysis. Chronic Poverty Research Centre Working Paper 111. http://www.chronicpoverty.org/uploads/publication_files/WP111_Ponte.pdf (accessed December 8, 2015).

Porter, M. 2008. The Five Competitive Forces That Shape Strategy. *Harvard Business Review* 86 (1): 78-93.

Russell, D. and S. Hanoomanjee. 2012. Manual on Value Chain Analysis and Promotion. Report prepared for ACPFish II and Pescares Italia Srl: http://acpfish2-eu.org/uploads/projects/id278/Manual%20SA-4.1-B20.1-39.pdf (accessed December 8, 2015).

Stewart, J. 2013. 'Evolving' US Seafood Industry Turning Attention to Value Adds, Marel Says. *Undercurrent News.* November 25. http://www.undercurrentnews.com/2013/11/25/evolving-us-seafood-industry-turning-attention-to-value-adds-marel-says/ (accessed December 8, 2015).

Taylor, J. 2008. *Determinants of Development Success in the Native Nations of the United States.* Report prepared for Native Nations Institute for Leadership, Management, and Policy, University of Arizona. http://nni.arizona.edu/resources/inpp/determinants_of_development_success_english.pdf (accessed December 8, 2015).

Thayer-Scott, J. 2012. *An Atlantic Fishing Tale 1999-2011.* Ottawa: MacDonald-Laurier Institute. E-Book.

Ulnooweg Development Group. 2015. About. *Ulnooweg Development Group Inc.* http://www.ulnooweg.ca/about.php (accessed December 8, 2015).

Wien, F. 1986. *Rebuilding the economic base of Indian communities: the Micmac in Nova Scotia.* Montreal: The Institute for Research on Public Policy.

World Bank. 2010. The Hidden Harvests: The global contribution of capture fisheries. Conference Edition. Report prepared for the World Bank, Food and Agriculture Organization and, WorldFish Center. http://siteresources.world-bank.org/EXTARD/Resources/336681-1224775570533/TheHiddenHarvest-sConferenceEdition.pdf (accessed December 8, 2015).

Chapter 12

The mining sector is highly regulated in Canada and crosses both federal and provincial legislative jurisdictions. Supreme Court of Canada decisions and constitutional amendments speak specifically to Aboriginal rights and the requirement for consultation before mining development can occur on traditional lands. Where Aboriginal title has been established by the courts, the Crown must seek consent from the Aboriginal interests.

Impact and benefit agreements (IBAs) are increasingly being entered into by mining companies and Aboriginal communities. Oftentimes these agreements are negotiated years before any actual development occurs. Some Aboriginal communities are developing their own resource laws, which serve to better clarify processes around mineral development and to properly convey community issues and expectations surrounding employment, procurement, revenue sharing, and independent development.

Aboriginal Communities and Mining
Angelique Slade Shantz

Aboriginal communities are playing an increasingly important role in the entire life cycle of mining and other resource-based industries, from initial prospecting through to closure and environmental remediation. Due in part to recent shifts in the institutional forces that recognize human rights and land rights (O'Faircheallaigh and Ali 2008), communities have growing power to grant or withhold a social licence to operate for projects that will affect them, based on the risks and/or benefits that leadership and members believe may result from industrial activities. By "social licence to operate," I mean a community's decision about whether or not to accept and approve the activities of a business operating in its area that will have an impact on them. There is a widely held understanding that communities can and should reap long-term, sustainable, and culturally appropriate benefits from the opportunities that these operations bring. At the same time, firms are starting to recognize and, in some cases, even embrace their

> **Social licence** to operate is the community's decision to accept the presence of an enterprise (e.g., extraction company) on their land and to allow them to engage in business activities that will affect the community.

Corporate social responsibility (CSR) refers to voluntary actions beyond those required by regulators that recognize and ameliorate the social and environmental impacts a company has on a locale.

role in helping to facilitate these benefits, and are beginning to update traditional corporate social responsibility (CSR) policies with more sophisticated approaches to community partnerships (Esteves and Barclay 2011). However, many questions still remain about how (and whether) communities and firms can work in partnership to maximize the benefits and minimize the risks of these opportunities.

The aim of this chapter is to highlight and discuss some of these questions, taking as a starting point that resource projects can indeed bring both opportunities and risks to local communities. A more complete understanding of these potential benefits and costs, and how communities and firms might navigate them individually as well as in partnership, is an important first step toward building a more mutually beneficial industry. Although the focus of this chapter is on the mining industry, much of what I'll discuss may apply to other resource-based industries. This chapter is also oriented toward the Canadian context, where there are at least 1,200 Aboriginal communities within 200 km of 180 producing mines, and more than 2,500 exploration properties (Mining Association of Canada 2014a), making this an especially important topic for Canadian Aboriginal communities and Canadian mining firms. However, I draw insights from other international contexts and, similarly, what I discuss also has relevance on an international level, as well as to non-Aboriginal communities affected by mining.

The chapter is organized around two themes: the various layers or levels of governance or oversight present in the mining industry; and the different forms or levels of involvement Indigenous communities may have in mining projects. When I say "governance," it's just another way of saying how the "rules of the game" get decided, including who decides and how they're enforced. The first section gives an overview of the institutional context that governs the Canadian mining field as it relates to Aboriginal communities, and at each level of governance I'll highlight relevant actors, important issues, and governance mechanisms. The section on levels of involvement focuses on concrete, actionable insights for communities, and describes the different type of engagement opportunities available in typical mining projects.

LEVELS OF MINING PROJECT GOVERNANCE

Legislative and Regulatory Governance

The major actors at the legislative and regulatory level are the federal and provincial/territorial governments, but delineating their governing limits can be difficult (as discussed in chapter 6). For example, while provinces typically claim ownership of the underlying legal title to the land within their borders, and have power over matters such as property rights and natural resources, Aboriginal legislation takes place at the parliamentary level (Isaac and Knox 2004). This means that some regulatory decisions happen at the federal level, like Supreme Court of Canada cases—which have been important in establishing Aboriginal rights as they relate to mining—and others at the provincial level, such as environmental impact assessments (EIA), although some EIAs do take place at the federal level, depending on the type of anticipated impact. EIAs are processes that are meant to assess environmental and social impacts of a given resource project with respect to the people and environments that may be affected by them. Also, the duty to consult, which I'll talk about below, can be breached at the provincial level, as was the case in the recent Tsilhqot'in case, when British Columbia breached its duty to consult by issuing forestry licences without consulting the Tsilhqot'in on the uses of their land and without accommodating their interests.

> An **environmental impact assessment** (EIA) is a process that attempts to identify the potential positive and negative outcomes that could likely arise from activities in a given setting or habitat, taking into account socio-cultural factors such as health.

Provinces can also pass acts that have an impact on mining industry-Aboriginal relations. For example, the *Ontario Mining Act*, which took effect in 2013, addresses issues related to mining industry-Aboriginal consultation in exploration and development activities. Some of the rules in the act include the recognition and affirmation of existing treaty and Aboriginal rights, including, but not limited to:

> **Duty to consult** is an obligation to engage in discussions or negotiations with Aboriginal peoples about project plans and intentions prior to making decisions about resource development that affect Aboriginal or treaty rights.

- the duty to consult;
- a requirement that Aboriginal peoples are notified when mining claims are recorded within their traditional use areas;
- a requirement of notification and consultation with Aboriginal communities that may be impacted by exploration activities, with opportunities to provide feedback before activities take place; and

- the ability for the Ministry of Northern Development and Mines to withdraw land from prospecting, staking, and mining or surface rights (Webb and Hohn 2013).

Taken together, these requirements are a significant modification to Ontario's old approach, and may be seen as a response to both international and federal pressure, as well as to a number of highly public instances of conflict between mining firms and Aboriginal communities, such as with Platinex Inc., God's Lake Resources, and the De Beers' Victor diamond mine (Webb and Hohn 2013).

Internationally, there is a growing consensus around the respect and protection of Indigenous peoples rights. This is demonstrated by a number of policies and covenants passed by international political organizations, including:

- the 2007 United Nations Declaration on the Rights of Indigenous Peoples, which outlines the principle of free, prior, and informed consent;

- the International Labour Organization Convention 169 on Indigenous and tribal peoples;

- the United Nations Guidelines on the Protection of the Cultural Heritage of Indigenous Peoples (Fidler 2010); and

- the International Covenants on Civil and Political Rights and Economic, Social and Cultural Rights.

Several major governance mechanisms that establish the boundaries and rules around mining and Aboriginal peoples include Aboriginal rights, Aboriginal title, treaty rights, modern treaties or land-claim agreements, treaty land entitlement, and the duty to consult and accommodate. These are all terms that you've probably heard before, but may not know exactly how they relate to mining and other resource developments.

"Aboriginal rights," according to the *Constitution Act, 1982*, are rights held by Canadian Indigenous people, including First Nation, Inuit, and Métis, that are part of a practice, custom, or tradition within the cultural heritage of the group claiming the right (Isaac and Knox 2004). Of most importance in the mining context are rights that take place in a specific area, such as hunting, fishing, and trapping. These rights are related to a specific kind of Aboriginal right, an "Aboriginal title," which is the right to the land those activities take place upon, if it isn't covered by a treaty. "Treaty rights" are rights that were established in historic agreements, or treaties, although there are also modern treaties, which are often called "land-claim agreements" (see chapter 13 for more on the different types of treaties). Mineral and other resource-extraction projects can affect these rights by impacting upon the environment, which might thus negatively affect traditional activities like hunting or fishing. If Aboriginal title is established, or if treaties are in place, firms wanting to undertake projects that might affect these rights are required by law to engage in consultation and, possibly, fair compensation or other forms of accommodation (Isaac and Knox 2004). Here is how this is laid out in the Supreme Court of Canada judgement on *Tsilhqot'in Nation v. British Columbia*:

> Aboriginal title confers ownership rights ... including: the right to
> decide how the land will be used; the right of enjoyment and occupancy
> of the land; the right to possess the land; the right to the economic
> benefits of the land; and the right to pro-actively use and manage the
> land.... The right to control the land conferred by Aboriginal title means
> that governments and others seeking to use the land must obtain the
> consent of the Aboriginal title holders. If the Aboriginal group does not
> consent to the use, the government's only recourse is to establish that the
> proposed incursion on the land is justified under s. 35 of the *Constitu-
> tion Act, 1982*. (Tsilhqot'in 2014: par. 73-76)

The duty to consult and accommodate is the last mechanism I'll discuss here. This is clearly laid out in the *Tsilhquot'in* case (and elsewhere):

> Prior to establishment of title by court declaration or agreement,
> the Crown is required to consult in good faith with any Aboriginal
> groups asserting title to the land about proposed uses of the land and,
> if appropriate, accommodate the interests of such claimant groups....
> After Aboriginal title to land has been established by court declaration
> or agreement, the Crown must seek the consent of the title-holding
> Aboriginal group to developments on the land. (Tsilhqot'in 2014: par.
> 89-90)

Although consultation is a government responsibility, it was determined by the Haida Nation case, below, that the Crown can delegate some aspects of consultation to industry actors (Haida Nation 2004 par. 53). It has also been determined that Aboriginal communities have an obligation to engage in the consultation process (Mikisew Cree First Nation, par. 65; Ingelson and Passelac-Ross 2013).

It all sounds pretty straightforward when it's on paper, but in reality it is far more complicated, and many issues and questions still exist. Even though the constitution protects Aboriginal and treaty rights, they are not absolute, and can be violated if the violation can be "justified" (Isaac and Knox 2004). How is appropriate justification determined? In other words, what happens when the use of a piece of land negatively impacts a small group of people, but positively impacts a much larger group of people? The Supreme Court of Canada ruling from *Delgamuukw v. British Columbia* provides insight. To quote the judgement of the chief justice:

> In my opinion, the development of agriculture, forestry, mining, and
> hydroelectric power, the general economic development of the interior of

British Columbia, protection of the environment or endangered species, the building of infrastructure and the settlement of foreign populations to support those aims, are the kinds of objectives that ... in principle, can justify the infringement of [A]boriginal title. (Delgamuukw 1997: par. 165)

What does accommodation really mean? The Crown does not have an obligation to reach an agreement with affected Aboriginal communities, nor do communities have veto power over development, although accommodation may involve moving the project location, altering construction schedules to fit traditional livelihood activities, or establishing revenue-sharing arrangements (Ingelson and Passelac-Ross 2013). Another question that often comes up is about the extent of consultation. In the 2004 case of *Haida Nation v. British Columbia* (Ministry of Forests), the Court affirmed a "spectrum of consultation," ranging from talking together for mutual understanding to obtaining consent from the Aboriginal group involved (Isaac and Knox 2004). The court, in addressing that spectrum, said that the scope of the duty to consult and accommodate Aboriginal interest "is proportionate to a preliminary assessment of the strength of the case supporting the existence of the right or title, and to the seriousness of the potentially adverse effect upon the right or title claimed" (Haida Nation 2014: par. 39).

As you can see, there are still many unanswered questions about how the governance of natural resources affects Aboriginal communities. Nonetheless, taken together, the mechanisms described above lay out some of the groundwork for the potential for productive participation of Aboriginal peoples in Canada's natural-resource economy, although many argue that participation in a manner that fully acknowledges and respects Indigenous values would require a much more fundamental systemic shift than current governance mechanisms allow.

Industry and Firm Governance

In addition to the federal and provincial levels, resource governance also takes place at the industry and firm level, sometimes referred to as "private governance." Relevant private-governance bodies at the international level include the International Council on Mining and Metals, an international, member-based organization governed by the CEOs of all member companies. The council requires each of its member companies to make public commitments to improve their sustainability performance and report their progress annually (International Council on Mining and Metals 2015). Another important example is the Extractive Industries Transparency Initiative (2015), a global standard that promotes openness and accountable management of natural resources at the country rather than the firm level. Canada also has its own industry-specific initiatives, such as the Mining Association of Canada's (MAC) "Towards Sustainable Mining" (TSM) initiative. TSM is a set of tools and indicators that is mandatory for all MAC members, who commit to guiding principles that were agreed upon through a stakeholder-consultation process. In addition to this commitment, they have to publicly report their performance against 23 indicators each year, and their performance is also verified by external auditors (Mining Association of Canada 2015). While these "soft law" initiatives are not binding and participation is voluntary, they are gaining in influence, and non-compliance can result in economic repercussions, such as difficulties in accessing capital, loss of social licence to operate, and withdrawal of permits or licences in the mining industry (Drost and Pariseau 2013).

At the firm level, participation in initiatives such as TSM can be seen as part of firms' CSR strategies. Because CSR is typically considered to be voluntary, mining companies often have very different approaches to it. Some mining companies approach CSR with an eye to maximizing public-relations benefits, and make commitments that may look good in glossy sustainability reports, but have little input from or relevancy to impacted communities or environments. Other firms take a longer term and more holistic perspective, recognizing that in order to extract natural resources, they must contribute to society in ways that go above and beyond what they are legally required to do or actions that are in their economic self-interest (O'Fairchalleigh and Ali 2008). In the resource-extraction industries, these activities are often referred to as firms obtaining (and maintaining) a social licence to operate. Although the duty to consult and accommodate refers to a government obligation, industry actors have just as much at stake in achieving a successful outcome from a consultation and accommodation process as communities do, since some communities have demonstrated that they have the power to halt or terminate prospective and even existing projects (Diges 2008). It's also important to remember that a firm's CSR policies take place in a broader political, social, and legal context, and within Canada this varies regionally due to province-specific approaches to mining policy. For example, some provinces, like British Columbia, have existing revenue-sharing arrangements with Aboriginal communities for mining and other resource projects (Coates 2015). How this interacts with firms' bilateral approaches to negotiating agreements directly with communities, without government intervention, is far from clear. Nonetheless, firms that take the second approach described above are often more likely to conceive of their relationship with

> **External auditors** are qualified analysts independent of the organization being reviewed, who assess an organization's activities and performance against standards and established indicators of sound practice.

> **Private governance** refers to the oversight structures that maintain industry standards. They are external to private organizations, with no official authority or decision-making power, but serve a purpose by setting and privately enforcing standards for industries.

> **Bilateral approaches** are those involving or entered into by two parties.

Aboriginal communities as more of a partnership in the governance of a given project's resources.

Partnership Governance

Savvy mining companies increasingly understand their mining projects as a partnership between a community or group of communities and a firm or firms. To provide a flavour of this, table 1 provides just a few of many examples of prominent corporate pledges toward community partnerships.

Unlike the legislative and regulatory mechanisms discussed earlier, the governance mechanisms related to corporate-community partnerships are

Table 1: Corporate-Community Partnership Statements		
Company	**Community Partnership Statement***	**Source**
Lundin Mining	"We work consultatively with our **community partners** to ensure that our support matches their priorities."	Lundin Mining (2015)
Goldcorp	"A Collaboration Agreement was signed by Goldcorp, the Cree Nation of Wemindji, the Grand Council of the Cree, and the Cree Regional Authority. This agreement outlines and signifies **a unique partnership** for sustainable value through the future success of our Éléonore project."	Goldcorp (2015)
New Afton Mining	"New Afton has successfully developed a **Partnership Agreement** with the Skeetchestn Indian Band and the Tk'emlúps te Secwepèmc."	Mining Association of Canada (2014b: 114)
Rio Tinto's Iron Ore Co.	"IOC has been **partnering with communities** in Labrador West and Sept-Îles for more than five decades, and hopes to continue for many more."	Mining Association of Canada (2013: 90)
BHP Billiton	"Management encourages outreach to the mine's stakeholders and communities of interest, including engagement in dialogue on sustainable **community partnerships**."	Mining Association of Canada (2011: 28-9)
*Emphases added		

generally voluntary, and often governed by negotiated agreement among the parties. These are also commonly referred to as an impact and benefit agreement (IBA), and I'll use the two interchangeably.[1] Although I said that these agreements are voluntary, some modern land-claim settlements do require proponents to negotiate IBAs before proceeding with mineral development (Fidler 2010). These agreements are typically confidential negotiations between a mining company and a community. In some cases, where there are several communities involved in a project, an agreement may be made with an umbrella entity or with the assistance of a third-party intermediary. On one

> An **impact and benefit agreement** (IBA) is a negotiated agreement between (e.g.) a resource-extraction company and an Aboriginal community that sets out the responsibilities of each party and how it will share the benefits arising from resource development prior to development.

hand, several communities negotiating jointly may strengthen bargaining power (Weitzner 2006) and ensure that one community is not negotiating a confidential agreement that could potentially adversely affect another community downstream (Hitch and Fidler 2007). On the other hand, this plurality can also be a challenge. For example, communities comprised of both Aboriginal and non-Aboriginal sub-communities, or communities with multiple First Nations living in the same geographic location, may have multiple governments, each operating simultaneously in the same "community," thus possibly posing challenges for the formation of a partnership. As an example, the so-called Ring of Fire mining region in Ontario has an estimated $60 billion of minable resources, spread across the traditional territories of nine First Nations.

These challenges may be mitigated by the presence of an umbrella organization representing and negotiating community interests. These entities can include tribal councils, alliances, and development corporations, which have been touted as contributing significantly to communities' ability to benefit from natural-resource extraction (Coates and Crowley 2013). Whereas an umbrella organization represents the interests of a community or communities, a third-party arbiter or mediating organization, acting as a neutral party, has also been shown to facilitate positive interactions between parties looking to collaborate (Sharma and Kearins 2011). Even individual communities are often divided by opposition or support of mining activities because of competing interests or values (Calvano 2008), although this conflict can sometimes be minimized by a thorough community-planning and visioning process that takes place well ahead of formal consultation by the government and firms.

> An **umbrella organization** is an association that represents and acts on behalf of its member organizations.
>
> A **third-party arbiter** is a neutral individual or organization selected to facilitate an agreement between two parties.

The timing of partnership activities is an important factor. In many cases, firms have already gained access to explore an area before the legislated consultation process begins, and infringement on Aboriginal interests can occur prior to Crown involvement and prior to a formal EIA process. IBAs, on the other hand, can take place earlier and negotiate the terms of engagement over the lifespan of a mine (Fidler 2010). While we're talking about timing, it's important to note that there are several different stages of a mine cycle, and it is often not the same firm taking the lead at each stage of the cycle. The initial stage, or mineral exploration, is the search for mineral deposits. This stage can take up to ten years before a mine is actually developed, and fewer than one in 10,000 mineral showings are developed (NRCAN 2013). Early on, this work is done by prospectors, and once they find a promising area, they will stake a claim so that they can continue to explore the area more carefully. This can be done on any Crown land, including land used by Aboriginal communities, although First Nation reserve land cannot be staked in most provinces. If anything is found, a junior mining company will likely be brought in and will usually be involved throughout the rest of the exploration phase.

Although full IBAs are not typical at this stage, and opportunities for communities to be involved are somewhat limited, letters of intent or memoranda of understanding maybe signed to begin the process. If mineral resources are found, interests are often sold to major mining companies, whose role it is to develop and construct the mine. Mine development can take another seven to ten years, and it is at this stage that an impact and benefit agreement is typically negotiated, after community consultations have taken place. It is not unusual for conflict to arise when ownership shifts from a junior mining firm, which may make certain commitments to a community, to a "major" or large mining company who will take the project to the next stage, and who may have a different approach to community relations.

The next stage of the mineral cycle is the operational stage, which can be as short as a few years or as long as several decades. Mine closure is the final phase, although a closure plan is often put in place during the development phase. The senior mining company is responsible for honouring their commitments for full and proper closure and environmental reclamation of the land, and there is typically a deposit or bond that is held by the government to ensure reclamation activities are honoured (NRCAN 2013).

The idea of a true partnership between a firm and the community or communities that are impacted by its activities is a positive one. However, issues and questions often well up. How does the confidentiality of the negotiated agreement process and contract help or hinder Aboriginal communities from sharing knowledge? How can a social licence to operate be transferred from one company to another? What should the role of the government be in these negotiations to ensure a fair process? How can trust be fostered when firms and communities often have such different goals and values? What's the best way to mitigate conflict when there are multiple communities with competing interests? How can an inclusive socio-environmental impact assessment be ensured? Who should be responsible for proper mine-closure procedures when a mining company goes bankrupt and cannot honour its land reclamation and other closure commitments? You can see that these questions are difficult ones to answer, and the answers may also be different for different projects and communities.

Resource Governance at the Community Level

While an IBA typically governs the partnership at the company-community level, there are also important governance issues and processes to be considered at the community level. Some communities, such as the Kaska Nation, an alliance of Kaska communities

> A **comprehensive community plan** is a document that outlines a community's vision and framework to guide future decision-making. Its goal is to facilitate sustainability, improved governance, and self-sufficiency. It is created through a holistic, community-led process.

located in the Yukon, British Columbia, and the Northwest Territories, are passing their own resource laws, often in collaboration with other First Nations. The Kaska Nation is in the process of passing a resource law that will provide a set of guidelines and policy for industry to follow, in an attempt to simplify the process for mining companies, decrease investor uncertainty, and ensure benefits for the nation (Thomson 2015). An important first step is the development of a comprehensive community plan (CCP), which can be used to create a community-based vision and framework to guide future decision-making (see discussions in chapters 2 and 6). This process can often be lengthy, but, as I mentioned earlier, it can also be useful in ensuring that a community is negotiating an agreement that is representative of the entire community and is reflective of broader goals. A truly comprehensive visioning and planning process can take up to a year or more, but if done well can result in not just a vision or set of goals, but a fully elaborated action plan that has the support and "buy in" of the entire community and its leadership. For example, T'Sou-ke Nation, on Vancouver Island, spent a full year on their comprehensive visioning and planning process, which they called "Visions in Progress." They came up with innovative ways to engage the whole community at different times throughout the process, such as canoe trips, community feasts, and engagement with their school. In particular, marginalised voices—which are sometimes lost in planning exercises that focus on the leadership level—can be heard through this process, such as the perspectives of women, who are often most negatively impacted by mineral activities without having access to many of its development opportunities (Keenan and Kemp 2014), or youth, through engagement with local schools or community-centre programming. As another example, the Teslin Tlingit Council engaged in a ten-year capital-development plan that took over three years to prepare, which included participation by the municipal government. The final product was a plan with significant community input and support for more than $75 million dollars of future planned infrastructure, with stipulations on local contractor procurement, local employment, local training, and greater local retention of economic impact. A planning process is a useful exercise to have completed before starting to negotiate an agreement with a mining company, as time limits can rush this process and result in a lack of full community buy-in. However, the prospect of mineral discovery can also be a great motivation for starting this process, and, in some cases, where the timeframe for negotiation of the IBA allows, can even intersect conveniently with the process of negotiating an agreement.

Throughout the comprehensive community planning stage, it's important to consider what sustainable development looks like in the context of mining development. Sustainable development goals and priorities may be different for every community, but "sustainability" remains a controversial term when it's applied to the development of a non-renewable mineral resources (Fidler 2010). One version of sustainability, sometimes called "strong sustainability," implies that natural resources are maintained at levels that will support their use indefinitely. The other version, sometimes called "weak sustainability," includes both natural and human capital in the equation, and calls an activity sustainable if "there is an effective conversion of the natural capital, represented by the resource, to social capital that would allow for long-term livelihoods ... assum[ing] that the resilience of the natural environment is not compromised" (Ali and O'Faircheallaigh 2007: 6). Even assuming sustainability in its weaker form, the question remains as to how to avoid the boom-and-bust cycle that often comes with a short-term activity like mining, and how to convert economic benefits that stem from the activity into long-term economic resilience once the cycle of the mine has run its course. This is a particular challenge in light of the geographic isolation in which most of these projects take place, as communities are often cut off from market opportunities outside of the mining industry. The temporary nature of revenue streams, jobs, and other resources that come from mining activities make a CCP process even more critical.

> **Boom-and-bust cycle** refers to the predictable phases of growth and decline of an economy resulting from industrial development. Periods of expansion (boom) result in economic growth and increased employment and business opportunities, while periods of contraction (bust) result in decreased activity and relatively fewer employment opportunities.

It also makes transparent accountability mechanisms to govern and allocate the resources that do flow from mineral extraction very important. Aboriginal communities in a number of sectors have used structures such as community trusts to avoid unfair fiscal-management practices. For example, in the context of Indigenous-owned renewable energy, "Community Clean-Energy Trusts" are sometimes used. These trusts are the corporate structure into which all revenue, dividends, and royalties from the project flow and are held. They are typically 100 per cent owned by the community, governed by a board of trustees, and are responsible for the distribution of funds to purposes agreed upon by community members through a voting process, as well as the transparent reporting of all aspects of any

> A **dividend** is a sum of money paid to a shareholder from the earnings of a company.
>
> A **royalty** is a percentage of revenues paid to an individual or group for the use of the property that they legally own.

funds, including both social and financial returns (Henderson 2013). In the Yukon, for example, many self-governing First Nations have established advanced business/investment trusts that not only act as an accountability mechanism, but also provide tax benefits. The limited-liability corporate structure can also be embedded within these trusts to manage businesses with potential liability risk.

LEVELS OF COMMUNITY INVOLVEMENT IN MINING PROJECTS

Aboriginal communities can structure their level of involvement in mining or other resource-based projects in the way that best suits their vision and development goals. These levels may include:

- employment, which is often accompanied by education and training opportunities;
- local-content clauses, which typically stipulate that a firm purchases certain goods or services from local entrepreneurs or community-based enterprises;
- various forms of revenue-sharing arrangements, either through the firm or province;
- joint venture, where the community is an investor or share-holder in the project; or
- independent development, whereby the community is the primary developer of its resources (although this level is less common in the mining industry, it is increasingly common among Aboriginal communities in the clean-energy sector, and is the goal of several Aboriginal communities in the Northwest Territories).

Regardless of the level of involvement, it is critical to consider both the benefits of having a mine site nearby and the potential risks. The benefits can include jobs, training, new business opportunities, infrastructure, and revenue streams. With these benefits can also come environmental risks, such as changes in water quality, impacts on wildlife, or vegetation changes, and social risks, such as family separation, intercommunity conflict, income inequality, challenges to traditional lifestyles and culture, and addictions. These trade-offs are complex, and should be weighed carefully, and continually, with input from the entire community, throughout the decision-making process.

Employment

"Thousands of Jobs Coming to Northern Ontario," claims an eye-catching headline of a recent Ontario press release. But what are those jobs, how long will they last, who will they go to, and what will happen when they're gone? These are the important questions that the impressive statistic doesn't address. Going back to our earlier discussion of a mine site's project cycle, different jobs become available at different times in the life of a mine project.

At the exploration phase, jobs may only last a few weeks to a few months, and can include field positions, such as drill helpers, line cutters, truck drivers, earth-moving operators, mechanics and welders, or camp-support positions, such as cooks and kitchen helpers, and accommodation janitors and housekeepers (NRCAN 2013). That said, although there may not be many long-term jobs in this phase, the period during exploration can be an important and often-overlooked opportunity to create a culture of transparent and honest interactions that build long-term trust (Rios and Thomson 2013). At this stage, firms are responsible for providing clear and honest messages that help create realistic expectations and dispel rumours. These messages should include both the benefits and risks of a project that moves to the development stage, as well as the high likelihood of a project not getting past the exploration phase. They should also include a transparent discussion of the process of exploration, how absent or present the company might be in the near future, and establish communication norms, such as how frequently meetings should be held to keep communities in the information loop (Rios and Thomson 2013). Communities are responsible for ensuring a broad level of participation at meetings, so that the entire community can participate in future decision-making. If the company is not forthcoming with details, it is the community's responsibility to dig in with questions, such as of the company's past experiences with other communities. When approached by project developers, some communities have even gotten in touch with other communities that have had experience with these developers to ask about their experiences with the company in question (Weitzner 2006). As with any future partnership, it's important to do your research on prospective partners before making a final decision.

At the development and construction stage, entry-level jobs such as those described in the exploration stage are typically available, as well as semi-skilled and skilled jobs, such as administrative roles, trades occupations, and environmental technicians, and professional roles requiring a university degree, such as managers, engineers, and geologists (NRCAN 2013). At the operation stage, miners, heavy-equipment operators, truck drivers, electricians, surveyors, engineers, instrumentation technicians, administrators, mechanics, IT specialists, and many others are required

(NRCAN 2013). However, it is important to remember and plan for the fact that these jobs are temporary, and critical that the community's initial planning takes into account how to diversify and transition to new economic activities well before the mine is scheduled to close. How to create economic resilience once the mine has closed and the mining company has left should be a major priority in all such community decision-making. It's true that mining projects create jobs and revenues for a period of time. However, there is a wide variance in communities' successes in using those jobs, training, and revenues as a springboard for a prosperous future, as opposed to the boom-and-bust cycle of mining that is sometimes the reality for local communities.

One example of this is the community of Elliot Lake, Ontario, a mining town crippled by the closure of the local uranium mine that had employed a large majority of the community's population. The community, acting collectively, decided to reinvent itself as a Florida-style retirement community, and in doing so has revitalized the local economy, restored its population, and re-invigorated the community's way of life (Peredo and Chrisman 2006).

Education and Training

Many of the jobs described above require qualified education and training. A useful framework to think about these capacity-building opportunities, particularly their usefulness to the community after the life of the mine is over, is the distinction between a top-down and bottom-up capacity building (Buitrago 2013). Whereas top-down capacity building might be defined as companies investing in infrastructure and training that address skill shortages in the area, and is driven by corporate priorities, bottom-up capacity building would take a long-term approach, and be characterized by providing the local community with alternative livelihood options that reflect the aspirations of community members beyond the life cycle of the mine (Buitrago 2013). Communities evaluating the costs and benefits of partnering with a mining company wishing to work nearby may want to ask about educational and training opportunities offered by the mining company, as in: How will the skills and capabilities I'm receiving from these opportunities be transferred to another industry so that they continue to serve me once the mine is closed? Similarly, mining companies may want to ask of their own training programs: How can we augment our programs so that we are providing community trainees with opportunities that will provide sustainable benefits beyond the life of this mine? What other mechanisms can we use to provide lasting value, such as ensuring that the communities we work with have easy access to banking and financial advising, so that saving money from paycheques is easy, financial advice is accessible, and financing is available to foster the creation of thriving and resilient local economies?

Local Content

Local content means different things to different people. In this chapter, "local content" means sourcing contracts locally, with the goal of providing mutual benefit to both the company and the community. In the context of mining, this can mean contracts for catering, housekeeping, recycling and waste-disposal services, aircraft support, trucking, environmental monitoring, and many others (NRCAN 2013). For example, Tli Cho Air invested in a Dash 7 aircraft and has multi-year, multi-million-dollar contracts to service the Ekati and Diavik diamond mines (NRCAN 2013). Good local-content policies should have benefits for companies by ultimately lowering their costs related to importing goods and services critical to a mine's supply chain, and by building support for their project. It should also benefit communities, building economic capacity and resilience at the local level, by offering local businesses equal or preferential access to contracts within the mine site's supply chain (Esteves, Franks, and Vanclay 2012), always with an eye to focusing on opportunities that will still be fruitful at the end of a mine's life cycle.

Communities negotiating local-content clauses in their IBAs should keep several things in mind. First, local content can be defined in a number of different ways, including having an entity that is registered locally, owned at least 50 per cent by a previously existing local entity, or having a majority local workforce (Esteves, Franks, and Vanclay 2012). So, it's important in the negotiating process that the ultimate goal of local-content policies that contribute to building local economic capacity and resilience are being met. It's also important for both mining companies and communities to make sure that the same local-content policies that are meant to help develop local economies are not creating unintended negative consequences. For example, the allure of high wages paid through mining contracts can lead to locals being drawn away from other businesses or important community roles, such as education, health, and governance roles (Esteves, Franks, and Vanclay 2012). Also, small local businesses that have either been developed or scaled up to service mining projects are often vulnerable to the boom-and-bust cycles inherent in mining and other resource-extraction industries, particularly in remote areas void of other economic opportunities. Conflict or discontent among community members can also result from perceptions of unfair allocation of business opportunities (Esteves, Franks, and Vanclay 2012). Finally, while well-structured local-content clauses may have the potential to have the greatest collective impact on the community, they can also be the most difficult to properly implement. For example, in

1990 the province of Nova Scotia began a $400 million rehabilitation of the Sydney Tar Ponds, with an Aboriginal set-aside procurement-strategy agreement with Mi'kmaw First Nations of Cape Breton, including a multi-million dollar bundle of contracts on which Aboriginal companies (i.e., an incorporated entity having more than 50 per cent Aboriginal ownership) could bid. However, because of the unique capital structure of reserve-based companies (see discussion of land in chapter 2 and financing in chapter 8), majority-Aboriginal-owned contractors were not eligible for bonding, a type of insurance that all contractors on government projects are required to have, because their capital could not be used for collateral. The government agency overseeing the project eventually found a work-around to this issue, but the case illustrates the complex legal challenges that are associated with Aboriginal businesses participating meaningfully in local-content contracts, and highlights the importance of appropriate corporate structuring for maximum community benefit.

Government or Firm Resource-Revenue Sharing

In addition to indirect benefit sharing such as employment and local-content opportunities, direct benefits, namely resource-revenue sharing, are becoming increasingly commonplace, despite the policy fragmentation and lack of standardization leading to a variety of arrangements across Canada (Coates 2015). Many IBA agreements include some form of direct payment by the firm to the community, either in the form of revenue sharing, fixed payments, or investments. Government resource-revenue sharing is distinct from IBAs and other agreements that Aboriginal communities and mining companies sign bilaterally; rather, it refers to funding from provincial or territorial governments that is a percentage of revenues they receive from companies for resource-extraction privileges. For example, in New Brunswick, First Nations receive 5.3 per cent of the allowable cut of timber cut on Crown lands, providing them around $12 million per year, plus another $3.35 million of Crown royalties (Coates 2015). Discussions on revenue sharing focus primarily on resources off-reserve, as on-reserve resources typically generate returns from developed resources.[2]

Regardless of where the revenues come from, these revenues can represent an important opportunity to develop a diversified portfolio of investments that can ensure a community's economic resilience well into the future. This may include investing in businesses, education, or infrastructure. One recent example of a sustainable infrastructure investment is a partnership between Tugliq Energy Co. and Glencore plc's Raglan nickel-copper mine, in the Nunavik region

> A **diversified portfolio** is an approach to investment that focuses on a variety of different securities. Because this approach reduces the relative impact of any one investment or type of security in a group of investments, it helps the owner offset or balance the risk of rapid change in one stock.

of northern Québec, where an ambitious multi-year wind trial is set to demonstrate the potential of Canada's first industrial-scale wind-power and energy-storage facility. This project is partially Inuit-owned and leverages the IBA negotiated by Glencore and several nearby Inuit communities, and could be a model for the many diesel communities with nearby mineral resources, where energy can cost more than $1.50 per kilowatt hour. A similar project has been undertaken by Rio Tinto plc's Diavik diamond mine in the Northwest Territories, with a farm of four turbines, and with an estimated saving of $4 million in energy costs in 2013 via wind energy (Van Praet 2014).

Project Ownership: Joint Venture and Independent Development

Finally, there are levels of involvement that include various degrees of ownership. A joint venture (JV) is a business arrangement where ownership of a company is shared by two or more entities, such as between a mining company and a community or its development corporation (see chapter 5 for other types of partnerships). An Aboriginal economic-development corporation (EDC) is the economic- and business-development arm of an Aboriginal community, and is typically used as the business vehicle that invests in, owns and/or manages subsidiary businesses that benefit the Aboriginal communities they represent (Canadian Council for Aboriginal Business n.d.). EDCs can have an ownership stake in the mining project itself, or in peripheral businesses, such as Rescan Tahltan Environmental Consultants (RTEC), a joint venture between the Tahltan Nation Development Corporation and Rescan Environmental Services. RTEC conducts environmental assessments of projects in Tahltan territory, including environmental consulting, ecological-risk assessments, environmental-effects monitoring, tailings management, reclamation/site closure, water treatment, and social and economic sciences (NRCAN 2013). Social- and environmental-impact assessment and monitoring is an important ongoing role for Indigenous communities to play in mining projects, and combining it with a business venture is a strategic win-win opportunity. As with any of the models of involvement, joint-venture participation and other types of equity ownership can be subject to misuse or exploitation, and due diligence is required.

Although it's not as common, there is no reason why Aboriginal communities can't be full owners in a mining project, and some are indeed moving toward this model. For example, in 2013, the Dene First Nations of the Northwest Territories formed an exploration and mining company through their corporate arm, Denendeh Investments Limited Partnership, and purchased four nearby "brownfield" (lightly contaminated) mineral properties on which they intend to develop a metal mine. Not only does being "resident owners" provide added value to potential investors, but by wholly owning the project they are able to generate more income and retain more control than a traditional IBA would provide (Moore 2014). However, this route also assumes significantly more risk and responsibility than an IBA or revenue-sharing arrangement, and communities interested in this possibility should carefully consider the pros and cons of each level of involvement, as each one carries its own level of risk and reward.

Conclusion

Aboriginal communities are playing an increasingly important role in mineral and resource development across Canada. What those roles are, how communities can stand to benefit or lose out from them, and how they are governed are all important and as yet unanswered questions that cannot be resolved in a textbook chapter, but require broad and inclusive debate among Aboriginal communities, mining executives, and all other Canadian citizens who enjoy the benefits of living in a resource-based economy.

Implications for Practice

Every industrial sector has its own specific regulations; however, some of the lessons learned from this mining case study are more broadly applicable. Any commercial activity related to resources, whether natural or renewable, is connected to traditional territories in some way. It is important not only to understand the governance structure of the particular industry, and by extension the international factors that influence decisions in that industry, but also the communities on whose territory the development is occurring. Each community will have its own "rules of the game" and one cannot make assumptions that the same process will work across different communities or territories. Further, there is much more to consider than what is mandated by federal and provincial government. The communities themselves are often interested in discussing legal and cultural obligations (both the written and the unwritten). Commercial activities can have long-term implications for land use and community well-being. Comprehensive community planning was discussed here with a practical example of how planning may play out within industry negotiations. Long-term community impact and benefits agreements are presented because short-term profitability is no longer the only discussion point. More and more communities want to put in place strategies that will ensure their leaders are being included in negotiations, community knowledge is considered during planning stages, and members are developing skills that will enable them to contribute in meaningful ways during and beyond resource development.

Key Points:

- In addition to obtaining permits required by government, resource-extraction companies also need a "social licence" to operate.

- Resource-extraction companies are increasingly moving beyond traditional notions of corporate social responsibility and entering into partnerships with Aboriginal communities.

- Comprehensive community plans form an important foundation upon which decisions about resource development can be made by Aboriginal communities and leaders.

- Environmental-impact assessments are critical for resource development, and should take a holistic approach.

- Impact and benefit agreements are often negotiated between resource-extraction companies and Aboriginal communities before development proceeds, outlining the responsibilities of both parties and identifying how profit will be shared.

- Local-content benefits both resource-extraction companies and their partner Aboriginal communities.

Questions for Review:

1. What is duty to consult and how does it apply to business?

2. What is an impact and benefit agreement? What is an environmental impact assessment? How do these relate to corporate social responsibility?

3. What is a comprehensive community plan and how does it relate to resource development?

4. Describe the life cycle of a mine. How will different phases impact upon an Aboriginal community?

5. What are the benefits of using local content?

Suggested Assignments:

1. How do Supreme Court decisions impact mining activities? What difficulties exist in executing or acting on these decisions?

2. Compare the life cycle of a mine to that of another business or industry. Consider how the different phases could impact upon an Aboriginal community.

3. What is the issue when small (first-stage) prospectors transfer "rights" to larger firms?

4. Describe the governance challenges in the mining industry. Are these different from those of other industries? How and why?

5. Is there a practical difference between consultation and approval and a so-called social licence to operate? Discuss the approaches.

Notes

Thanks to Jennifer Keith, Ben Bradshaw, Kevin McKague, and the anonymous reviewers for their feedback on this chapter.

1. Although several important issues related to the negotiation of these agreements will be discussed, it is outside the scope of this chapter to address them in detail. For an in-depth treatment of this topic, see Gibson and O'Faircheallaigh (2010).

2. Due to the fragmented regional approach of this topic, it is difficult to do justice to its complexity. However, a recent report on resource revenue sharing has been published—see Coates (2015).

References

Ali, S. and K. O'Faircheallaigh. 2007. Extractive industries, environmental performance and corporate social responsibility: Special issue introduction. *Greener Management International* 52: 5-16.

Buitrago, I. 2013. Mining, capacity-building and social license: Making the links. In *2013 World Mining Congress Proceedings*. Montreal: Canadian Institute of Mining, Metallurgy and Petroleum, 1-15. http://www.disandesinternational.com/uploads/1/4/9/5/14955598/wmc2013paper116.pdf (accessed December 3, 2015).

Calvano, L. 2008. Multinational corporations and local communities: A critical analysis of conflict. *Journal of Business Ethics* 82 (4): 793-805.

Canadian Council for Aboriginal Business. n.d. *About CCAB*. https://www.ccab.com/about (accessed December 8, 2015).

Coates, K. and B.L. Crowley. 2013. New beginnings: How Canada's natural resource wealth could re-shape relations with aboriginal people. Report prepared for the Aboriginal Canada and the Natural Resource Economy Series. Macdonald-Laurier Institute, Ottawa. http://www.macdonaldlaurier.ca/files/pdf/2013.01.05-MLI-New_Beginnings_Coates_vWEB.pdf.

Coates, K. 2015. Sharing the wealth: How resource revenue arrangements can honour treaties, improve communities, and facilitate Canadian development. Report prepared for the Aboriginal Canada and the Natural Resource Economy Series. Macdonald-Laurier Institute, Ottawa.

Delgamuukw v. British Columbia. 1997. 3 SCR 1010, 1997 CanLII 302 (SCC), http://canlii.ca/t/1fqz8.

Diges, Carmen L., Canadian Mining Law & Finance. 2008. "The Aboriginal Tool-kit: What every Mining Principal needs to know when dealing with Aboriginal Peoples in Canada." Toronto: McMillan Binch Mendelsohn.

Drost, A. C. and J. A. Pariseau. 2013. The Evolving Legal Regime Governing Ethics And Sustainability In The Mining Industry. In *2013 World Mining Congress Proceedings*. Montreal: Canadian Institute of Mining, Metallurgy and Petroleum, 1-15. http://www.disandesinternational.com/uploads/1/4/9/5/14955598/wmc2013paper116.pdf (accessed December 3, 2015).

Esteves, A. M. and M. A. Barclay. 2011. New approaches to evaluating the performance of corporate–community partnerships: A case study from the minerals sector. *Journal of Business Ethics* 103 (2): 189-202.

Esteves, A. M., D. Franks and F. Vanclay. 2012. Social impact assessment: The state of the art. *Impact Assessment and Project Appraisal* 30 (1): 34-42.

Extractive Industries Transparency Initiative. 2015. What is the EITI? Extractive Industries Transparency Initiative. https://eiti.org/eiti (accessed December 8, 2015).

Fidler, C. 2010. Increasing the sustainability of a resource development: Aboriginal engagement and negotiated agreements. *Environment, Development and Sustainability* 12 (2): 233-44.

Gibson, G. and C. O'Faircheallaigh. 2010. *IBA community toolkit: Negotiation and implementation of impact and benefit agreements*. Report prepared for The Gordon Foundation, Toronto. http://gordonfoundation.ca/sites/default/files/publications/IBA_toolkit_web_Sept_2015_low_res_0.pdf (accessed December 3, 2015).

Goldcorp. 2015. Responsible Mining: Aboriginal & Indigenous People. *Goldcorp*. http://www.goldcorp.com/English/Responsible-Mining/Partnerships-and-Programs/Aboriginal-and-Indigenous-People (accessed January 26, 2016).

Haida Nation v. British Columbia (Ministry of Forests). 2004. 3 SCR 511, 2004 SCC 73 (CanLII), http://canlii.ca/t/1j4tq.

Henderson, C. 2013. *Aboriginal power: Clean energy & the future of Canada's first peoples*. Erin, ON: Rainforest Editions.

Hitch, M. and C. Fidler. 2007. Impact and benefit agreements: A contentious issue for environmental and aboriginal justice. *Environments Journal* 35 (2): 45-69.

Ingelson, A. and M. M. Passelac-Ross. 2013. Mine Development, Consultation With Indigenous Peoples And Sustainability . In *2013 World Mining Congress Proceedings*. Montreal: Canadian Institute of Mining, Metallurgy and Petroleum, 1-15. http://www.disandesinternational.com/uploads/1/4/9/5/14955598/wmc2013paper116.pdf (accessed December 3, 2015).

International Council on Mining and Metals. 2015. About Us. *International Council on Mining and Metals*. https://www.icmm.com/about-us/about-us (accessed December 8, 2015).

Isaac, T., and Knox, A. 2004. Canadian aboriginal law: Creating certainty in resource development. *University of New Brunswick Law Journal* 53 (3): 3-42.

Keenan, J. C. and D. L. Kemp 2014. Mining and local-level development: Examining the gender dimensions of agreements between companies and communities. Brisbane, Australia: Centre for Social Responsibility in Mining, The University of Queensland.

Lundin Mining. 2015. Corporate Responsibility: Corporate Commitment. *Lundin Mining*. http://www.lundinmining.com/s/CR_Sustainability.asp (accessed January 26, 2016).

Mikisew Cree First Nation v. Canada (Minister of Canadian Heritage). 2005. 3 SCR 388, 2005 SCC 69 (CanLII), http://canlii.ca/t/1m1zn.

Mining Association of Canada. 2015. *Towards Sustainable Mining*. http://mining.ca/towards-sustainable-mining (accessed December 8, 2015).

———. 2014a. Facts & Figures: A Report on the State of the Canadian Mining Industry. http://mining.ca/sites/default/files/documents/Facts_and_Figures_2014.pdf (accessed December 3, 2015).

———. 2014b. Towards Sustainable Mining Progress Report. Ottawa: Mining Association of Canada. *mining.ca/sites/default/files/documents/TSM_Progress_Report_2014.pdf* (accessed January 26, 2016).

———. *2013. Towards Sustainable Mining Progress Report*. Ottawa: Mining Association of Canada. *mining.ca/sites/default/files/documents/TSM_Progress_Report_2013.pdf* (accessed January 26, 2016).

———. *2011. Towards Sustainable Mining Progress Report. Ottawa: Mining Association of Canada*. http://mining.ca/documents/tsm-progress-report-2011-0 (accessed January 26, 2016).

Moore, E. 2014. On the land: Mining and First Nations have not always gotten along, but what if they were one and the same? *Canadian Institute for Mining Magazine*. https://magazine.cim.org/en/2014/May/cover-story/On-the-land.aspx (accessed December 3, 2015).

NRCAN (Natural Resources Canada). 2013. Exploration and Mining Guide for Aboriginal Communities. http://www.nrcan.gc.ca/sites/www.nrcan.gc.ca/files/mineralsmetals/files/pdf/abor-auto/mining-guide-eng.pdf. (accessed December 3, 2015).

O'Faircheallaigh, C. and S. Ali. 2008. *Earth Matters: Indigenous Peoples, the Extractive Industries and Corporate Social Responsibility.* Sheffield, UK: Greenleaf Publishing.

Peredo, A. M. and J. J. Chrisman. 2006. Toward a theory of community-based enterprise. *Academy of Management Review* 31 (2): 309-28.

Rios, J. M. and I. Thomson. 2013. Contributing To Community Sustainability During Mineral Exploration: Lessons Learned From Mesoamerica. In *2013 World Mining Congress Proceedings.* Montreal: Canadian Institute of Mining, Metallurgy and Petroleum, 1-15. http://www.disandesinternational.com/uploads/1/4/9/5/14955598/wmc2013paper116.pdf (accessed December 3, 2015).

Sharma, A. and K. Kearins, K. 2011. Interorganizational collaboration for regional sustainability: What happens when organizational representatives come together? *The Journal of Applied Behavioral Science* 47 (2): 168-203.

Thomson, N. 2015. Industry Applauds Kaska Nation plan to pass resource law. *CBC News.* http://www.cbc.ca/news/canada/north/industry-applauds-kaska-nation-plan-to-pass-resource-law-1.2940206 (accessed December 8, 2015).

Tsilhqot'in Nation V. British Columbia. 2014. 2 SCR 257, 2014 SCC 44 (CanLII), http://canlii.ca/t/g7mt9.

Van Praet, N. 2014. In Québec, the energy future of the North id blowing in the wind. *Financial Post.* http://business.financialpost.com/news/energy/in-quebec-the-energy-future-of-the-north-is-blowing-in-the-wind?__lsa=9226-6083 (accessed December 8, 2015).

Webb, K. and M. Hohn. 2013. Mining Industry-Aboriginal Engagement Pursuant To The New Ontario Mining Act Rules: A Preliminary Examination Of Potential Impacts. In *2013 World Mining Congress Proceedings.* Montreal: Canadian Institute of Mining, Metallurgy and Petroleum, 1-15. http://www.disandesinternational.com/uploads/1/4/9/5/14955598/wmc2013paper116.pdf (accessed December 3, 2015).

Weitzner, V. 2006. *Dealing full force: Lutsel K'e dene first nation's experience negotiating with mining companies.* Ottawa: The North-South Institute.

PART FOUR

Chapter 13

Treaties and Land Claims in Canada

Katie K. MacLeod

Treaties and land claims can dictate or alter the ways in which Aboriginal peoples, the Canadian Government, and third-party companies operate on particular tracts of land. There are several different types of Aboriginal treaties in Canada, depending on the governing bodies in place at the time of negotiation and signing. If you are a non-Aboriginal person working in Aboriginal territory, it is critically important to understand the type of treaty or land claim that pertains to the area in which you hope to work. In most instances, Aboriginal populations are able to control what type of development occurs on their ancestral lands under a given treaty. In 1973, *R. v. Calder* was the first case to press the issue of Aboriginal rights to land in court.[1] As a result of that decision, the Nisga'a Nation was able to claim Aboriginal title to their traditional lands in British Columbia. This decision opened the door for subsequent court decisions addressing Aboriginal title, as well as to land claims and implementation of modern treaties and territories.

Historic treaties were established between 1726 and 1921 in both pre- and post-confederation Canada. There are two primary categories of historic treaty: treaties of peace and friendship and the numbered treaties. Beginning in 1973, modern treaties—or comprehensive land claims—began to be negotiated between Canada and Indigenous governments. These modern treaties are negotiated for land that was claimed by historic treaties and grant ownership and self-governance to the Indigenous population claiming the given land (AANDC 2015). Examples of modern treaties include the provincial treaty process established in British Columbia and the comprehensive land claim process that established Nunavut as a territory. These different types of treaties in Canada are described in detail below.

Historic Treaties

Historic treaties were made between Aboriginal communities and the British Crown (and later Canada) in order to establish what rights settlers and Aboriginal peoples had to land.[2] For example, beginning in 1726, treaties of peace and friendship were made with the British; however, a series of eleven numbered treaties (negotiated between 1871 and 1921, largely pertaining to Western and Northern settler expansion and resource extraction) were made with the Government of Canada, post-confederation. Historic treaties also include a number of smaller treaties, such as the so-called Williams treaties and Upper Canada land surrenders in southern Ontario, the Douglas Treaties on Vancouver Island, and the Robinson treaties concerning Lake Huron and Lake Superior. In some cases, Aboriginal land was ceded to Europeans; in others, there was co-management of the land. The promises made in these treaties are used to establish what development can or cannot occur on the land in question, as well as to establish what title and rights the Aboriginal population has to that land and its resources.

Treaties of Peace and Friendship

In 1713, the Treaty of Utrecht was imposed upon the colony of Acadia (present-day mainland Nova Scotia) to cede French sovereignty to the British Crown. The Maritimes were thereafter subject to struggle between French and British powers, leaving the Mi'kmaq and the Maliseet of the area caught in the crossfire. The British, significantly outnumbered by the Indigenous and French populations, were concerned with the Aboriginal population's stronger alliance with the French. A period of oppression, hostility, and war resulted. In an effort to mend relations, between 1725 and 1762 a series of treaties of peace and friendship were signed between the Mi'kmaq, the Maliseet, and the British Crown. The British perceived the treaties signed in 1760-1761 as thereby establishing control of the territory. These treaties included Mi'kmaw and Maliseet communities as signatories across the Atlantic provinces and into the Gaspé region of Québec.

The treaties signed in this period promised that the Mi'kmaq and Maliseet would retain hunting, fishing, and trading practices in return for an agreement to "keep the peace and to respect British law" (Issac 2001: 25). Unlike other treaties signed with the Crown and Canada, these treaties did not speak to land cession or to the extinguishment of Aboriginal title without land cession or release of Aboriginal title to the land. As a result, in Atlantic Canada, it is possible for rights within treaties to exist alongside Aboriginal title and land rights.

As did most Aboriginal peoples, the Mi'kmaq experienced a decline in their resources due to increased populations of settlers, resulting in an increased dependence on the Canadian government (Fox 2006; Paul 2000).

Mi'kmaw rights were not recognized due to federal government policy on land claims and Aboriginal treaty rights that placed restraints on Mi'kmaw access to resources. Beginning in the 1970s, the Mi'kmaq began asserting their rights under the peace and friendship treaties through treaty litigation, which continued through the 1980s and 1990s, with *Simon v. the Queen* (in 1985), *R. v. Denny* (1990), and *R. v. Marshall* (1999).

In 1985, James Matthew Simon was arrested for transporting a firearm and ammunition outside of hunting season. In prosecution of the case, Simon advocated for his rights under the Treaty of Peace and Friendship, 1752, which were recognized at least on reserve land. This decision resulted in the Union of Nova Scotia Indians establishing governance over Mi'kmaw hunting rather than regulation by the province. Following this decision, *R. v. Denny* determined that appellants David B. Denny, Lawrence John Paul, and Thomas Frank Sylliboy possessed the right to fish for food under the 1760 peace and friendship treaty, after they were charged with catching and retaining salmon without a licence in 1987, in contravention of the *Fisheries Act*.

In 1999, Donald Marshall Jr. was charged in Nova Scotia with the fishing of eel in a closed season and without a licence. Marshall maintained that the fishing he had undertaken was within his rights, according to treaties of peace and friendship signed in 1760 and 1761 between the Mi'kmaq and the British Crown. Mi'kmaw pre-contact practices indicate they were involved in trade networks and managed resources such as food, shelter, and trade to support their settlements (Allen 1994; Wiber and Milley 2007).

R. v. Marshall found that within the treaties of peace and friendship of 1760 and 1761, the Mi'kmaq, Maliseet, and the Passamaquoddy peoples have the treaty right to use natural resources for "moderate livelihood" as harvesting and trading would have occurred prior to European arrival and the establishment of the treaties (Wiber and Kennedy 2001: 164; Wiber and Milley 2007: 173).[3]

Questions and interpretations concerning the right to self-governed commercial fisheries have come to surface among Mi'kmaw fishers using resources to gain "a moderate livelihood" (Coates 2003; Fox 2006). However; the case of *R. v. Marshall* (No. 2), also in 1999, "stated that the Federal Minister of Fisheries has overall authority and that the right to livelihood fishery had limitations" of good governance (Wiber and Milley 2007: 169). There have been many projects and agreements made by the Department of Fisheries and Oceans (DFO) and the federal government that have both placed limitations upon Mi'kmaw harvesting activities and advanced community control (Wiber and Milley 2007: 165).

The Mi'kmaw world view of *Netukulimk* has always come into conflict with governmental regulation of trading, hunting, fishing, and trapping. The Mi'kmaw Grand Council (2014: 46) defines *Netukulimk* as: "the use of the natural bounty provided by the creator for the self support and well-being of the individual and community at large." *Netukulimk* is therefore in contradiction with the implementation of the fishery resulting from the Marshall decisions as capitalist resource management has a focus on individual gain. As a result, community benefit needed to be considered when moving forward in fishery implementation, since *Netukulimk* has a strong focus on community resource management (Wiber and Milley 2007; Barsh 2002; Prosper, McMillan, and Moffitt 2011).

Fishery development was not absent of governmental regulation. Interim fisheries agreements were implemented between DFO and Mi'kmaw and Maliseet First Nations that focused on "harvesting activities, with First Nations receiving vessels and training gear to support native fisheries" (Wiber and Milley 2007: 169-70). The objective of the Canadian government was to maintain DFO authority on the definition of "livelihood activity" within the Mi'kmaw fishery, despite the Supreme Court deeming it within treaty rights in *R. v. Marshall* (Wiber and Milley 2007: 170).

The Marshall cases increased opportunities in Mi'kmaw communities through participation in the commercial fishery. In 2009, ten years after the Marshall decisions, First Nations in Atlantic Canada had generated $35 million in commercial fishing revenue (APCFNC 2009). First Nations and the federal government have continued to work together to develop commercial fishery-management strategies (Wiber and Milley 2007: 121). After the decisions, there were meetings held throughout Mi'kma'ki (the traditional territory of the Mi'kmaq) to discuss the advancement of fishery management (168). As rights were not limited exclusively to harvesting, there were increased opportunities within communities and among Mi'kmaw leaders in community management and self-governance structures (167). Mi'kmaw communities have adopted administrative and corporate structures to manage the First Nation's fishery, and others have adopted community-based models for resource development, as these systems have been proven effective in terms of conservation and sustainability (Charles 2001). For more on the Mi'kmaw fishery specifically, see chapter 11.

Numbered Treaties

The numbered treaties were made between Aboriginal peoples and Canada post-confederation. These treaties range from one to eleven and pertain to parts of Ontario, Manitoba, Saskatchewan, Alberta, the Northwest Territories, and the Yukon. The treaties were instated to increase development across these provinces and territories for mining, farming, and other resource development, as settlement and development moved westward, and are sometimes characterized as "land sharing" treaties rather than "land cession" treaties.

Earlier historic treaties in this area, the aforementioned Robinson treaties of 1850, commonly referred to as the Robinson-Huron Treaty and the Robinson-Superior Treaty, were land-cession agreements made between the Crown and the Aboriginal peoples of Lake Huron and Lake Superior. The treaties were made by William Benjamin Robinson and later approved by Lord Elgin. These treaties also included a number of Métis communities prior to the implementation of the *Indian Act,* the rubric of which removed the Métis from the treaties. Reconfigurations of the Robinson treaties are contained within Treaty 3 and Treaty 9, with Treaty 3 addressing parts of the Robinson-Huron Treaty and Treaty 9 addressing aspects of the Robinson-Superior Treaty.

The Government of Canada negotiated many of the numbered treaties without concern for the land and water requests of the First Nation peoples, because of federal economic interest in the provinces. The state wanted control over resources. Due to these interests, and the fast pace of these negotiations, the Lubicon Cree, of northern Alberta, were excluded from the signing of Treaty 8, which sparked a legal dispute beginning in 1899 (Gerber 1990). This exclusion left the Lubicon Cree without reserve land and with difficulty claiming rights as Aboriginal peoples.

The Lubicon Cree requested to be included within Treaty 8 and for the Government of Canada to grant them reserve land; however, they were only granted sixty-six square kilometres of land (which was never surveyed) in 1939, and there were no steps to include the Lubicon Cree in Treaty 8 (Goffard 1991). As a result of an arbitrary registration process that occurred in 1942 and 1947, not all Lubicon Cree were registered within Treaty 8. The majority of the Lubicon Cree were denied official Indian status as only one of the six communities was registered (Gerber 1990).

In the late 1940s, the growing tar sand and oil development in Alberta had disastrous effects on the Lubicon Cree. The settlement at Marten River was destroyed, with forced relocation for resource exploitation (Gerber 1990). As companies continued to profit and the oil industry moved further into northern Alberta in the 1970s, there was destruction of the Lubicon way of life and traditional lands. Industrial activity drove wildlife from the area, destroyed forests, and, by 1984, 90 per cent of the Lubicon population had developed a dependence on the federal government. Prior to the 1970s oil boom, 90 per cent were living subsistence and self-sufficient lives (Gerber 1990; Huff 1999). After the destruction of Lubicon territory in 1984, the Lubicon took their case to the United Nations Human Rights Committee, which determined there was a fundamental human-rights violation due to the historic inequalities of Treaty 8 and to recent resource developments that endangered the lives and culture of the Lubicon Cree (Westra 2009). The Lubicon Cree continue to face threats of destruction on their lands with increased natural gas extraction, also known as fracking, occurring on non-treaty land.

Negotiations on Treaty 9, or the James Bay treaty, as it's often called, began due to an increased concern from Aboriginal peoples about the development of the Canadian Pacific Railway and the increasing settler population moving into the area. The construction of the railway is believed to be one of the most significant factors in Aboriginal peoples seeking treaty agreements with Canada. In addition to the railway, there was an increase in non-Aboriginal hunting, fishing, and trapping, and Aboriginal dependence on the trading posts hindered the overall subsistence livelihood (McKlem 1997: 102). On the side of the government, there is evidence to support the notion that they went into Treaty 9 negotiations in order to speed up the construction of the railway, which was necessary for early 20th-century expansion (McKlem 1997: 104-105).

The original Treaty 9 agreement included Aboriginal peoples surrendering certain rights to 336,700 square kilometres (130,000 square miles) of land. The adhesions to this treaty between 1929 and 1930 extended an additional 331,500 square kilometres (128,000 square miles) reaching the border between Ontario and Manitoba (McKlem 1997). Treaty commissioners Duncan Campbell Scott and Samuel Stewart began negotiations in 1905 with representatives from the Aboriginal communities along with representatives from the federal and Ontario governments. The resulting treaty was signed in 1906, with members of Cree and Anishinaabe communities living within the treaty limits. As with most early treaties, there are questions regarding the interpretations of the written and oral terms of the treaty (McKlem 1997).

After a draft of the treaty was reviewed by provincial and federal governments, Ontario requested a clause "that no site suitable for development of water power exceeding 500 [horsepower] was to be included within the boundaries of any reserve" (McKlem 1997: 108). Within the treaty itself, there are explicit references to economic activity and resource development; however, there are differences as to whether third-party activity on the treaty land is authorized by the treaty itself, and to what capacity it can be authorized by legislative action (McKlem 1997: 98).

Treaty 9 also limited Aboriginal subsistence practices, noting that hunting, fishing, and trapping can be restricted from time to time by governmental regulation. Furthermore, hunting, fishing, and trapping rights do not extend onto portions of land "as may be required or taken up from time to time for settlement, mining, lumbering, trading and other purposes" (James Bay Treaty 1931). It is clear that the rights established in Treaty 9 were to protect the traditional economic, social, and commercial practices of the Aboriginal population from the economic development of settlers.

Third-party companies have attempted to conduct mine exploration and hydroelectric activity on the territory protected by Treaty 9 and the clauses for hydroelectric activity are strong. There was an increase in demand for hydroelectric development within the boundaries of Treaty 9 as indicated by the clause proposed by the Province of Ontario; however, within the terms of Treaty 9 and the *Constitution Act, 1867*, Aboriginal title was not entirely extinguished, nor was hydroelectric development established as an exception to land use, as were "settlement, mining, lumbering, trading, and other purposes" (James Bay Treaty 1931). The Government of Ontario argued that hydroelectric development would fall into the category of "other purposes"; however, the court held, in reference to the *Constitution Act, 1867*, that treaties should be read to favour the "Indians." Employing this lens, it does not fall into the category of "other purposes" because the Aboriginal communities would not have signed the treaty under those terms (McKlem 1997: 125, 128).

Although the treaty presents protection over hydroelectric development, there have been additional concerns in northern Ontario around mining development. The treaty states:

> And His Majesty the King hereby agrees with the said Indians that they shall have the right to pursue their usual vocations of hunting, trapping and fishing throughout the tract surrendered as heretofore described, subject to such regulations as may from time to time be made by the government of the country, acting under the authority of His Majesty, and saving and excepting such tracts as may be required or taken up from time to time for settlement, *mining*, lumbering, trading or other purposes. (James Bay Treaty 1931; emphasis added).

As highlighted above, mining is specifically mentioned as an activity that can occur upon treaty land. The Fort Albany First Nation, of the Mushkegowuk Cree, has been subject to threats of mining and hydroelectric development in the past on Treaty 9 lands, and there is growing concern regarding the Ring of Fire developments (Restoule, Gruner, and Metatawabin 2013). The discovery of significant mineral deposits presents opportunities for third-party companies to pursue extractive mining development near First Nation communities without their consent, as First Nations have little power to prevent resource exploration on their territories.

Modern Treaties and Land Claims

Comprehensive land-claim agreements now allow Aboriginal peoples to negotiate with federal, provincial, or territorial governments to potentially develop a modern treaty. Modern treaties create a discomfort in Canada, as the process is dealt with in the courts and tends to place Aboriginal peoples and their rights in a pre-contact context where only "traditional" practices and economies can ensue (Scott 2012). There is an increased focus on rights in modern treaty processes and land-claim agreements that allow for First Nation economic development with the resources made available in the treaty negotiation. In addition to the comprehensive land-claim agreements as a process for modern treaty-making, British Columbia has also implemented a provincial-treaty process with the British Columbia Treaty Process for the First Nation people of the province.

British Columbia

In 1763, the Royal Proclamation required authorities to acquire or purchase Aboriginal land prior to any "molestation or disruption" occurring. According to the guidelines set forth by the proclamation, Sir James Douglas, governor of Vancouver, set out to "manage" the "Indian situation." In doing so, Douglas signed fourteen treaties with the Aboriginal peoples of Vancouver Island between 1850 and 1854. These treaties are known as the Douglas treaties or the Vancouver Island treaties. It was significant that Aboriginal title had not been settled in British Columbia prior to its confederation into Canada in 1871 and, as a result, neither the provincial or federal government addressed the issue of title or treaties (Roth 2002: 144).

In addition to the Douglas treaties, Treaty 8 is the only numbered treaty that covers land that extends into British Columbia. Treaty 8 was signed in 1899, and the majority of the treaty pertains to land in Alberta; however, it extends into the northeast portion of British Columbia and was signed by residents of Peace River Country. No other historic treaties were made in British Columbia, as at the time of the Royal Proclamation in 1763 there was little concern about the allegiance of the northwest coast to other powers (Scott 2012: 47).

The Supreme Court of Canada cases of *R. v. Calder, R. v. Sparrow*[4] and *R. v. Van der Peet*[5] established tests for Aboriginal title and the Aboriginal inherent right to land and territory for Aboriginal peoples across the country. *Delgamuukw v. British Columbia*[6] took this a step further as its outcome established the test for Aboriginal title in Canada. In 1997, *Delgamuukw v. British Columbia* presented a claim over British Columbia territory as hereditary land of the Gitksan and Wet'suwet'en. Arguments made by the Gitksan and the Wet'suwet'en nations were based within land succession that was passed on through matrilineal descent lines (Roth 2002).

The arguments and evidence presented in the case placed an emphasis on their political and legal system, more specifically, within the importance of the ritual of the potlatch (see chapter 1). As it was described in *R. v. Denny*, the Gitksan and the Wet'suwet'en nations described and presented "the laws of the feast hall as a fully operating, coherent, and sovereign system of authority and land tenure that regulates every corner of Gitksan and the Wet'suwet'en political, social and economic life" (Roth 2002: 146).

Despite the presentation of oral histories and testimonies from historians and anthropologists, in 1991, the chief justice of the British Columbia Court of Appeal, Allan McEachern, denied the Gitksan and Wet'suwet'en claims to traditional territory. Justice McEachern also denied the "very existence of an Indigenous legal and political system," stating that "I am quite unable to say that there was much in the way of pre-contact social organization among the Gitksan and the Wet'suwet'en" (Delgamuukw 1991: 508).

In response to *Delgamuukw v. British Columbia*, in 1992, the Government of Canada, along with that of British Columbia and the First Nations Summit, established the British Columbia Treaty Commission (BCTC) to begin treaty negotiation with BC First Nations. This commission oversees the stages of modern-day treaty processes that are negotiated with First Nations within the province. The BCTC proceeds in six stages:

1. Statement of Intent to Negotiate

2. Readiness to Negotiate

3. Negotiation of a Framework Agreement

4. Negotiation of an Agreement in Principle

5. Negotiation to Finalize Treaty

6. Implementation of Treaty

Maa'nulth First Nations and the Tsawwassen First Nation have implemented modern treaties though the BCTC and many other nations are at various other stages of treaty implementation. Even with the success rate, there are many First Nations in British Columbia choosing not to enter into the treaty process (Roth 2002). Alfred (2000) argues that the British Columbia treaty process has failed due to its focus on the natural-resource industry and assimilatory agendas on the part of the provincial and federal government. As a result, issues within the commission concerning extinguishment of title, rights to land, and self-government have left many First Nations deciding to distance themselves from the BCTC (Alfred 2000).

In 1997, the appeal process of *Delgamuukw v. British Columbia* ended with the decision that the Gitksan and Wet'suwet'en had title to their territory of 58,000 square kilometres (Roth 2002). Although there was a lack of historical evidence to support the claim in court, in the appeal case Supreme Court of Canada Chief Justice Lamer accepted oral histories from Elders as evidence and granted the land to the Gitksan and Wet'suwet'en. This outcome is greatly based in the terms of pre-contact matrilineal descent patterns as their hereditary names are passed down from mother to daughter, which was confirmed through the use of oral histories in the court.

The Delgamuukw decision established the following test for proving Aboriginal title:

- the land must have been occupied prior to sovereignty;

- if present occupation is relied on as pre-sovereignty proof of occupation, there must be a continuity between present and pre-sovereignty occupation; and

- at sovereignty, that occupation must have been exclusive (Delgamuukw 1991: par. 143)

This test creates issues for First Nations attempting to establish title due to the definition of occupation and their ability to prove that land was occupied pre-sovereignty; however, the case did increase the recognition of oral evidence in the court.

The Nisga'a final agreement (NFA)[7] is an example of a modern land claim that came into effect in 2000, recognizing 10 per cent of Nisga'a traditional land, with the remaining 90 per cent subject to co-management and Nisga'a Aboriginal rights (Scott 2012: 10). The NFA established title, rights, and jurisdiction, along with control over the lands and resources, for the interest of economic development. This is in contrast to the agreements commonly made with First Nations that are often based upon the continuation of traditional uses of land, which was integral to subsistence pre-contact.

Similar to other First Nations, Nisga'a relations with Europeans began with economic exchanges, and the rights and title to their territory have been in high contention since the arrival of settlers (Scott 2012: 46). Located on the northwest coast of British Columbia, Nisga'a First Nation occupies a traditional territory that covers 26,000 square kilometres along the Pacific Coast (Scott 2012: 45).

Influenced by the Delgamuukw decision, the Nisga'a final agreement became a contentious case as it has been interpreted by some as extinguishing Aboriginal title. As a result, many First Nations see the Nisga'a agreement as a negative example of the modern land-claim and treaty process, and it has contributed to the hesitations of groups entering the BCTC. The Nisga'a, however, assert that they have enshrined their Aboriginal rights in the treaty and that "the negotiating parties have agreed to rights—rather than extinguishing them" (Nisga'a Lisims Government n.d.). Although these issues raise concern, the Nisga'a have experienced a number of benefits though their agreement.

In the NFA, it was determined that the Nisga'a would develop commercial fisheries in addition to their members' continued fishing rights (Scott 2012: 10). The agreement was negotiated in order to meet Nisga'a law and give the Nisga'a Nation power over their own land. In the agreement, it was established that all fish and aquatic plants harvested in fisheries on Nisga'a territory may be traded or sold by Nisga'a citizens within the Nisga'a Nation or with other Aboriginal peoples and non-Aboriginals. The Nisga'a Nation holds all fish entitlements and is exempt from governmental licences (Scott 2012: 27).

On June 26, 2014, in a landmark Supreme Court decision *Tsilhqot'in Nation v. British Columbia*, Tsilhqot'in Nation was granted Aboriginal title to approximately 1,900 sq km of claimed land. This decision was the first to grant Aboriginal title over land that was on a reserve and will be governed by Tsilhqot'in laws and people (Tsilhqot'in National Government 2014). This case also resulted in the Tsilhqot'in Nation attaining all resource rights over the claimed land. Attaining resource rights presents complications and jurisdictional issues related to industry and economic development, and increased opportunities for Aboriginal title owners to develop partnerships and joint ventures with the resource industry, for example (Bankes 2015).

Nunavut

In 1993, the Nunavut Land Claims Agreement (NLCA) granted a land claim in co-management concerning a northernmost territory that encompassed 1,800,000 square kilometres, 353,000 square kilometres of which would be owned by Inuit. The Inuit have mineral rights to 36,000 square kilometres of the Inuit-owned territory. Within the agreement, the Inuit have rights to all minerals on Inuit-owned lands and the federal government must comply with the political aspirations of the Inuit in their agreement of self-governance (Légaré 1996; Hicks and White 2000).

Nunavut remained undivided from the Northwest Territories at the time of the NLCA. In 1992, the Nunavut Political Accord, a part of the NLCA detailing the establishment of Nunavut from a part of the Northwest Territories, confirmed that the territories would be divided establishing an independent self-governing territory for the Inuit, Nunavut Territory. This process was monumental in Aboriginal land initiatives in Canada in terms of land-claim agreements and modern treaties.

Inuit Tapirisat of Canada (ITC) used federal financial aid received in 1974 to study Inuit land occupancy in the Arctic. The Nunavut proposal was submitted to Ottawa in 1976 using information gathered in the 1974 study (Légaré 1996). After the first proposal was withdrawn by the ITC in 1976, it was resubmitted in 1977, which was then rejected by Ottawa. The third version of the proposal, titled "Political Development in Nunavut," was accepted in 1979 and became the starting point for the NLCA (Légaré 1996: 147).

The proposed was as follows:

(1) ownership rights over portions of land rich in non-renewable resources; (2) decision making power over the management of land and resources within the settlement area; (3) financial indemnisation

and royalties from resources developed in the area; (4) a commitment from Ottawa to negotiate self-government given a land-claim agreement. (Légaré 1996: 147)

Although the final agreement was signed in 1993, there was a process of developing a government and other issues that delayed the official establishment of the territory and government of Nunavut until 1999 (Campbell, Fenge, and Hanson 2011). The development of the Government of Nunavut focused on issues such as promoting gender equality and dissemination of government operations across the territory (ibid.). In addition, the inclusion of Inuit values, culture, and use of Inuktitut[8] was incorporated into the government, along with Inuit traditional knowledge, also known as Inuit Qaujimajatuqangit, to continue to promote Inuit societal values (Van Dam 2008; White 2001; Campbell, Fenge, and Hanson 2011). In addition to issues of land ownership and land management, the final version of the NLCA entitled Inuit to royalties from resource development projects in Nunavut over a period of fourteen years (Légaré 1996; Van Dam 2008).

Notes

1. See full Calder decision at http://scc.lexum.org/decisia-scc-csc/scc-csc/scc-csc/en/item/1362/index.do.

2. A map of historic treaties is available at http://www.aadnc-aandc.gc.ca/DAM/DAM-INTER-HQ/STAGING/texte-text/htoc_1100100032308_eng.pdf.

3. See full (first) Marshall decision at http://csc.lexum.org/decisia-scc-csc/scc-csc/scc-csc/en/item/1740/index.do.

4. See the full Sparrow decision at http://scc.lexum.org/decisia-scc-csc/scc-csc/scc-csc/en/item/609/index.do.

5. See the full Van der Peet decision at http://csc.lexum.org/decisia-scc-csc/scc-csc/scc-csc/en/item/1407/index.do.

6. See the full Delgamuukw decision at http://csc.lexum.org/decisia-scc-csc/scc-csc/scc-csc/en/item/1569/index.do.

7. See full agreement at http://www.parl.gc.ca/Content/LOP/researchpublications/prb992-e.htm.

8. The Inuit language most widely used, though one of many dialects in Nunavut.

References

AANDC. 2015. *Comprehensive Claims*. https://www.aadnc-aandc.gc.ca/eng/1100100030577/1100100030578 (accessed December 8, 2015).

Alfred, T. 2000. Deconstructing the British Columbia Treaty Process. University of Victoria, August 2000. http://web.uvic.ca/igov/uploads/pdf/GTA.bctreatyprocess.pdf. (accessed December 3, 2015).

Allen P. 1994. *Metpenagiag. New Brunswick's Oldest Village.* Fredericton, NB: Goose Land Editions and Red Bank First Nation.

APCFNC (Atlantic Policy Congress of First Nations Chiefs Secretariat). 2009. Report. Marshall 10 Years Later: Atlantic and Gaspé First Nations Participation in Fisheries. http://www.apcfnc.ca/images/uploads/Post_Marshall_report_10_years.pdf. (accesssed December 3, 2015).

Bankes, N. 2015. The implications of the Tsilhqot'in (William) and Grassy Narrows (Keewatin) decisions of the Supreme Court of Canada for the natural resources industries. *Journal of Energy and Natural Resources Law* 33:3, 188-217. http://www.tandfonline.com/doi/pdf/10.1080/02646811.2015.1030916 (accessed December 3, 2015).

Barsh, R. L. 2002. Netukulimk past and present: Mikmaw ethics and the Atlantic fishery. *Journal of Canadian Studies, 37*(1), 15.

Campbell, A., J. Fenge and U. Hanson. 2011. Implementing the 1993 Nunavut Land Claims Agreement. *Arctic Review on Law and Politics* 2 (1): 25-51.

Charles, A. 2001. *Sustainable Fishery Systems.* Oxford: Blackwell Science.

Coates, K. 2003. Breathing New Life into Treaties: History, Politics, the Law and Aboriginal Grievances in Canada's Maritime Provinces. *Agricultural History* 77 (2): 333-54.

Delgamuukw v. British Columbia. 1991. CanLII 2372 (BC SC). http://canlii.ca/t/1g2kh (accessed December 8, 2015).

Fox, G. 2006. Mediating Resource Management in the Mi'kmaq Fisheries Canada. *Development* 49 (3): 119-24.

Gerber, P. R. 1990. Exploitation of Resources against Land Rights: The Lubicon Cree and their Struggle for Survival. *Schweizerische Amerikanisten-Gesellschaft.* Bulletin 53-54:23-34.

Goffard, J. 1991. *Last Stand of the Lubicon Cree.* Vancouver: Douglas and McIntyre.

Grand Council of the Mi'kmaq Nation. 2014. The Convent Story. In *Dawnland Voices: An Anthology of Indigenous Writing from New England*, ed. S. Senier. Lincoln, NE: University of Nebraska Press.

Hicks, J. and G White. 2000. Nunavut: Inuit self-determination through a land claim and public government. In *Nunavut: Inuit regain control of their lands and their lives*, ed. J. Dahl, J. Hicks and P. Jull. Copenhagen: International Work Group for Indigenous Affairs Document No. 12: 30-115.

Huff, A. 1999. Resource development and human rights: A look at the case of the Lubicon Cree Indian Nation of Canada. *Colorado Journal of International Environmental Law and Policy* 10: 161.

Issac, T. 2001. *Aboriginal and Treaty Rights in the Maritimes: The Marshall Decision and Beyond.* Saskatoon, SK: Purich Publishing.

James Bay Treaty. 1931. The James Bay Treaty - Treaty No. 9 (Made in 1905 and 1906) and Adhesions Made in 1929 and 1930. *Indigenous and Northern Affairs Canada*. http://www.aadnc-aandc.gc.ca/eng/1100100028863/1100100028864 (accessed December 8, 2015).

Légaré, A. 1996. The Process leading to a land claims agreement and its implementation: The case of the Nunavut land claims settlement. *The Canadian Journal of Native Studies* 16 (1): 139-63.

McKlem, P. 1997. Impact of Treaty 9 on natural resource development in northern Ontario. In M.Asch (Ed), *Aboriginal and treaty rights in Canada: Essays on law, equity, and respect for difference.* Vancouver: University of British Columbia Press.

Nisga'a Lisims Government. n.d. Understanding the Treaty. *Nisga'a Nation.* http://www.nisgaanation.ca/understanding-treaty (accessed February 4, 1016).

Paul, D. N. 2000. *We were not the savages: A Mi'kmaq perspective on the collision between European and Native American civilizations.* Halifax, NS: Fernwood.

Prosper, K., L. J. McMillan, and M. Moffitt. 2011. Returning to Netukulimk: Mi'kmaq cultural and spiritual connections with resource stewardship and self-governance. *The International Indigenous Policy Journal* 2 (4): 1-17.

Restoule, J.-P., S. Gruner and E. Metatawabin, E. 2013. Learning from Place: A Return to Traditional Mushkegowuk Ways of Knowing. *Canadian Journal of Education* 36 (2): 68-86.

Roth, C. 2002. Without Treaty, Without Conquest: Indigenous Sovereignty in Post-Delgamuukw British Columbia. *Wicazo Sa Review* 17 (2): 143-165.

Scott, T. L. 2012. Postcolonial sovereignty?: The Nisga'a final agreement. Saskatoon, SK: Purich Publications.

Tsilhqot'in National Government. 2014. Summary of the Tsilhqot'in Aboriginal Title Case (Williams Case) Decision. *Tsilhqot'in National Government.* http://www.tsilhqotin.ca/PDFs/2014_07_03_Summary_SCC_Decision.pdf. (accessed December 3, 2015).

Van Dam, K. 2008. *A place called Nunavut: multiple identities for a new region.* Circumpolar Studies 5. Groningen, Netherlands: Barkhuis.

Westra, L. 2009. *Environmental Justice and the Rights of Ecological Refugees.* New York: Earthscan.

White, G. 2001. And Now For Something Completely Northern: Institutions of Governance in the Territorial North. *Journal of Canadian Studies* 35 (4): 80-99.

Wiber, M. and C. Milley. 2007. After Marshall: Implementation of Aboriginal Fishing Rights in Atlantic Canada. *Journal of Legal Pluralism* 55: 163-186.

Wiber, M. and J. Kennedy. 2001. Impossible Dreams: Reforming Fisheries Management in the Canadian Maritimes after the Marshall Decision. *Law and Anthropology* 11: 282-97.

Chapter 14

Indian Residential Schools, the Royal Commission on Aboriginal Peoples, and Truth and Reconciliation
Katie K. MacLeod

Indian Residential School System

Indian residential schools emerged as a result of a partnership between the Canadian government and participating churches. They were implemented as an assimilation tactic to "take the Indian out of the child."[1] The goal was to destroy Indigenous languages, cultures, and traditions, and, to achieve this end, children were removed from their parents' care to attend residential schools. The first of these government-sponsored religious schools opened in western Canada in the 1880s, and more subsequently opened across the country. The only provinces that did not operate Indian residential schools were Prince Edward Island, New Brunswick, and Newfoundland; however, Atlantic Canadian Mi'kmaw and Maliseet children did attend the Shubenacadie residential school in Nova Scotia (Miller 1996).

With the establishment of the *Indian Act*, residential schools prospered in the 1920s as a result of compulsory attendance, with First Nation, Métis, and Inuit children attending (Stanton 2011: 1). The structure of the school system was discriminatory and racist in order to alter Indigenous life in Canada under the policy of the *Indian Act* (Jung 2011: 12). There were 130 such schools in operation in the 20th century, and roughly 150,000 Aboriginal children attended (RCAP 1996: 353; Jung 2011: 6). Children experienced forced physical labour, physical harm, and mistreatment by staff. Due to malnutrition, abuse, and exposure to diseases (such as tuberculosis), schools had mortality rates as high as 25 to 60 per cent (Jung 2011). In addition, children were also the victims of nutritional experimentation, as well as mental, physical, and sexual abuse (Mosby 2013; Jung 2011).

The residential-school system has left a lasting impact on survivors and is responsible for significant cultural gaps in Aboriginal communities. It is also a major factor in many socioeconomic problems in those communities today. Survivors of residential schools suffer from "drug and alcohol addictions, depression, higher rates of suicide, and poor relationship and parenting skills" (Jung 2011: 10).

The impact extends beyond the survivors, as many Aboriginal peoples in Canada continue to experience intergenerational trauma as a result of the experience. Even individuals who did not attend residential schools experienced, and continue to experience, a loss of culture, language, and spirituality, substance abuse, family violence, parenting challenges, and a loss of knowledge of the land. Communities and families often suffer from low socioeconomic conditions, an increase in illnesses, and fragmented political, social, and familial systems (Jung 2011; Stanton 2011).

In 1969, the Canadian government decided that the residential-school system was not effective for assimilation and withdrew its partnerships with the various denominations of churches involved (Stanton 2011). Despite this, however, residential schools continued to operate, in some cases with ownership of the school transferred to respective Indian bands. Most schools ceased operation in the 1980s, with the last closing in 1996 (Stanton 2011). In 2008, Canada entered a period of reconciliation with the establishment of the Truth and Reconciliation Commission to address the travesties of the residential schools and to hear from school survivors (see below).

The Royal Commission on Aboriginal Peoples

The Royal Commission on Aboriginal Peoples (RCAP) was initiated in 1991 following the conflict known as the "Oka Crisis," which ensued between the Mohawk Nation at Kanesetake and the residents of Oka, Québec (Hughes 2012). The RCAP's mandate was to provide an overall analysis of the relationships between the Aboriginal peoples of Canada, the Canadian government, and the general Canadian public, and to provide education on these issues to Canadian society. This mandate was constructed through consultation with Aboriginal representatives, who urged the RCAP to consider Aboriginal self-government and self-determination within its mandate in order to "examine all issues which it deems to be relevant to any or all of the Aboriginal Peoples of Canada" (RCAP 1996: 11).

The main objectives of the RCAP mandate were:

- To develop a theory of constitutional law on the status of Aboriginal-state relations; and

- to develop a policy framework and programming for improving social conditions among Aboriginal individuals, families, and communities. (Hughes 2012:112)

The final report, submitted in 1996, contained 440 recommendations to improve the state of Aboriginal-settler relations in Canada. Major recommendations addressed legislation, recognition of an Aboriginal order of government, replacement of the federal Department of Indian Affairs (now Indigenous and Northern Affairs Canada) with two separate departments, creation of an Aboriginal parliament, expansion of Aboriginal lands and resource base, recognition of Métis self-government, and initiatives to address social, education, health, and housing needs (Hurley and Wherrett 1999). RCAP recommendations concerning economic development called for the improvement of human-resources development and the building of Aboriginal institutions. The majority of recommendations, however, were not implemented. The RCAP was also not successful in its goal to educate the general public about the issues addressed by the commission, partly because the commission ran out of funding and partly because of the distance the Canadian government kept from the RCAP over the years (Hughes 2012: 107).

In 1998, the government responded to the RCAP's recommendations with an action plan (Indian Affairs and Northern Development 1998) intended to outline how the government had successfully implemented the recommendations throughout Canada. A progress report (Indian Affairs and Northern Development 2000) on the action plan briefly outlined examples from successful Aboriginal communities. It focused on the settlement of land claims on treaty-free lands, partnership development, Aboriginal governance, and economic-development opportunities.

The action plan also acknowledged the $350-million "healing fund" outlined in the final RCAP report that was to address the legacy of the "widespread neglect, governmental underfunding, health-related problems, as well as sexual, physical and emotional abuse endured by students over many years, and called for a public inquiry into the policy" in the residential-school system (see RCAP 1996: 383). Despite the release of the action plan, however, the U.N.'s Human Rights Committee reported their concern about the Government of Canada not implementing the recommendations from the RCAP (see Jung 2011).

Despite the federal government having overlooked many of the 440 recommendations, the lack of engagement by government and by non-Aboriginal Canadians, and the many other criticisms of the RCAP, the commission did have some success and benefit. For example, RCAP findings have been used to support Aboriginal policy demands, and many Aboriginal organizations and groups have used its recommendations to engage in advocacy, along with the development of a theory on Aboriginal self-government that is both cohesive and constitutionally sound (Hughes 2012). In addition, the $350 million in "healing funds" established by the RCAP and the recommendation for public inquiry into the residential-school system led to the establishment of the Truth and Reconciliation Commission (TRC).

Truth and Reconciliation Commission

In the 1996 "Report of the Royal Commission on Aboriginal Peoples" (see RCAP 1996) it was recommended that a commission be formed to address the hardships faced by the residential-school survivors. In April 1997, there was a national day of protest organized by the Assembly of First Nations (AFN) in response to federal government refusal to discuss the RCAP report, which led to members of the AFN insisting on the formation of a truth and reconciliation commission.

In 1998, there was a "Statement of Reconciliation" given by the minister of Indian and Northern Affairs. This addressed the "healing fund" that was recommended in the RCAP report, with a commitment of $350 million, as well as a revised litigation strategy and alternative dispute-resolution mechanisms being implemented (Indian Affairs and Northern Development 1998; Jung 2011: 7).

By late 2002, there were approximately 11,000 court cases filed against the federal government and churches regarding abuses and mistreatment in the residential-school system (Kaufman & Associates 2002: 251). In response, the Government of Canada announced the out-of-court Indian Residential Schools Settlement Agreement (IRSSA) in 2006. This agreement was the result of discussions and deliberations among the AFN, the government, churches, legal representatives of former residential-school students, and with other Aboriginal organizations to determine an appropriate settlement for survivors (Jung 2011). The IRSSA, approved by the courts in 2007, is the largest class-action settlement in Canadian history (Jung 2011).

On June 11, 2008, Prime Minister Stephen Harper delivered an apology on behalf of Canada to those who had suffered in the residential schools. Within his speech, there was an acknowledgement of the role of the Canadian government in the residential-school system and the damage that these schools caused survivors, the generations to follow, and Aboriginal communities and cultures broadly. Of utmost importance, the apology explicitly stated, "We are sorry."[2]

The apology made by the prime minister was significant and generally well-received by residential-school survivors, as well as by the Canadian public. With the Canadian population becoming more aware of the legacy of the school system, the timing of the apology coincided with the launch of the TRC (Stanton 2011). The TRC mandate was to:

1. Acknowledge Residential School experiences, impacts and consequences;

2. Provide a holistic, culturally appropriate and safe setting for former students, their families and communities as they come forward to the Commission;

3. Witness, support, promote and facilitate truth and reconciliation events at both the national and community levels;

4. Promote awareness and public education of Canadians about the IRS [Indian residential school] system and its impacts;

5. Identify sources and create as complete an historical record as possible of the IRS system and legacy. The record shall be preserved and made accessible to the public for future study and use;

6. Produce and submit to the Parties of the Agreement a report including recommendations to the Government of Canada concerning the IRS system and experience including: the history, purpose, operation and supervision of the IRS system, the effect and consequences of IRS (including systemic harms, intergenerational consequences and the impact on human dignity) and the ongoing legacy of the residential schools;

7. Support commemoration of former Indian Residential School students and their families in accordance with the Commemoration Policy Directive (Schedule "X" of the TRC Agreement). (Truth and Reconciliation Commission of Canada 2009)

The TRC and its commissioners were given the task of revealing the truth behind the residential schools in Canada by gathering, documenting, and archiving survivor testimonies (Jung 2011). Individuals, such as the chief commissioner of the TRC, Justice Murray Sinclair, have noted that reconciliation may not be possible for many survivors of the system, and that this needs to be accepted through the truth-telling process (Hughes 2012). In that regard, Kymlicka and Bashir (2008) see reconciliation as a transformative process rather than a restorative process, when achieved within a colonial setting such as that of the Canadian context, for the reconciliation of residential-school survivors.

In addition to providing a medium for testimony, the TRC was tasked with conducting research into the residential-school system itself. The TRC gathered existing documentation on the system from the Canadian government and the churches involved, and engaged in new research on their roles in the system's implementation, policy creation, development, and proliferation. The TRC contained within it an opportunity to provide both Aboriginal and settler-society Canadians a better understanding of the tragic and disproportionate effects that the residential schools had on the Aboriginal population of Canada. The final report of the TRC was released in June 2015, with ninety-four recommendations, many of which pertain to education and economic development.[3]

Notes

1. Stephen Harper, "Apology to former students of Indian Residential Schools," June 11, 2008, full text can be found at http://www.parl.gc.ca/HousePublications/Publication.aspx?DocId=3568890.

2. Ibid.

3. These recommendations, as well as additional information about the Truth and Reconciliation Commission, can be found at http://www.trc.ca/.

References

Canada & Institute of Indigenous Government. 2000. Final report of the Royal Commission on Aboriginal Peoples (RCAP). Vancouver, BC: Institute of Indigenous Government.

Hughes, J. 2012. Instructive Past: Lessons from the Royal Commission on Aboriginal Peoples for the Canadian Truth and Reconciliation Commission on Indian Residential Schools. *Canadian Journal of Law and Society* 27 (1): 101-27.

Hurley M. C. and J. Wherrett. 1999. The Report of the Royal Commission on Aboriginal Peoples. Ottawa: Parliamentary Research Branch, Library of Parliament. http://www.parl.gc.ca/Content/LOP/ResearchPublications/prb9924-e.htm.

Indian Affairs and Northern Development. 1998. Gathering Strength: Canada's Aboriginal Action Plan. A Progress Report. Year One. Minister of Public Works and Government Services Canada. http://publications.gc.ca/collections/collection_2012/aadnc-aandc/R32-192-1998-eng.pdf.

——— 2000. Gathering Strength: Canada's Aboriginal Action Plan. A Progress Report. Minister of Public Works and Government Services Canada. http://publications.gc.ca/collections/Collection/R32-192-2000E.pdf.

Jung, C. 2011. Canada and the legacy of the Indian Residential Schools: transitional justice for Indigenous people in a non-traditional society. In *Identities in Transition: Challenges for transitional justice in divided societies*, ed. P. Arthur. Cambridge: Cambridge University Press.

Kaufman, T. & Associates. 2002. Review of Residential Schools Dispute Resolution Projects, Final Report. Ottawa: Indian and Northern Affairs.

Kymlicka, W. and Bashir, B. 2008. *The Politics of Reconciliation in Multicultural Societies.* Oxford: Oxford University Press.

Miller, J. R. 1996. *Shingwauk's Vision: A History of Native Residential Schools.* Toronto: University of Toronto Press.

Mosby, I. 2013. Administering Colonial Science: Nutrition Research and Human Biomedical Experimentation in Aboriginal Communities and Residential Schools, 1942-1952. *Social History* 46 (91): 145-72.

Royal Commission on Aboriginal Peoples. 1996. Report of the Royal Commission on Aboriginal Peoples. Final Report. Volume 4: Perspectives and realities. Ottawa: Royal Commission on Aboriginal Peoples.

Stanton, K. 2011. Canada's Truth and Reconciliation Commission: Settling the Past? *The International Indigenous Policy Journal* 2 (3): 1-18.

Truth and Reconciliation Commission of Canada. 2009. Mandate for the Truth and Reconciliation Commission. Truth and Reconciliation Canada. http://www.trc.ca/websites/trcinstitution/File/pdfs/SCHEDULE_N_EN.pdf (accessed December 3, 2015).

Timeline of Exploration, Settlement, and Development

Date	Event
1372	Basque Whalers Reach Newfoundland and Labrador and Nova Scotia
1497	John Cabot Contact with Mi'kmaq
1534	Jacques Cartier First Voyage
1535-36	Jacques Cartier Second Voyage
1541-1542	Jacques Cartier Third Voyage, Contact with Iroquois (Haudenosaunee)
1560	Martin Frobisher First Voyage
1577	Martin Frobisher Second Voyage, Contact with Inuit
1603	Samuel de Champlain Contact with Mi'kmaq and Algonquin
1604	Establishment of Acadia and Port Royal
1608	Establishment of New France and Québec City
1672	Establishment of the Hudson Bay Company
1713	Establishment of Louisbourg
1713	Treaty of Utrecht
1713-63	Peace and Friendship Treaties
1763	Royal Proclamation of 1763
1776	Establishment of the North West Company
1812	Selkirk Settlers Reach Winnipeg
1812	The War of 1812
1850-54	Robinson Treaties
1867	Constitution Act, 1867
1867	Indian Act
1869	The Red River Rebellion
1870	The Manitoba Act, Métis Rights Recognized
1871	Treaty 1
1871	Treaty 2
1873	Treaty 3
1874	Treaty 4
1875	Treaty 5
1876	Treaty 6
1877	Treaty 7

1885	The Métis North-West Rebellion
1899	Treaty 8
1905	Treaty 9
1906	Treaty 10
1921	Treaty 11
1929	Extension of Treaty 9
1973	Calder Decision
1982	Constitution Act, 1982
1990	Nunavut Land Claim
1990	Sparrow Decision
1991	The Royal Commission on Aboriginal Peoples
1992	Establishment of B.C. Treaty Commission
1997	Delgamuukw Decision
1998	Nisga'a Final Agreement
1999	Establishment of Nunavut Territory
1999	Marshall Decision
1999	Corbière Decision
2003	Powley Decision
2008	Establishment of the Truth and Reconciliation Commission
2009	McIvor Decision
2013	Manitoba Métis Federation Decision
2013	Daniels Decision
2013	First Urban Reserve in Manitoba, Winnipeg

Notes on Contributors

Robert Anderson (PhD) is Professor, Entrepreneurship and Management Accounting at University of Regina. His research has focused on economic development, entrepreneurship, corporate social responsibility, and sustainable development. He is the editor of the *Journal of Enterprising Communities*.

Keith G. Brown (PhD) is Vice President, International and Aboriginal Affairs and Purdy Crawford Chair in Aboriginal Business Studies at Cape Breton University. His professional and academic experience spans local, regional, and national First Nation issues and he is recognized as an international educator, author, and speaker on the subject of cultural tourism marketing.

Derek M. Bruno is an award-winning entrepreneur with a passion for community economic development. He has previously served as Band Councillor for Samson Cree Nation, President and CEO of Samson Oil and Gas Ltd., Founder of Mikwan Financial, and a Board Member for Peace Hills Trust. He is currently completing his MBA (Community Economic Development) through Cape Breton University.

Teresa Callihoo (BA) has more than ten years of experience in community development, working mainly in Aboriginal communities. She is currently completing her MBA (Community Economic Development) at Cape Breton University. She is passionate about bringing a holistic approach to community development that is spiritually grounded.

Brian Calliou (LLM) is the director of Indigenous Leadership and Management program area in the Lougheed Leadership Institute at The Banff Centre. He is Cree and a member of the Sucker Creek First Nation in the Treaty 8 area of northern Alberta. He practised law for eight years before taking on his current role and has taught as a sessional instructor. His research interests include Indigenous leadership, self-government, economic development, Aboriginal and treaty rights.

Tom Cooper (PhD) is an associate professor in the Faculty of Business Administration at Memorial University. His research interests include Indigenous people's business issues, risk management and strategic planning. He has published extensively on Aboriginal business access to capital and financial issues.

Léo-Paul Dana (PhD) holds the title of Professor at Montpellier Business School. He has published extensively in a variety of leading journals, including the *British Food Journal*; *Cornell Quarterly*; *Entrepreneurship & Regional Development*; *Entrepreneurship: Theory & Practice*; *Journal of Small Business Management*; *Journal of World Business*; and *Small Business Economics*.

Mary Beth Doucette (MBA) is the executive director of the Purdy Crawford Chair in Aboriginal Business Studies at Cape Breton University. An industrial engineer with an MBA in community economic development, she has extensive knowledge of quality assurance and ISO compliance stemming from her experiences working in industry, most recently at Membertou First Nation.

Harvey Johnstone (PhD) is a professor with Cape Breton University's Shannon School of Business. He holds a PhD from Durham University where he studied the economic geography of new firm formation. His current research interests focus on place-based entrepreneurship occurring within depleted communities. He is also a member of the Global Entrepreneurship Monitor (GEM) research team for Canada and has recently completed a study of Entrepreneurship in Nova Scotia using the GEM approach.

Miriam Jorgensen (PhD) is research director of the University of Arizona Native Nations Institute and for the Harvard Project on American Indian Economic Development. Her work in the United States, Canada, and Australia has addressed justice systems, land and natural resources, enterprise management, financial education, cultural institutions, and philanthropy.

Bob Kayseas (PhD) is Professor, Business and Associate Vice-President, Academic at First Nations University of Canada. He is from the Fishing Lake Nation located in east central Saskatchewan. His research interests revolve around Aboriginal entrepreneurship, strategic alliances, and Aboriginal economic development.

Jeanie Lanine (LLB) has acted as in-house counsel for the Penticton Indian Band since 2008 and has worked with First Nations and Aboriginal organizations across Canada since 2003. She acts as a facilitator and curriculum developer for the Aboriginal Financial Officer's Association of BC in the areas of employment, governance, policy development, strategic planning, and economic development. She is a past contributing editor to the taxation section of *Native Law*, one of the most widely used Aboriginal Law texts in Canada.

Katie K. MacLeod (MA) is a doctoral candidate in the Department of Sociology and Social Anthropology at Dalhousie University. Her research interests lay in identity, ethnohistory, legal anthropology, memory, settler states, and colonialism, specifically within the context of Aboriginal and minority populations in Canada. Her current and past research focuses on the diversity and complexities of ethnicity and indigeneity in the Maritime Provinces.

Peter W. Moroz (PhD) is currently an associate professor at the Hill School of Business at the University of Regina and primarily teaches entrepreneurship and economics related courses. His research interests include process theory and entrepreneurship, regional and economic development, technology transfer, and social enterprise creation.

Joanne Pyke (PhD) is an associate professor of marketing in the Shannon School of Business at Cape Breton University. Her doctoral research at Bournemouth University (United Kingdom) focused on Aboriginal cultural tourism in Nova Scotia.

Lori Ann Roness (MES) is a lecturer at Mount Allison University and an independent consultant who has been working in the area of Aboriginal community development since 1997. As a researcher, facilitator, policy analyst, and strategic planner, Lori Ann works extensively with Aboriginal communities in a range of areas, including Aboriginal economic development, labour and employment, education, training, health, governance, evaluation, and strategic planning.

Angelique Slade Shantz (MBA) studies institutional drivers and barriers to entrepreneurial and economic development activities in contexts of poverty. She is currently a PhD candidate at the Schulich School of Business at York University. Prior to this she worked with First Nations to develop sustainable economic strategies, particularly focused around clean energy opportunities.

Rachel Starks (MA) is senior researcher at the University of Arizona Native Nations Institute. Her research has focused on per capita distributions of tribal revenue, growth, and change in tribal economies from 1990-2010, Native arts leadership, tribes, and U.S. borders, tribal justice systems, Native nation control of health care, and First Nation land management and resource development.

Janice Esther Tulk (PhD) is Senior Research Associate for the Purdy Crawford Chair in Aboriginal Business Studies at Cape Breton University. Her doctoral research focused on Mi'kmaw music and culture, and over the past five years she has researched best practices in Aboriginal business, particularly in Unama'ki (Cape Breton).

Wendy E. Wadden (BComm Hons; LLB) has been a practising member of the Nova Scotia Barristers' Society since 1985 and is an instructor of law in the Shannon School of Business at Cape Breton University. She was appointed by the Privy Council as a member of the Canadian Forces Grievance Board from 2000 to 2006 and served as a member on the Service Nova Scotia and Municipal Relations, Regional Assessment Appeal Court. Her research interests are in areas associated with business law.

Index